HOSTAGES OF EMPIRE

France Overseas: Studies in Empire and Decolonization

SERIES EDITORS: A. J. B. Johnston, James D. Le Sueur, and Tyler Stovall

HOSTAGES OF EMPIRE

COLONIAL PRISONERS OF WAR IN VICHY FRANCE

Sarah Ann Frank

UNIVERSITY OF NEBRASKA PRESS
Lincoln

Portions of chapter 9, "The Long Road Home, 1940–1945,"
originally appeared as "'Meet the New Empire, Same as the
Old Empire': Visions and Realities of French Imperial Policy
in 1944," in *Reading the Postwar Future*, ed. Kirrily Freeman
and John Munro (London: Bloomsbury, 2019), 79–95.

Library of Congress Cataloging-in-Publication Data
Names: Frank, Sarah Ann, author.
Title: Hostages of empire: colonial prisoners of
war in Vichy France / Sarah Ann Frank.
Other titles: Colonial prisoners of war in Vichy France
Description: Lincoln: University of Nebraska Press, [2021] |
Series: France overseas: studies in empire and decolonization |
Includes bibliographical references and index.
Identifiers: LCCN 2020037910
ISBN 9781496207777 (hardback)
ISBN 9781496227027 (epub)
ISBN 9781496227034 (mobi)
ISBN 9781496227041 (pdf)
Subjects: LCSH: World War, 1939–1945—Prisoners and
prisons, French. | World War, 1939–1945—Prisoners
and prisons, German. | France—History—German
occupation, 1940–1945. | France. Armée. Troupes
coloniales—History—World War, 1939–1945. | France—
Colonies—Africa—History, Military—20th century.
Classification: LCC D805.F8 F658 2021 |
DDC 940.54/7244—dc23
LC record available at https://lccn.loc.gov/2020037910

Set in Garamond Premier by Mikala R. Kolander.

Designed by N. Putens.

For the monsters

CONTENTS

MAPS AND TABLES

Maps

Tables

ACKNOWLEDGMENTS

I was privileged to receive generous funding for the research and writing of this book. My thanks go to the Irish Research Council for funding my doctoral thesis, the Grace Lawless Lee Fund and the Trinity Trust Postgraduate Travel Grants for research funding for travel to archives in France and Senegal, and the International Studies Group at the University of the Free State for funding final research trips to London, Aix, and Paris.

This book would not have been possible without the generous assistance and contribution of many friends and scholars, far too many to name here. In particular, I appreciate the support and patience of my PhD supervisor, Professor John Horne, during the long doctoral process. I thank my colleagues at the International Studies Group and the University of St. Andrews for creating two collegiate and welcoming spaces for research and writing. I am especially grateful to the following people for their advice or support throughout the research and writing process: Amy Blakeway, Jenny Chapman, Andy Cohen, Ana Del Campo, Kate Ferris, Aileen Fyfe, Matt Graham, Kevin Grant, Lorna Harris, Emma Hart, Dónal Hassett, Bridget Heal, Tomás Irish, Ilse Le Roux, Géraud Létang, Clare Makepeace, Emily Michelson, Claire Miot, Ian Phimister, Raffael Scheck, Jennifer Sessions, and Alex Sutton.

Special thanks go to Helen Garnett, who made the beautiful maps for the book, and to Léan Ní Chléirigh, Kieran Fagan, Jonathan Frank, Nathalie Genet-Rouffiac, Kate Law, Rebecca Scales, Emma Thompson, and Abaan Zaidi, who read draft chapters, fixed comma use, and gave helpful feedback.

I appreciate the generous support of both Ruth Ginio and Claire Eldridge in reading and providing the blurbs for this book. Ruth and Claire are two of the most brilliant and generous scholars of the French Empire, and I am especially grateful for their positive comments on this book and the previous conference papers that shaped it. My gratitude also goes to the reviewers of my proposal and manuscript. Their careful comments helped shape and improve the book. The editorial team at the University of Nebraska Press has been absolutely wonderful throughout the entire publication process; particular thanks go to Bridget Barry, Emily Wendell, and Ann Baker. I am indebted to Joyce Bond, an absolutely brilliant copyeditor, who made sense of my prose.

Finally, I would like to thank my family and friends. I am very lucky to have such wonderful friends who keep me going and inspire me (and most importantly, cook for me). My thanks go to Kate Law for being the absolute best cheerleader and person I know (I am so grateful for all the times you rescued me in Bloem and beyond); Sally Fagan and Veronika Vaclavek for decades (and decades) of friendship; Ozge Senay, my first friend in St Andrews, who always has brilliant advice and a cup of tea; and my friends Abby and Zoe Stephenson and Stefania Pasare and her wonderful family, who saw me through lockdown and this ongoing pandemic. Last but certainly not least, I thank Alexandre and Arthur for their patience and understanding while I traveled, wrote, revised, wrote, and wrote some more. I did tell you that I was writing a book, and here it is, dedicated to you.

ABBREVIATIONS

DSPG   Direction du service des prisonniers de guerre

ICRC   International Committee of the Red Cross

MBF   Militärbefehlshaber (German military command in France)

OKW   Oberkommando der Wehrmacht (German High Command)

HOSTAGES OF EMPIRE

1. Map of Frontstalags housing colonial POWs in occupied France, March 1, 1941. Created by Dr. Helen Garnett.

2. Map of Frontstalags housing colonial POWs in occupied France, January 1, 1943. Created by Dr. Helen Garnett.

INTRODUCTION

At 6:35 a.m. on a cold February morning in 1941, a young philosophy student, Ginette Eboué, and her friend set out from the Gare de l'Est in Paris to find Ginette's brother Henry, a prisoner of war interned in Charleville, eastern France. Henry, from French Guiana, had been captured by the Germans during the Battle of France in the summer of 1940. Whereas white prisoners were taken to Germany, prisoners from across the French Empire, including North Africa, were instead interned in camps called *Frontstalags* across the occupied zone of France. After the Franco-German Armistice of June 1940 France was divided into occupied, unoccupied, and forbidden zones, within internal border checkpoints throughout the country. Without the proper papers to cross into the forbidden zone, traveling was a risk, but Ginette was determined to see her brother. As the train stopped in Rethel, at the border between the occupied and forbidden zones, armed German guards forced everyone lacking papers off the train. While the other passengers were grouped in the station room, the two women disappeared into a nearby restaurant, seeking lunch and a way to travel the last thirty miles to Charleville. The locals, despite their surprise at seeing Black women in the Ardennes, nevertheless greeted them warmly, especially after hearing their mission was to visit a prisoner of war. Ginette recalled that the food was delicious and copious, and they were offered a good bottle of wine and several digestifs. Later, a local wine merchant offered to drive Ginette and her friend to the next train station, from where they would be able to travel to Charleville, avoiding further checkpoints. Armed with beer, lemonade, a bottle of his champagne, and delicious ham sandwiches, which had already become rare in Paris, the women boarded the train and arrived without incident at a friend's house in Charleville at 10 p.m.[1]

Nothing about Ginette's or Henry's experiences of the war was typical, as their visit in Charleville would confirm. In the weeks and months following the French defeat, many other families also tried to locate their sons and brothers who were now German prisoners. Yet these visits were usually in vain, as camps were closed to civilians. It was particularly surprising, then, when Henry, accompanied by a German guard and a friend, arrived the next morning to have breakfast with Ginette. His education and privilege gave Henry more freedom of movement than most prisoners. At Charleville, he was placed in charge of camp provisions. This gave him access to supplies, bought locally or donated, and to civilians. While most colonial prisoners of war benefited from regular movement between the military world of the camp and the civilian world of work, Henry's job was exceptional. He used his access to increasingly rare food and alcohol to cultivate a network of sympathetic French civilians and German guards, further increasing his freedom of movement.[2]

While the extent of Henry's autonomy and influence were atypical, many colonial prisoners found that captivity brought certain freedoms, of movement and for friendships, regularly denied to them in the French colonial army. Until his release in April 1942 Henry sent Ginette parcels of chocolate, meat, rice, pasta, butter, margarine, and stockings, which "helped them tolerate the strict restrictions" in Paris.[3] During Ginette's visit, Henry arranged a meeting with the camp commander, who was "so taken by the women's beauty" that he gave Henry permission to spend the next day with Ginette outside the camp. In return, Ginette felt obligated to invite the commander to have lunch with them, where Henry plied him with alcohol.[4] This meeting and the lunch that followed highlighted the extraordinary captivity of Henry Eboué. Ginette, Henry, and Robert, also a prisoner in Charleville, were Felix Eboué's children. As governor general of Chad, Felix Eboué was the highest-ranking Black man in the French colonial service. The previous August, he had helped rally French Equatorial Africa to Charles de Gaulle and the Free French. Despite sharing their father's name, it took at least six months, and an informant, before the Germans realized who Robert and Henry actually were.[5]

Robert and Henry's race, like that of the other eighty-five thousand colonial prisoners, was a determining factor in their experiences of captivity. However, in contrast to the majority of the existing literature, this book shows that the colonial prisoners held a surprising and paradoxical importance for the Vichy regime and its collaboration with Germany. The very status of being a prisoner was a military and political question between the French state and the German occupiers. The period of greatest latitude, when the struggle over the colonial prisoners was the most intense, was when the Vichy regime had the greatest autonomy and the empire, their home, was nominally under Vichy control. That changed in November 1942, when Germany retreated at El Alamein and Stalingrad and shifted to a total-war economy. All of this means the colonial prisoners' experiences, and French control, changed substantially at this moment and explains the predominant concern of this book with the period 1940–42.

This book has three main arguments. First, after defeat and significant territorial losses in the metropole, the future of "French greatness" depended on having, and being, an empire. Therefore, the Vichy regime actively improved conditions of captivity for colonial prisoners in an attempt to guarantee their continued and future loyalty. Second, French "magnanimity" toward the colonial prisoners was part of a broader framework of racial differences and hierarchy. Thus the relatively dignified treatment of colonial prisoners must be viewed as a paradox in light of Vichy and Free French racism in the colonies and the Vichy regime's complicity in the holocaust. Finally, the colonial prisoners' experiences of captivity, combined with persistent French rhetoric of imperial solidarity, led many to believe that France's relationship with the colonized was changing; the subsequent backtracking further strained relations between France and its colonial prisoners.

For the Vichy regime, maintaining control over the empire was paramount, especially in the early years. Keeping the empire French and neutral boosted its negotiating power with victorious Germany, which was tempted by French bases in the Mediterranean and wary that the rest of the empire might join de Gaulle and the British. The French felt that their colonial interests were threatened by their former allies and longtime colonial rivals, particularly after the British sunk the French fleet at Mers-el-Kébir in July 1940. German, Spanish, and Italian encroachments in the French colonies were also a real possibility. With the colonial prisoners, the Vichy regime believed it had an opportunity to influence a group of men who would hold sway upon their return home to the colonies. After French Equatorial Africa joined the Free French, cultivating colonial loyalty seemed more effective than demanding it through force.[6] For the Vichy regime, protecting the colonial prisoners from the rigors of German captivity was a concrete demonstration of solidarity with the colonial soldiers and a means of counteracting German propaganda. It was based on the assumption that colonial prisoners needed French protection to survive captivity—which itself sprang from the broader belief that the colonies needed France to modernize and civilize them.

Surprisingly, and contradicting much of the previous scholarship, this paternalism led to solicitude and not to neglect. Instead, the colonial soldiers' experiences were dominated by the minutiae: their daily work, lunch provided by civilians or employers, cold weather, their ever-deteriorating clothes, and how the guards' mood would affect them. Colonial prisoners ate and worked alongside French civilians, certain friendships were encouraged, and aid agencies worked together to improve the physical and affective conditions of captivity. The French administration treated the colonial prisoners' complaints about conditions, guards, or fellow prisoners as legitimate and worthy of consideration. As prisoners of war, they had more contact with white French than they had during peacetime in the colonies. More importantly, individual prisoners could shape these interactions, choosing whether to seek a godmother to send them letters during captivity or a friend who might help them escape. The increased interactions between colonial prisoners and white French, and the ability to raise concerns and receive considered responses, signaled to many colonial prisoners that some of the rigid delineations of French colonialism had been suspended during this liminal period between war and peace. Blaming most complaints on the Germans, the French showcased their solidarity with and support of the colonial prisoners by addressing their physical and emotional needs. In return, colonial prisoners were expected to remain loyal to France. French support continued while French authorities believed the colonial prisoners were at risk of "contamination" by German propaganda.

This surprising leniency toward colonial prisoners, especially when placed in the larger context of the Vichy regime's racist policies in the colonies and its absolute refusal to protect Jews from the Nazi regime, must be understood as part of the regime's desire to keep the power conferred by controlling the empire. Thus the French desire to protect the colonial prisoners from a worse experience than if they had been interned in Germany was paradoxical. Indeed, once the former colonial prisoners were back under French control, either in the unoccupied zone or in the colonies, the solidarity evaporated and was replaced by discipline. Their complaints and desires were no longer viewed as legitimate; instead, protests were seen as a stepping-stone to outright rebellion and suppressed as such. Much to the colonial soldiers' justifiable frustration and anger, this reasserted their place as racialized subjects in an imperial nation.

Colonial captivity served as a reminder that race remained the silence qualifier of belonging in France in the twentieth century. Expressions of French imperial solidarity did not begin with the Vichy regime. The people subject to French colonial rule were well aware that solidarity, like liberty, equality, and fraternity, meant different things for white citizens than for people of color. For example, when war was declared, imperial "solidarity" meant conscripting men from the colonies to fight in Europe for lower pay, a smaller pension, and fewer rights than white soldiers. While the colonial prisoners were in captivity, however, French calls for solidarity were backed up by concrete efforts to bring them food, improve shelters, and ease the tedium of being a POW. Still, differences along racial lines persisted. When the Vichy POW services asked the French public to help the colonial prisoners as they would their family members in captivity, this meant through official means designed to maintain a suitable distance between giver and receiver of assistance. For example, sending parcels or appropriate educational material was encouraged. White prisoners in Germany were actively recruited to support Pétain's National Revolution, and political debates were encouraged, as these prisoners were seen as the building blocks of the new France. Colonial prisoners were discouraged from political thought, however; instead, they received food parcels with pictures of Pétain. The white French were encouraged to act as role models for the colonial prisoners, not as equals.

However, something changed during the colonial prisoners' captivity. As solidarity became increasingly vernacular, small acts, such as bringing a colonial prisoner food or smuggling letters to avoid censorship, created bonds between giver and receiver. Larger acts, such as helping colonial prisoners escape from captivity and cross the demarcation line, created shared experiences between men and women from the metropole and empire, which would not have occurred under ordinary circumstances. The combination of official rhetoric and unofficial and sincere support from some locals made a significant difference in the colonial prisoners' experiences in France. After release, interactions with civilians were much rarer, as the French government and military leaders reasserted the imperial hierarchies of race and citizenship. The French regrouped former colonial prisoners into large camps in the southern zone to reduce contact with civilians until repatriation to the colonies, where the French had a vested interest in upholding the imperial, and thus racial, order. The French feared that the loss of prestige after the defeat in 1940 would negatively impact their hold over the French Empire. In the end, the real turning point came after they broke a series of implicit and explicit promises made to the colonial prisoners, which contributed to the increasing disillusionment of the colonial prisoners specifically and the people under colonial rule generally. The events that followed the rapid defeat of France after only six weeks of fighting would fundamentally alter French political and imperial culture for decades to come.

Shocked by the rapid German invasion and seeming inability of republican institutions to deal with the crisis, on July 10, 1940, the French National Assembly overwhelmingly voted to give Philippe Pétain "full powers" to rewrite the French constitution. This signaled the end of the Third Republic and the beginning of the Vichy regime. By October Pétain was publicly committed to collaborating with Germany in hopes of obtaining the early return of the 1.8 million prisoners and giving France a better place in the new German-dominated Europe than Britain, which had kept fighting. To convince the French people of the same, prisoners of war and the French

Empire became two pillars of the Vichy regime's political agenda and a focus of its propaganda efforts. Under the new regime, with its distinctly religious undertones, prisoners of war were portrayed as an edifying group whose physical sacrifice in defending the land would bring about France's redemption. If the prisoners' return was a goal widely supported by French opinion, the role of the empire as a source of French strength and status in the world seemed a potential asset for Vichy in dealing with the Germans, since it remained beyond the latter's control. These goals highlight the tensions between past and present, defeat and greatness, metropole and empire that shaped the Vichy regime's political program. The colonial prisoners sat at an uncomfortable juncture within this agenda. They were individuals who suffered as the white prisoners did, but for the racially bound France, as non-Europeans they could not represent France's rebirth through suffering and sacrifice as Pétain claimed the white prisoners did. Instead, as a group, the colonial prisoners were held up as examples of loyal colonial subjects who had given their freedom for the motherland, thus reinforcing the importance of the empire. As soldiers, they were viewed as potentially influential men in their home communities, and it was hoped that upon return, they would shore up continued support for French rule.

Thus the colonial prisoners were seen as both part of, and separate from, the prisoner-of-war question. In a purely geographic sense, they were physically separated from the white French prisoners. Over the summer of 1940 and into the early months of 1941 the Germans segregated the prisoners according to their racialized worldview. This process would take until the spring of 1941 as the Germans struggled to manage the 1.8 million men they had captured. Indeed, approximately thirty-eight thousand colonial prisoners had initially traveled to Germany before the racial separation was officially enacted. Most prisoners from French West and Equatorial Africa, Indochina, Madagascar, the Antilles, and indigenous populations of French North Africa were grouped in camps across the occupied zone of France with only fifty thousand white prisoners. The remaining white prisoners, including the Europeans settlers from North Africa (*pieds-noirs*), were moved to camps in Germany and beyond. However, the separation between European and colonial prisoners was not just one of distance.

Despite the rhetoric of solidarity, the colonial prisoners posed problems for the French, who did not fully trust their colonial soldiers. They had witnessed the defeat of France and would eventually return home to the colonies, where they would share their experiences of the short-lived war. The French feared that if news of the defeat spread throughout the empire, it would harm French prestige and splinter the fragile presumption of racial superiority on which the colonial order was built. The fact that the colonial prisoners were under German control complicated matters, as the Vichy regime feared anti-French propaganda might take root among them. The Vichy government took advantage of the colonial prisoners' internment in France, believing that their proximity to the white French population would help maintain loyalty and that if cultivated properly, the colonial prisoners could be an important group in shaping the discourse of defeat in the colonies. With 10 percent of the white male population of France absent in Germany, the colonial prisoners were pushed into spaces previously denied to them, like French homes and dinner tables, sharing meals and creating friendships. Just as white prisoners were revered as the building block of the new France, Pétain's regime believed the colonial prisoners had a role in maintaining the colonial order. While praising the white prisoners' sacrifices, the French struggled to reframe those of colonial prisoners to discourage any future claims for rights. Therefore, the colonial prisoners' experiences of captivity were largely defined by their status as the "other."

Thus race became a defining characteristic of a prisoner's experiences of captivity. In many ways, this is not surprising. Nazi racial views were well known. The fury of some German troops at facing nonwhite soldiers whom they assumed to be savages or cannibals led to the massacres of up to three thousand Black troops during the six weeks of battle.[7] Likewise, race was, and remains, problematic for the French.[8] Technically, one's degree of civilization, and not race, determined access to citizenship and the rights it conferred. The educated elite from across the empire were held up as proof against French racism; Black men, such as Blaise Diagne from Senegal, were even elected to the French National Assembly. French reluctance to acknowledge that their colonial rule rested on the fundamental assumption of white superiority meant that racism was often hidden behind paternalism.

Paternalism was enshrined in France's civilizing mission with the belief that the French had a duty and a right to forcibly spread French values abroad. The French army was no exception; white officers and enlisted men often viewed the colonial soldiers as childlike and naive. Under Philippe Pétain, the self-designated father of the French nation, this paternalism expanded. Through examining these paternalistic interactions, this book contributes a social history of racialized colonial subjects (and a small minority of citizens) in the metropole.

Who Were the Colonial Prisoners?

France's complex imperial history and the fragmentary nature of wartime records make it difficult for historians to define and quantify the colonial prisoner population. The French Empire was an agglomeration of colonies of different statuses, French departments, and territories under mandate, each contributing differently to the French armies. In 1940 three territories composed French North Africa: Algeria, legally part of France, and not a colony, and the protectorates of Morocco and Tunisia. White settlers, the pieds-noirs, some of whom had been in Algeria for generations, felt the distinction was particularly important and worth defending. In Algeria, the indigenous Jewish population had French citizenship (since 1871), while the Muslim population did not. French West Africa, with its capital in Saint-Louis, comprised the colonies of Senegal, Sudan (Mali), Upper Volta (Burkina Faso), Dahomey, Guinea, Côte d'Ivoire, Niger, and Mauritania, as well as the mandate territory of Togo. Collectively, West African soldiers were known as the Tirailleurs sénégalais, or Senegalese infantrymen. They fought in units with other colonial troops, and some units were mixed with white soldiers. Occasionally, soldiers from French Equatorial Africa were also called Tirailleurs sénégalais, showing that "Senegalese" often became a shorthand for "African."

Cameroon in Equatorial Africa and Lebanon and Syria in the Middle East were also under French mandate. The colonies of Gabon, the Congo, Chad, and Oubangi-Chari made up French Equatorial Africa. Djibouti was the only French outpost in Eastern Africa. In the Indian Ocean, France ruled Madagascar and Reunion. There were smaller territories in the Pacific and along the Indian Peninsula. The Caribbean held the older French colonies of Martinique, Guadeloupe, and Guyana. Men from these older colonies, as well as the *originaires* of the four communes of Dakar and the naturalized, were all French citizens. They served in metropolitan units with white citizens, and thus the German policy of pulling them out of metropolitan units and grouping them with "regular" colonial soldiers was unorthodox and contrary to French military policy. While some contemporaries considered North Africans "white," this was not the case with the colonial prisoners. Much to the frustration of the prisoners concerned, and to a lesser extent the French, the Germans ignored many of these nuances of citizenship in their treatment of the colonial prisoners, preferring to use visual racial identifiers.

Because of these different statuses, "colonial prisoners of war" is a slight misnomer, but for the purposes of this book it remains a useful term. It is worth noting that even contemporary sources had difficulty with terminology that was generalized and overapplied. Without much consistency, colonial prisoners were usually separated into two groups based on geography: nord-Africains (North Africans) and *indigènes* ("natives") or *indigènes-coloniaux* (colonial "natives"). *Indigènes* usually referred to soldiers from sub-Saharan Africa, but depending on the context, it could include men from North Africa, Madagascar, and Indochina. More often, Madagascan prisoners (*Malgaches*) were considered separately from other African prisoners and were grouped with prisoners from what is now Vietnam. Vietnamese prisoners were referred to interchangeably as Annamites or Indochinois, even though the Annamites were one of the ethnic groups in French Indochina. For consistency, this book uses "colonial prisoners" to refer to the soldiers of color, citizens and subjects, who spent the majority of their captivity in France. The German separation of prisoners along racial lines, regardless of origin or citizenship, determined the prisoners' experiences and thus justifies this designation. However, whenever possible, this book describes the prisoners in question in terms of the available identifiers, such as name, rank, nationality, origin, social class, or previous occupation, to reinforce the fact that they were individuals and not simply anonymous "colonial prisoners."

A variety of factors make it difficult to establish exact statistics for prisoners of war in general and colonial prisoners in particular. The chaos surrounding defeat and capture allowed many soldiers to escape and disappear into civilian crowds, although it was easier for white prisoners to blend into civilian crowds. Official statistics were not compiled until prisoners reached a semi-permanent or permanent camp, where they could complete a "capture card" for the International Committee of the Red Cross (ICRC). An official list of prisoners captured by the Germans, including French, British, Danish, and Norwegian soldiers, was published in September 1940.[9] The first French statistics that specifically included colonial prisoners, published on December 16, 1940, were wildly inaccurate. Georges Scapini, head of the French POW service, reported that 300,000 "colored prisoners" had been captured, of whom 80,000 were Senegalese and the remaining 220,000 North African.[10] This statistic is over three times higher than any other found. As Martin Thomas warns, German newsreels exaggerated the numbers of captured colonial soldiers to prove German racial superiority.[11] This was easier to do in the early months of captivity, before an organizational system was put in place. Later statistics are more realistic but remained inconsistent until 1941. On March 1, 1941, the German authorities counted 81,301 colonial prisoners in France.[12] This number can be confirmed in other sources and must be considered a reliable estimate. French sources from 1941–42 under-estimated the number of colonial prisoners in France at 55,400 or 70,000.[13] The German authorities were not always forthcoming about the location and population of the Frontstalags. So in May 1941 Gen. Joseph Andlauer, head of the overseas section coordinating aid for prisoners, asked French prefects to count the number of colonial prisoners interned in their departments. Each prefect responded separately, and Andlauer never amalgamated the figures. However, adding the individual reports results in a total between 85,937 and 87,330.[14] The prefects used their own racial categorizations to classify the colonial prisoners, hence the slight variation in numbers. This total confirms the German count and provides the most accurate reckoning of the colonial prisoners.

Secondary sources are equally divided on the subject, which is problematic for drawing conclusions on sickness and mortality rates. Nancy Lawler cites a French colonel in charge of Section d'etudes d'information des Troupes coloniales, who calculated that there were 58,500 *tirailleurs* held in stalags in 1940.[15] This is confusing and incomplete for several reasons. First, the word *stalag* generally refers to the camps in Germany, but sometimes French archives use stalags as a shorthand for Frontstalags when talking about camps in France. Second, Lawler was writing only about West African prisoners, and not colonial prisoners as a whole. West African prisoners made up 18 percent of the total prisoner population, which would suggest a total of over 325,000 colonial prisoners, a number that is far too high based on what we know from other primary sources.[16] On the other hand, the German count of 68,550 colonial prisoners cited by Armelle Mabon and Martine Cuttier is too low.[17] Raffael Scheck estimates between 90,000 and 100,000 colonial soldiers were captured during the summer of 1940.[18] Scheck's estimate is consistent with most of the data I found from 1941, confirming that a realistic estimate is 85,000 colonial prisoners in German captivity in early 1941.

This book contributes a new statistical analysis that changes how we quantify and analyze the colonial prisoner population and fundamentally alters our understanding of the colonial prisoners' captivity. To fully examine the colonial soldiers' experiences of captivity, I built a database from ICRC capture cards held in the Bureau des archives des victimes des conflits contemporains, a branch of the French military archives in Caen. Captured soldiers filled out these cards in triplicate: for the ICRC and for the French and German governments. The Swiss copies are not open to historians, but the French copies are routinely used to establish pension rights for veterans. This is the first work to exploit this source in a comprehensive and quantitative manner. These capture cards constitute an extremely useful, albeit flawed, source that reveals surprising details about the colonial prisoners, their prewar lives, and their experience of captivity.

There are several concerns with the data these cards provide: multiple cards can potentially exist for prisoners, not all cards contain the same level of information, and there can be errors. Prisoners filled out new cards each time they moved camp or if there were complaints from prisoners or families about a lack of communication. There are over three hundred thousand individual cards wedged into 130 metal cartons, meaning approximately three cards per prisoner. Unfortunately, the duplicates are not necessarily filed together as a result of discrepancies in how names were spelled phonetically or first and last names being inverted. The information recorded varies considerably, though it usually includes the prisoner's name, rank, place and date of birth, regiment, occupation, location of capture, and movement between camps. Sometimes health records of illness and treatment were documented. Finally, some cards contain obvious errors, as in the case of Trân-Vân Hôi from Tonkin. According to the dates on his card, he was reportedly buried seven days before he died. If the dates were not recorded in error, it would certainly explain his cause of death.

In order to extract the data effectively and control for errors, I took a random sample of sixteen hundred colonial prisoners from across the cards and a control group of all the records from one test colony. I then compared the data set with the control group, demonstrating that the issues were consistent throughout both the random sample and control group. This means the data can be used to detail the proportion of prisoners from each country, along with their demographic data, and to map movement throughout the Frontstalags. These capture cards provide valuable information not found in other archival sources. Much of the data and statistical analysis is inconsistent with the findings of previous scholarship. Through these cards we can see a larger trajectory of the prisoners' lives before and after the war, from their prewar careers and their hometowns to their descendants who would later claim their pensions. This kind of individualized information helps build dynamic biographies of men whose experiences in Europe were fundamentally determined by their place in a racial, gendered, and social hierarchy.

The work with the capture cards, and a rigorous reading against the grain of the varied archival sources, draws out the colonial prisoners' voices from a source base dominated by white opinions, observations, and decisions. This forces us to dig deeper, to cross-reference claims and documents to gain multiple perspectives, until we can read between the lines and do justice to the subject. Many colonial prisoners were illiterate and could not leave written records of their captivity. Long letters sent from colonial prisoners to their families were rare. The few postal control records found in the Senegalese National Archives reveal that the censor judged that colonial prisoners' letters contained nothing of interest beyond personal greetings. On the other hand, the administrative documents are rich for the period.

Most accounts of the colonial prisoner experience in capture and captivity were filtered through a white lens and recorded by French officers, doctors, social workers, or ICRC representatives. I used these documents both to determine the Vichy regime's reaction to the colonial prisoners and to glean available details on the colonial prisoners' experience. As is particularly important when the documents are written from the colonizers' point of view, the assumptions within must be scrutinized, challenged, and supplemented where possible with firsthand testimony.

A handful of exceptional prisoners left written accounts of their captivity. These include the reports from the three Eboué siblings that opened this introduction, as well as those of Michel Gnimagnon, a teacher from Dahomey; Ahmed Rafa, an Algerian officer; and Léopold Sédar Senghor, intellectual, poet, politician, and the first president of Senegal. These men represented an elite minority, as their postwar careers indicate. Rafa became the first Algerian to reach the rank of general in the French Army. Senghor was an intellectual without equal who shaped the postwar political and cultural world. Ginette Eboué, who joined the external resistance in Brazzaville in 1943, married and divorced Senghor and later spent twenty years working to support anticolonial movements with Unesco. Senghor's captivity report was unnamed, but Raffael Scheck identified Senghor as the author in 2011, in part because Senghor was the only Black history professor who had passed the highly competitive and prestigious *agrégation d'histoire* before the war.[19] With the exception of Gnimagnon, all had relatively protected jobs while in captivity, with privileges and freedoms not accorded to the others. Luckily, these are not the only reports on captivity we have. Prisoners who escaped captivity or returned to the colonies in the early years of the war were often interviewed.

This is the first work to study testimonies from escaped prisoners sent to the Commission sur les replis suspects. These constitute the largest body of records of colonial prisoners' captivity experience, containing first-person narratives from their surrender, capture, camp life, and escape. In 1940 the Vichy regime created this agency to investigate and eventually bring to justice French officers who had retreated or surrendered against their orders. Its work was continued by the provisional government until after the liberation. The French also used this structure to question escaped colonial prisoners about German propaganda, morale, relations with French civilians, and importantly, to assess their loyalty. The reports are in the French military archives but were not categorized until 2008. They provide extremely valuable insight into the lived experiences of colonial prisoners of war, as told in their own words and recorded by French military officers. Most of these interviews occurred before 1942, further highlighting the importance of colonial soldiers during the first half of the war. As colonial soldiers dictated their experiences during captivity and escape to French officers, this necessarily affected the tone and content. These reports are silent on whether the colonial prisoners questioned the Vichy regime's legitimacy or the extent of anti-French or anti-imperialist movements that may have taken root during captivity.

Reported to French officers, it is natural that these narratives condemn, often violently, those prisoners or civilians seen as too friendly with the Germans. The colonial prisoners of war were a heterogeneous group of men from across the globe, united primarily by the fact of their captivity. Their different socioeconomic, religious, and intellectual backgrounds influenced how they experienced their captivity and how historians are able to view it. It can prove tricky to decipher the kinds of relationships that existed between prisoners of different elite backgrounds or indeed the general race relations within the camps. Those with religious, rather than secular, education were often solicited by the Germans to become propaganda agents, sometimes visiting Germany, touring Berlin, in exchange for better food and conditions and sometimes early release. Some did so out of genuine conviction, others to go home sooner. As much of the recent scholarship has shown, binaries like "resistant" and "collaborator" are imprecise and flatten the diversity of experiences and relationships during the occupation. The same can be said for imprecise categorizations of colonial prisoners' loyalty, which is often arbitrary or even ridiculous. For example, Senghor, the first president of an independent Senegal, was fluent in German and became lifelong friends with a German guard, but no one accused him of being anti-French during his captivity.[20] Perhaps this is because Senghor and his friends wrote the reports on which much of our understanding of captivity is based.

By historicizing evaluations of colonial loyalty, we learn how limited French understanding of the colonial prisoners was, how colonial prisoners adopted French vocabulary and categories for their own benefit, and how many of the socioeconomic inequalities of the colonial regime were reproduced in captivity. The elite, like Senghor and the Eboué brothers, had better camp jobs with benefits because they were articulate intellectuals with diverse language skills. This gave them greater access to supplies and freedom than those recruited for propaganda efforts. Henry did not hesitate to use—some might say steal—Red Cross donations for himself or his family, while criticizing prisoners who informed on his escape plans in exchange for lesser rewards than Henry obtained through his job. The mass of prisoners, who had received a limited education because of French colonial education policy, had far fewer opportunities to improve their conditions of captivity unless they accepted one of the "distasteful" jobs like camp police. Working directly under the German guards, camp policemen reinforced discipline, kept tabs on the other prisoners, and informed on escape plans, in exchange for extra supplies and favors.

The captivity reports universally condemn those who denounced their fellow prisoners to the guards, and understandably so. The difficulty in evaluating these positions is that the most eloquent condemnations of these men came from writers who were predisposed to dislike them, such as the prisoners whose escape plans were betrayed or those who joined the Resistance after captivity. Even before the war, Henry Eboué's path was not a standard one. He was one of two colonial prisoners, the other being his brother, Robert, who had the chance to hear "Papa" on the radio calling to continue the war and support de Gaulle.[21] It is hardly surprising that for Henry, the Resistance began in the summer of 1940, which painted his view of captivity and of his fellow prisoners. Other prisoners, like many French, bet on German victory, which felt inevitable in 1940. Still others did what they could to thrive in difficult situations. These differences among the colonial prisoners were highlighted by the agency prisoners had to redefine the conditions of their captivity. No colonial prisoner was without agency, but what each individual prisoner could control changed over time and often depended on external factors.

Historical Roots and Chapter Organization

Generally, previous scholarship on the Second World War has treated the French Empire as an issue apart rather than relating it to the domestic history of Vichy France, a false divide between metropole and colony that Ann Stoler and Frederick Cooper identified twenty years ago.[22] *Hostages of Empire* draws these entangled histories, which colonial prisoners saw as intimately linked, together. The overlapping identities that many colonial prisoners proudly held are revealed in the archival material and helped structure this book's arguments by analyzing how the Vichy regime dealt with its colonial subjects in mainland France as it struggled to rebuilt French prestige overseas within the context of metropolitan defeat and occupation. To do so, the book engages with, and challenges, a number of excellent military and imperial histories, improving our knowledge of the military, legal, political, and imperial stakes at play in the wartime captivity of eighty-five thousand colonial POWs.

By drawing on a number of excellent histories of captivity, covering French, British, American, and Commonwealth prisoners, this book challenges us to reconsider how we imagine prisoners of war in western Europe.[23] Captivity was not just a white experience. It was a shared experience for millions of men during and after the Second World War, and yet those experiences depended on race, class, and nationality. Many French and German decisions between 1940 and 1945 were based on the legal precedents and informal traditions of POW labor and violence toward POWs during the First World War.[24] The First World War brought a quarter of a million colonial soldiers and half a million colonial workers to metropolitan France. Their experiences of battle, captivity, leisure, race relations, and repatriation fundamentally shaped French policies in 1939 and created a generational memory of warfare in Europe.[25] Accordingly, French reactions to the colonial prisoners were based on their long experiences of recruiting colonial soldiers, the changing political landscape of the Vichy regime, and the wider context of imperial rule.[26] While historians and scholars have long been aware of the colonial soldiers' contributions to the French Army, public interest in the topic is relatively recent, creating a subset of work on the twentieth-century "memory wars" that has served to arouse public interest in the colonial prisoners and the French colonial archives.[27] In many ways, scholarship on the political, morale, and gendered backdrop of the Vichy regime contributes more to this study of the colonial prisoners' captivity than traditional POW histories do.[28] The colonial prisoners were interned in this landscape where the Vichy regime's imperial, racial, and gendered politics intersect.

Over the past forty years, only six major works have substantially engaged with POWs from the French colonies, in comparison with the wealth of material written on "Western" prisoners of war. The scholarship tends to adopt two positions: that the experiences of colonial prisoners were worse than those of white French prisoners, and that experiences across 1940–44 can be examined uniformly.[29] *Hostages of Empire* pushes back on these two assumptions, revealing that colonial prisoners fared better in France in the early phases of the war than white French prisoners did in Germany, and expounds on the fundamental differences in experiences in three distinct phases of the war. Raffael Scheck's important monograph *French Colonial Prisoners in German Captivity during World War II* has effectively challenged the first assumptions by arguing against the theory of systematic neglect.[30] Scheck's comparison of German and French policy decisions reveal how Scapini tirelessly argued for the colonial prisoners' release. Outside of the Scapini negotiations, the majority of Scheck's book focused on the period of 1943–45, providing useful detailed analysis of this difficult period of German occupation.

One distinguishing aspect of *Hostages of Empire* is how it uses periodization to create three distinct phases of the war, changing our understanding of colonial captivity. Much of the previous literature accurately describes the first and last periods of captivity. However, a more nuanced vision of imperial captivity emerges when one considers three distinct phases: first, capture and chaos during the summer of 1940, when colonial prisoners were at higher risk for violence, mistreatment, and neglect; second, a period of relative stability through early 1943, when most white prisoners had been released from camps in France and French aid to colonial prisoners was at its highest; and third, a period of decline through the liberation of France in 1944. By ignoring the shifts in both French and German policy toward the colonial prisoners, one risks flattening their experiences or, worse, applying the events and conditions of 1940 or 1944 to the entire war. The harsh conditions at the end of the war, difficulties in repatriation, and an unfair payment system, combined with the well-documented racism of the Vichy regime and French military hierarchy, make it easy to understand the assumptions of neglect. This new periodization also reveals that the solidarity among colonial soldiers that Myron Echenberg and Gregory Mann identified in the postwar era actually took root in the earlier second phase. It is during this period (1941–42) that the colonial prisoners could legitimately believe the imperial order might bend. This solidarity increased in the disappointment and frustration after 1944, when wartime promises were eclipsed by peacetime imperial normalcy.[31]

As this book maintains, the crucial period for the colonial prisoners was between capture and the Allied forces' landings in North Africa. It is during this period that the colonial prisoners' had the greatest agency within the camps and carried the greatest weight in Franco-German negotiations. For as long as the Germans remained interested in the French Empire (for bases or supplies), the Vichy government had something to negotiate with. The colonial prisoners' political weight is somewhat surprising in light of previous scholarship and their status as non-European soldiers. Working under the assumption that after the war, Germany would take Great Britain's colonies but not France's, and facing substantial territorial losses in the metropole, the Vichy regime saw the empire as key to its postwar role as a facilitator between Africa and Europe. As living symbols of imperial loyalty, and potentially influential men upon their return home, the French hoped that the colonial prisoners would be a conduit to that end. Quite quickly, both the French and the Germans realized that the colonial prisoners could be useful. The Germans, precisely because they were not interested in the colonial prisoners and did not want them in Germany, were willing to concede on certain political points concerning these prisoners. In exchange, the Germans made ever greater demands on the French, including access to the French colonies, supplies for the war effort, and reduced financial contributions for the colonial prisoners.

Hostages of Empire presents a new social history of captivity, imperialism, and global humanitarianism during the Second World War. It puts the colonial soldiers at the heart of the story and argues that French attitudes toward colonial POWs were directly connected to imperialism and were clinging to colonial rule at a time when that seemed increasingly under threat. Furthermore, the captivity of the colonial prisoners was inherently imperial, based on a different political and military agenda than that of the white French prisoners. The French developed an imperial vision for maintaining future control of the empire in which the colonial prisoners were implicated. The colonial prisoners were not mere pawns in this larger diplomatic game. Despite the difficulties, many managed to shape their conditions of captivity through friendships, cooking their own food, or sending their salaries home. The French, worried that German propaganda would lead their colonial prisoners "astray," wanted them released or, failing that, in closer contact with the French, and they were willing to contribute financially to obtain this. However, Vichy's loss of the empire was devastating for the colonial prisoners. They could not go home, as maritime routes were cut. Since the Vichy regime could no longer use them as tools for maintaining the colonial order, it preferred to return to more traditional methods of controlling colonized peoples in the metropole: increased discipline and surveillance. By this stage, the French had proved to the Germans that they would not refuse even the most egregious demands, so the Germans no longer made concessions regarding the colonial prisoners. Instead, they were caught up in the Reich's total-war economy.

Examining the colonial prisoners' experiences expands the traditional narratives of Western captivity and challenges assumptions about international law. An entire system of international humanitarianism and law, which was rarely designed with the colonized people's rights in mind, was based on the promise that signatory nations, like Germany and France, would uphold the conventions in wartime. The first major decision on colonial prisoners, to leave them in France, contravened the spirit of the 1929 Geneva Convention Relative to the Treatment of Prisoners of War, which assumed that captured enemy combatants would be housed within the borders of the detaining power. Instead, the colonial soldiers were kept within their own armies' country. Yet these prisoners were not at home. They were an exiled group of colonial soldiers whose survival depended on how important they were to the new Vichy regime. Despite this decision, and their increasing integration into the German economy as the war advanced, the colonial prisoners continued to receive Geneva Convention protections. This is particularly surprising, as Germany denied similar protections to Soviet and Polish prisoners, also viewed as racially inferior.

The question of the colonial prisoners' race affected their fate in captivity in ways white prisoners did not face. Colonialism, despite claims of bringing improved infrastructures or civilizing power, was a fundamentally racist institution. The conscription of colonial soldiers in defense of this institution was by its very nature problematic. Racism was not a static position; it took many forms, changed over time, and affected the colonial soldiers in different ways before, during, and after their captivity. French and German racial views shaped the legal and physical framework for the colonial soldiers' experiences of war. When all remaining "French" prisoners were released from the Frontstalags in 1941, French citizens of color were excluded from the German releases despite being as French as the white POWs. The French generally viewed colonial soldiers—and indeed, most colonial subjects—as children in need of French guidance. This paternalistic attitude, influenced by the importance of the French Empire, their home, to the Vichy regime, meant the colonial prisoners were not neglected, which is a significant departure from the previous literature. However, it is essential to remember that solicitude founded on assumptions of white superiority is not equivalent to benevolence.

This book turns on two central questions: How did the colonial prisoners survive daily life in captivity? And what does the colonial prisoners' captivity tell us about French imperialism generally and Vichy's imperial goals specifically? Spread over nine chapters, it begins with the roots of the colonial POW question and ends with the long-term consequences of their captivity on relations between France and its empire. Chapter 1 examines the colonial soldiers' long prehistory of fighting in Europe and how that shaped German and French reactions to them on and off the battlefield. It traces how an evolving vicious circle of French determination to exploit German discomfort fighting nonwhite soldiers affected the colonial soldiers' experiences of combat. Chapter 2 addresses how colonial soldiers became colonial prisoners. It examines the chaotic defeat of France in June 1940, the rise of empire and prisoners as pillars of the Vichy regime, and the roots of an administrative and physical structure built to deal with prisoners of war.

Chapters 3–5 present an in-depth social history of the colonial prisoners' everyday experiences in the camps, their work regime, and how the physical conditions affected their health during captivity. As prisoners' accounts of captivity are limited, not all aspects of prisoner life can be compared. Questions of sexuality and personal relationships are intrinsically important, but this information simply does not appear in the sources. The colonial prisoners' own accounts of their captivity were almost always given to French officers, and the prisoners were acutely aware of the boundaries determined by their race, status, and education. All references to relationships with the French were therefore suitably deferential. Looking in detail at what those everyday experiences entailed reveals the centrality of POWs and the French Empire to the Vichy regime's political legitimacy and long-term imperial goals. Every aspect of the colonial prisoners' captivity—and indeed, immediate postcaptivity life—was politicized by the French. For the French hierarchy, even small requests for cigarettes or better food were scrutinized for signs of impending revolt. This fundamental distrust paradoxically spurred French efforts on the colonial prisoners' behalf while in German captivity and then pushed the return to strict discipline after release.

Chapter 6 brings the political and social strands of the book together by examining how and why the French mobilized humanitarian intervention on behalf of the colonial prisoners. The history of captivity in the twentieth century is also the history of global humanitarianism. In the Frontstalags, humanitarian, military, and imperial goals collided. Vichy saw providing material and moral aid to colonial prisoners as a way to offset the effects of the defeat and reinforce the status quo while underlining the obligations of loyalty and obedience that accepting the aid implied for its recipients. The Vichy regime took credit for all assistance from the Swiss ICRC, the American YMCA, and the French Red Cross given to the colonial prisoners during their captivity, even placing the French Red Cross under its jurisdiction and co-opting its organizational network.[32] This chapter also examines how Vichy's imperialist goals collided with the "neutral" humanitarianism of the ICRC, whether the colonial prisoners benefited from the aid sent to them, and the repercussions aid had on the former prisoners' postwar relations with France.

Chapters 7 and 8 work together thematically to discuss the top-down political implications of the colonial prisoners and the empire in Vichy's policy of collaboration. Chapter 7 examines the imperial framework to Franco-German negotiations and how that changed after the Allies landed in North Africa and the Germans invaded the previously unoccupied zone of France in November 1942. This chapter explores how the colonial prisoners' treatment and experience became an important political issue in Vichy's relationship with Germany and thus in "collaboration." Woven around the colonial prisoners' everyday experiences were the political and economic implications as the Vichy regime and Germany negotiated payments, the Geneva Convention, rights to the French Empire, humanitarian intervention, and access to the colonial prisoners. Chapter 8 discusses how and why both Germany and Vichy targeted the colonial prisoners with propaganda. Determined not to allow the defeat or Gaullist dissidence to weaken the colonial prisoners' loyalty to France, Vichy actively combated German propaganda in the Frontstalags, the southern zone, and the colonies.

While the primary focus of this book is the colonial soldiers' experiences as POWs in France, their experience of war did not end with release from captivity. Chapter 9 deals with the time period of the future and their return home. Colonial soldiers were demobilized in the colonies, unlike metropolitan soldiers, who were generally free to return home after release. Indeed, for many colonial prisoners, release from German captivity merely signaled a change in guards as they were moved from camps under German control to camps under Vichy control until they were eventually sent home. As the French anticipated, the colonial prisoners' return home was a crucial component of maintaining loyalty in the colonies. Worried about German propaganda in the camps and the colonies, colonial governors were constantly asked to evaluate the morale of the European and indigenous populations, paying particular attention to the thoughts and actions of the former colonial prisoners. Unfortunately for the colonial prisoners, the political stakes they represented changed dramatically after November

1942, fundamentally altering their captivity, as well as their repatriation and reintegration into civilian life at home. The frustration and anger that arose on these long roads home, and the French reaction to complaints from its colonial veterans, negatively affected postwar relations between France and the colonies.

As a social and political history of war captivity, this book traces the continuities and disruptions of mid-twentieth-century French imperial history. In many ways, the Vichy regime appears like a rupture in French history, something that early historiography was quick to emphasize.[33] In a country under occupation, the Vichy regime abandoned republican values of liberty, equality, and fraternity for a "return to the land" reactionary agenda of family, nation, and work. The Vichy regime blamed the defeat on the Third Republic's "decadence" and deliberately distanced itself, promising French rebirth through traditional values. Freed from the tensions between the reality of French colonialism and republican ideals of equality and freedom, the Vichy regime could renegotiate its relationship with the colonies and the colonized. Charles de Gaulle allegedly took up the gauntlet of republican France, arguing that he was defending the True France and its values.

Yet for the indigenous populations in the colonies, the French defeat, even the change of allegiance to Free France, represented a continuity in the repressive practices of French imperialism, which included forced labor and conscription. During captivity, the colonial prisoners experienced a brief reprieve in the harsh realities of colonial rule as the Vichy regime attempted to uphold its rhetoric of imperial solidarity. However, that solidarity was limited in time and entirely dependent on the regime's interest in maintaining control over the colonies. For the colonized peoples, the move between the Third and Fourth Republics via the Vichy regime and provisional government was a confirmation and continuation of forced labor, lower salaries, and fewer rights—all the characteristics of a law based on race rather than equality.

1

GENESIS

French Colonial Soldiers under the Third Republic

French and German reactions to the colonial prisoners in 1940 hinged on the long history of colonial soldiers serving in the French Army. The colonial army was a source of French pride and for many a sign that French colonialism was ultimately successful and good. Mobilization drew men together from across the farthest corners of the globe supposedly to defend fundamental French values like democracy and civilization. This vision willfully ignored the violence inherent in conscription and an economic system in which voluntary military service was a means to avoid backbreaking forced labor.

Having mobilized the empire in 1939, France was not just preparing for war; it was solidifying an imperial identity that had eluded the Third Republic for decades. When France was defeated little more than nine months later, the empire remained an asset in the eyes of the Vichy regime, while the colonial soldiers who had been taken prisoner by the Germans became a liability of a different order than the far more numerous white prisoners of war. Whereas the Germans, as they had since 1870, considered it illegal and immoral to use colonial troops in European theaters of war, the French felt bound to protect their own colonial soldiers in captivity both for their own sake and as a guarantee of the Vichy regime's ability to still lay claim to its imperial role. The French were well aware of how uncomfortable the Germans were fighting colonial soldiers, and they took advantage of this unease as much as possible. The genesis of what was to be the colonial prisoners' experience in 1940 dated back to the Franco-Prussian War of 1870–71.

Colonial Soldiers and the Third Republic, 1870–1920

The recruitment of indigenous soldiers was deeply rooted in western conquest of the African continent. The Senegalese served as soldiers from the earliest French and British incursions into Senegal. In 1857 Gov. Louis Faidherbe established the first permanent African troops, called Tirailleurs sénégalais, in French West Africa. They became an icon of French imperial power, symbolizing loyalty and obedience. Initially, these troops were used to maintain stability, and French rule, in West Africa. Fifteen years later, France brought the first colonial soldiers from North Africa to Europe during the Franco-Prussian War. Otto von Bismarck and Moltke the Elder, the German commander in chief, vehemently protested against the North African soldiers, but the French considered the colonial soldiers a useful addition to their armed forces and continued to deploy them abroad. They were used, in particular, to pacify other colonies. Senegalese soldiers represented between 9 and 15 percent of the French conquest army in Morocco between 1908 and 1913.[1] Their numbers increased dramatically in the early years of the twentieth century.

The debate on where and how to deploy indigenous soldiers changed with Charles Mangin's 1910 publication of *La Force noire*. Mangin participated in the Fashoda expedition and during the late nineteenth and early twentieth centuries had extensive experience in North Africa, Senegal, and Sudan (Mali), where he learned to speak Bambara. Despite Mangin's reputation, his vision for changing the racial makeup of the French Army was controversial. He believed that a professional West African army raised for deployment in Europe could be an effective counterweight to France's declining birthrate.

Some colonial administrators were uncomfortable arming and training the indigenous peoples their administrations were simultaneously trying to dominate. Much of the greatest opposition came from French officers with extensive military experience in North Africa, who insisted that men there would make better soldiers.[2] They believed that "for the Arabs, soldiering is the most noble career. For a North African, the French army represents an ideal: to serve is not shameful: the act of serving under arms is noble: it represents the force that protects, that attracts, the force of the Muslim God. To join that force is a supreme honor."[3] Mangin believed, on the contrary, that "the Arab is the least governable of all the peoples."[4] The French military ascribed different motivations for fighting to their diverse colonial subjects based on stereotypes and conjecture. The idea that men from North Africa fought for honor while men south of the Sahara had bloodlust in their veins was an absurd, but persistent, notion.

Racial stereotypes firmly in place, the French sought to recruit the ethnic groups considered "warrior material." In West Africa, nomadic ethnic groups like the Moors, Touaregs, or Peuhls were deemed "unsuitable" for fighting, despite being able to effectively resist the French colonial administration.[5] While in Indochina, the French authorities were keen to recruit the "warlike" men from Tonkin. Overall, the political, cultural, and administrative divisions determined military recruitment more than assumed racial hierarchies.[6] Yet these stereotypes persisted and would later affect how the French judged the colonial prisoners' loyalty and capacity to survive the rigors of captivity. They also revealed that French officers had favorite ethnic groups, as well as a deep conviction that "natives" enjoyed fighting. Believing that the colonial soldiers were natural warriors helped shape another fundamental colonial army certitude: military service did not and would not guarantee civic rights for its colonial soldiers.

While the tirailleurs were perhaps the best known of the colonial soldiers, with their striking red hats called *chechias*, France recruited and conscripted from all over the empire. The First World War brought half a million colonial troops and a quarter of a million civilian workers from the empire to metropolitan France. The French Army had three distinct branches, each contributing differently to the mystique of the imperial armies: the Armée métropolitaine (Metropolitan Army), Armée d'Afrique, and Troupes coloniales (La Coloniale). The Armée métropolitaine was formed to defend France and was composed of white men from mainland France.[7] The Armée d'Afrique was effectively a North African army recruited from the Nineteenth Military Region in Algeria (legally part of France), and later the protectorates of Tunisia and Morocco.[8] It had separate European and indigenous regiments. The Chasseurs d'Afrique (cavalry), Légion etrangère (Foreign Legion), and infantry Zouaves made up the European contingents.[9] The Zouaves included French settlers from Algeria, or pieds-noirs, as well as the occasional French-born soldiers. Generally, most indigenous North African men served as soldiers in the light infantry units, with a small number of convicts, but they could also serve in North African cavalry units, the Spahis or the Compagnies Sahariennes on camelback.[10] The Moroccan Goums were specialized units. One particular characteristic of the Armée d'Afrique was its mixed European and native units, which after the Great War also included tank and infantry units.

The Coloniale was composed of units raised in both metropolitan France and the empire for the purposes of extending and protecting the colonies. It consisted of both white and indigenous soldiers. The Coloniale Blanche regiments were composed almost entirely of volunteers from the metropole and conscripts from the older colonies in the Caribbean, who had full citizen status. So Black men also served in the Coloniale Blanche. Colonial subjects, without French citizenship rights, were conscripted into the Coloniale's various infantry units.

Recruitment leading up to the First World War revealed the limitations of military policy based on conjecture and stereotype. Mangin had wanted a professional volunteer army. Despite his conviction that Africans, being innate warriors, would be grateful for the chance to fight for France, volunteers were not forthcoming.[11] As historian Marc Michel argues, images of the "loyal native ready to serve France" hid the reality of enforced mobilization.[12] Differing conscription laws throughout the empire led to unequal recruitment. Forty-five percent of colonial soldiers were from North Africa, and 30 percent came from sub-Saharan Africa.[13] In West Africa the February 7, 1912, law allowed for the partial conscription of men between the ages of twenty and twenty-eight. Recruitment began in earnest from September 1914, but each annual class was smaller than desired.[14] In Vietnam a 1908 decree permitted conscription, but by 1912 there were only 1,350 conscripts.[15] Eventually, approximately 30,000 Indochinese soldiers fought in France and North Africa during the First World War.[16] North African soldiers, mostly volunteers, were sent to the front as early as August 1914.[17] General conscription was brought to Algeria in the fall of 1915 and to Tunisia a year later. French officials in Madagascar claimed that all soldiers were volunteers, but the local administration had paid local recruiters for each volunteer, creating a system of corruption and coercion.[18]

Imperial mobilization was both a call to arms and an opportunity for France to showcase pride in its empire. As France prepared for war, the empire was a valuable representation of what France symbolized. Unlike Germany, France, home to one hundred million, colonized included, believed it embodied civilization and racial enlightenment. The "spontaneous" support showed by the colonies offering up "the blood of her children and the wealth of their labor" was held up as proof that French republicanism would triumph over German barbarism.[19] This effusion masked the reality of the colonial soldiers leaving home to the sounds of their mothers singing funeral songs.[20]

Using colonial soldiers to defend the metropole remained contentious. Critics were unconvinced that African soldiers could sufficiently reinforce the white French forces. Vigorous opposition came from civilian authorities in the colonies who recognized that the increased recruitment would further strain urban labor, leading to shortages.[21] Colonial recruitment pitted military needs against economic ones, as France needed men and food from the colonies. In the end, military requirements prevailed.[22]

As the war progressed and news of its devastation reached the colonies, recruitment stagnated and protest increased. There had been real, if exaggerated, expressions of solidarity in 1914, but they transformed into rebellion the following year with increased economic pressures and the return of the soldiers' corpses.[23] Revolts broke out in Algeria in 1916, but the famine of 1917–18 changed the situation dramatically, as military service became more appealing than starvation; the class of 1917 was filled completely.[24] Riots spread across West Africa in early 1917, reaching the Upper-Senegal Niger region, Guinea, Dahomey, and Ivory Coast.[25] In response, Joost van Vollenhoven, the governor general of French West Africa, stopped recruitment. On January 11, 1918, deputy Blaise Diagne was named commissioner for the republic for the recruitment of troops in French West Africa. This gave Diagne, a Black man, the same rank as van Vollenhoven, a white man. Van Vollenhoven immediately resigned, supposedly in protest of recruitment and not because of Diagne's appointment.[26] Diagne recruitment tourney was a roaring success for the French military. Even after the violent rejection of the previous year, he raised twenty thousand more volunteers than requested.[27] In 1927 Diagne's role in recruiting West African soldiers, and his support for France, would be vigorously attacked by anticolonial leader and First World War veteran Lamine Senghor.[28]

The presence of a quarter million colonial soldiers in Europe sparked popular imagination, both negative and positive. The Germans were explicitly opposed, as they had been in 1870. Their own experience of colonial warfare, especially with the Herero in South-West Africa in 1904–7, reinforced this hostility, which was reapplied to Europe in 1914. In particular, they accused colonial soldiers of "enemy barbarism" for mutilating wounded and dead German soldiers.[29] Capitalizing on German prejudice and fear of the colonial troops' "savagery," the French used the African soldiers as shock troops, while also glorifying their "ruthless barbarism." The colonial soldiers' supposed "warlike characteristics" and "simplistic minds" allegedly made them better suited for simple frontal attacks without complicated strategy.[30] This backfired after some French elements purposely emphasized images of Africans decapitating their victims, which allowed the Germans to complain that the French employed cannibals against their enemies.[31] German author Leo Frobenius's 1917 *Le Cirque ethnique de nos ennemis* (Our enemy's ethnic circus) criticized French "domestication" of Africans and Asians, while promoting racial segregation as a means to protect cultural differences.[32]

Among the French, opinions on the colonial soldiers oscillated between praise and derision. Gen. C. R. Huré wrote in 1977 in glowing terms about the 2nd Régiment de marche de tirailleurs, who captured one thousand German prisoners, praising this "assault regiment which has maintained the harsh and vibrant traditions of the bladed weapon and the French bayonet during this war."[33] On the other hand, critics claimed the colonial soldiers were more susceptible to disease and cold, had bad aim, were undisciplined under fire, and did not maneuver well.[34] Others argued that despite their bravery and endurance in battle, the colonial soldiers lost focus and panicked without their European officers.[35] Similar criticism would resurface in 1940.

The most important development from the First World War was the generally accepted idea that the colonial soldiers were special and different. As such, they needed to be both accommodated and protected to ensure they would remain loyal and effective in combat. This meant expensive training and maintenance costs, especially during winter. The wintering policy, known as *hivernage*, moved soldiers who were originally from warmer climates and were believed to be susceptible to cold and disease away from the front to the warmer regions in the Midi during the winter. However, this policy interrupted some soldiers' training. In 1914 the Senegalese troops arriving from Morocco fought well at Dixmude (Belgium) but were immediately removed from the front for winter. They remained in the Midi, training until May 1916, when they finally returned to the front.[36] Unlike the West African troops, Madagascan soldiers remained on the front throughout the winters of 1917–18 and 1918–19.[37]

During the First World War prisoner treatment was violent, brutal, and part of a carefully coordinated propaganda war among France, Germany, and Great Britain. Each country emphasized its enemy's callousness in caring for prisoners, and collective punishments and humiliation were commonly used as leverage over the enemy.[38] The Germans' clumsy attempts to turn captured Algerian soldiers against the French Army backfired and had the opposite effect.[39] As the First World War drew the European empires into conflict, the French capitalized on German discomfort with colonial spaces and people being used to disrupt their racialized worldview. German prisoners found internment in the French colonies and having colonial soldiers as their guards particularly humiliating.[40] So France moved captured German soldiers to POW camps in Morocco and Dahomey, which prompted Germany to move French POWs to extremely harsh camps in Latvia.[41] This set off a spiral of retaliation. When photographs and drawings showing German soldiers in "inferior" positions to their indigenous guards surfaced in 1916, Germany sent thirty thousand French prisoners to Russia, where they were subjected to brutal work conditions, reduced food packages, and insufficient accommodations.[42] Other French prisoners were moved to the front to dig German trenches, in violation of international law.[43] The Germans encouraged the French prisoners to write home about these terrible conditions, hoping that their families would complain, which in turn might force the French military to improve conditions for Germans POWs in the French colonies.[44] These reciprocal punishments created an uncomfortable association between treatment of POWs and the French Empire as a place of German humiliation. Eventually, neutral negotiations were required to deescalate the treatment of prisoners of war. Yet the fundamental tension endured: under international law, France was entitled to use colonial soldiers in Europe, and Germany continued to consider this fact unacceptable.

The inclusion of French colonial soldiers among the postwar occupation troops in the German Rhineland in 1919 gave this Franco-German disagreement an international forum. The number of colonial troops varied from two hundred thousand during the winter of 1919 to forty-five thousand in 1921.[45] Their presence in Germany was nicknamed the "black shame" as claims of their unrestrained appetite for sex and violence multiplied. While the reactions of the German population should not be generalized, propaganda reflected a response to these soldiers that was visceral, vitriolic, and totally ungrounded in reality. As evidenced during the war, France continued to exploit German fear of Black men.[46]

Unfortunately for the French, international opinion turned rapidly against them. Pamphlets published in the United States, Sweden, and Great Britain criticized the colonial soldiers and mourned the fate of innocent German girls allegedly raped by the hundreds. As Julia Roos argues, a deep-seated fear of "African" sexuality allowed the accusations to gain traction.[47] German politicians issued a joint statement in May 1920 condemning the colonial troops' continued presence in Germany, claiming, "These savages pose a horrifying danger. . . . This situation is disgraceful, humiliating, and insufferable!"[48] The international attention and condemnation demonstrated that the Germans were not the only people steeped in racist stereotypes of "oversexed" Africans. Indeed, a number of brothels for the occupying soldiers were installed in the Saar to keep the soldiers away from "good" women.[49] In May 1919 an anonymous group of French soldiers wrote to Gen. Georges Brissaud-Desmaillet to complain that the colonial soldiers were taking too long in the brothels, leaving little time for white soldiers. In response, Brissaud-Desmaillet took the French civilizing mission to the extreme, explaining that until more sex workers could arrive, "the tirailleurs must expedite their antics. They will be given instructions on this subject."[50]

Despite integration into the army, and its brothels, colonial soldiers remained "others," revealing the multileveled and often contradictory French views of their colonial soldiers. That French soldiers had racially integrated brothels in 1919 while the American army remained segregated until well after the Second World War reveals as much about French and American racial thought as the "black shame" did about the Germans'. While defending its colonial soldiers who were innocent of the accusations of rape, France bowed to increasing international pressure and quietly removed Black soldiers from Germany while retaining other troops from the empire in the occupation force.

The Empire between the Wars

The Great War changed popular attitudes toward the empire and colonial soldiers, both now seen as a positive asset. The shock of the First World War, combined with a lingering feeling of vulnerability against a populous Germany, created a sense that France's survival depended on having, and being, an empire.[51] While the war certainly improved French opinion on the empire, criticism of French imperial expansion arose across the political spectrum. Some politicians opposed capitalist imperialism; others thought it too expensive; still others simply did not understand the point. Some had strong dissenting opinions, fearing that colonial expansion would only benefit Germany in the long run.[52] The Socialists accepted a left-leaning civilizing mission with a view to improving conditions in the colonies, while the Communist Party declared itself implacably opposed to imperialism. Still, the successive Third Republic governments used the euphoria of victory in the Great War to strengthen ties to the empire. The relatively successful deployment of a quarter million colonial soldiers inspired French military thinkers to imagine future possibilities. The colonial soldiers had a major, if mostly symbolic, role in defining French imperial identity, and this evolving imperial identity influenced how the French viewed the colonial soldiers throughout the twentieth century. The 1919 peacetime code for French West Africa altered how France raised its colonial army. It created a universal military service for African men, shifting the dynamics of the Tirailleurs sénégalais from being a "mercenary slave army" to including conscripts from all parts of society.[53]

To move the colonial army forward, a three-volume training manual for white officers and soldiers serving with colonial troops was published in 1923.

It combined detailed ethnographic research with lessons learned during the war. Some of the findings were unambiguous; after the Madagascan soldiers' success in battle, "the long-retained doubt on their bravery has fallen. We can say today that not only did the Malagasy become good soldiers but they are brave under fire."[54] Similarly, Vietnamese troops at the front had also given a "good show in combat," provided they were closely supervised by (white) leaders they knew well.[55] To obtain the best from these soldiers, new officers were instructed to provide regular breaks and assume the soldiers would never be able to march in formation correctly.[56] It seems obvious that training, and not race, would determine a soldier's success in battle, but the legacy of "warrior races" persisted, and ultimately these manuals replaced one set of outdated stereotypes with another. Combining notions of nature and nurture, officers were taught that the "black race" made excellent soldiers because "as far back as we can go in history, the state of war is normal in Africa, [and] his society teaches him discipline; the harsh conditions of his existence give him endurance: from his insouciance which makes him tough in drawn-out struggles which characterize modern battles, to his hot-headed and bloodthirsty nature which make him terrible in the shock."[57]

Colonial soldiers were viewed as several different but essentially homogeneous groups with uniform characteristics and flaws, specifically arrogance and pride. For example, the Hovas, from Madagascar, were seen as docile and disciplined, with above average intelligence "for natives."[58] Officers were told to avoid "using hurtful words in front of [a soldier's] friends; bullying is not acceptable, and it is worth remembering that violence is totally prohibited."[59] Unsurprisingly, these training manuals reveal more about how the French Army viewed and valued its colonial soldiers than provide actual insight into the different populations of the empire.

The French military took its contribution to the civilizing mission seriously. Colonial soldiers were deemed only as good as their French officers, and a paternal relationship between a white officer and an indigenous soldier was considered the ideal.[60] The inherent paternalism fit nicely into republican colonization by presenting France as a benevolent parent willing to raise its children (the colonial subjects) up through education.[61] However, for colonial subjects to rise up would violate the racial stereotypes on which colonial rule was founded and exacerbate tensions with republican values of liberty, equality, and brotherhood. A successful civilizing mission would eventually bring everyone to an acceptable level of French civilization and give them equal political and legal rights of citizenship. However, that was never the goal of imperialism.

The French Army believed that with the right support and encouragement, colonial subjects could become valuable soldiers. Love, not respect, was one of the guiding tenets of the French colonial officers' training. As A. Charles Roux wrote in 1939, "Those who are destined to instruct, educate and lead the black Africans must love them for all their qualities and despite their defects, that they be instilled with the idea that the white man's role, especially that of a French man, is a paternal role vis-à-vis the black man."[62] The training manuals also evoked the "legendary" love and devotion West African soldiers showed the white officers "who know how to conquer their simple hearts, for those who love them really."[63] It seems odd to talk of love in a military context, but it reinforced the French conviction that colonial soldiers were children who needed the benevolent discipline of a father figure to cultivate their potential. The racism is clear, but it took a different form than that of Nazi Germany or the segregated American army. French officers and soldiers were proud of their ability to lead and shape "their" colonial soldiers, contributing to a sense of responsibility that persisted through the Second World War and permeated French civilian culture.[64] It also infantilized and othered people under French rule, helping justify their continued domination without providing them the rights that were increasingly given to white workers in the metropole.

The French felt they had an obligation to help their subjects along the path to civilization. The training manuals carefully explained that not all "natives" were "savages," but rather they were just taking longer to evolve. Central Africa was viewed as particularly slow to develop compared with Vietnam, which had its own modern civilization.[65] Military service or mastering the French language would draw the colonial soldiers closer to the French way of life, which benefited the army and society at large.[66] Access to education was determined by a soldier's place in an assumed and invented racial hierarchy. Madagascan soldiers were considered more intelligent and better able to speak and understand French than other colonial subjects.[67] The Indochinese, despite having a "primitive language," were seen as slightly more intelligent, so they could be forced to speak French.[68] It had been previously assumed that most Africans could not learn "proper French," and soldiers were taught pidgin French, or *petit-nègre*, to get by in the army. The experience of the First World War had shown the limitations of this language policy, which became a barrier to the cohesive society of the French Armed Forces. After the war, select soldiers, especially those with longer contracts, were encouraged to learn French. In theory, providing the colonial soldiers with "proper" French lessons would prepare them for the same jobs as white soldiers in the colonial metropolitan armies.[69]

In reality, however, opportunities for advancement were limited to colonial soldiers from already privileged backgrounds. Indigenous officers and NCOs could be recruited in one of two ways: those who had received the same professional training as white officers and thus held an officer rank, and those who were recruited and trained specifically to be a "native NCO."[70] Men with access to these exclusive officer schools came from the colonial elite. For them, the army was one of several potential careers. Some indigenous North African soldiers were promoted to the rank of lieutenant, second lieutenant, and more exceptionally, captain. Within the Troupes coloniales, however, only Senegalese and Madagascan units had indigenous NCOs.[71] White officers were warned to consider local customs when choosing the NCOs. Among ethnic groups with strict hierarchies, the manual explained, formerly enslaved men or men from socially inferior groups would be universally rejected as leaders.[72] In this manner the French Army limited upward mobility based on social status and not technically on race. As with most systemic inequality, it benefited from the implicit consent of important families, who had access to better opportunities for their children. The French Army integrated young men from influential families into "French settings" so they could "familiarize themselves with our mentality."[73] The inclusion of small groups of elite "natives" helped reconcile hierarchies in colonial society with the republican concept of a nation formed not by individuals of the same race but by ones who had embraced the same culture.[74] Without forcing major changes, the army could point to a few success stories, like that of Blaise Diagne, as examples of republican victories. Meanwhile, the majority of colonial soldiers received less pay, lower pensions, and longer contracts. Their ties to France were bound by domination.

Despite the concrete links forged by the First World War, many French people lacked a personal connection to the empire. On May 6, 1931, the Third Republic launched the ambitious Colonial Exhibition on the outskirts of Paris to create that attachment by promoting the technological advances the French had brought to "virgin" lands. Thirty-four million visitors came to see the replicas of temples of Angkor-Wat, Tunisian marketplaces, and mosques from the Sudan and gawk at the indigenous men and women who populated the reconstructed colonial villages.[75] Chaired by Marshal Hubert Lyautey, the "maker of Morocco," the Colonial Exhibition reinforced the idea, born of the First World War, that France was strong because of the empire.

Hidden behind the impressive installations and poignant symbols of colonial exploitation were doubts and disagreements over the empire's necessity and France's actual status.[76] In a subtle message, Blaise Diagne praised the French government's attention to its colonial obligations and urged France to show the colonies that they shared the same long-term goals and opportunities.[77] By now French victory in the Great War had given way to general malaise. Minister of Colonies Paul Reynaud, later the center-right French premier, tried to rally support for the empire by explaining:

> The French are not a race but a nation. Therefore, they do not speak on behalf of a race, proud and cruel criterion, unbridgeable gap, but in the name of a humane and gentle civilization whose character is to be universal. Many thought that extending French power throughout the world would dilute it, weaken it, making it less able to ward off the ever-threatening danger. But experience has spoken. The republic, after giving France far-off territories, returned its lost provinces [of Alsace and Lorraine]. During those tragic days, the colonies came to the motherland's side, and the unity of our empire was forged in suffering and blood.[78]

The importance of the First World War to French colonial unity was highlighted in various ways at the fair. Colonial veterans were paid to attend in ceremonial roles. An outpouring of procolonial literature accompanied the exhibit, including a publication on colonial regiments in the First World War.[79] French politician Jean Odin, who would vote against Pétain in June 1940, claimed that the First World War had "achieved to a dizzying extent, through the ordeal of blood, pain and tears, and despite the diversity of races, the unalterable fusion of the greater French Fatherland."[80]

By mixing a fantastical vision with a utilitarian one, the fair tried to give France a new definition of what it was to be French.[81] In 1931 imperial France was in a strong position, spanning over 4,767,000 square miles. In the empire, most resistance movements had been violently quashed a few years earlier. While other countries were already suffering from the Great Depression, a timely devaluation of the franc in June 1928 gave France a temporary advantage in international trade. France had ceased lending abroad and had repatriated its funds, but the reprieve proved to be temporary. The end of the export-led boom and the sterling devaluation brought France firmly into the Great Depression.[82] The political and economic crisis of the 1930s had a devastating effect on French self-confidence. The prices of tropical foodstuffs dropped between 60 and 70 percent. To help the affected colonies, France reduced the cost of importing colonial goods, but this required metropolitan interest in colonial products.[83] Political instability felled many successive Third Republic governments, until the Popular Front in 1936 brought new optimism to the left and the colonies. However, that too faded as the economic recovery stalled and the promised reforms were recalled.

This image of a greater France of one hundred million was in direct contrast to Nazi German views on nation and race. Hitler specifically and repeatedly criticized French pride in its empire. In *Mein Kampf*, he argued that France "complements her army to an ever-increasing degree from her enormous Empire's reservoir of colored humanity, but racially as well, she is making such great process in negrification that we can actually speak of an African state arising on European soil."[84] Germany had been deprived of its colonies in 1919, but under the Nazis, interest in an empire outside Europe was renewed. This became even more apparent once Germany was at war again with the two major empires, Britain and France.

Between June and September 1940 Dresden hosted its own colonial exhibition exploring the economic, political, and social questions surrounding a German return to their former colonies.[85] In March 1940 German prisoners in France explained, among complaints of undercooked steak, Germany's motivation for war: "England and France have all the colonies. They have taken our 'vital space.' We are fighting for our Lebensraum."[86] Lebensraum, or the sacred space Germany needed to fulfill its destiny, was generally argued to be in the east. However, these prisoners were echoing Hitler's 1939 speech in which he demanded the restitution of all the German colonies. A German radio show complained that forty German prisoners were held in Morocco, where they were mistreated by French colonial soldiers. It concluded by criticizing the French for "behaving in Morocco as they did before 1914."[87] The German government protested the French and British violations of the mandate system by stationing troops in Syria and recruiting colonial soldiers in Cameroon.[88] This helped legitimize Nazi claims, dating from their First World War alliance with the Ottoman Empire, that Germany was anti-imperialist and pro-Islam. At home Germany continued to promote distaste of racial minorities. The fall of France in June 1940 created unimagined opportunities for German colonial expansion, while simultaneously reigniting French passion for the empire as a symbol of greatness.

Much of the political discourse in the aftermath of the 1938 Munich conference resonated with the language later used by the Vichy regime. The conference proved that appeasement had failed and Hitler's territorial demands were insatiable. More importantly, it revealed a major shift in French national identity from a defender of Europe to a country ready to fall back on its empire. As the Alliance démocratique claimed, "The development of our magnificent Empire is of much greater importance to our destiny than the unappealing role of gendarme or banker of Europe which in the flush of victory we felt ourselves called on to play."[89] Even before the defeat of 1940, France was looking inward for its identity and sense of grandeur.

Colonial Soldiers and the Second World War

After France declared war on Germany on September 3, 1939, French colonial subjects, volunteers and conscripts, were called to arms once again. Not everyone who fought in the French Army supported France or French colonialism, and not everyone who opposed the war remained at home. Serving in the French Army meant a loss of freedom and perhaps of life. It contributed to the destruction of families and gender imbalances as the men went to war and the women remained at home. For some it was an adventure with exposure to new lands, foods, languages, for others an obligation they would have willingly forgone. The colonial soldiers' attitudes toward the French and the war were multifaceted and malleable, shifting over time.

The French stifled voices of opposition and amplified those who supported French rule. In West Africa, most reservists went willingly because they feared repercussions against their families.[90] Similarly, in Indochina, few men volunteered for service, but conscription was generally accepted without protest.[91] The begrudging acceptance was reinterpreted by colonial administrators, who reported that spontaneous declarations of loyalty and support for the war flowed from the colonies. In some cases it did, especially among those with strong influence in colonial society, like reservists, marabouts, religious leaders, and chiefs, whose support for France guaranteed their positions. Aguibou Barry, chief of Dabola, a village in the center of Guinea, announced that he and the other village chiefs would encourage their children to defend the motherland, as they were all French in their souls.[92] In Senegal, the heads of the influential religious brotherhoods spoke in support of France and implored their followers to defend France as France defended Islam. Older, influential leaders like Seydou Norou Tall in Senegal and the Moro Naba in Côte d'Ivoire publicly declared their intentions to enlist despite their advanced age, which prompted their followers to volunteer instead. The governor of Guinea recognized that mobilization had brought complications but declared that most Guineans quietly accepted it and set to work preparing for the departure of the colony's young men.[93]

The colonial soldiers came from diverse socioeconomic backgrounds, with French citizenship as one of the greatest dividers, which sometimes exacerbated religious tensions. Once someone had French citizenship, the person had, in theory, the same rights and responsibilities as every French citizen, as French republican values were based on "civilization" and not race.[94] In practice, the racial hierarchy was dependent primarily on skin color or religion. In Algeria, the Crémieux Decree of October 24, 1870, gave French citizenship to Jews but not to Muslims or European settlers. Elsewhere, citizenship was granted to "evolved natives," or residents of certain areas, including the four communes of Saint-Louis, Rufisque, Gorée, and Dakar in Senegal and the older colonies of Martinique and Guadeloupe in the West Indies. Voting rights for the originaires were protected by the October 15, 1915, law, which also established the corresponding obligation for military service.[95] By 1939 metropolitan and colonial citizens had the same obligations toward military service, but that did not guarantee the same rights.[96] As during the First World War, citizens from the colonies constantly had to fight to have their rights respected in ways that white citizens did not. The distinctions between citizens and subjects created divisions among the indigenous populations, which ultimately helped maintain the colonial hierarchies and thus French dominance. Generally, the French military respected the nuances and distinctions within the colonial populations. To the frustration of the colonial prisoners, the Germans routinely ignored them.

Less than two weeks after mobilization began in Senegal, tensions arose between citizens and subjects at the Thiès garrison. Citing their lukewarm welcome upon arrival, unacceptable accommodations, and bad conditions generally, a number of reservists from the four communes complained that their position as citizens had been disrespected. Some of them were so appalled about the quality of food supplied by the army that they felt obligated to bring their wives to cook for them.[97] Others complained about the difficulties they faced in having their citizenship recognized by the French Army. These citizens wanted the right to defend the metropole like the white citizens and believed their delayed departure proved that France did not respect them as citizens or soldiers.[98] These rumors spread among the rest of the soldiers, one of whom suggested they all be sent home if they were not going to France. Agent auxiliaire de la sûreté Abdou N'Diaye asserted that these complaints revealed "the Senegalese pride and compulsion to always claim their rights, regardless of the circumstances."[99] While N'Diaye might have had a point about the timing, the citizens were absolutely correct in insisting that their rights be upheld. Without constant pressure from the French citizens of the empire, many of those rights would have been ignored for the sake of the war effort. Eventually, the Senegalese soldiers did sail for

France, where they were joined by soldiers from across Africa, Madagascar, Reunion, Indochina, the Antilles, and territories in India and the Pacific.

Generally, as in the First World War, colonial soldiers served either in regiments with their own countrymen under white officers or in mixed infantry regiments alongside white soldiers. These Régiments d'infanterie coloniale mixte, created in August 1914 in Morocco, had been particularly successful during the First World War. In 1939 North African regiments were stationed in Lyons, Avignon, Bourg, Metz, and Verdun.[100] During the winter, the Tirailleurs sénégalais, the term used for all West African soldiers, moved to the warmer climates of the south between Mont-de-Marsan and Toulon. Five Régiments d'artillerie coloniale with mounted divisions and Madagascan gunners were stationed in Agen, Bordeaux, Joigny, and Lorient. Finally, there were two half brigades of colonial machine gunners: the Madagascans in Pamiers and the Indochinese in Carcassonne.[101] From the onset, the colonial soldiers were an integral part of the French defense.

Upon arrival, the colonial soldiers found themselves in the Phony War. The term was probably coined in September 1939 to designate the period between mobilization and the beginning of active fighting. In French, it was known as a *drôle de guerre* (strange war), because the French and German armies remained behind their lines until May 10, 1940. Despite the relative calm, there were skirmishes along the front, and both sides took prisoners. In a significant reversal from the First World War, where, as Heather Jones argues, POWs were constantly associated with violence and atrocities, now France and Germany went to great lengths to prove how well captured enemy prisoners were treated.[102] In France, German-language copies of the Geneva Convention of 1929 were posted where German prisoners could read them.[103] Michael Wilson, with the International News Service, interviewed one German officer who reported marvelous treatment even after attempting an escape.[104] After recapture, the officer was restricted to his barracks, with access to books but not his parcels. This punishment was much less severe than the Geneva Convention allowed.

Similar positive stories were published in Germany; the *Deutsche Allgemeine Zeitung* reminded readers that unlike during the First World War, now the belligerent countries forbade reprisals against prisoners.[105] Germany also made judicious use of radio propaganda throughout the war. Radio Stuttgart encouraged captured prisoners to send messages to their families over the air "to ease the plight of the victims of a senseless war."[106] A similar line of propaganda asserting that Germany had opposed the war was later used with the colonial prisoners. Reaching out to prisoners' families was a particularly effective form of propaganda, and French soldiers were warned that it was their patriotic duty to remain silent if captured.[107]

For the colonial soldiers, the Phony War seemed long and uneventful. During this time, the population adapted to their presence in France. Official efforts to simultaneously support and monitor the colonial troops began as soon as they arrived in France. To fight against boredom, the Senegalese soldiers gave a concert of traditional music and dance for the French soldiers.[108] Lack of news from home was a common complaint among colonial soldiers and could be dangerous for morale. Léon Cayla, governor general of French West Africa, encouraged local chiefs and government officials to facilitate communication by distributing writing supplies, helping illiterate families with correspondence, and removing the postal tax on letters to soldiers.[109] Soldiers from Mali were given preaddressed postcards to send home.[110] This correspondence then passed through the military censor, providing the French military and colonial administrations with valuable insights into the morale of the colonial soldiers and home populations. Unfortunately for historians, the records of postal censorship for the colonial POWs under the Vichy regime do not appear to be found in France. Luckily, some summaries of censorship reports from West African prisoners' letters are held in the Senegalese National Archives.

In May 1940, after eight months of stagnation, the Phony War suddenly became real. Over the following six weeks, the German Army advanced with the unprecedented rapidity of blitzkrieg warfare. Combat was ferocious and marked by the use of aerial bombardment. Colonial soldiers shared the brunt of combat, facing tank attacks in the Aisne and Argonne, along the Somme, and defending the Maginot line.[111] Decades of recruiting the "warrior races" had permeated French military culture down to the rank and file. One French soldier wrote home enthusiastically, "Talk about the job the Senegalese are doing! Without them the Krauts would already be in Paris, they have only one word engraved on their minds: 'Win.'" Often the white soldiers believed the stereotypes and described the colonial soldiers as fearless warriors born to fight and not afraid to die.[112] A soldier with the 220th Régiment d'artillerie nord africain wrote, "In a few days we will return to 'kick their ass' and we'll show them what a mix of black and white really is, because our Senegalese are ready for ferocious fighting and aren't afraid, as for us, we have friends to avenge."[113] This soldier believed that the French fought for country and for vengeance for their fallen comrades, whereas the African soldiers were "naturally bellicose." The letters from white and indigenous soldiers reveal the discrepancy between how French soldiers viewed their colonial counterparts' motivation and how the colonial soldiers saw themselves. The military censor repeated the commonly held belief that the colonial soldiers could not fully comprehend the reasons for war and the few who did had accepted the situation with their usual fatalism. However, the colonial soldiers' letters often contradicted the censors' interpretation. For example, one colonial soldier explained to his family that his unit had gone to fight to help the Belgian civilians.[114]

A strange dichotomy existed, where colonial soldiers were seen simultaneously as naive and childlike and as vicious warriors. When the French were faced with the reality that their colonial soldiers were normal men who could be brave or cowards or both, the criticisms were harsh. For many soldiers, the style of warfare prevalent in May and June 1940 was terrifying. Overall, the colonial soldiers had less training and experience under fire than their white counterparts.[115] One Senegalese soldier wrote home, "Here we don't fight with the gun, but only with airplanes, lots of noise, lots of fear."[116] Unsurprisingly, the colonial soldiers were not the only ones affected by the bombing raids. Marc Bloch's memories are worth quoting at length:

> A blitz is probably not, in itself, actually more dangerous than many other threats to which the soldier is exposed. . . . But it possesses, this bombing descended from heaven, a capacity for terror, which really only belongs to itself. Projectiles fall from very high and appear, incorrectly, to fall straight down. Their combined weight and altitude allows them a tremendous visible momentum, to which the strongest obstacles appear unable to resist. There is something inhuman in this kind of attack coupled with

such force. The soldier bows his head under this unleashing, as before a cataclysm of nature, inclined to feel absolutely helpless. . . . The sounds are heinous, savage, unnerving to the extreme: as much the whistling, deliberately intensifying, that I was just talking about, as the detonation where the whole body is shaken in its marrow.[117]

The colonial soldiers' normal reactions of fear to this brutal and oppressive form of warfare fed the diverging views on their worth as soldiers and their motivations for fighting.[118] Paternalism was widespread; even enlisted soldiers looked to protect "their" colonial soldiers.[119] When three enemy planes bombed the 7th Company of the 53rd Régiment d'infanterie coloniale mixte, a junior officer saw that the colonial soldiers were so excited that he let them believe they were French or English planes coming to assist rather than attack.[120]

Stereotypes were more than simple racism. They influenced all belligerents to sometimes dangerous degrees. Some German soldiers believed the colonial soldiers to be savages who desecrated German corpses. Views varied from simply assuming African soldiers were uncivilized to believing they were cannibals.[121] German colonel Walther Nehring warned, "It is proven that French colonial soldiers mutilated German soldiers in a beastly manner. Any goodwill toward these native soldiers would be an error. It is rigorously forbidden to send them to the rear unguarded."[122] The colonial soldiers' faithlessness was attributed to their use of the *coupe-coupe* (machete), which the Germans contended was an illegal weapon, although it was legal under the rules of law. The colonial soldiers had been taught that the Germans were racist and would not take "colored" prisoners. This was to encourage the colonial soldiers not to surrender early, and it worked. This kind of resistance "to the end" surprised the Germans, and in some cases, they reacted badly. German responses to the captured colonial soldiers varied from uncomfortable, forcing them to keep their hands on their heads, to the extreme, refusal to accept their surrender and killing them outright.[123] So the vicious circle continued. The colonial soldiers fought tooth and nail to avoid capture, and German soldiers felt that proved the stereotypes of "savage African fighters," which could justify treating them with violence.

Consequently, the repercussions of the French defeat were worse for colonial soldiers than for white soldiers. Ingrained racism, ferocious close combat, and rumors of illegal warfare made surrender and capture the most dangerous time for colonial soldiers. While all French soldiers might be exposed to enemy maltreatment, African soldiers were at particular risk. Any evidence, real or imaginary, that soldiers had fought "dirty" inspired vengeance and often death. Murdered British and white French soldiers had been accused of using dumdum bullets.[124] In the case of the colonial soldiers, the machete was held out as visible proof that they used illegal weapons, but the protests went further. Sergeant Langenfeld, a white officer with the 7th Moroccan Regiment, was forced to watch the execution of West African soldiers. Langenfeld was told that for every allegedly beheaded German soldier, twenty Black soldiers were killed.[125] The French and North African prisoners who survived the attack were forced to bury their dead comrades. A French officer, Colonel Bouriand, reported that these massacres occurred all along the front and were often witnessed by French mayors or colonial soldiers who managed to escape.[126] Unable to prevent the massacres, the local populations carefully recorded the locations of colonial prisoners' graves. This information was later passed along to the families.

This period of violent uncertainty continued during the transfer between the place of capture and a temporary camp. In more than one instance, the Germans surrounded a group of colonial prisoners with machine guns and fired on them. Malian soldier Aboulaye Maiga reported one incident where he was the only survivor.[127] Another survivor, Dibour Cissé, reported that while transporting captured colonial soldiers to Lyon, the Germans rounded up one hundred men and fired on them with machine guns, twenty-five-centimeter cannons, and a tank.[128] Cissé survived by falling to the ground with the men who had been shot and pretending to be dead for three hours. Some of these massacres occurred as the colonial soldiers were preparing to surrender, others after the colonial soldiers had been recognized as prisoners but before they were taken to a camp. In at least one instance, the organized violence followed the prisoners east. In Austria, soldiers from Dakar were placed in a muddy field and decimated by machine guns. For the survivors, the men they were forced to bury were not anonymous soldiers, but their friends and well-known members of their communities.[129]

The assumption that the colonial soldiers were duplicitous meant that any gesture that could be interpreted as undisciplined was severely punished. In a well-documented case, Capt. Charles N'Tchoréré was killed after insisting that his military rank be respected.[130] In another example, three captured West African soldiers were shot after capture for refusing to be disarmed.[131] Sergeant Hassen-Ladjimi recalled that while marching to a temporary camp, any prisoner who deviated from the line or fell from exhaustion was shot.[132] Reports of these massacres traveled quickly among the prisoners. Colonial soldiers were left trying to rationalize the killings and navigate the beginning of a captivity that felt dangerous and volatile. It is unsurprising that they viewed this early period of captivity through a lens of exhaustion and fear. These incidences of violence continued through the first weeks of captivity, but then generally, and surprisingly, stopped. While only a minority of colonial soldiers were massacred, their deaths affected the experience of colonial prisoners who had fought a legitimate war according to the rules of war.

In searching for an explanation or simply trying to make sense of their captivity, the colonial soldiers found three main rationales for these massacres: revenge, racism, and rumors of illegal warfare. Corporal Leonanci, from Morocco, was told his comrades had been killed due to their persistent resistance and strong fighting against the German troops.[133] White, British, and other Allied prisoners were also at risk during the critical phase of surrender. Historian S. P. MacKenzie has documented the difficulty soldiers have in shifting between fighting an enemy and protecting him.[134] On June 20, 1940, a day between France's request for an armistice and its signature, seventy West African soldiers capitulated after fighting all day while being severely outnumbered.[135] Instead of accepting the soldiers' surrender, the Germans killed forty-five men and wounded the other twenty-five. In certain cases, like that of the German 6th Infantry Division, rage and fear after close combat with Black soldiers provoked the violent reactions.[136] A French report described the situation as "very peculiar," saying, "The Germans, surprised and overexcited by the unexpected resistance, acted cruelly and harshly after the combat, but one should not conclude that they have adopted this behavior generally toward our blacks whom they have captured."[137]

The evidence seems to confirm this: German massacres of African soldiers were generally limited in time and place to after the battles in France. Historian Raffael Scheck estimates about that three thousand West African soldiers were massacred in May and June 1940.[138] This represents less than 3 percent of the total number of colonial soldiers captured. Revenge for a surprisingly intense defense as a justification for the murders held some appeal for the colonial soldiers but did little to reassure them about their imminent captivity. However, the consequences of this explanation endured; after the war, many former colonial prisoners believed that they had fought better than the white soldiers had in 1940 and thus deserved equal, or at least fair, treatment.

Most soldiers had a basic knowledge of the rules of war, so why did these massacres occur? Using the assumed status of indigenous enemy soldiers as "rebels" or "uncivilized" as justification for death was standard German practice in South West Africa, and later East Africa, at the beginning of the twentieth century.[139] The Germans considered the colonial soldiers to be illegal combatants. Some German soldiers who participated in the massacres rationalized that if the colonial soldiers were savages and illegal combatants, the rules of war and Geneva Convention could be suspended. The oft-cited Jean Moulin, prefect of the Eure-et-Loir and later a major figure in the French internal resistance, attempted suicide rather than sign a German document falsely blaming the Senegalese troops for atrocities that would have been used to justify their murder. The German soldiers had sought to legitimize their actions after the fact by forcing Moulin's signature.

The German attitude did not reflect a new Nazi racism, but rather the old hostility toward colonial troops being used in a European theater that was evident from 1870 and 1914–18. The Germans assumed that the colonial soldiers fought in a barbarous and illegal manner. More fundamentally, they considered the colonial soldiers' deployment in Europe unacceptable, and that was communicated to captured colonial prisoners. One German officer kicked a Moroccan soldier who was lying on the ground while yelling, "The great French nation declared war on Germany, but Morocco did not declare war on Germany! Dog!"[140] Indeed, France was blamed for dehumanizing everyone's war experience by using colonial troops, which explains in part why the colonial prisoners were subsequently left in France.

Some German soldiers no doubt felt that the assumed status of indigenous soldiers as "savages," who violated international law through illegal warfare and desecration of corpses, justified killing them even after surrender. In direct opposition to French pride in their colonial troops, Hitler wrote that to be the "salvation of the nation," the Germany Army could only depend on "the strength and unity of its own nationality."[141] However, as Scheck argues, even for Nazi regiments, "hallucinatory racism" was not enough to justify the massacre of prisoners, especially since not all German units killed Black prisoners, and most colonial prisoners were not killed.[142] Given German racial theory, as evidenced by the Germans' reaction to Soviet prisoners, it is unsurprising that some colonial soldiers suffered a similar fate. However, the contrast with the future conflict in the east is striking. Germany's war against Soviet Russia was a war of extermination; Russian prisoners were fed the bare minimum.[143] Between 3.3 and 3.5 million Soviet prisoners (60 percent) died in German captivity, whereas less than 5 percent of colonial prisoners died during captivity.

The French reaction to the massacres showed that France was prepared to defend its use of colonial soldiers as legitimate. Jean Moulin, a man of exceptional moral character, nevertheless set the stage for the French refusal to accept German racist violence. Even though most men and women were not ready to give their own lives to safeguard the colonial soldiers' honor, there was a general sense that the colonial prisoners needed to be protected. The sheer number of reports, both civilian and military, of the violence showed that the French did not consider this acceptable behavior, even in wartime. Although these massacres occurred before the Vichy government was installed, we can see the roots of the Vichy regime's reactions to both the Germans and the colonial prisoners in the French reaction to the violence and the soldiers affected. Despite its pride in its colonial armies, the French remained conscious of the racial divides and hierarchies between colonizer and colonized and between whites and "others." The massacres were noted as "peculiar" and limited, but no sanctions or reprimands were demanded as the French focused on their government's collapse.

French confidence dissolved with the defeat, forcing the government to search for other means to preserve French "greatness" (*grandeur*). With significant and symbolic territorial losses in France, only the empire remained. The theme of the empire returned—or, rather, continued—with the Vichy regime as one element of "collaboration" with the occupying Germans. Despite repudiating the ideals and politics of the Third Republic, Vichy echoed much of its imperial rhetoric. This was as much by necessity as from conviction. Pétain reminded France that the armistice had saved the empire, allowing France an honorable defeat. Indeed, an intact empire allowed Vichy to imagine that it had a real measure of power in the face of Germany and a postwar role as the linchpin between Europe and Africa. In its rhetoric, at least, Vichy attempted to establish connections with the empire from a supposed position of strength and not as the last resort of a nation defeated and impotent in Europe.

2

PHASE ONE

Building the Frameworks for Colonial Captivity

The summer of 1940 shaped the precarious position of the colonial prisoners. Once the armistice was signed on June 22, 1940, an administrative framework was required to implement its conventions. At the same time, the next steps were still undecided. Pétain and de Gaulle defined what it meant to be French in 1940 in starkly different ways, but both felt the empire had an important role to play. In the colonies, leaders debated whom to support, while in the metropole, France was in turmoil with almost two million prisoners parked in fields along the front and the roads clogged with eight million civilian refugees who had fled the German advance. The Germans struggled to set up an infrastructure to care for the prisoners. Nowhere in France was equipped for this number of captives. Until a working political and organizational structure was created, the colonial prisoners lived in chaotic and disorganized captivity on the ground. Over the first six months, administrative, legal, and physical frameworks emerged that would shape the Vichy regime and thus the experiences of the colonial prisoners.

With the benefit of hindsight, it is easy to forget how malleable the situation was in 1940. Allies became enemies, and enemies became collaborators; France split into occupied and unoccupied zones, Free French, and Vichy colonies; and all the while, colonial prisoners struggled to adapt to their new realities as prisoners of the German Reich. This chapter follows the series of decisions made in the metropole and the empire that created the domestic and international contexts for the colonial prisoners' captivity. The paradoxically important position the colonial prisoners came to occupy developed out of the chaos of this first phase of captivity, when the role of the empire, evolving attitudes and jurisprudence on war, and the new Vichy regime's ability to negotiate with Germany collided.

Armistice or Empire

From the minute the battle for metropolitan France was lost in June 1940, the empire came into focus like never before. Previously a malleable but vague symbol of French prestige, progress, and civilization, it now risked becoming something more concrete. The German advance had shown that the French government could abandon Paris and fall back to Tours and then Bordeaux. But could it fall back to Oran or Algiers or Dakar? If it did, what would happen to the racial hierarchies if a colonial city suddenly became the capital of France? Although history has shown that the unlikely city of Brazzaville could have legitimized an alternative French government, in June 1940 this seemed impossible, as opinions on the role and place of the colonies varied widely. For a moment, everything hinged on the empire.

Before the war, over half of the French population had declared that losing part of the empire would be as painful as losing metropolitan territory.[1] The French defeat would put that conviction to the test and reveal discrepancies between the empire's symbolic and practical value. The continual political and economic crises of the 1930s had weakened faith in the republic, and for some the defeat felt almost unsurprising. For Pétain and supporters of the armistice, it became essential to convince the French population that the empire had enough value to merit saving it, but not enough to support a government in exile, as French premier Paul Reynaud had half-heartedly suggested. On June 16, 1940, Reynaud resigned, ceding his place to Philippe Pétain. Pétain believed that saving metropolitan France was the only way to save the empire and that accepting the armistice was the "necessary condition for the survival of our eternal France."[2] Opponents of the armistice wanted to retreat to the unoccupied empire and use the powerful and undefeated French Navy to continue the war.

The day after Pétain announced his intention to request an armistice, Charles de Gaulle spoke to the French via the BBC. In a rousing speech, he called across the airways, "France is not alone. She is not alone! She is not alone! She has an immense Empire behind her. . . . Whatever happens the flame of French resistance must not and shall not go out."[3] This rallying call has come to symbolize the bravery of the Free French and the ideals of resistance, but relatively few people heard it until a rebroadcast several days later. The contrast between de Gaulle and Pétain could not have been more extreme. Pétain, a hero of the Great War, was a known quantity. Charles de Gaulle was a relatively unknown general (*à titre provisoire*) with a challenging personality. De Gaulle evoked the empire as a force for victory, while Pétain saw it as a symbol of French prestige that must be preserved. Surprisingly, the decision between armistice and renewal with Pétain, or war and rebellion with de Gaulle, was not made in the metropole; instead, the colonies, seen as holding the key to France's survival, seemed to decide the future. The French colonial leaders had a massively important role in tipping the balance. The decisions were made in a climate of chaos, stress, and fear, exacerbated by communication difficulties between the colonies and the metropole.

Continuing the war from the empire meant accepting certain risks, such as potential guerrilla warfare in the metropole or reprisals against those left behind.[4] Furthermore, the logistical undertaking involved in moving the government and the military was extensive. One report on France's shipping estimated that it could move only fifteen thousand to twenty thousand men to North Africa, and if that proved possible, the territories lacked the industry to equip them.[5] In the empire, French administrators had other concerns: proximity to enemy colonies, fear of a punitive armistice that might strip France of its colonies, and potential for "native" insurrection.[6] North Africa, in particular, had a history of uprisings against imperial rule, including the Grande Kabylie in 1871, a revolt in the Aurès Mountains in southern Tunisia in 1916–17, and the Rif rebellion in 1925–26. In 1940 there was the added fear that a potential rebellion would take on a new political dimension and begin a push for independence.[7]

In the tense days that followed, de Gaulle and Pétain had their eyes on French North Africa, where the fleet was anchored. North Africa was paramount to the success of both Pétain's project to rebuild France after the armistice and de Gaulle's plan to liberate France from a base within the empire. In the Levant, both High Commissioner Gabriel Puaux and Levant

Army commander Eugène Mittelhauser contacted Pétain, Gen. Maxime Weygand, commander in chief of the armed forces, and Gen. Charles Noguès in Tunisia about continuing the war from North Africa. De Gaulle reasonably believed that North Africa might rally to him, as Noguès appeared willing to organize an army of 270,000 troops.[8] Believing they were moving the government to North Africa, members of the Bordeaux government, including former French premier Edouard Daladier, Minister of Colonies Georges Mandal, Camile Chautemps, Jean Zay, and Pierre Mendès France sailed for Casablanca on June 21. This decision was supported by the United Kingdom, which wanted France to honor its alliance and continue fighting from North Africa. However, some doubted that Britain could continue fighting and that it would provide military, financial, and economic support to the French colonies if they remained in the war.

Hitler recognized the delicate situation in the French Empire and understood the terms of the armistice agreement would be a deciding factor. The political and military clauses of the armistice, signed on June 22, 1940, imposed significant burdens and territorial losses in the metropole. The empire and the French fleet remained untouched. A demarcation line divided France into occupied and unoccupied zones, with a "forbidden zone" following the Atlantic coasts and border regions. The Germans annexed Alsace and Lorraine and administered the northern departments directly from Brussels. The Armistice Army was limited to one hundred thousand men, and Germany imposed huge occupation costs on France. To ensure the Armistice Army was essentially composed of white French soldiers, the Vichy regime repatriated many of the colonial soldiers who had not been captured to the colonies to be demobilized. Article 20, which required that the 1.8 million French prisoners remain in captivity until the conclusion of peace, was devastating for the French and their economy.[9] The armistice was harsh but not humiliating.

Overall, political legitimacy, military obedience, and imperial stability outweighed the desire to keep fighting. The climate had shifted completely while the parliamentarians were at sea. Upon arrival in Casablanca three days later, they were accused of desertion and arrested by the government, now officially loyal to Pétain. Helping de Gaulle's precarious position, Winston Churchill recognized him as the head of the Free French on June 28, but that was insufficient to draw French military leaders into treason and desertion. General Weygand argued that continuing the war from North Africa in 1940 would mean losing that region.[10] Once it became clear that North Africa would support the armistice, Damascus and Beirut, despite British pressure, followed suit. High Commissioner for the Levant Territories Gabriel Puaux and Gen. Eugène Mittelhauser, commander of the French forces in Lebanon and Syria, waited ten days before declaring their support for Pétain. This delay cast a shadow over Puaux, who was replaced by Gen. Henri Fernand Dentz in December 1940. French West Africa, under Pierre Boisson, supported Pétain, as did Indochina. Historian Jean Suret-Canale is not alone in blaming the decision to follow Pétain on "bureaucratic pusillanimity" and a lack of "imagination."[11] Imagination notwithstanding, Pétain was the legal and legitimate leader of France, which was enough to command loyalty, if not stability. In July 1940 the British blockade of the French colonies posed a real threat to Vichy sovereignty in the colonies and metropole, as well as being detrimental to the colonies' markets. Still, de Gaulle was in Britain, not France, and risked being viewed as an illegitimate rebel leader or, worse, as a puppet who would give the British a foothold in the French colonies.[12]

The "Three Glorious Days" of August 26–28, 1940, changed everything for de Gaulle. First, the Guyanese governor general of Chad, Felix Eboué, declared his support for de Gaulle. The remaining territories of French Equatorial Africa, Cameroon (Douala and Yaoundé), under Col. Philippe Leclerc, and Congo-Brazzaville followed quickly. On October 27, de Gaulle created the Conseil de défense de l'empire in Brazzaville, which would help legitimize him as French leader and provide desperately needed resources to the Free French. De Gaulle was not yet independent; his territory was bordered by British colonies, and the industry needed to exploit its resources remained in British and American hands.[13] Joining the Free French renewed the possibility of trade with the British colonies and brought other financial advantages. The British treasury bankrolled the Free French soldiers and promised to ensure the financial stability of any colony that rallied to the Free French.[14] French Equatorial Africa's decision to break rank with Pétain and the metropole shattered the image of colonial unity, which in turn affected the position of the colonial prisoners.

With de Gaulle's regime in Brazzaville and Pétain's government in Vichy, the colonies were suddenly presented with two "Frances," each claiming to be the legitimate government. As Ruth Ginio's brilliant work on French West Africa established, for the first time, France felt obligated to bargain for its subjects' loyalty.[15] This need to ask for allegiance, rather than impose it by force, had a positive impact on the colonial prisoners' experiences of captivity, and for a short while, it reshaped how they were seen by the French authorities. Ultimately, the decisions made between June and October 1940 did more to split the unity of the French Empire over the next three years than any Axis intervention or "native" revolt.[16] From his headquarters in Vichy, Pétain hoped that the threat or promise of allowing use of the empire's strategic bases, or alternatively, keeping the empire neutral, would entice the Germans into negotiations. Almost immediately after the armistice, prisoners and the empire became key issues for the new regime and a "restored France."[17]

A Future for the Vichy Regime

Questions surrounding prisoners touched vast swaths of French society, and the government was aware of their symbolic and economic value. The absence of the prisoners, of whom 57 percent were married and 39 percent had children, touched almost every aspect of French life and industry.[18] Agriculture and industry lagged without their manpower, which affected France's ability to pay the massive occupation costs. The prisoners also came to symbolize France's moral restoration and the healing power of quiet suffering.[19] They were omnipresent in the press, films, posters, and political discourse.[20]

"The fate of our prisoners is my first thought," Pétain reminded the nation. "I think of them, because they suffer, because they fought to the very limit of their strength and by clinging to the soil of France they have fallen into the hands of the enemy."[21] In October, two weeks after that speech, Pétain shook Hitler's hand, highlighting lingering complications over the notion of the enemy. Hitler was returning from an unsatisfactory encounter with Spain's Francisco Franco, and Pétain hoped the promise of collaboration would give France leverage to negotiate reduced occupation costs and the early return of the French prisoners. Hitler promised little but came away convinced that Pétain was not in secret contact with de Gaulle.[22] Collaboration became the scaffolding on which Pétain built a regime dedicated to French renewal and imperial strength. Having elevated the prisoners to a redemptive status, the Vichy regime needed their support for the National Revolution and collaboration. An internal memo warned that errors or inadequate funding could awaken the hostility of 1.5 million prisoners, bound together through the "solidarity of suffering."[23] Pétain and his supporters believed that if collaboration could facilitate the prisoners' early return, the Vichy regime could count on popular support for its policies and its National Revolution. The fatal flaw of the Vichy governments, from Pétain in 1940 to Pierre Laval in 1942, was the miscalculation that collaboration would necessarily diminish internal French sovereignty over time.

Still, the Vichy regime actively courted prisoners and their families by helping both until the prisoners could return home. Evidence of shipments to prisoners in captivity of tobacco, blankets, clothing, and food was posted in public spaces.[24] Brochures reminded prisoners that they owed their packages, food, letters from home, and especially their release to Marshal Pétain.[25] Posters were displayed in German POW camps to educate the prisoners on their rights and responsibilities.[26] Meanwhile, the strictly controlled French press attempted to shape public opinion on both prisoners and the empire.[27] Greatly exaggerating the success of the Montoire meeting, the right-wing newspaper *Je suis partout* declared that opponents of collaboration were enemies of the prisoners and France.[28] In Vichy's rhetoric, prisoners became a shorthand for France in a way that the empire never could.

The Vichy regime, like previous French governments before it, found it harder to create a personal attachment to the empire. The image of the empire was used to move France beyond the defeat by reminding the French, with language reminiscent of Third Republic publications, that strong bonds tied them to Africa.[29] One such publication, *L'Empire, notre meilleur chance* (The empire, our best chance), promised, "In this tragic situation, [France] turns her eyes toward her empire to try to find, not just a consolation and comfort, but a reason for national pride and hope."[30] Other publications highlighted the empire's loyalty and its vast potential resources. Large infrastructure projects, such as the trans-Saharan railroad or the development of the Niger Delta, were advertised to inspire popular imagination and "reanimate the mystique of the empire builders."[31] Yet for many, until the British attacked it, the empire remained an abstract symbol.

On July 3, 1940, the British navy bombarded the French fleet anchored off the coast of Algeria, killing thirteen hundred men.[32] In September Free French ships unsuccessfully attacked Dakar. In response, the Vichy Air Force bombed Gibraltar. In France, the attacks were generally condemned and provided a rallying call for the Vichy regime. Its military success boosted morale, and under these circumstances, collaboration with Germany seemed a plausible alternative to British imperial domination. Now the real advantages for Germany of a neutral French Empire became clear. Adm. François Darlan proclaimed, "In spite of [Britain] treating us like a continental Ireland or even as a colony, I intend to act so that France will retake its place of power in Europe and in the world."[33] Protecting the empire, and thus the colonial prisoners, became one of the Vichy regime's top priorities.

The combination of French paternalism toward colonial subjects and the significance of the empire to Vichy's future endowed the colonial prisoners with political importance and a profile that went beyond their small numbers. The French imagined that the colonial prisoners would return to their homes in the colonies grateful for French protection during their captivity. Former prisoners would thus exhibit the two most important qualities a colonial subject should have: obedience and loyalty. Until that time, colonial prisoners could be visible symbols of imperial devotion, through both the loss of their freedom in the defense of the motherland and their anguish often evoked by Pétain. Paternalism allowed the French to believe that its colonial subjects were simple and childlike and needed French protection from German influence. Unlike the white prisoners, whose participation in the National Revolution was seen as an integral component of Vichy's political agenda, the colonial prisoners were systematically excluded from political discussions. Behind the Vichy regime's discourse of imperial solidarity lay the colonizers' fear of revolt. Through its discourse on white prisoners, it is evident that the Vichy regime understood that captivity had the power to unify prisoners, making them an important group to keep onside. The risk for the colonial regime of sending home unhappy former colonial prisoners who had both served in France and witnessed the French defeat drove French efforts on their behalf. The duration of the war, however, became a major complicating factor.

The Legal Framework

The evolving codification of warfare and the protection of soldiers was the greatest external factor affecting the colonial prisoners' experiences of captivity during the Second World War. Attempts to regulate warfare took root in the seventeenth century, gained traction during the nineteenth century, and culminated with the Geneva Conventions of 1929 and 1949. The beginning of a conscious effort to humanize and limit warfare is often linked to Henry Dunant's *A Memory of Solferino*, in which he described the traumatic aftermath of battle and how sympathetic but untrained civilians tried to help wounded soldiers. Dunant, a wealthy Genevan heavily influenced by Christian ideas of charity and with business ties to North Africa, proposed that European elites form an international agency that would be charged with protecting all wounded soldiers. The founding of the International Committee of the Red Cross (ICRC) and the beginning of humanitarian law, while far from perfect, established a legal framework to protect soldiers in war and changed the history of emergency humanitarianism.[34] In 1863 Dunant, Guillaume-Henri Dufour, and Louis Appia founded the Red Cross in Geneva to mitigate the effects of war rather than to end it altogether.[35] The Red Cross sought to professionalize the assistance provided during wartime. Twelve governments signed the convention in 1864. Upholding the convention was voluntary, and there was no punishment for not respecting the terms except the risk that other powers would retaliate in turn.[36]

The codification of war continued throughout the early twentieth century. The 1899 and 1907 Hague Conventions and the 1906 Geneva Convention for the Amelioration of the Condition of the Wounded and Sick in Armies in the Field were among the first multilateral attempts to define acceptable behavior during war. The Hague Conventions built on the Lieber Code, used during the American Civil War, and established the rights of neutral powers, guidelines for treating prisoners, and laws and customs for battles on land and at sea, but did not outlaw reprisals against captured soldiers. The conventions affirmed that all soldiers, regardless of origin, deserved the same treatment and access to care. These enlightened rules were imagined for a white European, "civilized" context and were not applied to European warfare or conquest in the colonized world.[37]

During the First World War, belligerents violated and abused the newly written laws of war. Despite having signed the conventions, the actions of France, Britain, and Germany during the First World War pushed their limits. Instead of stopping violence toward their own captured soldiers, the dependence on reprisals to keep the enemy in check escalated violence toward prisoners. As Heather Jones argues, it was precisely the fear of reprisals against one's own prisoners, and not a rigorous adherence to international law, that eventually tempered abuses.[38] While the ICRC did visit POW camps starting in 1915, their inspectors were regarded with suspicion by the French and German Armies. The threat of reciprocal violence toward one's own prisoners meant that prisoners were treated differently depending on their nationality, and not based on the universal standards imagined before the war.[39] However, the principle that war could and should be regulated also endured. During the war, the ICRC gained significant financial and political weight and grew to over twelve hundred staff members. The repercussions of the change in attitudes toward prisoner labor can be seen long after the end of the Great War. The disillusionment of many delegates in the field and a growing conviction that war was no longer "chivalrous" led to the drafting of the text that would become the 1929 Geneva Convention Relative to the Treatment of Prisoners of War.[40] This text was signed by most of the world powers, with the Soviet Union noticeably absent. This new convention defined how soldiers temporarily removed from warfare should be treated. It imposed financial and moral responsibility for the prisoners' well-being on the detaining powers and created a network of neutral "protecting powers" to ensure the prisoners' rights were respected. It became the standard against which all POW treatment in western Europe during the Second World War was measured.

French prisoners, like other "Western" POWs, continued to benefit from a list of protections during their captivity; crucially, this included colonial captives. The protection of the colonial prisoners was therefore in sharp contrast to the experience of Soviet POWs and Slav civilians. German officers warned soldiers posted in France that violations would "reflect poorly on the honor of the German soldier."[41] Interning the colonial prisoners in "their" country was unorthodox. Rather than protest, the French saw the advantages of having them closer to home and felt this opened the possibility to imagine other extralegal options for the prisoners. One month after signing the Franco-German Armistice, Charles Huntziger declared that "the Geneva Convention did not fit perfectly, it did not provide for such a large number of prisoners of war in such a short time," saying that "everyone [was] surprised by the amplitude of the problem."[42] Establishing the idea that the Geneva Convention could be revised or improved created a negotiable space where other treaties, including the armistice agreement, might also be amended. French and German reactions to this flexibility developed and evolved throughout the occupation, often in conjunction with German war aims.

The 1929 Geneva Convention Relative to the Treatment of Prisoners of War created the legal framework for the colonial prisoners' experiences. It determined living standards, ensured neutral observers could verify conditions, and placed financial responsibility for captivity on the detaining power. International aid organizations, such as the ICRC and the national Red Cross societies, were present from the beginning of the conflict. In July 1940 the Red Cross, under German supervision, distributed goods to prisoners in France.[43] However, by August only the American embassy, acting as the protecting power to French POWs, could access camps in Germany and France.[44] Article 78 gave legally formed charitable organizations the right to visit and assist prisoners of war. Often the ICRC was seen as a neutral alternative to the national committees and was allowed access when others were not. When local actors, such as the prefect of Vienne, were unable to work directly with the camp administration to check on prisoners' conditions and ensure the POWs were receiving locally donated food, they could request support from a American or Swiss Red Cross delegation or sometimes use back channels to contact the colonial prisoners directly.[45] Access to the colonial prisoners was never unfettered or total.

On September 14, 1940, the French and German committees for prisoners of war met to clarify how French prefects could coordinate with the

German military administration to visit camps in France.[46] The agreement was never signed, and French access to the camps in France remained severely limited, which impeded the prisoners' legal right to inform their families and governments of their capture and their address.[47] French civilians tried visiting the Frontstalags to look for missing family members, ignoring German warnings prohibiting these visits.[48] These ad hoc stopovers were particularly problematic, as the Germans kept the locations of the Frontstalags secret until October 1940.[49] In November the French POW services had still not received an official list of colonial prisoners by camp, which prevented the ICRC from inspecting the camps.[50] Even as relations between the two governments stabilized, the German High Command (Oberkommando der Wehrmacht, or OKW) reminded the French that only George Scapini's service, in charge of all French POWs, could contact the colonial prisoners, and technically, even Scapini could communicate only with the German officials and via the Foreign Office, where German ambassador Otto Abetz was a representative at the military command.[51] Luckily, Scapini's personal relations with high-ranking German officials allowed him to circumvent some of these restrictions.

While the German decisions on access to the colonial prisoners from July to November 1940 appear to have been reactions to the disorganization of the post-armistice era, they were in fact precedent setting. The Germans used this period to establish their priorities for the occupation, test French resolve, and identify areas where the French would cede easily or push back. In 1940 the Vichy regime could have evolved in any manner of ways. One of the defining moments of the Vichy regime's POW politics was the signature of the November 16, 1940, protocol making France the protecting power for all French prisoners.[52]

The change was not without controversy. The rights of the protecting powers, and indeed of the ICRC, codified by the 1929 Geneva Convention, had been a huge step forward in the protection of prisoners.[53] It gave the protecting powers legal status to ensure that humanitarian, and not military or political, aims determined its implementation.[54] Now the French prisoners were no longer protected by a powerful neutral nation, the United States, but by a defeated France that held no German prisoners. Scheck argues that refusing to become the protecting power would have jeopardized the French prisoners, as Hitler seemed unprepared to accept any other power.[55] Instead of protesting, the French believed the change would grant greater access to their prisoners.[56] Even skeptics acknowledged that a successful deployment of the November protocols could benefit the French prisoners.[57] With Vichy acting as the protecting power for French prisoners, there was no neutral participant to ensure negotiations remained fair. As Yves Durand argues, this created unequal negotiation where the powerful country, Germany, could use French prisoners as hostages.[58] The significance of this change should not be underestimated; it reveals much about the reigning mentalities within the Vichy administration in October 1940. After British attacks on the French colonies and the United States' continued neutrality, collaboration with and demonstrations of goodwill toward Germany were considered legitimate means to ensure France's status after the war. Unfortunately for Scapini and the prisoners, by the end of 1940 Hitler had already begun to focus his interest on the east and was less inclined to concede to the French.[59]

A month later the German minister for war withdrew permission for the American YMCA, an aid organization with significant experience helping prisoners during the First World War, to visit French prisoners in Germany. Demonstrating German willingness to use French concessions against them, "the reason given for this prohibition [was] that the Scapini Commission is responsible for all French prisoners of war and the French know better than anyone how to help their countrymen and arrange a program of activities that best suits them."[60] The Scapini Mission depended on YMCA donations and camp inspection reports throughout the war. Interestingly, this restriction was not enforced in the occupied zone, as YMCA delegates visited Frontstalags during this time. Generally, the Germans respected the spirit of the Geneva Convention in relation to indigenous and white French prisoners but almost immediately began negotiations to lessen its financial responsibilities.

The Administrative Framework

As summer moved into autumn, the battle lines between the Free French and Vichy colonies seemed to stabilize, and in France, an administrative structure for dealing with POWs emerged. The Germans set the rules, and the French pushed back in a variety of ways. Colonial and white prisoners generally fell under the same administrative structure. Lt. Gen. Hermann Reineke of the General Wehrmacht Office in Berlin was placed in charge of all prisoners of war. In Germany, the High Command of the German Army (Oberkommando des Heeres) oversaw captured prisoners, while the Reserve Army Command administered the stalags and oflags.[61] Hitler took a personal interest in France and prisoners and directly influenced many decisions on both.[62] In France, local military commanders, *Feldkommandantur*, instructed the camp commanders and the French administration regarding colonial and French prisoners. While politically less important, camp commanders and guards had real influence over the colonial prisoners' experience and controlled who could access them.

Subcommittees with slightly different names and roles were formed to facilitate negotiations and create an improved administrative and logistical system for dealing with prisoners.[63] Article 22 of the armistice agreement created the French Armistice Delegation (Délégation française auprès de la commission allemande d'armistice) to negotiate with the German Armistice Commission (Waffenstillstandskommission); both had subcommittees dedicated to prisoners. The French Armistice Delegation worked closely with the prisoner section of the Délégation des services de l'armistice to obtain the release or temporary leave of certain categories of prisoners.[64]

In July 1940 the first organization dedicated solely to the emotional and material well-being of prisoners and their families, the Direction du service des prisonniers de guerre was created and placed under Gen. Benoît Besson's control.[65] This agency continued to function throughout the occupation, but negotiations changed dramatically with the appointment of Georges Scapini. A half-blind First World War veteran, he was a close friend of Otto Abetz from their interwar participation on the Franco-German Committee. Pétain had sent Scapini as his personal emissary to Berlin on several occasions before Scapini received an official mandate. Scapini's first request, on July 30, for the mass release of French prisoners was categorically denied. In Germany, Scapini met with top officials to argue that as a colonial power, France could play an important role in Hitler's Europe.[66] The fates of prisoners and colonies were linked in the person and actions of Scapini, who believed that the French Empire was key to France's new future.

Benefiting from his German connections, Scapini was given the administrative rank of ambassador of France in September and made head of the Service diplomatique des prisonniers de guerre, known as the Scapini Mission. He was given total control over all prisoner matters. While the Scapini Mission officially worked to improve the material needs of all French prisoners, it was fundamentally a political organization designed to convince white prisoners of the virtues of the National Revolution.[67] Carl-Henrich Jacques Benoist-Méchin, another member of the Franco-German Committee, ran Scapini's Paris office and had great influence over the prisoners in France.[68] Scapini, Darlan, and Benoist-Méchin worked closely with General Reineke in Berlin and his deputy, Major von Rosenberg, in Paris and with Otto von Stülpnagel, the military commander of France.

German policy toward the colonial prisoners was different, as exhibited by Hitler's refusal to have them in Germany. However, that decision set in motion a series of events that would, ironically, make the colonial prisoners important for the Germans. Being on French soil increased the colonial prisoners' visibility and significance for the French authorities, who hoped to promote France's imperial agenda through them. Understanding the Vichy regime's interest, and believing France was wrong to use colonial soldiers in a European conflict, Germany used the eighty-five thousand colonial prisoners as leverage to exact increasing financial concessions from the French.

Despite Nazi racism and long-standing German contempt for the use of colonial soldiers in Europe, the French appealed to German humanity and goodwill in requests concerning the colonial prisoners. The question of where to intern the colonial prisoners arose immediately. In anticipation of the harsh winter to come, the French delegation, and later Scapini, explained the French tradition of hivernage for housing colonial soldiers in the metropole, hoping the Germans would defer to their expertise. The French warned that the combination of cold weather and the mental anguish of captivity would infect the colonial prisoners with fatal afflictions.[69] Scapini, whose blindness reportedly appealed to the "chivalrous instincts" of his German counterparts, argued that the gesture of releasing the French prisoners was powerful enough to create feelings of goodwill among the population, which would be to Germany's advantage in the long run.[70] French Lieutenant Colonial Chauvin warned Rosenberg, Reinecke's deputy in Paris, that the French believed the Germans wanted to physically and morally exhaust an entire generation of French men. To improve relations, Rosenberg agreed to let French prefects inspect the POW camps in France so the government could see how the prisoners were treated. Chauvin suggested two alternative arrangements to safeguard the colonial prisoners' health: move them to the warmer regions of the unoccupied zone, under joint French and German authority, or send them to southern Italy.[71] Rosenberg rejected the latter suggestion on the grounds that the Italians would never allow the colonial prisoners in their country. Instead, he stated that twenty-two thousand colonial prisoners had already been moved camps south of Orléans, and thirteen thousand more would follow. Rosenberg's numbers were exaggerated and still only accounted for less than half of the colonial prisoners.

Colonial prisoners' vulnerability to the rigors of the climate in northern France, which featured so largely in their experience, became a key issue in Franco-German negotiations. Sick and injured colonial prisoners, who were unable to work, had been released to the unoccupied zone, where the French were legally and financially responsible for them.[72] While never successful in obtaining preventative releases, the French continued to request that all indigenous soldiers, and white prisoners with tuberculosis symptoms, be released on humanitarian grounds.[73] The question of colonial prisoner health was politically and racially charged. In the midst of the first round of negotiations, the Scapini Mission was given sole charge of French prisoners. French requests to move Senegalese prisoners south that had started before the Scapini Mission received its mandate were forced to be resubmitted while the prisoners waited.[74] By sticking strictly to the new procedure when convenient, the German authorities postponed decisions instead of refusing outright. This allowed them to maintain an illusion of good faith in negotiations and forced the French to redouble their efforts to obtain releases. There was little consistency as to how this rule was upheld. Political maneuvering on both sides of the table meant that other French agencies talked directly to German officials who hoped to cut the OKW out of talks.[75]

As the first winter approached, Scapini reexplained that hivernage would have moved the colonial prisoners farther south and that the French "climate is hardly healthier for them due to its humidity," stressing that "not only does the threat continue, but our fears [of fatalities] are coming true."[76] According to white prisoner and doctor Jean Prost, the German authorities maintained that the colonial prisoners would be moved to a warmer climate.[77] In December the Germans falsely told the colonial prisoners that the French authorities had refused to organize camps in the southwest, forcing them to remain in northeastern France. The issue was exacerbated by Vichy propaganda, especially that of the Scapini Mission, which presented itself as more politically powerful and effective than it was in reality, prompting the colonial prisoners to blame their lengthening captivity on the French.[78]

Getting the prisoners home was the top French priority from the signature of the armistice to the Allied victory in 1945. Scapini took a two-pronged approach to negotiations. First he requested the release of specific categories of prisoners: farmers, miners, or fathers. Then, leveraging the promise of French collaboration and concessions, he repeatedly asked for the collective return of all prisoners, fearing that ongoing captivity was detrimental to their health.[79] Negotiations with Reinecke were somewhat successful, particularly in solidifying Scapini's position as sole negotiator for the French. The Scapini Mission opened an office in Berlin and had two early diplomatic successes with agreements signed on November 16, 1940, and in May 1941. These agreements improved conditions for prisoners by organizing faster repatriation for the wounded, assigning jobs related to their skill sets, and arranging for Christmas parcels.[80] The May 1941 agreement secured the release of Great War veterans, wounded soldiers requiring lengthy rehabilitation, fathers of large families, nonessential medical personal, and civilian workers who had been mistakenly captured.[81] These limited and publicly celebrated successes gave the Scapini Mission and Pétain's government unfounded confidence. Germany, still at war, viewed France as a supplier of resources and manpower for exploitation. Allowing the French to believe in German good faith in collaboration was part of Germany's negotiating strategy; French requests were rarely denied outright, but rather were delayed or sent to different committees for consideration. Germany's policy toward

French prisoners was determined by its labor requirements, which only intensified over time.[82]

The French armistice delegation expressed fundamental doubts about the Scapini agreements, fearing that the 1.5 million French prisoners were too important as pawns to be released. The delegation's report anticipated that "the winner will, in fact, cede nothing and play by his own rules, even against international law and the agreements."[83] As the armistice delegation no longer controlled the prisoner negotiations, it could do little more than highlight potential issues. Even in December 1940 the delegation understood that French prisoners would never be released, as they were "systematically and methodically used by the Germans as laborers."[84] Abetz had told Scapini the same during one of their first meetings, where he implied that French prisoners would be released only in exchange for concessions.[85] Blinded by their commitment to collaboration, Scapini and Pétain interpreted any gesture, even the release of prisoners of war, which, as Julian Jackson argues, cost the Germans nothing, as confirmation of their diplomatic success.[86]

Scapini took his role seriously and struggled throughout the war to get as many prisoners released as possible. Although they represented less than 10 percent of all prisoners, colonial prisoners were not neglected in the negotiations. A detailed report released in January 1941 showed the Scapini Mission had raised thirty-five points with the German Armistice Commission; 11 percent related directly to colonial prisoners, and 28 percent concerned both colonial and white prisoners of war.[87] By April 1942, despite being told no more colonial prisoners would be released, Scapini's service continued to request their release.[88]

Scapini's agreements only minimally concerned the colonial prisoners, but their politicization had a great impact on their experiences. Even before Scapini's May 1941 agreement, approximately six hundred colonial workers mistakenly identified as soldiers were released in November 1940.[89] Additional colonial prisoners would have qualified for release as veterans or fathers. Questionnaires revealed that between 20 and 60 percent of colonial prisoners were fathers of large families, but few had the legal documents to prove it.[90] In January 1941 Pierre Boisson instructed the colonial governors of West Africa to coordinate with the local military authorities and prisoners' families to create lists of those eligible for release under the Scapini agreement. As colonial subjects had an inferior legal status to citizens, the colonial Registry of Births and Marriages was adapted to streamline official records.[91] These efforts were time-consuming and frustratingly inefficient, leading many colonial prisoners to blame the French and not the Germans for their continued captivity.[92]

Outside assistance proved necessary for more than one colonial prisoner to get early release, but it was challenging to obtain without personal relationships. One prisoner, Mamadou Kane, an officer and a civil servant for the French government in Mauritania and St. Louis, Senegal, mobilized all his connections to get released. He asked his cousin to contact a friend, Jean David, in Vichy to help confirm that Kane's wife was receiving an official family allowance from the French government in Senegal.[93] As he explained to David, his position and his wife's allowance could be confirmed by the minister for colonies or the War Ministry. Kane's message was received, and Adm. Charles Platon, the colonial minister, sent Governor General Boisson an official request for his documents.[94]

Despite the fundamental changes resulting from the French defeat, one constant remained: the privileged kept their privileges throughout captivity and release. The vast majority of colonial prisoners did not have the influence to have high-ranking French ministers count their children. Another prisoner, Moussa Baccouche, sent two unsuccessful requests for captivity leave, with all the necessary documents to justify his status as a father and the only supporter of a large family. Baccouche's four young children and two younger brothers had all been under his father's care until the elder man's untimely death. In a last attempt to get released, Baccouche sent a scathing letter to the president of the French Red Cross in Algiers expressing the frustration shared by many colonial prisoners: "In order to complete my duty for France, Mr. President, must my family suffer in misery, and my children be left, without support, to disease and perhaps death? Is that the reward that we, the colonial soldiers, deserve?"[95] Despite Baccouche's legitimate rage and frustration at the unfairness, something had shifted temporarily in French-colonial relations. The fact that colonial prisoners like Baccouche were able to criticize the Vichy regime's work on their behalf demonstrated that the colonial prisoners had moved out of the chaotic limbo and into a period where they could expect more than the bare minimum of food and shelter. Similar criticisms at the end of the war were handled quite differently.

When it became clear that the German government was unwilling to release colonial prisoners, the Vichy government launched efforts to gain more control, direct or indirect, over the colonial prisoners.[96] Scapini tested a variety of different arguments with little success: the colonial prisoners could be used to defend the colonies; cold was detrimental to their health; the French unemployed could do the work the colonial prisoners were engaged in. The Germans simply replied that there was no unemployment and thus no need to send the colonial prisoners home.[97] Eventually, the French accepted that at least occupied France was a better option than Germany. Having the colonial prisoners in close physical proximity would facilitate control and influence over a population whose loyalty, they believed, was at risk from German propaganda. The Germans understood that and constantly undermined French prestige by blaming the Vichy government for not addressing the colonial prisoners' complaints. At the same time, German negotiators hid behind new policies or Geneva Convention requirements while delaying or obscuring negotiations.

Becoming a Colonial Prisoner of War

The magnitude of the French defeat was felt first by the soldiers captured by the German Army. The sheer number of prisoners overwhelmed infrastructure and food supplies, leaving many to fend for themselves during the first weeks after capture. They suffered physically from hunger, exhaustion, and strict discipline, as well as emotionally from the shock of such a rapid and thorough defeat. Corporal Leonanci from Morocco described a typical experience in June and July 1940: "We walked the St. Michel road. They left us, like beasts, for eight days, without water, without food. Always walking, they directed us toward Verdun to the Niel barracks where there were eighteen thousand of us. The food was only a quart of cooked barley per day (dysentery wreaked havoc)."[98] Colonial prisoners reported insufficient food, nonexistent hygiene, iron discipline, and harsh labor.[99] They were searched and anything that could be construed as a weapon was confiscated.[100] Food was an immediate and lasting concern. After several days the Germans began distributing watery, "foul-smelling soup" served with moldy bread or soldiers' biscuits.[101] There was never enough to eat. Early camps were often fields surrounded by barbed wire, containing a mix of nationalities. Overcrowding was a serious problem. A camp designed for one thousand men now held thirteen thousand prisoners, while fifteen thousand prisoners overran the camp at Meaux, sleeping in buildings and courtyards, and even on the bare earth.[102] Moreover, this June was unseasonably wet and cold.

The German Army's response to the prisoners during this initial period was more reactive than organized. However, almost immediately a hierarchy of treatment emerged, with French officers at the top and colonial soldiers at the bottom. Officers were treated in a relaxed manner, housed inside, often with beds, while colonial prisoners were left in fields or put in overcrowded shelters.[103] Crucially, and perhaps surprisingly, once colonial soldiers were recognized as prisoners of war, German attitudes toward them changed dramatically. Because of legal precedent and the French uniform, colonial prisoners were accorded the same international protections as the white French soldiers. At this stage, colonial prisoners were deemed the least important of the captured men, but they were no longer at risk for massacre. Still, the difference in treatment was noticeable, and the colonial prisoners would not have known that the risk of death had subsided, especially as essentials like food were lacking. One white military doctor remembered sharing his bread ration with colonial soldiers who were imprisoned in a separate room and not fed.[104]

Originally, the German Army had planned to intern all prisoners in Germany and by October 1939 had constructed thirty-one POW camps.[105] Some colonial soldiers were among the first prisoners transported to Germany between May and July 1940.[106] Transfer to Germany was arduous, as prisoners were forced to march great distances.[107] They were unanimous in their complaints about bad food and terrible accommodations.[108] One group of colonial prisoners was given coffee made from grilled barley (served without sugar), one loaf of rye bread for five men, and thin soup with beets, potatoes, and no meat. Their barracks were made from sheet metal and wooden planks, and soldiers slept on sawdust without blankets. These conditions were typical at the beginning of captivity in Germany and Austria.[109] At Neubrandenburg camp, the food was improved only after an epidemic of diarrhea caused fifty deaths.[110]

More concerning than the food and housing were the incidents of violence inflicted on the colonial prisoners in Germany. In Stalag VII-A, the guards shot prisoners allegedly attempting to escape and released dogs on others, some of whom died from bite wounds.[111] Abdoulaye Maiga from French Sudan (Mali) witnessed German soldiers hitting Black or biracial officers and described all younger guards as "wicked."[112] Generally, older guards and First World War veterans were seen as more humane.[113] During the transfer to Germany, the guards had often been armed civilians who were forty to fifty years old.[114] However, in the permanent camps, the guards were from the German Army. Some were consistently violent, while others were relaxed when alone but became "horrid" in front of their NCOs.[115] This tendency for different attitudes and actions depending on the presence of superior officers became increasingly common in the Frontstalags as well.

The occupation of France presented Germany with options for interning colonial prisoners that had not existed in previous conflicts. This segregation worked to make occupied France a geographic buffer zone between the "racially superior" German people and the "inferior" French colonial soldiers.[116] There were many inconsistencies in this policy: prisoners from the British Empire and Commonwealth interned in Germany were housed in the same compounds as British prisoners.[117] The separation of French colonial prisoners was inherently tied to German discomfort with French use of colonial soldiers during the First World War and the subsequent occupation of the Rhineland in the 1920s. Officially, refusing colonial prisoners in Germany would maintain the racial purity of the Reich, protect the Germans from colonial diseases, and force the French to pay for their own colonial soldiers.[118] The organization of racial separation, specifically what the French would finance, evolved with the situation on the ground.

Generally, a prisoner's race determined his captivity experience and ultimately his chance of survival, but even racial designations were subject to military and political objectives. The OKW's June 1941 orders confirmed that the Germans were following Geneva Convention rules.[119] A year later

Dr. Alfons Waltzog, chief OKW legal expert, restated that "the criterion was the uniform. A Polish man who fought in the French army, is, when captured by the Germans, a French prisoner of war and not a Polish one. This is important in determining the protecting power's actions."[120] The initial categorization as a French prisoner was the most important guarantee that the colonial prisoners' Geneva Convention rights would be respected. Other "inferior" races, such as the Polish or Russian prisoners, were not given the same protections. For the French Army, the Germans made additional distinctions based on skin color, which largely determined their experiences of captivity.

The sheer number of captured soldiers meant that the racial separation took several months to be implemented. As early as August 1940 Senegalese, Madagascan, Indochinese, and North African prisoners were transferred from Neubrandenburg to Orléans or Pithiviers.[121] By early 1941 almost thirty-eight thousand colonial prisoners, possibly 40 percent of the total, had traveled to Germany and needed to be returned to France.[122] This included officers like Capt. Ahmed Rafa from Algeria, who as an officer was initially interned in Oflag II-D. He was sent back to France in November 1940.[123] By October 1941 the OKW declared that no more Algerians or Tunisians be found in German POW camps.[124] While fundamentally, the French did not oppose the colonial prisoners' internment in France, they objected to separating them from their white officers, who might provide a layer of protection against German influence.[125] Among the 140,000 prisoners who remained in the Frontstalags, approximately 45,000 were white soldiers, who were not released until the spring of 1941; some had fought in overseas regiments, but many others had no ties to the colonies.[126]

Over time German attitudes toward colonial prisoners fell into two broad categories: racism tending toward mistreatment or a curious camaraderie. Both of these categories were far removed from the massacres in May–June 1940. The stark change in context for the German soldiers, moving from the heat of battle against "savage" foes to the euphoria of victory, partly explained this shift in attitude. For some German soldiers, the colonial prisoners were different and intriguing. For others, kindness was a key component of anti-French propaganda.

A white prisoner, Jean Cavaillès, reported that he had a "quarrel with the Germans about the blacks. They deck them out in straw hats—top hats, etc., and photograph them. Since I reproached a Senegalese man for allowing this, the German soldiers surrounded me [and] punched [me] in the nose, '*Schwein*.'"[127] The German military administration in France grew increasingly worried that their soldiers were becoming too friendly with the colonial prisoners and issued a memo in August 1940 stating that behavior similar to that described by Cavaillès was unbecoming of the German Army.[128] Cavaillès remembered that the prisoners were photographed in procession, with the Black soldiers directly behind the officers and in front of the French troops. Despite Cavaillès's worries, at this juncture it would be an exaggeration to claim that the colonial prisoners were treated better than the white prisoners. It is more likely that these photographs, like the German newsreels exaggerating the numbers of colonial prisoners captured, were used to demonstrate German racial superiority.[129] By placing the colonial soldiers in front of the white ones, the Germans flipped the accepted racial hierarchies, as they felt the French had done to German soldiers during and after the First World War.

A calculated middle approach to the colonial prisoners began to appear, reflecting Germany's ongoing efforts to destabilize French and British territories by encouraging independence movements. Makan Traore and Mamadou Kone felt they were "treated better and better by their guards. These guards were discreetly attempting to gain their friendship by taking good care of them and promising them an early release, etc."[130] A North African prisoner reported being told, "Eat and drink and if you want to go back to your country then go, but do not stay in the Frenchmen's country where you will be killed with them."[131] However, most of the colonial prisoners were not able to return home.

A series of physical and administrative frontiers separated the French from the colonial prisoners. The first and most visible boundary was the barbed-wire borders around the Frontstalags, creating enclaves of German control on French soil. The second, equally important, was the location of the new Vichy government. Article 3 of the armistice agreement gave the French the right to choose their capital. The government chose Vichy, a spa town in the unoccupied zone that had the advantage, for Pétain's regime, of having a great number of hotels and a limited number of left-wing politicians. Unfortunately, it was on the opposite side of the demarcation line from the colonial prisoners. Placing hurdles between the French and their colonial soldiers allowed Germany to exact financial contributions in exchange for greater access to the colonial prisoners. The colonial prisoners represented little more than a labor force for the Germans until Vichy's interest in them became clear. After that they became an arena where Germany could concede to some French requests, which in turn let the French believe that collaboration was effective and sincere. The cycle continued as the French took on more financial responsibilities in exchange for access to the colonial prisoners.

With temporary camps in France exceeding their limits, prisoners pushed for improvements. At the prompting of several NCOs, the Kommandantur at Meaux organized cleaning duties. Each NCO took responsibility for one of five sectors. Sergeant Paris and Corporal Sanchez organized a cleaning crew with six Moroccan prisoners, who received extra rations in exchange.[132] In another camp, officers of the engineering corps created the camp's physical infrastructure. First they built shelters for the prisoners using boards and corrugated iron. A log road to facilitate the camp commander's movements followed. Finally, they built wooden observatory towers along the camp's barbed-wire perimeter. It was unsurprising that the prisoners pushed for change, since they were the ones suffering, but it illustrated a German tendency to allow the prisoners, and as a consequence the French, to take over German responsibilities.

The lack of available camps forced the German Army to improvise. Buildings were requisitioned or renovated, and POW camps slowly appeared across occupied France. In the Somme, North African prisoners were housed in youth hostels, barracks, a partly destroyed building, and two castles.[133] The Dijon Air Base, whose water pipes had been destroyed by bombardment, became Camp Longvic.[134] Wherever possible, the Germans used existing camps; for example, Laharie had been intended to house German prisoners, but instead it welcomed colonial prisoners.[135] In Angoulême, construction to house civilian Indochinese workers had been halted by the fighting in May 1940. After the defeat, the Feldkommandantur wanted to complete the construction and use the space to house ten thousand colonial prisoners.[136] The German Army added barracks, water pipes, and roads to the unfinished Camp Airvault.[137] Over time, the Germans attempted to transform or build camps according to their standards. Most German prisoner-of-war camps had a comparable layout based on 1939 manuals.[138] Camps were surrounded by barbed wire, with a guard post at the entrance and a *Vorlager* (forecamp) containing administrative buildings, showers, a disinfection area, an infirmary, and a camp prison. Farther along, behind more barbed wire, was the *Hauptlager*, the main part of the camp.[139]

Bringing the improvised camps up to an acceptable standard and building new structures required French and German cooperation, which under the circumstances was not simple. Polo fields in Bayonne became a camp for five thousand prisoners. The German authorities contracted French engineers to install a sanitation system and waterworks to make the camp habitable for a cost of 325,000 francs.[140] In Angoulême, the Feldkommandantur's efforts to build a new, well-equipped camp for the colonial prisoners was stymied, he believed, by restrictive French labor regulations, material shortages, and French inefficiency.[141] The camp commander wanted to expedite the construction process and move the colonial prisoners into a permanent camp as soon as possible. However, to increase the work week beyond the forty-hour maximum established by the popular front in 1936, the camp commander was forced to obtain permission from the *inspecteur du travail*. The inspector conceded that since the war had interrupted work for months, the extra hours would not require overtime pay.[142] Another delay, this time due to the contractors' lack of trucks for moving the raw materials needed for barracks, showers, toilets, and roads, caused the camp commander to complain to the prefect, "I have tried in the last few weeks to create a spacious, clean, and hygienic camp for the prisoners already there and the thousands who will be arriving in the next few days. . . . All my efforts and all my labors are for the benefit of the French prisoners entrusted to me, and I request your kind assistance in completing my duties that benefit only your brave native soldiers from the colonial territories."[143]

Eventually, two months later, and because the Germans were financing the camp, the French Ponts et chaussés department allocated trucks to the contractors so that the camp could be completed.[144] This incident reveals

German and French attitudes toward cooperation, financial responsibil-ity, and the physical conditions for the colonial prisoners. The financial responsibility, which legally fell on the Germans, became increasingly up for debate. The camp commanders understood the benefits of having good conditions for prisoners under their care and did not hesitate to blame the French for deficiencies.

Article 4 of the Geneva Convention placed the financial responsibility for upkeep of the colonial prisoners on Germany.[145] However, the Germans argued that older legal texts, such as the 1907 Hague Law of Land Warfare and the recently signed Franco-German Armistice Agreement, left space for negotiation. Article 3 of the armistice agreement imposed the costs of the occupation on the French, without specifying what could be considered an "occupation cost" and what could not. This allowed the Germans to budget expenses related to the prisoners as occupation costs to be paid for by the French. In building the camp at Angoulême, the German authorities seized two fields without compensating the local farmers. This spurred a legal debate between the prefect of Charante and Colonel von Ploetz over whether the fields had been requisitioned or expropriated. Von Ploetz argued it was a requisition of land, which fell under the law for war benefits, and not an expropriation, which would have required compensation.[146] The prefect and von Ploetz exchanged letters until March 1941, alternatively citing the Hague agreement, the Geneva Convention, and the Franco-German Armistice to force payment. Eventually, a German directive was issued on March 13, 1941, requiring the French to pay the cost of quartering the colonial prisoners.[147] A few months later the directive was clarified: the French were required to pay for the maintenance of preexisting buildings, while Germany would pay for new construction, renovations, and expansions.[148] Even with the clarification, French towns and prefectures often advanced the necessary funds or supplies, forcing local mayors to request reimbursement from the Germans.[149] Drawing out legal debates and delaying reimbursement was a successful tactic to avoid remuneration. The financial question continued to evolve throughout the occupation, with the French assuming more and more direct financial responsibility for feeding and sheltering their colonial soldiers in German captivity.

The decision to keep colonial prisoners in France and not Germany defined the colonial prisoners' experience of captivity above all other factors. Instead of being interned in a racially segregated enemy country, colonial prisoners were surrounded by the French population, who generally recognized their contributions in defending France. Although it was an unintentional consequence, leaving the colonial prisoners in France forced them into the public eye, which, combined with Vichy's proimperial rhetoric, ensured that the French could not neglect the colonial prisoners in favor of white prisoners. It is ironic that German racism, which kept the colonial prisoners out of Germany, was exactly what made them a key question at stake in relations between France and Germany. Thus the colonial prisoners became an important component of the Vichy regime's political arguments with Germany, perhaps despite their original intentions. By early 1941 the prisoner-of-war system in France was fully established. Twenty-two Frontstalags had been built across occupied France, from the Ardennes to Brittany to the Landes near Bordeaux. The construction and habitation of the Frontstalags initiated the second phase of captivity, which lasted until the German occupation of the southern zone in November 1942. As diplomatic relations between Vichy and Germany stabilized, so did physical conditions for colonial prisoners.

3

EVERYDAY LIFE IN CAPTIVITY
Conditions in the Camps

The examination of the everyday reveals the impact of French imperial aims on the colonial prisoners and provides a measure to understand their experiences of captivity. Once the colonial prisoners were identified as a group that could be used for leverage in the political negotiations, every aspect of their captivity became negotiable. While this had a clear and profound effect on the overall conditions of captivity, most colonial prisoners were deliberately left out of the decision-making process. The colonial prisoners' major concerns—survival, food, physical comfort, and loneliness—were all subject to German control. The Scapini Mission viewed every aspect of the colonial prisoners' daily lives as a potential access point for French influence, which might allow them to regain some control over their colonial subjects and occupied metropolitan territory. The filtering process, which turned the Frontstalags into a world dominated by colonial soldiers, gave the colonial prisoners the unusual possibility of interacting with men from the rest of the empire. Standards set by the Geneva Convention provided the guidelines for camp life, but conditions could deviate significantly.

Over fifty overcrowded, often unfinished camps existed on September 24, 1940.[1] By the next summer only twenty main Frontstalags, spread throughout occupied France, were needed.[2] Camps were never static entities. Labor needs or sanitary conditions dictated the closure or opening of camps. Prisoners came and went for daily work or even moved out temporarily to smaller work groups (*Arbeitskommandos*) scattered throughout the surrounding areas. German organizational priorities dictated movement between camps, creating instability in the colonial prisoners' lives. The sheer size of the camps contributed to feelings of depersonalization. A midsize camp, like Chartres, would have five thousand prisoners. Epinal, which was both a Frontstalag and a transit camp for Germany, could hold over ten thousand.[3]

By the beginning of 1941 the Scapini Mission started visiting the camps in France, represented sometimes by Scapini himself; Marcel Bonnaud, a doctor at the Fréjus hospital specializing in colonial diseases; or René Scapini, possibly Georges's son.[4] These visits, and those by local politicians and international aid organizations, brought supplies to the colonial prisoners and served to reinforce the ties between the colonial prisoners and France.[5] The French wanted to believe that the colonial prisoners recognized and appreciated their efforts to facilitate their captivity.[6] As Scheck argues, French access to the Frontstalags gave colonial prisoners the impression that France had more influence than it actually had.[7] The inspection reports written after a camp visit provide valuable information on everyday life in captivity, particularly as few colonial prisoners left first-person accounts. They also reveal the inspectors' biases and what information was available to the French authorities. In western Europe, inspections were carefully orchestrated. Camps received advance notice, the delegations were closely supervised, and often the physical conditions and rations were improved beforehand, prompting the prisoners to exaggerate their complaints.[8] Overall, camp inspection reports in Germany provided a positive, pro-German approximation of the captivity experience in the camps.[9] René Scapini's inspections of Chartres reveal similar tendencies. During his first visit, he concluded that morale was low but acceptable and that the Germans "meant well." Two months later, clearly unaware that the number of escapes had doubled, he concluded that the camp had improved remarkably.[10]

Each aid organization saw its role and importance differently. The International Committee of the Red Cross (ICRC) had the diplomatic weight needed to negotiate with belligerent powers and the resources to send inspectors and material goods to prisoners all over the world. The YMCA took a typically American Protestant approach to constant self-improvement and viewed itself as a link between prisoners of all religions and the world.[11] This resonated well with the National Revolution but sometimes frustrated the colonial prisoners who preferred to play cards rather than organize orchestras or reading groups.

The reality for the colonial prisoners was austere. Camps varied drastically in cleanliness, situation, and organization. At Epinal in eastern France, prisoners worked on agricultural projects such as vegetable gardens and tending horses, rabbits, goats, and sheep. There was a cinema with seating for five hundred, as well as a thirty-five-person orchestra. The camp commander organized German classes and hoped to start football and sporting competitions within the camp.[12] Nonetheless, Epinal was considered a harsh camp, where African prisoners were allegedly not allowed medical treatment.[13] At Solferino in the southwest, the German officer in charge attempted to improve conditions. Prisoners received fresh vegetables and better rations, but they were critically short of clothes and woolens. Some of the Martinican and Madagascan prisoners were dying of cold, with only light canvas jackets.[14]

Housing, Food, and Clothing

The Geneva Convention established minimum standards for all POW camps: "Premises must be entirely free from damp, and adequately heated and lighted. . . . As regards dormitories, their total area, minimum cubic air space, fittings and bedding material, the conditions shall be the same as for the depot troops of the detaining Power."[15] In reality, the level of comfort depended on the camp's location, the prisoners' nationality, camp leadership, and relations with the local administration. The United Kingdom held German prisoners and could retaliate if its prisoners were mistreated. As a result, British prisoners were usually treated better than the other prisoners in Germany. At the other extreme, Germany decided that since the Soviet Union had not signed the Geneva Convention, Soviet soldiers were not covered by its protections. In the middle, French prisoners, and consequently the colonial prisoners, were an integral part of the German war labor economy and continued to benefit from the Geneva Convention protections.

There was no way for the colonial prisoners to forget they were prisoners; signs of captivity were omnipresent. Camps in Bordeaux were surrounded by a complex system of barbed wire and German sentinel posts.[16] Dijon had a similar setup, with guards posted about four feet from the barbed wire.[17] Longvic was organized into sectors or blocs and surrounded by walls, with machine guns posted at each corner and the front gate.[18] The German authorities paid for the purchase of the barbed wire for large camps and Frontstalags.[19]

Proper sanitation facilities for large numbers of men living in crowded conditions were essential to prevent disease outbreaks, which could spread to guards and the surrounding communities. Yet despite the importance of proper hygiene, standards varied widely across France. Unhygienic practices afflicted colonial prisoners in Brittany with scabies and other diseases.[20] Usually the fear of unknown "colonial diseases" encouraged the Germans to take sanitation seriously. Upon arrival in Poitiers, Lieutenant Paillet declared, "This pigsty is not suitable for the French Army!"[21] He had running water installed, covered muddy pathways with stones, and even built a sports field. Free access to individual showers made the difference between a mediocre camp and a good one. Prisoners at Montargis could shower only once every ten days while their clothes were disinfected.[22] Epinal had facilities for five hundred prisoners to shower daily, but disinfection was only available at the hospital.[23] In this domain, the Scapini Mission, local government leaders, and the camp commanders generally cooperated to improve the sanitation. German officers informed Scapini that the poor hygiene at Camp Laharie could be fixed with proper plumbing fixtures. Scapini wrote to the ICRC, and within two months the camp had individual showers and an eighteen-hundred-liter water tank.[24] In rare cases the infrastructure could not overcome a camp's natural disadvantages. At Airvault, the Germans had built "an admirable system of sanitation and hygienic installations," which would have been more effective if the camp had not been surrounded by mud.[25] Airvault was plagued with disease and was eventually closed.

Colonial prisoners reported that conditions began to improve at the end of 1940, with real beds, electricity, and stoves in the barracks.[26] When Léopold Senghor arrived at Poitiers in October 1940, prisoners were lodged in unheated hangars with corrugated metal roofs.[27] Despite the generous coal allowances, when temperatures in December fell below zero, Senegalese prisoners froze in the uninsulated barracks. It was worse for the North African prisoners living in converted hangars. The cold was the biggest complaint across the Frontstalag network.[28] Persistent fuel shortages forced camp commanders and local authorities to find creative methods to keep the colonial prisoners warm, especially those from warm climates. With only a few cast-iron stoves available in Loiret, the earthenware factory Gien created brick stoves specifically designed for the POW camps.[29] Wood cut by the colonial prisoners became a major fuel source. These measures were adapted across France, and the colonial prisoners' health stabilized in warmer premises. However, prisoners did not spend their days in the barracks, so the cold remained a concern throughout captivity because of the persistent shortages of warm clothes, shoes, socks, gloves, and jackets.[30]

Colonial prisoners shared overcrowded rooms and slept on bunk beds with two or three levels.[31] In Epinal, the rooms housed twice as many men as legally permitted.[32] Barracks might house one hundred men sleeping on straw mattresses with two or three blankets if lucky.[33] NCOs generally had better sleeping arrangements, often with their own rooms and bed linens.[34] At Charleville, Henry Eboué had his own room and even a piano.[35] Work assignments changed the housing situation as a great number of men moved out of the Frontstalags into smaller work camps. At Pithiviers, Mohamed Ben Brahim and Mohamed Ben Ali remembered prisoners were forced to sleep on a factory floor, sharing half a blanket between them.[36]

Colonial prisoners were generally housed with men from their home colony, which meant differences in living standards quickly became racial issues. At Joigny, only the colonial prisoners had mattresses, while the white prisoners slept on straw, a role reversal they did not appreciate.[37] It was the opposite at Epinal, where the camp commander claimed that all prisoners had received the same berths, but the colonial prisoners had burned them for warmth. The colonial prisoners' representative vehemently denied this accusation.[38] It was not unusual to find contradictions between the prisoners' and the camp staff's assessments. The colonial prisoners were at a clear disadvantage, as some believed that "certain races" were inherently dishonest, while a white gentleman's "honor" was seen as a guarantee of truthfulness.

When the colonial prisoners worked in their local communities (discussed in the next chapter), the French could assess their physical condition outside of coordinated inspections. That visibility increased pressure on French officials to replace the colonial prisoners' worn clothes and footwear. André Paul Sadon, prefect of the Nièvre, a traditionally left-wing rural department, repeatedly lamented that colonial prisoners in his department went barefoot and wore rags.[39] Prisoners at Epinal and Chartres were shod and clothed in a similar manner.[40] Indochinese prisoners at Joigny were unable to work and thus earn a salary "due to their physical conditions and their shoes."[41] The camp authorities often held back the leather shoes for the winter and provided the prisoners with wooden shoes instead.[42] Prisoners disliked the wooden shoes, and at Montargis, they asked Paul Anderson and Auguste Senaud of the YMCA for better shoes. However, the inspectors hesitated because of rumors that the North Africans had sold their clothes to their friends.[43]

The colonial prisoners had greater means of communicating issues regarding their captivity than white prisoners in Germany did, via inspectors or civilians met while at work. However, because of their race, they had a harder time being believed. Racist judgments by white inspectors, camp commanders, and politicians, such as considering some races "inherently dishonest," persisted and negatively influenced the colonial prisoners' access to aid. While this form of racism was certainly not new, during captivity, as seen at Epinal with beds or Montargis with shoes, it affected the colonial prisoners' ability to be heard. They prisoners were limited to the assistance that the inspectors felt they "deserved."

While certain aspects of captivity remained too abstract to attract much attention, hunger was universally understood.[44] Articles 11 and 12 of the Geneva Convention required that prisoners receive the same quality and quantity of food as the depot troops and have access to canteens and cooking areas. The French wanted to be reassured that their prisoners were not starving, and that included the colonial soldiers. French civilians, the Scapini Mission, the French Red Cross, the ICRC, and aid organizations in the colonies all worked to increase the quality and quantity of the colonial prisoners' food. Food shortages posed a real problem to their health. At Saint-Médard, undernourishment made between four hundred and five hundred colonial prisoners vulnerable to serious, sometimes fatal, illnesses like tuberculosis, pneumonia, and consumption.[45] Colonial prisoners in the Somme were fed only one meal a day, forcing them to beg for bread when outside the camps.[46] Prisoners in southwestern camps suffered greater food shortages due to overpopulation after many colonial prisoners had been transferred south.[47]

At Labenne, colonial prisoners refused the games and soap brought by a French Red Cross representative because they were not edible. Instead they called to her, "Come, come, see kitchen. Nothing to eat. Come see soup. Soup of water. Give food."[48] The prefect of the Loiret reported in February 1941 that the camp commander was overwhelmed by the number of colonial prisoners and the persistent disorganization in France. Instead of taking action, he appeared to have been paralyzed by the situation, and the colonial prisoners suffered.[49] Corruption forced French charities to take care of fifteen thousand colonial prisoners interned in Vesoul when the camp commander sent the Red Cross donations to Germany.[50]

Instead of supplying better rations, the German camp commanders preferred to request more food from the French rather than increase their own expenditure. Camp inspections confirmed the necessity of increasing the colonial prisoners' rations of bread, meat, and dried vegetables. Consequently, the colonial prisoners were better fed, worked better, and were in better sprits without affecting the camp's budget. At Ecly (Ardennes), the camp commander told the prefect that he urgently needed vouchers for bread, meat, and fats to feed his colonial prisoners.[51] France needed to retain the image of a strong colonial power that would not abandon its subjects to die of hunger as some prisoners feared. Working with the German commanders, the Vichy government and French aid organizations attempted to provide adequate and varied provisions to the colonial prisoners. This was as much about humanitarian aid as about political aims.

How the prisoners spoke about food changed as their situation evolved. When there was not enough food for them to survive, they generally asked for more of anything. Only when prisoners' minimal needs were met did they complain about unappetizing or bland food.[52] Once the Red Cross deliveries increased food rations to acceptable levels, the colonial prisoners did not hesitate to ask for further improvements, specifically food from the colonies.[53] When possible, these requests were honored. One camp received two monthly deliveries from the French Red Cross of fresh bread, tea, mint, couscous, dates, chickpeas, and jam.[54] The colonies remained a major supplier of colonial foodstuffs despite the British blockade, but after 1941 they were forced to supply Germany first.[55] Most colonial prisoners survived on bread or potatoes as a staple, with smaller quantities of proteins. The French press almost certainly exaggerated claims that prisoners at Epinal received seventy grams of meat per day. Colonial prisoners most likely received meat once or twice a week in soup.[56] Senghor remembered receiving "a small, scientifically calculated ration of fat or jam."[57] Most of the camps required additional food for the colonial prisoners, as the Germans did not provide enough. Instead, the colonial prisoners turned toward the French population for help, and they usually found it.

Colonial prisoners' morale was linked to the availability and quality of food. One significant improvement came with the replacement of the German cooks by chefs from among the colonial prisoners, after which morale improved greatly.[58] Deliveries of colonial specialties, increased individual food parcels, access to individual stoves, and a change in camp chefs greatly improved conditions for the colonial prisoners.[59] Prisoners earned salaries from work, which they could spend on food or drink in the camp canteen. In many camps, the "man of confidence," or group leader, was permitted to buy or collect donations in town for the canteen.[60] Canteens offered cakes, chocolates, beer, lemonade, even bread or cheese, usually sold at cost.[61] Alcohol was sold for a small profit, which was then used to purchase tobacco and bread for the prisoners.[62] Most colonial prisoners could buy wine, beer, or cider; the Indochinese prisoners were allowed to purchase one liter of wine per week.[63] Considering that France, during both wars, went to great lengths to ensure that Muslim culinary rules, including the prohibition of alcohol, were respected, it is surprising that alcohol was readily available. Photos and anecdotal evidence revealed that colonial soldiers drank more alcohol than the French military would have liked.

Internal Camp Hierarchies

As much as the French tried to influence the Frontstalags through aid organizations, they became an increasingly colonial world as the Germans filtered out the white prisoners. Most German POW camps followed the same internal organization. At Bulgose in the Landes, a German reserve officer assisted by six or seven N C O s ran the camp, while a different company supplied the guards.[64] These special guard battalions were composed of career soldiers, broadly representing Nazi Germany, often older or with slight handicaps, precluding them from active duty.[65] A formal multilevel hierarchy existed among the prisoners as well, usually organized by sleeping arrangements. Each barrack had a leader, usually a colonial N C O. The barracks were then grouped under the authority of one N C O representing a place of origin. For example, the barracks might have one Moroccan warrant officer, one Senegalese staff sergeant, and one Madagascan staff sergeant.[66] The oldest of these N C O s served as the man of confidence, as stipulated in the Geneva Convention. Armelle Mabon is quite critical of the prisoner representatives, arguing that they were responsible for executing German orders.[67] In many ways that was true; however, good group leaders could be effective liaisons between the prisoners, the Germans, and the Scapini Mission.

The man of confidence not only was the prisoners' advocate to the aid organizations but also effectively became the charities' representative in the Frontstalags. In Vesoul, Sgt. Maj. Tran Van Tiep verified the daily deliveries from the Red Cross, kept the only key to the depot, and controlled access to food and supplies.[68] It was a position of considerable responsibility. In Germany, prisoners were allowed to choose their own leader, as dictated by Article 43 of the Geneva Convention.[69] In France, the camp commanders imposed their own choice of leaders, sometimes over the colonial prisoners' protests. As Mabon highlights, this could allow opportunistic colonial prisoners to obtain favored roles from the Germans at their comrades' expense. However, these leaders faced multiple challenges: distrust from the fellow prisoners if they were not effective, interference by camp officials who wanted control over Red Cross deliveries, and physical distance from their fellow prisoners scattered in work groups.[70] If supported by the camp authorities, the man of confidence could improve conditions for his fellow prisoners by sending requests for godmothers or donations from aid organizations.[71] Sometimes white prisoners served as *chefs de camp* (group leaders), replacing the function of the man of confidence.[72] They liaised with the colonial prisoners and the German camp administration and distributed packages and goods supplied by the aid organizations. These roles were often assigned to men of a certain social standing, not simply white prisoners.

Fearing that without their white officers the colonial prisoners would be vulnerable to German influence, the French encouraged the few remaining white soldiers, often in health roles, to lead and "educate" the colonial prisoners. The YMCA also believed gentle guidance from the white soldiers would help the colonial prisoners feel "at home."[73] The white camp inspectors saw these paternalistic efforts as universally positive, especially when the white French who were "accustomed" to the African troops watched over them.[74] Unfortunately, we do not have the colonial prisoners' opinion on the subject. In this context, "watch over" was synonymous with "supervise," and being accustomed to the "ways" of the colonial soldiers was an important skill for French officers and NCOs. Most French soldiers with "colonial experience" went through the same training, ensuring a certain continuity in attitudes toward the empire and race. Until their captivity, colonial soldiers rarely interacted with French men and women with different backgrounds. When the remaining white prisoners were released from the Frontstalags in the spring of 1941, the French feared the Germans would now have unrestricted influence over the colonial prisoners.

Leadership roles placed these prisoners in a potentially awkward position above their fellow prisoners and below the German guards. Despite the challenges, many colonial prisoners navigated their positions well and improved conditions for prisoners beyond their circle of friends. The ICRC inspectors praised the man of confidence and the "native NCOs" at a camp near Rennes for their excellent job maintaining discipline.[75] Corporal Hamada used his position to circumvent the camp authorities and discuss his concerns about a Tunisian soldier, Ayade van Amor, with the mayor of Mailly. Van Amor had declared himself an NCO, encouraged indiscipline among the colonial prisoners, insulted France, and refused to obey the man of confidence, who was white.[76] Hamada's report prompted the mayor to launch a formal investigation, which was stymied because of a lack of gasoline. As the departmental delegate could not visit the camp personally, he suggested that the Red Cross delivery drivers continue the investigation. The outcome was unknown, but prisoners like Ayade van Amor existed everywhere.

In all German POW camps, guards cultivated prisoners to act as spies and betray their comrades in exchange for favors.[77] The other prisoners, often their victims, universally hated these men and went to great lengths to denounce them to authorities. At Solferino, an NCO named El Mouldi Benhassen wrote to the French Red Cross to accuse the Algerian chef de camp, Akob Bouabdallah, of a long list of crimes: conducting unauthorized searches of the barracks, pillaging personal parcels and stealing hashish (kef) from the Tunisian packages, selling the shoes and clothes provided by the Red Cross to civilians at exorbitant prices, confiscating money from games, and inciting racial hatred.[78] The colonial prisoners knew their rights and to whom to address their complaints while in captivity. If they felt their complaints were not taken seriously enough, prisoners reiterated the issues to local authorities on their return home.[79]

Sometimes French officials responded directly to the colonial prisoners' concerns. S.Sgt. Bonko Hambrié wrote to Pétain complaining that infighting had forced out a good NCO, leaving the colonial prisoners without any support.[80] The head of the Bureau de l'inspection des camps met with Hambrié during his next visit to Rennes to discuss the incident further. On another occasion, responding to accusations from colonial prisoners at Camp Hanneman that the man of confidence, Geromini, was selling Red Cross supplies to the prisoners and Germans, the Direction du service des prisonniers de guerre intervened, and the Germans had him transferred to Stalag VIII-A in Görlitz.[81] Stealing Red Cross supplies or parcels was punished severely.

New formal and informal hierarchies emerged in this relative vacuum, as the French feared, yet the privileged maintained their privileges throughout. Often the men of confidence were chosen from among the literate prisoners, which reinforced the previously existing colonial hierarchies. Wealthy, educated men like Henry and Robert Eboué continued, even in captivity, to enjoy significant advantages denied the rank-and-file soldiers.[82] Literate colonial soldiers were taken on as camp scribes, involved in documenting the prisoner population and writing correspondence for the German hierarchy. Sometimes they were sent into town on errands, allowing them to come into contact with French civilians and start creating personal networks of influence. Religiously educated Muslim prisoners might find themselves in a position to exchange influence over the other prisoners for early release or better conditions while in the camp (discussed in chapter 8). However, the vast majority of prisoners had few possibilities to change the conditions of their captivity without seeking favors from the German guards or becoming policemen.

Serving as part of the camp's internal police force was much more controversial than acting as a man of confidence.[83] NCOs or soldiers who gained the Germans' trust could become policemen and were generally hated by their fellow prisoners, who assumed they had gotten themselves appointed by scheming. In smaller work groups, colonial prisoners were under both the guard's supervision and the policemen's authority. A few policemen resigned as a result of their fellow prisoners' hostility.[84] In his captivity report, French doctor Pierre Jean Prost described at length the Algerian and Tunisian prisoners who accepted these positions:

> One should perhaps not generalize, but what made them unsympathetic is that they were very opportunistic; they sought to please our guards and eagerly accepted the job of camp police. (They were given helmets; they wore an armband with a "P"; and were armed with a gasmask hose that served as a baton. They earned one mark per day.) The Germans had suggested that Captain Cherchell of the colonial artillery (Martinican) entrust the colored officers (there were seven) with running the camp police. Of course, the officers refused this kind of collaboration, the Senegalese tirailleurs and Moroccans did as well; but the Algerians [and] Tunisians, perhaps through the intermediary of two warrant officers, agreed to guard the buildings where French prisoners, sometimes officers, were locked awaiting departure for Germany.[85]

By using North African prisoners to guard French officers, the German guards reenacted their biggest complaint about the French occupation of the Rhineland: placing Europeans in a position of inferiority vis-à-vis colonial subjects. For the prisoners, the police salary was enticing. One mark equaled twenty francs, double what prisoners earned working on farms or in forests. The French would have preferred that white men hold policing roles to avoid "awkward" racial tensions. Instead, the Germans favored North African prisoners as policemen, which allegedly exacerbated tensions with other prisoners.[86] Previous scholarship incorrectly argued that Vichy opposed using colonial soldiers as police because they preferred to maintain an apartheid regime in the army.[87] This argument underestimates the all-encompassing violent invasiveness of apartheid and sheds no light on the nuances of French imperialist policy. Contrary to the total and unequal separation promoted by apartheid, the French believed that their influence was essential to set the colonial subjects on the path to "civilization." Adoption of French language and culture through the example and advice of "superiors" was an essential sign of assimilation. The Vichy regime's opposition to the use of colonial soldiers as police was much more straightforward. It did not want them to be unduly influenced by the Germans or to get accustomed to positions of power, especially over the white soldiers or officers. While collaboration permeated every aspect of the political discussions around colonial prisoners, the French tried to keep it away from the colonial prisoners themselves, preferring instead that they continue to think of Germany as the enemy. Captivity and their deliberate exclusion from political debate facilitated this. Collaboration remained abstract and thus subservient to the realities of captivity, at least at this stage, when it was still the Germans who guarded the colonial prisoners, forced them to work, and shot those who attempted to escape.

It is unsurprising that many colonial prisoners felt isolated. They were without news from their families, sometimes for years, and were depersonalized or treated like "others" by their fellow prisoners. White prisoners seemed to view the Indochinese prisoners, a minority in the Frontstalags, as a group, to be admired as in Stalag VII-A or hated as at Ambroise.[88] When colonial prisoners were praised or noticed, it was usually for their excellent discipline, as loyalty and obedience were considered the highest qualities for a colonial soldier. In an odd decision, the Germans moved all Indochinese prisoners to Vesoul in November 1942, allegedly because they were too weak to work in the forests and the Germans wanted to separate them from the other colonial prisoners.[89] However, the French considered the Indochinese soldiers and civilians to be excellent workers who managed the cold better than the African soldiers. Without news from their families, the Indochinese prisoners felt a growing sense of isolation, and this move would not have improved it.[90]

Racial conflicts came to a head in the spring of 1941, when all remaining "French" prisoners were released from the Frontstalags. For the Germans, "French" meant "white," ignoring the important minority of French citizens from the older colonies in the West Indies and small enclaves in West Africa. Unsurprisingly, the Martinican prisoners were "offended at being considered natives, and [at the fact] that the Germans only see men of color and not the nationality and the position of French citizenship."[91] An aid organization representing Martinican soldiers asked General Andlauer to obtain the release of citizens from the West Indies who had been living in France before mobilization in 1939.[92] They had the same legal rights as any metropolitan white French soldier and therefore should have also been released. While individual prisoners may have been released, nothing was granted to the citizens as a group. This German decision badly affected the morale in the Frontstalags, especially among French citizens, who felt that the French government had deemed them second-class citizens and had shown an inability to fight for their rights.[93]

The French citizens of color posed a significant risk to the Vichy regime's desire for loyalty and stability, as the French had no power to release them. They were educated, literate, and accustomed to fighting for their rights. However, they were a small minority, mostly from Martinique and a few from the four communes of Dakar.[94] The French were therefore more concerned about the negative effect these citizens and other subjects might have, fearing a "contamination of the blacks by the protesting bad minds of some North Africans and Martinicans."[95] The postwar French tendency to dismiss legitimate complaints from colonial prisoners as the result of German propaganda demonstrated that this tendency to divide and ignore was French rather than Vichy-specific. One should hardly be surprised that after undermining the rights of French citizens, the postwar debates on citizenship and empire were fraught.[96] Rather than admit their impotence to a group with potential influence over the mass of colonial prisoners, the French preferred to ask the Germans to separate the colonial prisoners by race and origin.

Worry about German propaganda certainly preoccupied the Vichy authorities, but their desire for the separation of races went further. Behind the racist discourse of the French colonizers was detailed knowledge of the empire's populations based on racist ethnographic studies.[97] Despite publicly praising a vast empire brought together through love of the motherland, actual unity was difficult to obtain and even feared by the French. This fear, while inherently French, was heightened under the Vichy regime, as the colonial empire had already split into Free French and Vichy colonies. The colonial prisoners were expected to conform to assigned characteristics of "Algerians" or "Indochinese." However, the colonial prisoners had different cultures, languages, and religious traditions. Rural farmers from Burkina Faso had as little in common with urban workers from Algiers as with their German captors. Yet the French applied generalizations to most colonial subjects.[98] The French colonial administrators and military officers had experience with the different and distinct cultures within the colonial populations. This knowledge was combined with generalizations and stereotypes to create French imperialist policy.

Under Vichy, the French felt that keeping races separate would effectively limit potentially dangerous tensions among different races. The official reasoning was that different ethnic groups were inherently incapable of getting along. However, the comment about "bad minds" potentially contaminating loyal soldiers suggests that preventing squabbles over supplies by separating colonial soldiers by race had another benefit. While anticolonial resistance has existed since the beginning of the colonial conquest, the interwar period saw an increase in organized transnational anti-imperialist movements. By keeping the colonial prisoners out of political discussions and encouraging close supervision by white prisoners or loyal NCOs, the French hoped it would prevent the prisoners discussing radical ideas like *Négritude*, championed by Suzanne and Aimé Césaire and their friend Senghor, or the growing nationalism of Habib Bourguiba in Tunisia.

Germany, by contrast, had organizational power over the colonial prisoners but none of the colonialists' inside knowledge of the different peoples and cultures. More importantly, Germany had its own goals for destabilizing the French and British colonial regimes by supporting Arab self-determination and freedom of movement in the Middle East.[99] Bigard explained to the head of the German High Command how the French managed their vast empire: "Natives from Morocco, Algeria, Madagascar and Senegal are found in some camps in the east. These men, who are different races, live together with difficulty. In the French army, great care is taken, in the interest of discipline, to separate natives from different races, in different garrisons or at least different barracks."[100] In response, the German High Command declared that it would house colonial prisoners by religion, but the vast majority were Muslim.[101]

By November 1941 most colonial prisoners were separated by origin.[102] In Voves (Eure-et-Loir), the housing allocation reflected a racial hierarchy. Prisoners from Alsace or Lorraine had the best lodging, and Black soldiers were housed in the slaughterhouse.[103] Lo Samba, a Senegalese soldier, remembered camps being divided into four sections: "European prisoners, Arab prisoners, Yellow prisoners, Black prisoners."[104] Prisoners from the Caribbean were housed with the African prisoners, which, as seen, worried the French authorities.

Henry Eboué felt that tensions and racism plagued relations between North African and Black prisoners.[105] Inès Lyautey, widow of the military colonizer and herself symbolic of the empire, complained that at Camp Lerouville, "natives from Morocco, Algeria, Madagascar, and Senegal, due to a lack of sufficient food and warm clothes, are reduced to great suffering. They fight among themselves, which incites their guards to punish them."[106] Her explanation was ignored by members of the Comité central d'assistance aux prisonniers de guerre en captivité (Central committee for aid to prisoners of war in captivity), who dismissed the fighting as the natural result of mutual hatred between Moroccans and Senegalese.[107] However, many prisoners blamed the disagreements on conditions of captivity, not an "inherent" inability to get along. In one case gambling caused problems between the Senegalese and Indochinese prisoners.[108] Perhaps the committee felt Lyautey was criticizing its efforts for the colonial prisoners. If suffering in captivity was the cause of the fighting, the French could be expected to fix it, but they could not be held responsible for "innate" hatreds. Gnimagnon echoed Lyautey's belief. He remembered that "the prisoners maintained excellent relations among themselves, without regard for color, race or rank. They saw themselves as brothers-in-arms, united by the same misfortune. One could see at the beginning, and it was painful, some hostility between race and color due certainly to the shortages and the misery in which were brutally found ourselves. But immediately the brotherly instinct quashed the instinct for egoism and petty mindedness and [now] all fraternize in the common fate."[109]

The crux of French fears can be seen in Gnimagnon's phrase "united by the same misfortune." France wanted the colonial soldiers to be united and loyal to France, but not necessarily united with each other. Some conflict was tolerated, as it provided an excuse to keep the prisoners separate from each other. Captivity was the catalyst, but the German focus on North Africa and North African prisoners certainly exacerbated tensions (see chapter 8). For much of their captivity, until they moved into work camps, the colonial prisoners were in confined spaces, far from home in harsh conditions. As A. J. Barker argued, "Captivity breeds increased irritability in all men; some suffer a little more, others a little less. This is the so-called 'barbed-wire disease,' which is not particular to any nationality."[110] Ultimately, the colonial prisoners were just men adapting as best they could to captivity.

Within the constraints imposed by occupation, the Vichy government, aided by local and international initiatives, attempted to improve conditions for the colonial prisoners to ensure their continued loyalty. Despite the hardships, there was continuity and predictability in the colonial prisoners' captivity. The chaos of the summer of 1940 was over, and the colonial prisoners settled into a routine. The most revealing comment about the colonial prisoner experience came from Gnimagnon: "One can say that until recently, a prisoner's life in Epinal was not much different from that led in French garrisons during peacetime."[111] The status quo was exactly what the Vichy regime wanted: if nothing changed, then no colonial prisoners would get "unsavory" ideas. Overall, the basic camp experience of the colonial prisoners in France was better than that of their French and Allied counterparts in Germany through the end of 1942. However, the work regime and the health of the colonial prisoners were two additional crucial aspects of their life that require separate investigation (see chapters 4 and 5).

The reality of the fragmented French Empire better reflected the actual relations among the colonial prisoners than did the persistent French rhetoric of a loyal and united empire. Despite what French publications from the Third Republic to the Vichy regime proclaimed, the French Empire did not consist of a unified group of loyal French subjects and citizens. The French advised keeping the soldiers from different colonies separate, allegedly to avoid cultural clashes. In reality, it was to prevent ties or alliances from forming across colonial boundaries, which might prove detrimental to French rule. Without the imposed military order, colonial prisoners renegotiated the constraints of captivity and created new alliances to their own benefit. Interactions varied among the colonial prisoners and between the colonial prisoners and the French. However, this colonial space created within the Frontstalags did not free the colonial prisoners from racism or generalizations from the French, Germans, or even fellow prisoners.

The colonial prisoners' daily life presented certain difficulties that should not be minimized: hunger, cold, and harsh living conditions. However, from early 1941 the colonial prisoners had a means of communication with the French, first through international organizations and later through French ones. Being able to complain and having those complaints heard were two fundamental signs of a stable experience of captivity. Vichy used the colonial prisoners' complaints and needs as a way to access the closed German space in the Frontstalags. Eager to prove French commitment to collaboration, Vichy policies helped improve the camps and the colonial prisoners' experiences within them, to the colonial prisoners' benefit. With the exception of the work regime, physical conditions were the major factor influencing the colonial prisoners' experiences of captivity. As for discipline, most colonial soldiers would have been used to a highly regimented life in the French Army anyway, and one not dissimilar to the POW regime.

4

OCCUPYING THEIR TIME

Colonial Prisoners' Work in Occupied France

Work occupied the greater part of the colonial prisoners' everyday life and was the subject of extensive political negotiations based on legal precedents in Europe and the colonies. Diverging economic priorities set the French and German authorities at odds over the definition of prisoner labor. Germany saw France as an important potential material contributor to, but not partner in, its war economy, with the colonial prisoners a minor financial question. For the French, rebuilding the economy went further than financial necessity; it became entangled in the imagery of renewal and rebirth that characterized Pétain's National Revolution. In this vision, the continued presence of colonial prisoners working in French fields and forests was a poignant reminder of what France had lost to Germany: 1.5 million white men. Everything regarding the colonial prisoners' labor became a political tug-of-war between the German financial and military demands and the French desire to get their prisoners home. These competing goals had a direct impact on the colonial prisoners' experiences, as Germany and France defined and redefined the kind of work they could do.

The double legacy of the First World War and the tradition of forced labor in the colonies influenced the colonial prisoners' experience of work in France. In 1887 the *indigénat* legal code was imposed on French subjects. It created a legal system wherein white administrators could punish subjects without trials for a variety of crimes, and it imposed a complicated system of forced labor and taxation on men, women, and children. After the formal abolition of slavery in French West Africa in 1905, forced labor was justified as a practical method to ensure the "lazy Africans" would work to develop the colony.[1] By codifying a separate legal system for subjects and citizens based on race and religion, the indigénat was fundamentally at odds with the stated universalizing values of the French Republic. Labor requirements under the indigénat varied from mining to road building to working on private farms in conditions that ranged from uncomfortable to deadly. Work sites were often far from home, breaking family cohesion and imposing different climates and languages on workers.[2] While veterans of the Great War were exempt from the indigénat, forced labor persisted and came under international condemnation as a form of slavery.[3]

In 1936 the Popular Front considered implementing social legislation in the African colonies to create an African urban workforce. Its efforts were stymied by the belief, held equally by those who supported and opposed the reforms, that the Africans were peasants who, despite French civilizing efforts, would not work without being forced.[4] Some of these racist views on colonial subjects' work ethic resurfaced when colonial prisoners were sent to work in France; however, as prisoners of war, they were protected by international law, which guaranteed greater protections than those in the colonies. Forced labor continued throughout the French Empire in Free French and Vichy colonies, finally ending with the April 11, 1946, Houphouët-Boigny Law.

The integration of prisoners into the captor's war effort was technically a violation of the prisoners' legal status, creating disagreements on what constituted illegal war work and what was permitted.[5] As Heather Jones argues, during the First World War, the increase of collective reprisals against prisoners and use of prisoner labor expanded in a cyclical manner, pushing the boundaries of acceptable violence.[6] The desperate need for labor in wartime, combined with the systematic reciprocity and escalation of violence against prisoners, changed the definition of permissible prisoner labor. From 1916 it was no longer a question of whether prisoners would work for their captors but of how and under what conditions. Eventually, restrictions were established by the 1929 Geneva Convention.

The structure of prisoner labor in occupied France differed significantly from the POW regimes of the First World War. In 1914–18 prisoners worked for the detaining power's army and interests, while the home country protested and retaliated. Then the cycle repeated itself. Article 31 of the Geneva Convention was unambiguous: prisoners could not work directly for the war effort.[7] Yet from the outbreak of war, German interests took precedence over the country's legal obligations. Officially, instructions from the German High Command (OKW) held employers responsible if prisoners were used illegally to build weapons factories. In reality, the OKW and the Todt Organization coordinated to use prisoners to build explosive factories.[8] The Todt Organization, a German civil and military engineering firm founded under the Third Reich by Fritz Todt, was implicated in forced labor projects throughout the occupied territories. Indeed, abuses were reported as early as October 1940, while the United States still acted as the protecting power to French prisoners. The American ambassador was called to investigate claims that French prisoners in Germany were forced to work in a munitions factory.[9] Initially, the colonial prisoners were relatively protected from dangerous war work; that changed in the war's latter years, continuing through the D-day landings. Despite the Scapini Mission's many protests, colonial prisoners worked in munitions factories, transported explosives, and built military defenses along the coast and on the Atlantic Wall.[10]

In 1940 the Germans saw the colonial prisoners' unique position as a means to redraw the Geneva Convention restrictions on POW work. For eight months the French and German delegations debated the technical and legal differences between "roads" and "runways," because prisoners could legally repair the former but not the latter. The Germans argued that there was no practical reason to prevent the prisoners from working on runways, because tanks drove on roads and airplanes on runways.[11] Gen. Paul-André Doyen for the French delegation retorted that the question of road repair was more nuanced: during the First World War, prisoners were not allowed to build roads destined for military use.[12] However, Article 13 of the armistice agreement required the French to maintain or repair all harbors, industrial facilities, roads, railways, and transportation routes. Lacking a German response, Scapini, without explicitly abandoning the protections provided by Article 31, quietly informed the Germans in March 1941 that he would not protest against war work.[13] Even in his memoirs,

Scapini defended his choice, arguing that these restrictions were purely academic and sentimental.[14] As Raffael Scheck elaborates, once both the Scapini Mission and the Vichy government openly supported German victory, it became difficult to protest against the use of French prisoners to work for that victory. Additionally, Scapini feared that insisting on a strict interpretation of Geneva Convention would push the Germans to renege on previous "generous" decisions.[15]

Colonial Prisoners' Work for the French Economy

French agriculture was an immediate and persistent priority for both France and Germany. As a demonstration of Hitler's "generous" commitment to French economic recovery, he allowed prisoners to work on French farms.[16] Prefects sent the occupying forces requests for laborers, and prisoners went to work immediately. This calculated gesture was anything but generous. Germany had a war economy with huge expansionist designs, whereas France was a postwar regime in limbo, with one-third of its farmers interned in Germany.[17] Showing generosity to France early on was a calculated decision to encourage the French to uphold the armistice, thus reducing the number of occupation troops required. In the same vein, Germany had a vested interest in French agriculture, as France would become a major supplier of foodstuffs for Germany. Moreover, the early deployment of French prisoners encouraged the belief that they would be released soon, reducing the number of escapes and calming spirits.

The question of when colonial prisoners began working in the French countryside is somewhat complicated. Scheck argues that the German military command in France was reluctant to use colonial labor outside the Frontstalags before the spring of 1941, when they integrated agriculture, forestry, and public work.[18] However, the evidence suggests that an important minority of colonial prisoners worked outside the camps before the autumn of 1940. Hassen-Ladjimi from Tunisia remembered working outside during these early confused months.[19] Michel Gnimagnon, a teacher from Dahomey, remembered that at first only North African and white prisoners left the camps for work, but by September 1940 West African prisoners joined the work groups.[20] In August 1940 the camp commanders in the Eure-et-Loir department looked for suggestions for work for their colonial prisoners.[21] At the end of August Henry Eboué went to Amiens regularly on work duty, during which time he met Mr. Pagès, president of the Amis coloniaux de la Somme, who began sending him parcels several times a week.[22] Cpl. Amar Belkacem from Tunisia reported that many prisoners managed to escape while on work duty near Dijon sometime between August and October 1940, which suggests there were other North African prisoners working outside.[23] After November 1940 in Epinal, only the West African prisoners were sent on work groups, as the Moroccans and Algerians reportedly escaped too often.[24]

With the increased organization and racial separation of the prisoners, the colonial prisoners became a frequent visible presence in the French economy. Even if all eighty-five thousand colonial prisoners, a significant number, were able to work outside the camp, the prisoners were still a limited resource. The labor shortages in a peasant-based agricultural society were particularly severe during the occupation. Hence the colonial prisoners' labor was as important for the French as it was for the German authorities.

For the colonial prisoners, work offered a welcome change from the strict regime of captivity. In the summer and autumn of 1940 conditions were relaxed. Charles Metton simply collected four Algerian prisoners from their camp each morning and drove them, without guards, to his farm, where they helped drain the fields.[25] This allowed the colonial prisoners to interact with the French without German oversight and to shake off, at least for a while, the discipline of the Frontstalags. The prefect of the Nièvre, André Paul Sadon, reflected a commonly held opinion that the colonial prisoners were best suited to the unskilled spring work but that the autumn harvest required skilled workers.[26]

Although colonial prisoners were generally unfamiliar with agriculture in the metropole, they were physically accustomed to hard labor, unlike many of the metropolitan unemployed who had urban backgrounds.[27] Farm work was demanding and exhausting, especially for those unused to it, but nevertheless many colonial prisoners preferred working outside the camp.[28] Two months later Sadon acknowledged that the North African prisoners had been quite useful.[29] The colonial prisoners were welcomed as temporary relief while the French men were in Germany. The fact that their labor was useful came as a surprising bonus. The prisoners were not the only ones taking advantage of the distance separating them from the Frontstalag command. The guards' relaxed attitudes on work groups provided further respite from prisoner life.[30] However, French authorities feared that this relaxed attitude and close contact with German guards would influence the colonial prisoners and make them forget their loyalty to France. The guards' leniency also gave prisoners and civilians opportunities for contact when formal avenues were closed.[31] In the Ardennes, locals took advantage of this to slip packages and letters to prisoners, despite the risk that if they were caught, the local post offices would be closed as punishment.[32]

As agricultural work was an absolute priority in France and Germany, the majority of colonial prisoners, like most of Germany's prisoners, worked on farms. This shifted over time, with prisoners engaged in agriculture decreasing from 65 percent in the summer of 1940 to 31.5 percent by February 1944, as French prisoners became civilian workers and Germany was firmly engaged in a total-war economy.[33] In August 1940 the German agricultural agency Ostland occupied farms in northeastern France, especially those that had been abandoned during the German advance, becoming one of the major employers of colonial and white French, Polish, Russian, and Jewish prisoners.[34] Colonial prisoners working for Ostland farms had different experiences from those working on French farms. Ostland guards were closely supervised and pushed their prisoners for maximum productivity. Conditions could be quite difficult, and the Scapini Mission was aware of the abuses but understood that colonial prisoners often received higher wages and better rations.[35]

When not engaged in agricultural work, colonial prisoners generally did manual labor, such as repairing roads, clearing out ditches, cutting down isolated trees, breaking stones, excavating cesspools, cleaning bridges and quarries, digging fields, and repairing waterways.[36] The colonial prisoners were mostly peasant farmers, agricultural laborers, or unskilled workers. There were also skilled workers, including shopkeepers, secretaries, nurses, students, hairdressers, mechanics, blacksmiths, bakers, teachers, carpenters, butchers, cooks, writers, drivers, office workers, and career soldiers.[37] When possible, their skills were used in finding work assignments. In the Mayenne, the colonial prisoners were split into small groups and sent to different private and public jobs involving waterworks, forestry, communal road repair, and even driving the camp ambulance.[38] The mayor of Changé (Mayenne) assigned Algerian prisoners to each farm over twenty hectares, provided it was not run by an isolated French woman.[39] The racist and misogynistic undertones to his rationale of prisoner allocation cannot go unnoticed. In the Yonne, the colonial prisoners were divided between forests and farms, but all were required to spend a few hours daily collecting potato beetles, a local pest.[40] Technically, colonial prisoners assigned to one kind of work could not be used for another. In at least one case, a prisoner switched among several work groups without attracting German attention, while studying the possibilities of escape.[41] At Joigny, teams of colonial prisoners repaired the walls and ceilings of the former barracks to improve conditions for their own captivity.[42] Others built a sports field for the German soldiers.[43]

Racial stereotypes influenced the choice of work assigned to some colonial prisoners. Indochinese prisoners, who represented 4 percent of the colonial prisoners, with 2,753 men, were particularly affected by these stereotypes.[44] Indeed, their stories have often been overlooked in the literature and the sources on colonial captivity. During the First World War, the French believed the Indochinese and Madagascan prisoners to be more intelligent than other races and capable of holding specialized jobs, such as clerks, mechanics, butchers, and lumberjacks.[45] However, during the Second World War, some Germans believed the Indochinese prisoners and civilian workers had "weak constitutions," which made them "unsuitable" for difficult labor like chopping wood.[46] There was no proof to substantiate either of these beliefs. During their captivity, Indochinese prisoners worked on farms and forests, for French firms like the Lambiotte company, and directly for the Germans.[47] At Fort d'Uvegney, seventy-five Indochinese prisoners worked under heavy guard at a munitions depot with seventeen West African prisoners.[48] In Vesoul, the desire to keep the Indochinese inside the camp was an advantage to the eight prisoners working as camp chefs.[49] Positions where prisoners had control over the camp food and supplies or access to the civilian population were sought-after jobs and usually went to privileged prisoners.

Ironically, prisoners with jobs inside the camps often had more freedom of movement than prisoners on external work duties. In Epinal, prisoners working as batmen for the Germans were the only prisoners allowed to go into the town center.[50] In Vesoul, prisoners working as medical staff could also leave the camp, but the privilege was suspended until May 1941 as a result of abuses.[51] Henry Eboué was a prisoner in Amiens for a month in the late summer or early fall of 1940. He was allowed to wander around the camp and go into town without guards.[52] He maintained that rare level of freedom throughout most of his captivity. The German guards used the relatively few literate prisoners as camp secretaries or administrators. These privileged work placements allowed prisoners greater freedom of movement within the camp structure and sometimes throughout the surrounding area. At Poitiers, Henry and his brother, Robert, and their friend Léopold Senghor were "evaluated" and then made the Kommandantur's secretaries.[53]

At this stage, the camp hierarchy had not yet realized who Henry and Robert were, beyond the fact that they were educated. Their work routine was fairly relaxed: from 8:00 a.m. to 11:30 a.m. and from 2:00 p.m. to 5:00 p.m., they created lists of prisoners in Poitiers and the surrounding camps, noting religion, colony of origin, occupation, and "nationality," as the Germans did not recognize French citizens of color as citizens. Henry Eboué managed and trained the other camp secretaries and liaised with the French Red Cross to ensure regular deliveries of food, supplies, and especially cigarettes. He later wrote that the Kommandantur's office where they worked reported directly to the Nazi military intelligence office in Poitiers, allowing them to gather "useful intelligence."[54]

After a failed escape attempt, the Eboué brothers were sent to Charleville, where they found many of their old friends. Two Antillean prisoners, Paul Lucrèce, *chef du bureau français*, and Léopold Thémia, *ingénieur des travaux publics* and *chef de camp*, were essentially running the camp. Both brothers resumed secretarial duties; additionally, Robert ran the library, and Henry managed a group of Antillean prisoners and the laundry service.[55] The laundry job gave Henry three weekly trips into town to disinfect the prisoners' clothes and surreptitiously meet civilians. Thémia was eventually released because of his ill health. Lucrèce assumed day-to-day control of the camp, and Henry took control over the kitchens, which put him in contact with the French Red Cross. As Red Cross liaison, Henry left the camp daily to buy fruit, vegetables, and toiletries or to deposit the profits from their sale. He met with the Red Cross representatives to request food, clothing, or cigarettes. These frequent trips increased Henry's civilian contacts, who began receiving his personal mail and packages, presumably to avoid the camp censors. In exchange, Henry shared Red Cross food and supplies with his civilian contacts. To ensure his loose supervision and benefits continued, Henry also supplied the guards and local occupation staff with chocolate, sugar, biscuits, cognac, and butter.[56] These men were not the "average" colonial prisoners, and their experiences of captivity were not typical. Most colonial prisoners were engaged in physical labor outside the camps.

Further Restrictions and Forestry Work

At the beginning of 1941, coinciding with the natural winter lull for agriculture, the occupying authorities decided to further regulate colonial prisoner labor. These new restrictions meant the colonial prisoners lost some of the freedoms they had experienced during the first chaotic summer of captivity. Despite slowly imposing financial responsibility for the work on the local French authorities, the Germans maintained ultimate control over the colonial prisoners and their labor. They allocated and reassigned colonial prisoners, sometimes without informing the French or ensuring towns could absorb their numbers effectively. For example, Sambourg had a population of ninety-seven and received thirty colonial prisoners.[57] Two months later, they were all removed without an explanation.[58] It became increasingly common for companies or communes to be forced to accept colonial prisoners as employees.[59]

German guards accompanied the colonial prisoners to work, technically to prevent their escape.[60] In reality, the sentries gave the colonial prisoners two masters: guards for discipline and managers for productivity. As more colonial prisoners were sent to work in small communes, the German authorities published posters with instructions regarding escapes. The Germans reminded the colonial prisoners and the French that they were being trusted in order to rehabilitate the French economy. Despite contradicting the Geneva Convention, notices warned the prisoners and civilians that escape was considered desertion and carried the same punishment.[61] The intermingling of employers and prisoners brought ordinary French men under the influence of the local Frontstalag. Mayors and employers were held personally responsible for the prisoners quartered locally. This was standard practice for prisoners in Germany. What made the system different in occupied France was that the authorities and civilians were responsible for members of their own army. In this form, collaboration effectively made French civil servants agents of the detaining power.

At the beginning of 1941 the Germans announced that colonial prisoners must be grouped together for work assignments outside the Frontstalags.[62] The Germans claimed to "reluctantly" allow the colonial prisoners to continue to work on civic projects but would no longer allocate individual prisoners to farmers.[63] Most of these newly constituted work groups had between twenty and two hundred colonial prisoners.[64] As was common, implementation was uneven and depended on the local German authorities. Officially, the change was due to German authorities' fear that colonial prisoners would escape and incite disorder. As groups of disgruntled colonial prisoners could potentially endanger the peace more easily than individuals, the change was more likely a means of reducing the number of required guards. The occupying forces were short-staffed almost from the beginning of the occupation, and the situation only worsened over time.[65] A few work groups had attempted to substitute a French man of confidence instead of a German guard, but too many prisoners escaped.[66] This controversial solution was used again in 1943 with mixed results.

The new restrictions disproportionally affected small farms and reinforced the fact that French employers could neither control nor fully exploit their new employees' labor. Instead, the prefects were encouraged to find large farms where supervised groups of colonial prisoners could work effectively. However, family farms were much more common in rural France, especially in smaller communities like Beaulieu-sur-Oudon (Mayenne). Initially, the town was sent ten men: five African prisoners who each worked on a small farm and five Vietnamese prisoners who worked together repairing local roads and pathways.[67] The farmers and the town were happy with this organization and the prisoners' work. But in June 1941 the mayor was forced to assign all ten men to one work site. Since none of the small farms could use ten workers, the mayor essentially had to create jobs and pay for work to keep the colonial prisoners occupied. At the same time, the farmers who needed one additional person were deprived the help previously supplied by the colonial prisoners. This happened all over the occupied zone.

As the new restrictions were not uniformly imposed, towns found ways to work around them. In Loiret, the prefect proposed housing the colonial prisoners together so each local farm could take a worker during the day. After work, the men could return to their quarters.[68] In the Yonne, colonial prisoners continued to work individually on farms through the spring of 1942.[69] In other towns and departments, enforcement was stricter. Employment for colonial prisoners on public works or with private companies had to be found, and financed, when the farms could not use large groups of prisoners.

French businesses soon sent requests to hire the inexpensive colonial prisoners directly to camp commanders. Legal contracts between the companies and camp commanders were drawn up, and the colonial prisoners were allocated to a work site.[70] Generally, these contracts benefited the Germans, who could break them at any time, over the French employers. The colonial prisoners were not represented in the contract negotiations.[71] Private and public companies, like the French forestry department (*Eaux et Forêts*), signed similar contracts for colonial prisoners. Colonial prisoners working for the forestry department in Bordeaux logged, unloaded, and stocked wood and fought forest fires.[72] In the Yonne, a Parisian company requested forestry rights and the use of fifty colonial prisoners, tying the right to exploit the woods to the colonial prisoners. The company stated that "being former *coloniaux* we are particularly apt to lead this labor force, which, with your permission, we would like to choose directly from the camp."[73] It is unclear whether the employers were allowed to select specific colonial prisoners from the camp or the camp commander assigned them. Again, precedent of this kind of labor deployment was found in Germany, where employers could choose workers, often individual farmers, or request a certain number of POWs directly from the camp.

Moving colonial prisoners directly into the local economy left them vulnerable. In one case, German authority was exploited to circumvent French labor law. On request from their French employers, the Feldkommandantur increased the working day to ten hours for colonial prisoners at Mézilles (Yonne).[74] Eventually, the inspector for the French forestry department complained to the prefect about the increased hours, citing the "onerous conditions of the black prisoners employed in the forests of your jurisdiction."[75] After his intervention, the prisoners' working day was once again limited to eight hours.

Many of the companies employing colonial prisoners were involved in the logging industry. French fuel requirements were just as important as their agricultural needs. After the defeat, fuel shortages forced the French to exploit the forests for wood. Since 35 percent of the professional French lumberjacks were prisoners in Germany, untrained groups such as the colonial prisoners and the youth group Chantiers de la jeunesse were used to exploit the forests instead.[76] The German military command in France (Militärbefehlshaber, or MBF) had imagined that at least half of the colonial prisoners would work in the French forests, but in reality, only forty-two hundred were sent. Their progress was hindered by missing machinery and weak and malnourished pack animals.[77] By June 1941 the Billault company could no longer afford the twenty-five colonial prisoners assigned to it.[78] Instead, a Parisian company took advantage of the available labor and requested permission to exploit the Bois de Madeleine in Brienon (Yonne) with the colonial prisoners. The Feldkommandantur agreed and assigned thirty-five colonial prisoners to the Société d'exploitations des bois, which built a work camp to house them.[79]

Working in the French forests was particularly difficult. Scheck explains that the colonial prisoners were isolated in camps deep within French forests, cut off from camp life and French civilians.[80] The French did try, on a limited basis, to include those in the isolated camps in the religious celebrations. For example, for Aïd el-Kébir, the French authorities sent fifty sheep to the colonial prisoners interned in the Haute-Saône.[81] The Frontstalag commander forwarded lists of the isolated work camps, including the forest work groups, surrounding Vesoul with the number of prisoners so that the sheep could be divided among them.[82] The difficulty of the work they performed was exacerbated by the harsh conditions and lack of work supplies: one-third of the colonial prisoners were forced to use manual saws and to carry the wood on their backs or shoulders. They had shorter workdays, earning up to forty francs a day, but the work was harder.[83] Senghor confirmed that the winter conditions were difficult but noted that at least the barracks of those working in the forest were heated correctly.[84] René Scapini reported that the health of the men working in three forest work groups near Vesoul in May 1941 was good, but overall their morale was mediocre.[85]

Forestry work was so important that entire camps were structured around the exploitation of nearby woods. The camp at Mont-de-Marsan was initially a work group dependent on the Frontstalag at Angoulême. It was built in the middle of the Landes forests so that prisoners could work in the woods and return to the wooden barracks in the evening.[86] After the summer of 1941 all the colonial prisoners from Angoulême were transferred to Mont-de-Marsan, which was renamed Frontstalag 184A. As this was a bigger camp designated primarily for forest work, the prisoners avoided some of the disadvantages Scheck links to isolated forest work groups. The camp commander requested that the French Red Cross supply the prisoners with new shoes and undergarments. French doctors visited twice a week, and two North African medical workers were stationed permanently in Mont-de-Marsan. The prisoners had the opportunity for religious practice: a marabout led the Muslim prisoners in prayer, and a nearby Catholic priest visited the camp but stopped when only five Catholic prisoners from Martinique remained. Despite the camp's location close to the demarcation line, no prisoners attempted to escape in the first year.

A similar situation existed nearby at the Frontstalag Onesse-Laharie, also located in the Landes forest. Onesse-Laharie had eight work detachments (Mimizan, Ste-Eulalie, Tchoux, Lue, Escources, Labouheyre, Solférineo, and Morcenx) located in the forest, with an average of 300 men and a maximum of 560 prisoners.[87] The International Committee of the Red Cross representatives, Dr. Roland Marti and Dr. Jacques de Morsier, did not visit these smaller forest camps. Unlike at Mont-de-Marsan, at the time of their inspection, eight men were imprisoned for attempting to escape. Prisoners regularly took advantage of their work assignment to escape, and the forest camps were no exception. Two Algerian prisoners, Said Ben Derradji and Madani El Metai, ages thirty-seven and thirty-nine, had been shot while allegedly attempting to escape from another forest camp in the Landes.[88] Less than a year later, another prisoner, Arousi Yahya, was killed in similar circumstances.[89]

The irony of working in French forests was not lost on the colonial prisoners. Many Ivoirians had enlisted to escape the forced labor in forests in Côte d'Ivoire, only to be sent to work in French forests.[90] European planters exploited the fertile forests in Côte d'Ivoire, bringing in forced laborers to chop trees and plant cocoa, coffee, and bananas. Competition for this labor increased especially when, in the 1930s, wealthy Africans started their own plantations and wanted access to the inexpensive labor. Unsurprisingly, the white planters resisted the African competition, especially when it was compounded by military recruitment and immigration to the British colonies.[91] The white planters hoped the pro-Vichy regime would support their plantations and solidify their status to the detriment of the African planters. Indeed, the colonial administration created "sanitation crews," technically to prevent the spread of disease, but which were instead used to destroy the African planters' farms. The racist deployment of forced laborers for private European planters, and not the immorality of the legal system, had long-term political and economic consequences for both Côte d'Ivoire specifically and the entire French colonial empire.[92] In 1944, after observing the Free French continue this institutionalized discrimination, Félix Houphouët-Boigny, a planter, created the Syndicat agricole africain to oppose the principle of forced labor. In 1946 it became a political party, the Partie démocratique de la Côte d'Ivoire, and Houphouët-Boigny became an instrumental force in obtaining Côte d'Ivoire's independence. He would later serve as the country's first president.

Forced labor existed throughout the French Empire and continued during the Second World War. Its bloodstained legacy in French Equatorial Africa continued under the Free French, despite their condemnation of the Vichy regime's use of forced labor. Indeed, Felix Eboué, Free French governor general of French Equatorial Africa, and Pierre Boisson, Vichy governor general of French West Africa, shared many fundamental values and visions on forced labor. Wood and timber needs were as important for the Free French and Allied war effort as they were in France and Germany.[93] As the war continued, workers in the Free French colonies were faced with many of the same logistical problems as the colonial prisoners in French forests. Lack of transportation in French Equatorial Africa was the biggest hindrance to timber exports in 1943 and a major contributor to the difficult conditions for the African workers. Henri Laurentie had tried to replace dependence on porters with mechanized transport, but military needs prevailed, giving Gen. Philippe Leclerc's forces all the modern trucks. Instead, African workers were forced to carry material over land for extremely long distances.[94]

Forestry work, especially when lacking modern supplies, was as grueling in France as it was in the colonies. Yet the colonial prisoners benefited from two things denied to workers in the colonies: Geneva Convention protection as POWs and an unusual importance because of the Vichy's regime's imperial goals. Despite the differing conditions of the forced laborers in the colonies and of the colonial prisoners, a mounting resistance to these racist forms of labor was slowly beginning to take hold. The frustration felt by the colonial prisoners during their captivity was not in isolation; they were part of a growing movement of colonial subjects and citizens who were questioning the conditions of French colonialism. For some, like Houphouët-Boigny, opposition to racist labor policies would grow into support for independence. For others, including many of the colonial prisoners, it was a much quieter, smaller, and imperceptible shift. While the colonial prisoners may not have been aware of everything happening in the colonies, the French colonial administration was acutely aware of any dissent or anti-French feeling. These incidents, compounded by de Gaulle's success in the colonies and German propaganda in the camps, gnawed at French trust in their colonial subjects and influenced how the French responded to the colonial prisoners. Naturally, this in turn influenced how the colonial soldiers viewed their experiences in France.

Growing Expenses and Increasing Frustrations

As the occupation continued, tensions around the use of colonial prisoners as a labor force increased. Two factors frustrated the French employers:

the Germans controlled the colonial prisoners' work, and most colonial prisoners were unskilled in the tasks the employers chose and thus deemed "unproductive."[95] The work schedules were unpredictable: sometimes the guards took the colonial prisoners back to camp after only five or six hours of work.[96] Often colonial prisoners walked a significant distance, up to sixteen kilometers daily, before arriving at their physically demanding jobs.[97] Even at Mont-de-Marsan, a camp designed to be near work sites, colonial prisoners worked only four-hour days.[98] The teams were changed regularly, forcing the men to continually adjust to different jobs and colleagues.[99] Eventually, the Germans agreed that the colonial prisoners were traveling too far.

With the colonial prisoners dispersed among different employers, both public and private, they needed suitable lodgings closer to work. Under the Geneva Convention, the detaining power, Germany, should have paid for their quarters. However, as with most expenses relating to the colonial prisoners, the cost for these smaller work camps was imposed on the French.[100]

Despite the increased pressure and expense, some communities went beyond their responsibilities for the colonial prisoners. Local authorities built or provided small camps for locally employed colonial prisoners.[101] Farmers in Nitry, Montrel, and Vernenton were instructed to house their colonial prisoners throughout the winter of 1941–42 without a salary, while the camp commander decided how to proceed.[102] The mayor of Dollot (Yonne) asked if the colonial prisoners could remain with their employers during the winter, as their camp was uncomfortable.[103] By the spring of 1942 twenty-five camps for the Yonne department's agricultural services had been built, with plans for seventeen more.[104] To prepare for the colonial prisoners' arrival, the French cleaned and repaired the sites, added security to the doors and windows, installed electricity and heating in the rooms, and found beds, linens, and sanitation supplies.[105] Technically, the employers were to pay for the colonial prisoners' lodgings. However, as seen, many towns became the de facto employers. As a result, the secretary of state for war's exceptional budget was used to subsidize costs that outweighed the colonial prisoners' "economic contributions."[106] In rare cases, such as in the Gironde, the German authorities contributed two-thirds of the costs for a camp specifically designed so colonial prisoners could remove burned pine trees between Le Temple and Le Las.[107] The French forestry department paid the balance.

French towns were given more and more financial responsibility toward the upkeep of these prisoners. Over time, the diverse motivations for hiring colonial prisoners—solidarity with French prisoners, need for sporadic help during peak times, protectiveness toward colonial prisoners—were overwhelmed by frustration against the ever-increasing German demands. For all the assistance provided by colonial prisoners, communities often hesitated to employ them because of the accompanying restrictions.

Two developments regarding food and salary changed French attitudes toward colonial prisoner labor. Even while colonial prisoners remained mainly in the Frontstalags, the Germans already proved unwilling to pay for their food, which was greatly supplemented by French humanitarian mobilization in the metropole and colonies. By February 1941 German policy went a step further and required employers, be they small farmers or large businesses, to pay ten francs per working day for each colonial prisoner's food.[108] The Frontstalag commanders informed the prefects of the changes, and in turn, the prefects were expected to force compliance from mayors and local employers. The significance of the change from providing food to paying cash to buy the food should not be underestimated.

French budgets were stretched thin, and small farmers could not always manage the additional ten francs for food. These changes became a bureaucratic nightmare; confusion reigned over implementation. Technically, the French were only responsible for the colonial prisoners' food while they worked. In practice, employers were expected to pay the ten francs even when the colonial prisoners had remained in their camps.[109] Naturally, employers protested against paying for days without work. The French subsidized the cost for struggling employers: the "assistance for prisoners of war" budget covered the cost of food within the camps, while the "occupation costs" budget covered the guards' food at work sites and any costs related to preparing the work sites for the prisoners' arrival.[110] A further distinction was made between costs paid by the town where the colonial prisoners were lodged and those paid by their employer. The issue was complicated further when the towns became the de facto employers.

Feeding colonial prisoners was more than a simple monetary transaction. It meant ensuring the prisoners' most basic right, one protected by international law. The German authorities exploited Vichy's commitment to collaboration and the colonial prisoners in order to avoid their Geneva Convention responsibilities, and Pétain's government could not let the colonial prisoners go hungry on French soil while it struggled to maintain French sovereignty overseas. Here practical business sense and humanitarian concerns collided and revealed the multitude of French attitudes toward the colonial prisoners. Without any concessions from Germany, the French had additional financial charges, but the Vichy regime imagined that this gave it greater influence over the colonial prisoners. It was wrong.

Resistance to these extra costs grew as the occupation lengthened. The Frontstalag commanders placed responsibility for collecting payments on the French prefects.[111] The prefects in turn appealed to their mayors' feelings of solidarity to accept the additional charges, and failing that, they reassured the mayors that if the costs of hiring colonial prisoners outweighed their productivity, the local government would cover the difference.[112] Understandably, municipalities that had been forced to employ the colonial prisoners balked at the extra expenses.[113] For the mayor of Bais, it was not a question of principle; it was simply a lack of money.[114] In Villers-la-Montagne (Meurthe-et-Moselle), the mayor refused to feed the sixty-five colonial prisoners working in the commune.[115] This scandalized the local French population, and eventually the French Red Cross and the Germans provided food for these colonial prisoners. When payments were delayed or incomplete, the Frontstalag commanders summoned unlucky prefects to the camp for a reckoning.[116] Another camp commander sent the prefect a list of mayors that he believed were underfeeding the colonial prisoners, along with instructions to rectify the situation.[117] The complicated dynamic created by collaboration meant that the Germans were pressuring the French to ensure the colonial prisoners were fed. This effort cost the Germans nothing, and the unlikely support of the German camp commanders sometimes improved conditions for the colonial prisoners.

Elsewhere, food was used as a motivating tactic. Worms and Company employed five hundred North African prisoners near Nantes and used the promise of extra rations to increase productivity. The director felt that the prisoners' rations were "much lower than what they should be for forced labor, extracting peat is exhausting work; as a result, we have noted reduced production; we decided ... to distribute an additional meal to all those who have worked conscientiously: if we insist on distributing this extra ration ourselves and not adding it to their normal food, it is because we want it to be a reward for good workers."[118]

Presumably, prisoners who did not work "conscientiously" enough were left with the insufficient rations, highlighting how quickly the motivation behind feeding the colonial prisoners shifted from humanitarian to financial. A similar carrot-and-stick tactic was used in Germany to encourage productivity among white French prisoners.[119] The Ostland corporation also used higher rations and sometimes higher wages to motivate the colonial prisoners.[120] Still, acts of solidarity with colonial prisoners continued despite the increasing pressures of an unending occupation. Some French were spurred by religious conviction and encouraged by the National Revolution's return to Christian values to organize baptisms or classes for the colonial prisoners.[121] Others helped as an act of defiance against the occupying Germans, using food deliveries as a way to support colonial prisoners emotionally through their captivity.[122]

While food often drew the French and the colonial prisoners together, the second major development, a paid salary, drew out racist opinions on whether the colonial prisoners "deserved" to be paid. A prisoners' right to paid work was guaranteed by Article 28 of the Geneva Convention.[123] Normally, the detaining power benefited and paid for prisoner labor either directly, when prisoners worked for the camp or civic works, or indirectly, when local industries paid the camp for the prisoners' labor. Unsurprisingly, the Germans eventually decided that the French should pay the colonial prisoners' salary, even when French towns had been forced to create work for colonial prisoners. For the Germans, making the French responsible for the colonial prisoners' salary ensured the spirit of the Geneva Convention was respected, while reducing their own expenditure and further "punishing" the French for using colonial soldiers in a "white man's war." The change came as a shock to many employers who had hired colonial prisoners assuming that their only requirement was to feed them.[124] In Vienne, engineers had been told that the colonial prisoners' labor was "completely free."[125] At first only work outside the camps was paid. Prisoners worked in teams to give everyone access to paid work.[126] By mid-1941 the Germans expanded the salary requirement to include all colonial prisoners, even those on fatigue duty or cooking meals inside the Frontstalags.[127] The Germans justified imposing these additional expenses on the French because the alternative, hiring a white woman to cook for the colonial prisoners, would be more expensive.[128]

Work was the colonial prisoners' only opportunity to earn money while in captivity. Salaries could vary slightly, but most colonial prisoners earned ten francs per workday. They kept eight and gave two to the camps' communal fund.[129] Specialists, skilled workers, forestry workers, and those working for the German armament productions or directly for the Wehrmacht earned more.[130] Trained stretcher bearers could earn as much as two hundred francs every ten to twelve days.[131] The colonial prisoners could spend their wages in the canteen on chocolate, tobacco, or light alcoholic drinks or send it home for their families. Many were able to save considerable sums.

To ensure timely payments, the camp treasurer billed the prefects, who paid colonial prisoners and sought reimbursement from employers.[132] By forcing prefects to obtain payment from companies, instead of doing it directly, the Germans reinforced French responsibility for their colonial prisoners. This was a significant reversal from the summer of 1940, when the Direction du service des prisonniers de guerre had complained to the German Armistice Commission that prisoners' salaries had not been paid at Longvic, Beaune, and the camps in the Loiret.[133] If private businesses refused to pay the colonial prisoners' salaries, the prefectures were held responsible.

For some, these additional costs outweighed the importance of imperial solidarity. The mayor of Nitry complained that had the municipal council known the true cost of the colonial prisoners, they would have "left them in their quarters."[134] The mayor of Selle-Craonnaise felt likewise, explaining that the town could take fifteen white prisoners, "even Bretons," but "no farmer would want to employ Arabs, Indochinese or others."[135] In reality, many farmers had no difficulty employing and respecting the work done by colonial prisoners. The mayor of Chatelain insisted his commune could not employ, feed, and pay seventeen prisoners, especially as no farmer had requested a prisoner, and their work "was not worth a salary higher than their food."[136] It is hard to imagine a French employer saying the same about a white worker, especially a prisoner of war. In one case, the prefect of Yonne worried about the "potential inconveniences" of allowing colonial prisoners access to cash, suggesting holding their salaries in savings accounts, which presumably the colonial prisoners would not be allowed to access.[137] Limiting the colonial prisoners' access to funds was a manner to further limit their movements, and the German authorities at Frontstalag 124 rejected this idea.

These racist reactions, reflecting the disappointment of many small towns when their allocated prisoners were not white, were combined with frustrations over the increased costs and difficulties of the occupation.[138] Holding racist views about the colonial prisoners was not incompatible with helping them during their captivity. Commitment to notions of imperial solidarity and Christian humanitarianism often went hand in hand with a belief in French, and white, superiority. On a local level, feelings of duty and humanitarianism were inextricably linked.

French frustration grew, and in April 1942 three mayors refused to take the colonial prisoners back after the winter. They argued that the farmers in their towns had accepted prisoners only for the previous harvest.[139] The mayor of Saint-Agnan explained that "by patriotism as much as by humanitarianism, my farmers bravely accepted this burden. . . . [C]ould we not now pass these prisoners along to other nearby communes where agriculture is more important and farmers more numerous?"[140] The mayor of Cossé argued that his commune was too small for twelve prisoners and two German guards.[141] These demands moved through the French administrative hierarchy, and eventually prefects of the Nièvre and Yonne formally requested that the colonial prisoners be removed because of the lack of available work and supplies, low productivity, and high costs.[142] The Germans rejected all these requests. The towns were instructed to use the colonial prisoners' labor for "the greater good."[143]

The forestry industry lobbied the Vichy government to bring down the cost of colonial prisoner labor, suggesting that the employer pay the twenty francs for salary and food on workdays and the government pay any additional costs for food and installing camps. More importantly, the timber merchants wanted the guards to ensure that the prisoners worked for eight hours at a normal speed. In return, any output over the average would be paid at the normal local rate.[144] However, the Vichy regime subsidized only farmers, not the logging companies.[145] Private companies could more effectively resist the increased restrictions. Timber merchants at Chatel-Gérard (Yonne) did not rehire fifty colonial prisoners when their contracts ended. They estimated that the cost of POW labor was sixty francs per cubic meter of stacked wood, whereas civilian workers cost only twenty francs.[146] Historian J. Billig confirms that in other areas, such as coal mining, prisoners were less productive, being generally half as productive as civilian coal miners.[147] However, the timber merchants also believed that white prisoners were more productive than colonial prisoners, despite the lack of evidence to support this.

Sometimes French frustrations with growing expenses were blamed on the colonial prisoners' "arrogance" and "laziness." The mayor of Pont-sur-Yonne even questioned the inherent worth of the Indochinese prisoners assigned to his commune: "These men are good for nothing. The farmers have tried everything except violence. There is nothing to get from them: gluttonous and lazy, unsuited for all work. It is an inconvenience and sets a bad example if they decide not to work. Their attitude prevents others from working. This morning, Mr. Van Damme could not convince his prisoner to go to work. He refused and hid in an attic."[148] It is hard to imagine a colonial prisoner in June 1942 with enough food to become gluttonous, especially while engaging in difficult farm work. It is equally hard to imagine the same kind of racialized insults being directed at a white prisoner. Still, the complaint was taken up the hierarchy. The prefect of the Yonne complained to the local military commander, claiming the Indochinese prisoners had "a bad attitude and flagrant indiscipline, consequently, the cultivation is done under bad conditions and with practically no results. The brigadier of Eaux et Forêts charged with supervising this work has seen his authority sapped by the insidious action of the Annamite corporal and is not adequately supported by the German guards, to the extent that these acts, which challenge the discipline, happen daily."[149]

This kind of disobedience, especially if tacitly supported by the German guards, had both financial and imperial consequences. To maintain the racial hierarchies, any colonial prisoner who challenged French authority, even a farmer's instructions, had to be invalidated immediately. The French worried that isolated complaints could grow into larger, more generalized discontent and even revolt.

Attitudes that might be praised privately if expressed by white prisoners employed by an enemy were condemned when adopted by the colonial prisoners. French prisoners in Germany went on strike in December 1941 to protest their increased deployment in war industries. Reinecke, the OKW official in charge of prisoners, immediately threated to discontinue all advantages granted to French prisoners. Scapini broke the strike after speaking with the striking prisoners and getting Reinecke to agree to better food and a shorter work week.[150] Unsurprisingly, as the right to strike was not guaranteed across the empire, the colonial prisoners never organized a collective strike. By 1936 only workers in French West Africa had gained the right to join a trade union under certain conditions. A year later there were eight thousand union members for forty-two unions and sixteen professional associations.[151]

Under normal rules of war, prisoners worked for the enemy and could justify low productivity. The double effect of ensuring a slower work rhythm and the catharsis of thwarting the enemy's plans helped prisoners deal with the frustration of captivity. Colonial prisoners were technically working for "their" motherland, and any similar efforts were criticized. Instead, the French hoped that "good" colonial prisoners would recognize the efforts made on their behalf and respond to the work with enthusiasm. Without any explanations from the colonial prisoners themselves, it is hard to determine whether acts like hiding in an attic or working slowly were the beginning of organized resistance or simply the expressions of frustrated and exhausted prisoners. Nevertheless, their actions and the French reactions foreshadowed the conflicts during repatriation at the end of the war. For the colonial prisoners, the "rules" of French colonization overshadowed every aspect of their captivity, especially their interactions with the French.

The question of colonial prisoner labor revealed both the limits and benefits of the colonial prisoners for Vichy's policy of collaboration. Scapini understood he could not refuse German demands for prisoner labor and that the colonial prisoners would benefit from working closely with the French, another unintentional consequence of being left in France. Work changed the colonial prisoners' experience of captivity. Instead of remaining gathered together in the overcrowded Frontstalags, the colonial prisoners joined small groups and were sent to work across the occupied zone. This made them more visible to the French and provided the opportunity to foster relationships with French civilians outside of the Vichy regime's control. For the French who worked with them, the colonial prisoners were seen less as representatives of a political agenda and more as individuals who needed help.

Difficult labor conditions were normal for prisoners, including the colonial prisoners. At least in France, some of their employers saw the colonial prisoners as more than just workers and felt some responsibility for their conditions. While their work in France was somewhat protected compared with that in Germany, it remained difficult and strenuous, and they were far from home. Although it would be ridiculous to expect gratitude from the colonial prisoners for being "allowed" to work on French farms, some employers and officials did. The questions raised by the colonial prisoners' work reveal the racism and paternalism of the French government and many civilians. Despite the racism and perhaps because of the paternalism, the colonial prisoners were important to the French. Knowing this, the Germans found financial advantages in colonial prisoners' labor, which protected them from a fate similar to that of Soviet prisoners, who were systematically worked to death.

The prism of colonial prisoners' labor reveals the different interplays between French colonialism and Vichy collaboration. While generally, local farmers and small businesses were initially pleased with the colonial prisoners' labor, they became increasingly disillusioned with the situation. Employing colonial prisoners was presented to individual farmers and small employers as a French humanitarian gesture. However, it was actually fulfilling German military objectives. This became increasingly evident after turning points like the Battles of El Alamein and Stalingrad. Both France and Germany depended on the revival of the French economy, with Germany purchasing heavily from French agriculture. The exchange rate set by the occupying authorities gave the Germans huge purchasing power and depleted the French treasury. By 1944 German grain purchases had increased from six million to eight million quintals, and meat purchases had doubled to 270,000 tons.[152]

On an individual level, positive relationships formed between colonial prisoners and the farmers they worked alongside or individuals they met while working on public land. The addition of a paid salary changed the fragile dynamic, which was based no longer on solidarity and support, but rather on profits and budgets. Now the colonial prisoners were caught in a business interaction where their labor had been imposed on French employers. For many small businesses or farms, dependence on paid labor was unusual. Indeed, it was the continued absence of the prisoners in Germany that prompted some to seek outside help. When German constraints made the colonial prisoners' labor appear to be more expensive and restrictive than foreseen, feelings of solidarity were replaced by frustration against the occupation and the continued absence of the French men. The colonial soldiers were considered poor replacements. Nevertheless, despite the increased financial pressure and worsening conditions with the lengthening war, the solidarity never evaporated completely.

As the occupation continued, conditions in France worsened. Responding to a sense of solidarity, farmers and local employers had been willing to feed and sometimes even house colonial prisoners, even though some would have preferred to support white prisoners. The increasing rules and expenses changed the equation from one based on solidarity to a business decision, with many employers calculating that colonial prisoners cost more than they could deliver. Yet even these seemingly economic decisions were intertwined with preconceived notions of racial aptitude for productive work. Once the full cost of colonial prisoner labor, food, housing, and salary was revealed, employers were "stuck" with their prisoners.

The German authorities benefited more than the French from the use of colonial prisoners in the economy. Their prisoners were supervised and kept busy with minimum German intervention and infrastructure. Additionally, the colonial prisoners' labor pool allowed the Germans to address French concerns about rebuilding the economy without sending the white prisoners home. This allowed Germany to keep the "better" workers in its own economy while showcasing its generosity (in allowing the colonial prisoners to work in France) as a contribution to collaboration. Surprisingly, during the first two years of captivity, the colonial prisoners were the unexpected beneficiaries of this policy.

5

MALADIES AND MISTREATMENT
Colonial Prisoners' Health and Welfare

Two major factors influenced the colonial prisoners' health while in France: how they were treated by those in power and their vulnerability to disease. Both factors were influenced by their dual status as prisoners of war and men of color. German treatment of prisoners of war during the Second World War has been remembered as violent, cruel, and without regard to international law. Certainly, the massacre of twenty thousand Polish officers in 1940 and use of Soviet prisoners as a slave labor force under starvation conditions affirm these accusations. In France, the situation was different. German occupying forces deliberately demonstrated their "civility" through respectful behavior, and generally this was extended to the colonial prisoners. Still, racialized violence and even murder occurred in the Frontstalags. The biggest impetus toward aggression was if a guard believed a colonial prisoner was overstepping his position as a "native." Some guards became known as particularly dangerous and were not always mentally stable. Acts of arbitrary cruelty toward the colonial prisoners shocked colonial and white prisoners alike and were often reported to the French authorities. Despite the risk of extreme and unwarranted violence, disease was a more present and pressing menace to the colonial prisoners' existence.

Given the presence of eighty-five thousand colonial prisoners from warm or tropical climes on French soil, ill health was a particular source of vulnerability to the men and of concern to the Scapini Mission. The harsh climate, insufficient food, and often unsanitary conditions rendered the colonial prisoners susceptible to disease. The German authorities feared contagion and balked at the expenses related to treating sick colonial prisoners, preferring to release them instead. The German guards' often limited experience with colonial troops combined with racist ideas on "primitive diseases" facilitated these releases. Inaccurate and contradictory statistics fueled fears that tuberculosis had devastated the colonial prisoner population and prompted the Scapini Mission's renewed efforts to have the colonial prisoners released. Perhaps more than anything, the ability to respond to sick or brutalized colonial prisoners tested the Vichy regime's paternalism and its level of control over the lives of its colonial soldiers in enemy captivity.

Death and Ill-Treatment

Setting out standards for treatment of enemy prisoners of war in the 1929 Geneva Convention codified the humanitarian values of the International Committee of the Red Cross (ICRC). Its most important contribution was the idea that all prisoners shared the same basic humanity and thus deserved good treatment.[1] Yet this idea of a shared humanity was assumed to be shared across European or "civilized nations."[2] As S. P. MacKenzie explains, the German guards were generally considerate of those prisoners deemed "worthy of respect."[3] Considering Eurocentric views on humanity and Nazi racial hierarchies, it is unsurprising that much of the previous scholarship has concluded that the colonial prisoners were neglected and abused because of their race. Race and racism clearly had an impact on their experiences in German captivity on French soil. The politicization of race and health, seen through the nuances of the colonial prisoners' treatment by the Germans and the French, reveal much of what was at stake in wartime imperial planning.

While in some cases targeted abuse and violence toward prisoners was part of a larger war strategy, this was not true for France. Violence could be used for obtaining intelligence or breaking civilian morale in a long war, but it risked generating public and international condemnation.[4] For the occupation to be successful within the context of the wider war, the Germans needed to invest the least amount of manpower in dominating France, which meant keeping the French relatively calm. Restraining the behavior of the German guards was one way to maintain control over the

French and prisoner populations. Mistreating and abusing the prisoners in France ran the risk of inciting protests that might spiral. Furthermore, the situation in France did not warrant an official decision to systematically abuse colonial prisoners, and that is reflected in their overall experiences of captivity. Camp commanders at Bordeaux and Epinal were particularly conscious of their responsibility in running a Frontstalag and actively sought to improve conditions to boost the colonial prisoners' health and morale.[5]

Top-level German decisions provided the framework for the colonial prisoners' captivity, and individual guards had the real power to shape their health. Many guards were pleased to have a privileged posting in France, away from the front, with substantial purchasing power. Some had even been POWs in France during the First World War. At least one guard who had been treated well by the French during the previous war tried to do the same for the colonial prisoners.[6] Indeed, the German military administrator in France, Lt. Gen. Alfred von Streccius, worried that German soldiers might be intimidated by the French civilians and thus be too permissive in their treatment of prisoners. In August 1940 he issued a reminder to the Frontstalag guards to treat prisoners with "dignity, rigor and distance."[7] The Vichy regime also feared that close relations between the German guards and the prisoners would make the colonial prisoners forget their loyalty to France.

Individuals, German and French, good and bad, had a decisive influence on the colonial prisoners' experiences in captivity. In at least one case, violence was due to one man, Officer Speith, who was "a real brute, and not always sane. He would not hesitate to kick or use his cane to hit French or native prisoners for futile reasons. In January this officer shot a North African prisoner with a revolver during roll call."[8] Another guard, Corporal Sudau at Ychoux, was also singled out as particularly violent.[9] Colonial prisoners reported that discipline lessened over time. With German difficulties on the eastern front, the younger guards were replaced by older or injured ones who were generally less prone to fanaticism.[10] The reports on violence in the Frontstalags should be considered carefully, as some, but not all, were relayed secondhand. This consideration must be understood within the broader context of power dynamics in the POWs camps, the military, imperialism, and the archive itself. We must ask whose voices are heard and whose are believed when building a picture of captivity experiences. The accounts that follow are from a variety of sources over time. They paint a picture of a relatively stable camp experience in France, with episodes of extreme, unwarranted violence.

The colonial prisoners and camp inspectors highlighted a range of violations of the colonial prisoners' rights. These complaints ran the gamut from health and safety concerns like carrying heavy loads to acts of real brutality.[11] The colonial prisoners were mostly preoccupied with the strict discipline in the camps and mentioned it in almost every captivity report or declaration made to the French authorities. Touré Vamoutari maintained that "he could not complain too much about the Germans, who, according to him, were extremely severe, intolerant of any infringement of the rules, but who did show a certain fairness."[12] Gnimagnon identified a spectrum of German discipline, ranging from strict but manageable to grim and severe: "At Rambervilliers, we experienced misery unlike anything before. The discipline was severe: roll calls followed roll calls that lasted all day, searches followed searches, threats followed threats. [At Epinal,] life was better than in all the other camps in which we stayed. Without thriving, which is incompatible with the life of a prisoner, we had the minimum necessary to survive. The discipline, without being relaxed, was without austerity."[13] As Vamoutari and Gnimganon showed, prisoners acknowledged that a certain level of discipline was to be expected during captivity. It could be tolerated as long as it was predictable and somewhat fairly applied.

Physical abuse and arbitrary unjustifiable murder were the most extreme perils facing the colonial prisoners. Warrant Officer Fillet remembered that the guards at Troyes treated the French decently but mistreated the colonial prisoners, especially the Black prisoners.[14] Oumar Diallo made similar observations but felt the Moroccans suffered the most.[15] Another prisoner, Paul Mansire, believed that colonial prisoners were more likely than white prisoners to be shot by German guards.[16] The motives behind the violence could be retaliation for an alleged crime, such as giving water to French prisoners against orders, or for having an "incorrect" attitude.[17] A released Senegalese prisoner reported that in Germany, "the slightest hesitation in completing a task was punished by death (the prisoner actually said 'slaughtered like a chicken')."[18] Another colonial prisoner in the Meuse refused to work until the ragged condition of his clothing was addressed. In response, the German guard killed him on the spot.[19] The abuse was reported and limited, which neither excuses it nor minimizes its impact on the colonial prisoners' mental health.

The Scapini Mission was aware of acts of violence committed against its colonial prisoners, as incidents were reported by multiple witnesses. Violence was constrained and continued to shock prisoners and civilians alike. Three murders occurred at Frontstalag 194 in Nancy and its surrounding work groups. The first victim, Kadour Ben Mohammed, survived long enough to report his own murderer.[20] The incident transpired on a Sunday afternoon at 4:00 p.m. The German guard entered Ben Mohammed's room, where he was lying on the bed, and demanded that all the men report to work. Ben Mohammed replied that he was sick. The guard immediately took out his revolver and shot Ben Mohammed in the chest, saying, "*Nix* sick." Six hours later he was admitted to the Hôpital-Dieu de Mont-Saint-Martin, where he died shortly after an operation. The second victim, Abdelam-Ben-Safhili, had allegedly been fighting with another North African prisoner. In order to separate the two men, the guard fired on them. Abdelam-Ben-Safhili died thirty minutes after arriving at the hospital. The prefect of Meurthe-et-Moselle informed Scapini of the murders. The prefect reported a third murder of an unnamed Senegalese prisoner who was shot while on a work assignment.[21] Nothing came of the protests, and the camp authorities justified these types of murders as a "legitimate" response to some wrongdoing by the colonial prisoners.

When a prisoner died from gunshot wounds, the Germans often claimed he had been trying to escape. A twenty-three-year-old North African prisoner named Tayeb was killed because guards suspected he was having an affair with a white French woman who delivered milk to the camp.[22] While being escorted to the camp commander, Tayeb was shot after allegedly trying to run for freedom. However, the doctor's report revealed that Tayeb was shot from the front while walking. A fellow prisoner refused to sign a false declaration to support the guards' version of events. Seeking this sort of justification demonstrated that the German guards regularly pushed the limits of the

Geneva Convention, which only permitted shooting an actively escaping prisoner. Articles 2, 3, 50, and 51 of the Geneva Convention placed strict limits on disciplinary action allowed for escaping and recaptured prisoners and forbade reprisals on prisoners who remained behind. As white prisoner, Marcel Guillet, confirmed, "My friends and I were never treated badly. However, I saw a guard kill, without pity, a prisoner attempting to escape."[23]

Elsewhere, German reactions aligned more closely with international law. Over eighteen months, sixty prisoners escaped from the work groups at Camp Saucats. The ICRC inspectors reported that the remaining colonial prisoners were treated well and had not been punished for the multiple escapes. Only one prisoner had died as a result.[24] In France, if a colonial prisoner was recaptured after escaping, he was usually imprisoned while waiting disciplinary punishment.[25] Escape could not be treated as a crime, but only as a disciplinary offense with a maximum punishment lasting no more than thirty days. However, prisoners who were surprised in the act of escape ran the real risk of being killed immediately instead of being returned to quarters. Raffael Scheck argues that German guards were under enormous pressure to prevent prisoners from escaping and were encouraged to shoot at them, estimating that 5 percent of escaping colonial prisoners were killed.[26]

Prisoners attempting to escape in Germany were much more likely to be shot than those in France. About one-third of British prisoners killed in Germany between January 1941 and July 1943 died while attempting to escape. Perhaps because more British prisoners tried to escape, German guards were more likely to shoot at the British than the French.[27] White French prisoners in Germany also reported being slapped, hit, and abused. One prisoner explained that "when a prisoner disobeyed the occupying authorities, they locked him in a cell for three or four days without food or blankets or else they tied him up so his feet barely touch the ground. They left him in this position for one to nine hours."[28] Such treatment was illegal, and this was not the only complaint of its kind. Similarly to the acts of brutality in the Frontstalags, Yves Durand argues that in Germany, this violence was due to the behavior of certain individuals and was not symptomatic of French captivity.[29] While punishments for French prisoners were severe, they generally were treated better than the Polish but worse than the British.[30]

The reactions from the colonial and white prisoners and French civilians showed that violence in the Frontstalags remained anomalous. Had murder become a predictable characteristic of captivity in France, German guards would not have felt obligated to offer an explanation or justification for the prisoners' death, even one easily contradicted by the physical evidence, as in Tayeb's case. When the official explanation for another colonial prisoner's death deviated too much from the physical evidence, as was the case with a colonial prisoner shot after surrendering at Camp Bulgose, the doctor was forbidden to view the body.[31] Guards who simply liked violence, such as Speith, were the minority. What remained elevated was the number of suspicious deaths that were erroneously justified by blaming an escape attempt.

Official complaints and investigations were lodged after the murders of colonial prisoners. Besson, head of the Direction du service des prisonniers de guerre, reported to the Scapini Mission that colonial prisoner Nia Kouei had been killed for refusing to obey an order. While Besson believed that Kouei had been wrong, he objected to the use of violence: "Most of these cases where the prisoner was killed should have required a court martial and not summary execution; nothing can justify a guard firing on unarmed men. I would be obliged if you could intervene with the German authorities to ensure measures are taken to avoid this kind of incident from happening again, and if you feel it is appropriate, ask that the prisoners' families receive some kind of financial compensation."[32]

It seems unlikely that the German government would pay the family of a colonial soldier for a death they would claim was provoked. Cynically viewed, protesting cost Besson nothing and demonstrated his commitment to protecting French colonial subjects. His request could have been a means of deflecting responsibility from his services to the Scapini Mission or reflected a real desire to stop violence, or both. Several months later, the Direction du service des prisonniers de guerre requested that the Scapini Mission investigate or at least formally complain to the German authorities about the murder of two Moroccan prisoners at Nancy.[33] No official record was found of the success of these complaints. Only in rare cases were guards punished after official inquiries into their behavior.[34]

The repercussions of violence against the colonial prisoners were not contained by the walls of the Frontstalags. It seeped into the surrounding communities. French doctors were called on to operate on mortally wounded prisoners, and locals mourned their death. Funerals in Nancy were held for the three men who died there.[35] Similar funerals were held in Chaumont and Epinal and were usually attended by about thirty people. In Epinal, only religious funerals in the local church were permitted.[36] Death led to intertwined relationships between the local communities and the camps. Attending the funeral of a stranger whose only connection was that he died in one's town showed feelings of commitment to and solidarity with those men, who were temporarily neighbors because of the fates of war.

Overall, these murders appear to have been the exception. There is nothing in the diverse primary sources to indicate a climate of insecurity in the Frontstalags. The proximity of the occupation forces and the French population meant that widespread violence could not go unnoticed. Doctors and other prisoners, like the man of confidence who reported Tayeb's murder, felt confident enough to refuse to corroborate false reports. This suggests prisoners maintained a level of agency within the camps. While the majority of colonial prisoners were not abused or killed by their German guards, the images and reminders of unprovoked brutality justifiably lingered. But in general, diseases were much more devastating for the colonial prisoner population.

Health in the Frontstalags

The colonial prisoners' health was the greatest concern for the colonial prisoners and the French, through for quite different reasons. Close quarters, less-than-ideal sanitary conditions, and the harsh climate put the colonial prisoners at risk of contagious diseases. The prisoners naturally worried about themselves and their families if they fell sick. Fears of contagion, stereotypes, and racist ideas about "native" diseases informed and influenced the French and German responses to sickness among colonial prisoners. In addition, the Scapini Mission saw illness as an opportunity to get sick or weak colonial prisoners sent home and away from German influence.

Historians such as Nancy Lawler have long cited German fear of colonial diseases as a contributing factor to the colonial prisoners' internment in

France instead of Germany.[37] From the late nineteenth century, some German doctors believed that tropical diseases could have a lasting degenerative effect on the German race. Combating tropical diseases became an important step to successful German colonization. In fact, German scientists had found a cure for sleeping sickness in 1922, but without its colonial empire, Germany could not take advantage of the medical advances.[38] Continued German interest in tropical diseases involved the colonial prisoners directly. In November 1940 construction began for a hospital at Saint-Médard for colonial prisoners, containing a special section for training German doctors.[39] This section was closed to French inspectors and used for medical experiments on colonial prisoners. These ranged from simple studies on tropical diseases to more sinister medical experiments designed to "prove" racial differences, including injecting colonial prisoners with antibodies from other races to observe the effects.[40]

"Tropical diseases" such as sleeping sickness, yellow fever, malaria, typhoid, cholera, bubonic plague, and leprosy could be particularly frightening for those with limited experience of them. Yellow fever, for example, had "terrifying symptoms that cause panic: jaundice, high fever, internal hemorrhage and vomiting of black blood."[41] Naturally, outbreaks in the colonies affected both indigenous and white populations. However, white public opinion stubbornly associated "native hygiene" with disease. As Kalala Ngalamulume effectively demonstrates, the French in Senegal believed the "natives" were "natural targets" for disease and thus posed a risk for the European settlers unless they adopted French civilization and ideas of progress.[42] Martin Thomas confirms that this vision dominated views during the interwar period, when the high rates of illness in North African populations were explained by "moral degeneracy, criminality and cultural primitivism" rather than by the overcrowded and unsanitary living conditions created by decades of coercive French imperial rule.[43] With the increased recruitment of African soldiers during the First World War came evolving views connecting biological race and levels of civilization in creating a predisposition to illness.[44] In France, the main specialist centers for tropical illnesses were in Fréjus, where Marcel Bonnaud of the Scapini Mission had worked, and in Marseilles, where the Ecole du Pharo was an important research center for tropical diseases.[45]

Prewar stereotypes persisted and influenced French and German attitudes toward the colonial prisoners' health.

A variety of illnesses were recorded in the Frontstalags. Epinal had seven cases of leprosy and three or four cases of trachoma, an easily treated disease that often led to blindness when ignored.[46] Colonial prisoners also suffered from syphilis, chills and dysentery, fevers, bronchopneumonia, and bronchitis.[47] The hospital at Bayonne-Anglet requested more quinine used to treat malaria.[48] Malaria was, and remains, one of the deadliest diseases in the tropics, killing indiscriminately. Malaria death rates were high throughout the nineteenth century, until quinine was regularly used as a prophylactic. It had been a controversial cure in Algeria since the 1830s but was not widespread in France until after the Second World War.[49] Unsurprisingly, the colonial prisoners were susceptible to illness, having arrived into camps exhausted from battle and suffering from lack of food. To get to the battlefield, many had traveled across the world from different climates and regions.

Restricting the spread of disease was a priority for the Vichy regime.[50] Camp commanders strictly regulated doctors' access to the colonial prisoners. A white prisoner in France, Dr. Jean Guérin, was charged with the colonial prisoners' health.[51] However, Guérin was permitted to examine and treat prisoners only during a daily health visit or in the infirmary and always while under a German guard's supervision. The guard ensured that Guérin brought nothing for the prisoners and only discussed their health. He could not verify hygiene standards in the rooms or kitchens. Health specialists, doctors, and dentists were recruited first from among the Frontstalag population to care for the colonial prisoners. In their absence, unpaid civilian doctors were recruited from the local population, especially if camp hospitals had excessively high mortality rates.[52] Alternatively, hospitals could request the release of their nurses who were POWs in Germany. However, most nurses remained in captivity as part of the prisoner health services.[53] Generally, white French Army doctors, with the assistance of colonial prisoners, ministered to the colonial prisoners.[54] Thus all decisions and conclusions on colonial prisoner health were filtered through a white European lens.

Conditions and personnel varied from camp to camp. Larger camps were more likely to have medical facilities or at least a basic infirmary. There are no overall figures for the ratio of medical staff to colonial prisoners. Instead, we have examples from a few camps. At Montargis, three doctors, a dentist, and thirty-four medical professionals treated prisoners in an isolation ward (*lazaret*) with 150 beds, under the supervision of a French medical officer specializing in colonial diseases.[55] Nancy had nineteen doctors for five thousand prisoners, including ten doctors designated for the prisoners on work groups.[56] Colonial prisoners living near major hospitals, such as at Dijon, were more likely to be in better health.[57] The hospital at Chartres, run by a German chief medical officer, was actually installed in a wing of the local hospital, providing better access to medical supplies, surgical equipment, and personnel.[58] Other camps were seriously underserved. Bayonne had no medical supplies, forcing critically ill colonial prisoners to go to the nearest hospital.[59] As seen with Ben Kadour, hours could pass between injury and arrival at the hospital, with fatal consequences.

The French had irregular and limited knowledge about illnesses in the camps, mostly depending on camp inspection reports. As Scheck argues, the French rarely had the access needed to shape their negotiations on colonial prisoner health accurately.[60] Despite the full infirmary and frequent deaths at Airvault, in December 1940 inspectors were prohibited from accessing the camp and its doctor.[61] The next report, a month later, recorded frequent cases of tuberculosis and that the health of the Indochinese prisoners was "deplorable: tuberculosis, dysentery etc."[62] The camp was eventually closed, and doctors at La Roche sur Yon and Le Mans noticed that prisoners transferred from Airvault were quite sick.[63] By March 1941, if it had concerns about the health or sanitation, the Scapini Mission could request an inspection for camps or work detachments. However, as inspections were heavily coordinated, inspectors rarely spoke to all the prisoners and did not have access to every part of the camp.

Ultimately, the Scapini Mission did not need up-to-date data on the prisoners' health. Instead, it relied on a consistent argument in its negotiations with the Germans: all colonial prisoners were susceptible to disease, especially in cold climates, and should be released on humanitarian grounds. German ignorance and fear of colonial illnesses actually helped sick colonial prisoners. Usually, writing "contagious" on a door dissuaded even the most suspicious German doctors from examining the patient.[64] Many colonial prisoners, with the help of French doctors, faked madness or coughing fits, fasted, or used a leprosy diagnosis to get released for ill health.[65] As Scheck remarks, German indulgence in these releases was particularly difficult to explain, as they were well aware that the French authorities exaggerated the extent of illnesses.[66]

Mental illnesses also affected the colonial prisoners, although little is known about the diagnostic processes and treatments available. During the Great War, it was thought that prisoners were protected from "shell shock" by their presence in quiet camps far from the front, but as Clare Makepeace argues, by 1919 "barbed-wire disease" was recognized as a disorder.[67] Indeed, treatment recommendations for mental illnesses were included in the 1929 Geneva Convention, including internment in a neutral country for "grave chronic maladies of the central and peripheral nervous system; in particular grave neurasthenia and hysteria."[68] By the end of the Second World War, mental illness as a result of captivity was widely recognized, with symptoms including depression, weight loss, fatigue, and atrophied muscles.[69]

In France, the question of how colonial prisoners were coping with captivity was often framed as a question of morale, with a lack of news from home contributing to "low morale." References to depression or mental illness were rarer but do exist. A data sample of the ICRC capture cards have mental health recorded as the reason for the release of at least three colonial prisoners: one had a nervous breakdown, one suffered from melancholy, and another had general fatigue.[70] The psychiatric hospital Fleury Les Auchais admitted approximately thirty colonial soldiers between 1940 and 1944, some of whom may have been prisoners. At least one soldier, Private Second Class Deguety Gassam, age thirty-six, was admitted with anxiety immediately before the armistice was signed. He was later "cured" and released. The main diagnoses for these colonial soldiers were "mental agitation" and depression, with one case of alcoholism and another of hypochondria. Twenty-four soldiers were from North Africa; the remaining six hailed from Côte d'Ivoire, Madagascar, Sudan (Mali), and South Africa, including three from the British colonies in Africa. One suffered from a depressive state and two from dementia praecox, a term that was already fading from use in the 1920s and would be replaced by schizophrenia. Another seven French colonial soldiers were also diagnosed with dementia praecox, implying irreversible cognitive decline. Surprisingly, four of the patients suffering from dementia were later released in "much better health." Of the thirty indigenous patients, nine died in the hospital, including four cases of tuberculosis, one case of cerebral syphilis, one case of cardiac issues, and two cases of general paralysis.[71] The fascinating question of mental health and illness among colonial soldiers and prisoners deserves more attention.

TB or Not TB?

The degree of German fear in the face of "exotic maladies" was shown by the measures taken to control the risk of tuberculosis, the most prevalent malady among the colonial prisoners and a contemporary scourge.[72] Before 1914 tuberculosis was seen as a private and embarrassing illness that was too costly to prevent. The Great War changed public and private attitudes toward the disease. White French soldiers returned home infected with tuberculosis, prompting three major developments: ex-soldiers gained the right to proper treatment, the sick obtained access to sanatoriums, and the government financed an antituberculosis campaign.[73] War had also brought tuberculosis to the colonies, with the number of pulmonary infections and tuberculosis in French West Africa increasing in both 1919 and 1945, probably corresponding with the soldiers' return.[74] Since diseases spread in overcrowded areas with limited sanitation, the Frontstalags were ideal breeding grounds, while the work detachments where most prisoners spent their time were less crowded and healthier environments.

The destigmatization of tuberculosis did not apply to the colonial prisoners; instead, stereotypes of colonial soldiers and tropical diseases influenced medical opinion and political debate. Often the colonial prisoners were blamed for their illnesses. Marcel-Eugène Lacaze argued in his 1920 doctoral thesis on the Senegalese Tirailleurs and the Great War that "not only will [the native] not defend himself, but often, unconsciously, he courts trouble; he has no idea what precautions to take for the cold."[75] These attitudes were common during the First World War, when high levels of pneumonia among West African soldiers were argued to the be the result of "biological proclivity" and cultural factors like "poor hygienic habits, apathy and general ignorance."[76] Unfortunately, these ideas evolved little between the wars; instead, they were often combined with sincere fears that the colonial prisoners refused to take care of themselves when sick.[77] Much like the debate on which ethnic groups made the best soldiers, competing theories argued that certain "races" were more susceptible to tuberculosis. As Besson wrote to Scapini in December 1940, "The number of sick and dying increases in worrying proportions. The natives, overall, are having difficulties adapting to the conditions that they are forced to endure. They frequently get tuberculosis, and even though our climate is milder than that in Germany, it is not sufficient to stop this illness that develops very quickly."[78] The Scapini Mission argued that tuberculosis was almost always fatal for colonial prisoners.[79] The argument was boosted by multiple allegedly neutral sources, such as the ICRC, recording the high numbers of colonial prisoners with lung disease.[80]

Many high-ranking French politicians and military leaders had strong opinions on tuberculosis. Prime Minister François Darlan wanted all Madagascan prisoners repatriated, as he believed 70 percent of them were infected by tuberculosis.[81] The Scapini Mission refused to convey this request to the Germans, since releasing only the Madagascans might create tensions with prisoners of "other races."[82] Huntziger informed Scapini that about half of the colonial prisoners presenting with symptoms were already beyond treatment, arguing that the only way to combat the spread of tuberculosis was to detect it while it was still curable.[83] From December 1940 Besson and Scapini argued that colonial prisoners' vulnerability to tuberculosis meant they died shortly after the disease was detected.[84] Generally, West African prisoners were believed to be more susceptible to tuberculosis than North Africans. By 1943 French sources also claimed that 80 to 90 percent of released colonial prisoners suffered from tuberculosis, which was nearly always fatal.[85] ICRC reports confirmed the acute nature of the tuberculosis, which evolved quickly and was often fatal to colonial prisoners.[86] A week of X-rays at Camp Montargis showed that North African prisoners actually had the highest rates of infection, at 11.4 percent, and white prisoners and prisoners from sub-Saharan Africa had the same rate of 8.6 percent.[87]

Generally, all the Europeans involved in the colonial prisoners' captivity agreed that they were highly susceptible to tuberculosis. Disagreements focused on which prisoners should be released first.

The French achieved a major diplomatic success when Scapini was able to secure mobile pulmonary X-ray machines for use in the occupied zone, under the auspices of the ICRC and local volunteers. The same request had been denied for white French prisoners in Germany. Scapini celebrated the victory in his memoirs: "By focusing on the special vulnerability of indigenous troops, screening was done on a large enough scale. Seventy-seven thousand men were examined in 440 camps and work groups and more than 12,000 releases granted to natives and North Africans."[88] The earliest reports of systematic testing in the Frontstalags date from April 1941. Over the first year more than sixty-two thousand colonial prisoners were tested for tuberculosis, resulting in eleven thousand confirmed or suspected cases. An additional undated Red Cross report noted that twenty-five thousand additional prisoners were tested, with approximately thirty-four hundred confirmed or suspected cases. It is significant that practically all colonial prisoners were examined at least once, sometimes multiple times, for tuberculosis. In one case the German camp commander of Luçon personally requested that the ICRC organize X-rays, as the colonial prisoners in his camp had not been examined, and he felt too many had already died.[89]

Tuberculosis examinations were not carried out in Germany in the systematic way granted to the Frontstalags. British doctor A. L. Cochrane explained that the lack of medical supplies, food, and clothing in POW camps in Germany made them a breeding ground for tuberculosis. After 1942, out of fear that prisoners might infect the civilian workers, the Germans started X-raying prisoners. Cochrane discovered that the French, like the Indians and Serbs, often described tuberculosis symptoms in an attempt to be released. However, in Germany, the symptoms alone were not enough; German medical officers required confirmation with positive sputum, which was difficult to fake. Genuinely sick prisoners often remained in captivity, as samples rarely arrived at the testing facilities.[90] White French prisoners were required to have a German doctor's agreement to be excused from work or repatriated.[91] The Red Cross was able to send some supplies, but generally camps needed X-ray machines and medicine.[92] There were a few special hospitals in Germany for tuberculosis cases. For example, Königswartha was used for French prisoners despite its limited facilities. Cochrane concluded that repatriation was nonexistent, and "inevitably the hospital developed into a pleasant place to die, rather than a serious hospital, although much good work was done there." By 1943 Elsterhorst became a hospital for tuberculosis patients.[93] To maximize work efficiency, the Germans set daily limits on the number of prisoners permitted to be sick, with acceptable morality rates set at 5 percent for Western prisoners.[94] Yves Durand argues that despite these limitations, white French prisoners were cared for appropriately by French and German doctors, and most prisoners did not live in fear of sickness or death.[95]

Scapini's victory in getting systematic X-rays authorized for the Frontstalags did not signify a change in German attitudes toward tuberculosis specifically or colonial prisoners generally. Dr. Bonnaud had also proposed using a new diagnostic technique developed by Scapini's friend, Dr. Arthur Vernes, who had found that blood tests were successful in early detection of both tuberculosis and syphilis.[96] However, the German authorities refused on the grounds that this new treatment was not used in their own army.[97] Unsurprisingly, they did not believe colonial prisoners deserved better medical care than German soldiers.[98]

Nevertheless, the mobile screenings provided a quick and relatively accurate means of examining large numbers of colonial prisoners. Camp commanders facilitated access and coordinated the efforts of the Red Cross with French and German doctors. At a rate of one hundred prisoners per hour, all eleven hundred colonial prisoners at Montargis, Bourges, Chartres, Châteaudun, Nonant-le-Pin, and Le Mans were examined in one day. A German interpreter supervised the X-rays so that members of the Red Cross were not left alone with the colonial prisoners. Prisoners were classified as either "unfit for duty" (*Dienstunfähige*) or "not unfit for duty" (*noch nicht Dienstunfähige*), and suspicious results were given to the German medical officer (*Stabsarzt*) Honiger after each session. A mixed medical commission verified prisoners who were determined unfit for duty, while questionable cases were sent for follow-up X-rays at the civilian hospital in Montargis.[99]

At another camp, Morancez, the French doctor had total control over the process: he selected the prisoners to be released and informed the German doctor of his choice.[100] Overall, any prisoner with a confirmed case of tuberculosis was released.[101]

While the German authorities used the Red Cross's systematic X-rays as a basis for release, X-rays remained problematic for determining how widespread tuberculosis actually was among the colonial prisoners. Marc Daniels warned in 1949, "When one presents statistics of tuberculosis in Europe it is with a feeling that they are better than no information at all, but not much better."[102] This was particularly true when one considers the impact that preexisting beliefs about colonial health had on the plethora of studies commissioned by the French. The evaluations often produced different and contradicting results. At Camp Laval, for example, the Scapini Mission reported that between 15 and 18 percent of the colonial prisoners had tuberculosis, while the Direction du service des prisonniers de guerre claimed only 10 percent were infected.[103]

The most revealing result of the systematic Red Cross examinations (see table 1) was that infection was relatively consistent across race, with one exception: white prisoners had the highest infection rate of 50 percent, with seventeen out of the thirty-two prisoners examined showing signs of tuberculosis. The rates of infection across the racial breakdown used by the French Red Cross (including Algerian, Moroccan, Tunisian, "Yellow," Madagascan, Black, and Antillian) were consistently between 22 and 25 percent. Tuberculosis was spread through close contact with other infected individuals and was not due to racial makeup. As Scheck confirms, a predisposition to tuberculosis among people from tropical climates has never been proven, but it has permeated the historical record.[104]

The Red Cross published camp infection rates from their largest examination, which involved over fifty thousand prisoners. Montargis and Le Mans had the lowest infection rates, at 9.4 and 9.1 percent, respectively.[105] Chartres, Bourges, and Châteaudun were in the middle, at 13.1, 14, and 15.4 percent, respectively.[106] The most severe rate of infection was in Nonant-le-Pin, at 23.5 percent.[107]

Chapters 7 and 8 show that the strategic position of North Africa in

Table 1. Results of systematic X-rays in the
Frontstalags, January 1–February 10, 1942

Race	Number of X-rays	Total cases of suspected and confirmed tuberculosis	Percentage with tuberculosis
White	32	17	53.1
Algerian	3,497	882	25.2
Moroccan	2,164	472	21.8
Tunisian	1,117	263	23.5
Syrian	1		
"Yellow"	102	23	22.5
Malagasy	885	219	24.7
Black	2,761	608	22
Antillian	116	40	24
Guyannais	2	1	50
Reunionnais	2	2	100
French India	1	1	100
Total	10,730	2,528	23.5

SOURCE: Archives Nationales, F/9/2351.

the war effort translated into certain advantages, including early release for ten thousand North African prisoners as they became targets of German propaganda. However, this did not increase their chance of being released on the grounds of ill health, as only 13 percent of Algerian and Moroccan prisoners, compared with 31 percent of Senegalese prisoners or 43 percent of Ivoirian prisoners, were released due to illness. In total, approximately 18 percent of colonial prisoners were released due to illness, which included tuberculosis, other diseases, work-related injuries, mental illness, and credibly faked sickness.[108] This calculation of 18 percent falls between the Red Cross report of 23 percent and Armelle Mabon's low statistic of 14 percent, counting prisoners who were released through February 1943.[109] Sanitary conditions deteriorated as the war progressed, which would have only augmented the number of colonial prisoners with tuberculosis. Colonial prisoners' health was at its worst during the period immediately after the armistice and again in 1944 with the Germans' retreat.[110]

By politicizing the rates of tuberculosis infection among colonial prisoners during the occupation, the Scapini Mission, the Vichy government, and the French Red Cross sought to obtain the release of more colonial prisoners. Yet politicization did not stop with the prisoners' release nor even with the end of the war. A former president of the French Red Cross, Dr. Louis Bazy, wrote an article on the health concerns associated with repatriating prisoners from captivity. He used a rather high statistic for colonial prisoner infection rate to drive home his point that infections in France originated from the colonial prisoner-of-war population and not from among the French civilians, who had a peacetime infection rate of 1 percent. Despite the efforts that had been made during the interwar period, tuberculosis remained a stigma, something that reflected badly on a family and a community. However, during the occupation, Bazy comfortably talked about high tuberculosis rates and the need for action as a benevolent and humanitarian way to help "our" colonial prisoners.[111] Once the war was over, some white experts felt it important to stress that the diseases came from the "others."

Health in the Southern Zone

The German authorities' leniency in releasing sick colonial prisoners should have been an advantage for these prisoners. Unfortunately, release for colonial prisoners improved neither their heath nor their chances of returning home quickly. Following the established German policy of releasing prisoners unable to work or whose illness might become expensive to treat, severely ill prisoners were liberated almost immediately.[112] Leaving the Frontstalags was only the first step in a long journey south that not all colonial prisoners would survive. First, sick prisoners had to wait for liberation papers, which took forty-eight hours to obtain. Then they could travel to the southern zone, where they came under the Vichy regime's jurisdiction and care. However, because of gasoline shortages, this trip south was often delayed. Omar Diallo, not a unique case, was forced to wait for an available freight train to take him to Paris. From Paris, he was eventually transported via hospital train to the southern zone.[113] It took on average three weeks for a sick prisoner in Orleans to be evacuated to the southern zone.[114] When possible, Red Cross drivers tried to collect the most urgent cases weekly. Some colonial prisoners died as a result of these unnecessary delays; in other cases, the prisoners' condition worsened to the extent that recovery was no longer possible.[115] Mabon accurately attributes the high mortality in 1941 to the long delays, adding that once evacuations were better organized, the number of preventable deaths decreased.[116]

By the spring of 1942 the frequency of evacuations increased, and consequently fewer colonial prisoners were hospitalized in Marseille.[117] By October 1942 sick prisoners could expect evacuation from outside Chartres to Paris or Orleans in less than a week.[118] Myron Echenberg believes that the Vichy regime deliberately left five thousand African soldiers without resources in Paris.[119] This was most likely due to an oversight rather than a deliberate decision. Given the French desire to keep colonial prisoners separate from anyone who might influence them unduly, such as Communists or unhappy ex-servicemen, it seems unlikely that the Vichy regime would purposely allow such a large number of colonial prisoners to go unsupervised in occupied Paris. It is quite possible that soldiers remained in or went to Paris after the armistice instead of reporting to their lost units. Knowing that release meant demobilization in the colonies, some men perhaps decided to stay in Paris and work discreetly. Others went to Paris after escaping and chose not to report to the French authorities. Still others remained because they were unable or unwilling to risk recapture in attempting to cross the demarcation line.

Once sick colonial prisoners finally reached the unoccupied zone, they were directed according to French racial designations to hospitals in Marseille or Fréjus for examination. Generally, North African prisoners were sent to hospitals Sainte-Marguerite, Michel Level, and Montolivet in Marseilles, and most prisoners from sub-Saharan Africa were sent to Fréjus, Bordeaux, Marseilles, or Brive. Fréjus, with its major hospital for colonial diseases, typically housed four hundred to five hundred patients but could accept a maximum of eight hundred if large groups of colonial prisoners arrived from the occupied zone together.[120] As the risk of tuberculosis did not stop at the demarcation line, the number of recorded cases of infection increased, albeit slowly, in the southern zone hospitals. Fréjus reported infection rates of 1.7 percent in 1940, 1.4 percent in 1941, and 2.2 percent in 1942.[121] Interestingly, these rates were only slightly higher than the 1 percent of French civilians infected before the arrival of the colonial soldiers cited by Dr. Bazy.

While these hospitals specialized in "tropical diseases," the colonial prisoners were sometimes surprised at the negative welcome they received. The morale of the repatriated colonial prisoners concerned Darlan, who called for an investigation into the situation of the repatriated colonial prisoners in military hospitals and potential sanctions: "[Darlan] cannot accept that, through misunderstandings or personal failings, our natives might not be given all the moral and material aid that they deserve; with all the heart and spirit of national solidarity that the metropolitan French feel that the French of the empire particularly deserve."[122]

Darlan was right to be concerned. Much of the goodwill gained from close contact with the French populations evaporated during the colonial prisoners' stay in the southern zone. At the military hospital in Brive, seventy-five colonial prisoners lodged a complaint against Dr. Jokoum, who bullied them for being "constant moaners."[123] An inspector found the prisoners' complaints to be justified, because Jokoum had felt the formalities to obtain extra soup and cigarettes were too onerous to accomplish, choosing instead to distribute them parsimoniously. The inspector concluded that "the Senegalese are soldiers in every sense of the word: they are disciplined and only a few complain."[124] His choice of vocabulary to describe these West African soldiers is important. He underscored their discipline as proof that they had legitimate reasons for complaint. Indiscipline was seen as the result of German propaganda and not as a form of legitimate protest. The specter of German influence overshadowed French interactions with their colonial soldiers and affected policy toward their stay in the southern zone and eventual repatriation.

When white soldiers were released from captivity, they were demobilized and sent back to their families as soon as possible to recover. Others were released on "captivity leave," meaning they were not definitively freed, had to report to the authorities from time to time, and could be recalled. Colonial prisoners were not demobilized in France and were rarely given captivity leave. They remained soldiers subject to a strict military regime, in a country facing increasing hardships. Naturally, that had a negative effect on morale and health. Commander Wender noted in 1942 that the North African prisoners undergoing treatment in Marseilles were in low spirits, which he attributed to the residual effects of German propaganda. Wender did acknowledge that irregular payments, delays before repatriation to North Africa, and understaffed hospital wards with personnel unused to the "North African mentality" had contributed to their low morale.[125] Ignoring the effects on the colonial prisoners of inconsistent payments and prolonged stays in the metropole would have grievous consequences for the provisional government at the end of the war. Further distinctions in treatment emerged once the colonial prisoners returned under French control. Colonial prisoners who were French citizens received better treatment in the southern zone hospitals, which caused conflicts in the tuberculosis ward in Marseilles.[126]

Now that the colonial prisoners were back under French rule, following precedents set during the First World War, the Vichy regime sought to send them home quickly. The benefit for the colonial prisoners was obvious: they would return home to their families and take advantage of well-deserved comforts of home. For the French, sending the colonial prisoners back home removed the potential for unsupervised interactions with "unsavory" elements: those opposed to the Vichy regime or French colonial rule, workers, Socialists, or Gaullists. It also meant the former prisoners would return to strict imperial rule. Until Vichy lost access to the empire after the Allied landings in North Africa in November 1942, sick former prisoners were repatriated on hospital ships when available or regular ships when not.

In November 1942 the Vichy government made one last attempt to obtain the release of all colonial prisoners on humanitarian grounds. Gaston Joseph, the director of political affairs at the secretary of state for colonies, argued, "The toll of two years of captivity has left them with little physical resistance, at risk to contract a dangerous, or even mortal infection. It would be humane, while there is still time, to proceed with their release."[127] His request, arriving days after the German invasion of the southern zone, was likely designed to test the diplomatic waters. The Scapini Mission had been making the same suggestion in vain for almost two and a half years, and after the German invasion of the southern zone in November 1942, the Vichy regime had even less diplomatic weight than before. The request was denied, and the healthy colonial prisoners (and over half of the white prisoners in Germany) remained in captivity until they were liberated by the Allies in 1944–45.

With no means of repatriation available, and Germany's labor needs rapidly expanding with its increased war effort, sick colonial prisoners were rehabilitated rather than released. Colonial prisoners needing long-term care were sent to Toulon.[128] At this stage it was no longer feasible for the French authorities to keep the colonial prisoners fully separate from white soldiers or civilian workers from the colonies. The German occupying forces moved colonial prisoners suffering from short-term or mild illnesses into temporary hospitals. Once recovered, they were reassigned to large work groups employed directly by the Germans.[129] Seriously ill colonial prisoners continued to be released, but without the possibility of returning home, they found their situation virtually unchanged from captivity. Instead of being demobilized and released, they were healed, placed in "centers" rather than Frontstalags, and eventually sent back to work for the Germans. By 1943 *centres de regroupements et de réadaptations* were used to house sick or otherwise incapacitated colonial soldiers, members of the French Army, colonial workers, and discharged prisoners. The Indochinese and Madagascan prisoners, less numerous, were kept in the hospitals and not the centers. After years of requesting that the colonial prisoners be moved south and insisting that only the French understood how to handle their colonial soldiers, the Vichy regime finally got direct control over some of its colonial prisoners. Unfortunately, the French were unable and unwilling to protect their colonial prisoners in the southern zone from the deterioration of conditions as the war continued.

Most of the colonial prisoners' experiences of captivity were decided by the German authorities, but sick colonial prisoners and soldiers in the southern zone had also to contend with Italian rule. Without a peace agreement, France was still subject to the whims of the armistice commissions. One of the peculiarities of the armistice was the requirement that France sign one with Italy, which had declared war on France only a few days beforehand. Even though it could not act without German approval, the Commission italienne d'armistice was given a zone of influence in southeast France, including Grenoble and Nice. After the defeat, a number of colonial soldiers who had not been captured remained in the Vichy-controlled unoccupied zone. As with the released prisoners, Vichy tried to repatriate the soldiers as soon as possible, but many remained in France. The commission grew nervous about the presence of colonial soldiers so close to the Italian border and declared that by March 15, 1941, all colonial troops must be relocated west of the Rhone.[130] Initially, an exception was made for the colonial hospital in Fréjus. With the German invasion of the southern zone, the Italian forces occupied parts of southern France, including Toulon and up to the Rhone, at which time the exception for the colonial hospital was revoked.

With the closure of the colonial hospital, the Vichy regime lost its greatest advantage in caring for colonial prisoners.[131] While the number of patients had declined from a height of 5,000 in 1940, the hospital's closure was detrimental to the health of its remaining 3,144 patients, who were forcibly relocated.[132] The medical staff and the patients were dispersed across the southern zone. Despite official inquiries from Medical Officer Crozat, the German authorities refused to confirm whether the isolated detachments of sick colonial soldiers near Avignon would remain there permanently. Without official substantiation, it was increasingly difficult to organize supplementary care from local doctors.[133] During this period of greatest direct control over the colonial prisoners, the French had less and less authority. Once sick soldiers had recovered, their labor was allocated to the German authorities in conditions much like captivity. Vichy's sovereignty was all but an illusion.

Despite the advantages of captivity in France compared with Germany, and bearing in mind the limitations of statistical data on colonial prisoners, slightly more colonial prisoners died during captivity than white prisoners. Approximately 2 percent of all French prisoners died in German captivity, whereas about 3.4 percent of the colonial prisoners died, almost all from illness.[134] These statistics, even with Scheck's slightly higher mortality rate of 5 percent, are comparable.[135] The difference from the findings of previous scholarship is striking. Bob Moore has estimated that approximately half of the colonial prisoners survived captivity.[136] This is much closer to the rate of mortality for Soviet prisoners of war, at 60 percent. It seems more likely that this was actually the percentage of colonial prisoners who remained in captivity at the end of the war. Surprisingly, colony of origin significantly affected a prisoners' chance of survival, with mortality rates ranging from a low of 0.9 percent for Tunisian prisoners to a high of 18.8 percent for Madagascan prisoners.[137] This is most likely due to the length of time Madagascan prisoners spent in captivity.

When prisoners died in captivity, it was often due to lung disease. The Ministère des anciens combattants established that of the total 1,850,000 white and colonial prisoners, 183,330 were sick at some point and 37,054, or 2 percent of the total, died. Of the latter, 6,178 died from tuberculosis, 1,451 from other pulmonary diseases, and 1,186 from contagious diseases.[138] This meant between 19 and 25 percent of French POWs died from lung diseases. These statistics include both colonial and white prisoners together. We can calculate that approximately 18 percent of the colonial prisoners died from lung disease.[139] Again, these are comparable statistics, which show there was slightly higher potential for white prisoners to die of lung diseases while in captivity. Conditions were worse for white prisoners in Germany, with greater shortages and insufficient protection against the elements, leaving them more susceptible to disease. Another potential explanation for the difference in mortality rates is that the German authorities' fear of colonial prisoners' illnesses was greater than their fear of French or Allied prisoners' illnesses, so colonial prisoners were granted greater leniency in the identification of tuberculosis and thus had a greater chance of release. More difficult to quantify is the mortality rates for colonial prisoners who died several months after release from afflictions brought on by captivity.[140]

While fewer colonial prisoners caught tuberculosis, the white prisoners were more likely to survive captivity. Two possible conclusions arise: either the colonial prisoners' health was weaker in general, which we have seen was not the case, or postinfection treatment was crucial to recovery. White prisoners were more likely to recover even after contracting a disease. Colonial prisoners were sent to understaffed hospitals in the Vichy zone, then on to extended stays in camps. Some returned to harsh labor, even after their release from captivity. It was easier for the French authorities to accept the belief that men from the colonies were more susceptible to disease than to do a critical examination of conditions in the camps and southern zone.

The simplest explanation is that tuberculosis vulnerability has nothing to do with racial identity. In the Frontstalags, where prisoners of all races lived in comparable conditions, infection rates were generally stable. Differences occurred among camps and at different times of the year. However, there was no persistent, traceable evidence that prisoners from Abidjan, for example, were more likely to catch tuberculosis than prisoners from Pau. Then why did the French so fervently push the argument that tuberculosis was decimating the colonial prisoner population, and why did Swiss inspectors and German camp guards accept these arguments? The high number of positive X-rays among colonial prisoners did not imply greater vulnerability. Infection was common and led to illness only if accompanied by unhealthy conditions, meaning there was no justifiable medical reason for releasing all prisoners with signs of tuberculosis.[141]

As seen, racism and paternalism permeated all interactions between the French and their colonial soldiers, and indeed, between many of the European actors and the colonial prisoners. Medical studies of peoples from Africa, Asia, the West Indies, and beyond were couched in racial typecasts portraying the "native" as unable to understand the basic rules of hygiene and in need of European help.[142] Members of the Scapini Mission were most likely sincere in their worry about the colonial prisoners' health. More importantly, as chapter 7 demonstrates, they noticed that arguments for release based on humanitarian concerns were more effective than their previous requests for soldiers or workers for the colonies. The final reason for the difference in mortality rates concerns the rapidly deteriorating conditions in France and Germany as labor demands and food shortages increased. Colonial prisoners who were forcibly brought to Germany in 1944 faced grueling conditions, which affected their overall survival rates.

Once one accounts for the possibility of random violence in the

Frontstalags, the overall standard of treatment for prisoners in France was higher than that in Germany. Colonial prisoners were more likely than their white counterparts to be victims of brutality and murder at the hands of the guards. Considering that the colonial prisoners reported specific individual events and not a general atmosphere of violence, one can conclude that murder remained rare enough to shock and be remembered in detail. This conforms to Bob Moore's assessment that in western Europe, the Geneva Convention was generally upheld, and violations, violence, and prisoner deaths remained exceptional and were investigated as such.[143] German officers were lucky to have a posting in France, rather than in Germany or on the eastern front. Prisoners in France were also somewhat sheltered from the realities of the war, at least until 1943–44. The Germans' fear of contagious diseases combined with an unwillingness to financially support unfit prisoners meant that they granted concessions, such as systematic X-rays, for France that were not accorded in Germany. Improved rations from the French contributed positively to the colonial prisoners' overall health. The Vichy regime's paternalism showed great interest, and probably sincere concern, for the colonial prisoners' health. However, that concern remained grounded in racial stereotypes, which prevented optimal care.

6

HELPING "OUR" PRISONERS
Aid and Escape

French support for their prisoners of war was part of a growing consciousness of the humanitarian concerns affecting combatants. With the outbreak of war in 1939, aid organizations sprang up throughout Europe, North America, and in the French colonies to bring support to the soldiers. At its most basic level, helping both colonial and white prisoners served the same purpose: reminding them that they had not been forgotten.[1] The parcel from home, containing letters from loved ones, warm socks, and most importantly, food, was archetypical of the POW experience during both world wars. When families' financial situation did not permit them to send packages, the state and humanitarian organizations stepped in. A professionalization of the humanitarian sector continued throughout the Second World War, helped by many of the actors and agencies who had been present in the Great War. With this shift toward professional organizations and planning came increased interaction with, and even dependence on, the state.[2] While metropolitan civilians were recruited into the Vichy regime's humanitarian politics, the same cannot be said for the colonized populations. Settler communities with close ties to the French colonial administration and charities organized in the colonies were promoted to send aid and packages from the colonies. In rare cases, the indigenous populations were solicited for donations.

This concentration of aid in the hands of white Europeans reflected two tendencies: the growing professionalization of humanitarianism and its inherent paternalism. This paternalism flourished under the Vichy regime and served as a reminder to the French that they had obligations toward their colonial subjects, specifically the colonial prisoners of war. Fulfilling these obligations allowed the French to gloss over the inherent malevolence of imperialism while juggling the tensions between enlightenment values of liberty and equality and exploitative rule based on racial and religious hierarchies. The Vichy regime, worried because it could not entirely control the circumstances of the colonial prisoners' captivity, feared that German propaganda in the camps and de Gaulle's dissidence in the colonies would corrupt the hearts and minds of loyal, but "easily misled," colonial prisoners. Without control over their daily lives, the French had to seek another way to ensure the colonial prisoners toed the line, which they did by politicizing humanitarian relief for these prisoners.

Politics of Organization through Top-Down Assistance

The organizational requirements of humanitarian aid for the colonial prisoners cannot be dissociated from the political aims. Indeed, the increasing organization of relief efforts was indicative of an early split between those on the ground responding to observed needs and official visions of what aid could accomplish in the long term. The first efforts to help were spontaneous and unorganized: French civilians tried to give food and water to colonial prisoners on forced marches to temporary camps. Once the prisoners were in camps, people brought food to the gates. Often prisoners, like those at Ambroise, survived on local donations until the French Red Cross could organize regular aid.[3] Even after the Red Cross took over, civilians continued to help by supplying hot soup for workers or buying extra food or tobacco.[4] While in the early days the French government praised these efforts, this individual and spontaneous relief was difficult to regulate. Those who helped did so for their patriotism and desire "to recognize the courage and good behavior of the 'natives' during the war."[5] Both the Germans and the French officials took advantage of these unregulated humanitarian efforts, especially in chaos following the defeat, but neither power approved of these "illegitimate" methods.

Controlling the humanitarian aid for prisoners meant controlling the narrative that accompanied it. Realizing that on their return home the colonial prisoners would be potentially influential men, it was important to the Vichy regime's postwar imperial goals to ensure that they would support continued French rule. The Comité central d'assistance aux prisonniers de guerre en captivité (Central committee for aid to prisoners of war in captivity; CCAPG) explained, "Upon their return to their home countries, our natives, conserving the memory of the help and assistance they received during their time spent on French soil, will be the best representatives to their friends and families of upholding the unity of our great colonial empire."[6] Through the colonial prisoners, humanitarian aid was tied to the future of the French Empire and the Vichy regime's control over it.

The overwhelming number of prisoners in precarious situations necessitated an organized and dynamic network for humanitarian intervention. Article 78 of the 1929 Geneva Convention guaranteed the right of legally constituted relief agencies to bring aid to their prisoners.[7] In France, the Germans wanted to simplify their point of contact by limiting the number of interlocutors, so they refused to allow the French Red Cross deliveries into the Frontstalags until the August 7, 1940, law was applied.[8] This law fused three charities—the Société de secours aux blessés militaires, the Association des dames françaises, and the Union des femmes de France—into the French Red Cross.[9] The president of the French Red Cross protested against this and other changes that allowed the Vichy government to place the Red Cross under its jurisdiction, co-opt its logistical network, and ensure that all humanitarian aid to the prisoners followed its political aims.[10] The law imposed a centralized political structure, under the Direction du service des prisonniers de guerre (DSPG) and the Scapini Mission, over an inherently decentralized, disunified, and sometimes unwieldy collection of aid organizations in France and the colonies, all vying to help the prisoners. While this decision to centralize was imposed by the German occupiers, France was not the only country to bind its relief efforts to the state. In July 1942 the United States, only seven months after entering the war, created the War Relief Control Board, an organization linked to the State Department that controlled accreditation, budgets, fundraising, and advertising possibilities for all humanitarian work involved with the war.[11] In France, many charitable organizations resisted this new hierarchy; they were proud of their contributions and protective of their legitimacy.

Army Controller Bigard, head of the Paris section of the DSPG, was tasked with improving conditions for all French prisoners in France and Germany as thoroughly and rapidly as possible.[12] The newly created CCAPG, led by a man named De Bellaigue, served as an umbrella linking the DSPG above to the diverse relief agencies below.[13] Helping the prisoners of war was popular, and the CCAPG had branches in over six hundred French towns.[14] Its delegates facilitated the Red Cross drivers' access to Frontstalags.[15] A separate Overseas Section of the CCAPG was created to cater to the colonial prisoners' "specific needs," thus separating the relief efforts for the colonial prisoners from those aimed at white prisoners.[16] This separation allowed the different political, financial, and organizational priorities for colonial and white prisoners to flourish.

The seemingly linear organization flowing between the DSPG and CCAPG and the smaller relief agencies hid the much of the disorganization surrounding humanitarian aid for the colonial prisoners. In reality, there were many different state agencies and private charities, all trying to improve conditions for the colonial prisoners and motivated by different factors. Some, like the Algerian Comité de secours aux mobilisés et à leurs familles, which had been created in 1939 to care for soldiers from Algeria, shifted focus to the prisoners after the armistice.[17] Others, like the Comité d'aide et d'assistance coloniale, had existed during the First World War.[18] These "godmother" charities were recruited to fulfill the needs of a diverse group of colonial prisoners. Different colonies and territories' represented "their" prisoners' interests. There were charities for Black soldiers, North African soldiers, West Africans, Antilleans as French citizens, Indochinese and Madagascan workers and soldiers, and even ones for the numbers of soldiers from the Pacific Islands.[19]

After the French Red Cross, Amitiés africaines rapidly became one of the most important aid organizations. Created after the Great War, when colonial soldiers had been sent to fight without intellectual preparation for what they would experience, the agency tried to actively cultivate military spirit among African soldiers and tighten links with veterans.[20] Under Pétain this trend of linking material aid with intellectual influence expanded. Amitiés africaines had a large influential presence in Lyons, France's second-largest city, close to the occupied zone and home to an important French Red Cross depot.[21] From there the organization helped prisoners' families claim their benefits and payments and advised the government on measures it believed would protect the colonial prisoners from the physical and mental consequences of a long captivity.[22] The aid organizations with access to the Frontstalags became an integral part of Vichy's paternalistic supervision of the colonial prisoners.

Relief agencies publicized their contributions and sought endorsements from important figures to increase visibility and thus receive more funding. Generally, resources were allocated according to the number of prisoners the charities served, with smaller charities fighting for more government subsidies.[23] The press helped promote the idea that important French politicians and administrators were personally concerned with the plight of colonial prisoners. In North Africa, Resident General of Tunisia Jean-Pierre Esteva's donation of fifty thousand francs and Pierre Pucheu's surprising gift of one hundred thousand francs were praised as expressions of solidarity from France to the French Muslims in captivity. The article on Pucheu, a profascist propagandist and minister of the interior in 1941, reminded readers that the government of Algeria underwrote much of the aid for colonial prisoners.[24]

Colonial prisoners received individual and group assistance, with each type serving a different purpose.[25] The collective deliveries ensured that the prisoners had enough to eat by supplementing rations supplied by the detaining power and were also sent to white prisoners in Germany. Between April and December 1941 the Frontstalags received 460 tons of rations, including sugar, rice, chocolate, chickpeas, dates, figs, and cigarettes.[26] In the first eighteen months of the prisoners' captivity the Frontstalags received a quarter of all donated food, despite having less than 10 percent of the prisoner population.[27] Parcels were normally sent by families with food from home, woolens, letters, and other items intended to soften the conditions of captivity. The French government took over this role for prisoners who could not afford packages. It also classified all colonial prisoners as "needy," entitling them to a government parcel.[28] Government-sponsored parcels were designed to eliminate tensions between prisoners whose families could send items and those whose families could not. Yet these parcels were not all supplied by the same agency, and logistical problems quickly became morale problems when some colonial prisoners felt that others were receiving better packages. Some prisoners were on distribution lists and received packages in their names, while others received anonymous and uniform parcels.

Distance, cost, and availability of supplies complicated the procedure for the colonial prisoners, hence the creation of individualized government parcels. According to the CCAPG, "The individual package brings the native the proof of solicitude, not only of the nation but of a particular element in this community: the colonial organization, the governor or resident general, substitutes itself for the prisoner's far-off family."[29] Here the subordinate colonial authorities sought to replace the colonial prisoners' family, whereas helping white families with their packages was seen as a way to reinforce the familial bond, not sever it. In taking on the role traditionally held by the family, the Vichy regime reinforced the position of Pétain as the father of the nation and the empire. Pétain's photo was often included in the colonial prisoners' packages with a note explaining which colonial authority had sent it.[30]

The Overseas Section coordinated the numerous smaller charities that funded and assembled the packages, but it did not always communicate back up the ladder to the DSPG. Packages and supplies coming from different colonies or overseas territories arrived on different days. These discrepancies exacerbated tensions, which, according to Marcel Bonnaud of the Scapini Mission, risked becoming racial conflicts when prisoners from Senegal, Indochina, Martinique, or Madagascar did not receive the same monthly packages as the North African prisoners.[31] Among the North African prisoners, the Moroccans received more frequent and better parcels than the Algerian or Tunisian prisoners.[32]

The three North African territories were active in supporting prisoners from the indigenous and settler communities. The colonial administrations worried incessantly about the consequences of the defeat on French prestige in the colonies. Allowing the indigenous populations to fundraise or help supply packages for the colonial prisoners would have meant facing certain uncomfortable truths about the defeat and the situation of the colonial soldiers currently interned in France. According to Nancy Lawler, French administrators reluctantly asked the local population in Côte d'Ivoire for assistance with the colonial prisoners, but only after news of the camps had spread throughout the colony. By 1942 the Ivoirians had raised over eight hundred thousand francs.[33]

In North Africa, however, the large settler community and network of French and European administrators and their wives meant that humanitarian work for colonial prisoners could pass through the hands of white French women, such as Suzanne Noguès, married to the resident general of Morocco, and Marie-Renée-Joséphine Weygand, married to Gen. Maxime Weygand, general delegate for French Africa. Pushing parcels through the settler community under the sponsorship of high-ranking white women reinforced the paternalistic and hierarchal nature of humanitarian aid. As Johannes Paulmann argues, humanitarian mobilization requires a defined problem that can be solved in the name of "humanity," but doing so creates a hierarchy between those receiving aid and those delivering it, between the victims and the benefactors.[34] Here the identified problem was colonial soldiers who were suffering in German captivity but might potentially forget their ties to France, and the solution, rather than humanity, was "imperial solidarity." The resulting hierarchy and its underlying paternalism was an inherent part of France's civilizing mission and was considered a positive attribute by many of the French actors.

Suzanne Noguès's streamlined parcel operation in Morocco led Amitiés africaines to suggest that all North African packages be sent to France via Rabat. Individualized packages would be sent to named colonial prisoners, while extra parcels would be shared among any remaining Algerian, Tunisian, and Moroccan prisoners. The idea was to ship packages via the Red Cross to Marseilles in the unoccupied zone and on to distribution centers in the occupied zone, from which packages could be delivered to all the colonial prisoners simultaneously.[35] Unfortunately, the CCAPG's mandate was limited to the occupied zone. Despite a detailed study in 1942, the streamlining stagnated without an organizing committee whose purview spanned both zones.[36] The French Red Cross had been using a similar system since 1940, with a distribution center in Paris and three smaller centers in Bordeaux, Angers, and Chaumont. Those centers distributed packages sent from the colonies to local agencies that delivered them.[37] The efforts in North Africa did nothing to address complaints from the remaining 30 percent of the colonial prisoners from the rest of the empire but demonstrate the importance North African prisoners had.

Furthermore, the fluid nature of the work camps made it hard to ensure an even distribution of parcels to colonial prisoners scattered across farms and forests.[38] German camp commanders' discretion in allowing access to relief agencies was a major contributor to the disorganization. French requests to obtain permission for Red Cross drivers to deliver directly to the work camps, as protected by Article 33 of the Geneva Convention, were repeatedly denied.[39] Instead, the Germans required that donations be left at the Frontstalag for distribution by the men of confidence.[40] The French quickly learned to work around these restrictions. In Epinal, the local delegate chose to work outside official channels, allowing him to send news of the colonial prisoners to their families in North and West Africa.[41] Over time, the German occupiers loosened restrictions on which relief agencies could visit the Frontstalags.[42]

In addition to the logistical issues, corruption and theft existed at all levels of the humanitarian aid system. Anonymous letters to the French Red Cross detailed the issues. One author chose anonymity, fearing "starvation, prison, and exercise during an entire day" if caught complaining. He accused the colonial prisoner in charge of the packages of distributing items to his friends and selling the rest to civilians or other prisoners. Allegedly, the thief was in league with the translators, who were apparently all Jewish, leaving the author and his friends no reliable method to inform the guards.[43] The anonymous author's last comment is perhaps the most revealing, as it demonstrates an almost perfect reading of the political climate. The writer did not blame the Germans for the theft but, understanding the tolerance of antisemitism, blamed Jewish translators. Antisemitism was not a new feature in France or its overseas territories. In North Africa, the 1870 Crémieux Decree gave Algerian Jews French citizenship, thus codifying different legal statutes based on religion, which increased tensions between the three religious communities. The Vichy regime in Algeria overturned the Crémieux Decree in 1940. Perhaps in response to an increase in anti-Semitic legislation, in August 1940 returning North African Muslim soldiers caused considerable disturbances against Algerian Jews.[44] Despite the significant indigenous Jewish population of North Africa, there is little archival trace of Jewish colonial prisoners in general and no evidence that they were given better jobs.[45] However, the letter writer's other allegations are credible; localized theft by guards and prisoners was rampant.

Theft varied in scope and consequences. Sometimes prisoners stole entire parcels or took individual items like chocolate or cigarettes for themselves and their friends.[46] The man of confidence Geromini, at Camp de Hanneman, was transferred to Stalag VIII-A in Görlitz as punishment for selling food and clothing donated by the Red Cross to the other prisoners.[47] The German authorities appeared to know about his activities and agreed that the Red Cross should be informed. At Charleville, Henry Eboué "shared" extra Red Cross donations among his friends in the camp, including his brother, Robert, and Léopold Senghor, their families in the occupied zone, local civilians, and strategically chosen Germans within the camp hierarchy in order to cultivate their goodwill.[48] Having access to the "extras" certainly improved Henry's captivity experience, but the other prisoners dependent on parcels, like the anonymous author above, might have been more critical about his use of Red Cross supplies.

Yet were the two situations so different? Henry Eboué, in his opinion, was not stealing from the other prisoners; instead, he was putting the extra supplies the Red Cross provided to judicious use. His black-market trading allowed him to make contacts with civilians and German guards, who in turn helped him get supplies for the camp and provided personal favors. The advantages were shared among his friends, who represented the colonial elite, and their families living in France. Eboué does not mention selling goods to the other prisoners. Somewhat disingenuously, considering his friend's use of Red Cross goods, Senghor complained in his captivity report that at Saint-Medard, although unclaimed packages were supposed to go to the neediest prisoners, the Germans instead removed all the cigarettes and chocolates and sent the rest to the kitchen.[49] It is clear that this small group was unlike the majority of the colonial prisoners; these were highly educated intellectuals who had lived in France before the war and were directly connected to the Free French through Henry's father, Felix Eboué. The manner in which Henry wrote his captivity report conveys his belief that they were doing nothing wrong and were simply making intelligent choices for their captivity. Other colonial prisoners without these connections and advantages felt differently.

To keep goods from going astray, departmental delegates and men of confidence were given more control over receiving and distributing deliveries.[50] Response cards were included inside the packages to ensure they were being delivered to the colonial prisoners and not the German guards.[51] French law punished stealing from prisoners with forced labor.[52] However, it had no jurisdiction in the Frontstalags.

Institutional corruption was harder to distinguish from disorganization or incompetence. The DSPG, Amitiés africaines, and CCAPG were all accused of similar crimes including artificially inflating prices, giving prisoners rotten produce, general disorganization, and outright theft.[53] An investigation conducted by a military auditor named Honnorat concluded that some of the complaints were accurate but that it was unnecessary to reorganize the entire DSPG. The relief agencies were regularly audited to determine how they spent their donations; most kept good records.[54] However, Amitiés africaines came under scrutiny after a public auction. Instead of donating food directly to the colonial prisoners, the organization auctioned it off to wealthy buyers, allowing them to circumvent rationing and buy restricted goods. The auction raised 1.5 million francs, which were donated to help buy food for the colonial prisoners. The organization's own general secretary, Messel, blew the whistle on the auction, blaming Françoise Meifriedy, head of the women's section, for fear that news of it would damage the government's reputation.[55] The head of the Lyons branch of Amitiés africaines defended Meifriedy's decision to hold the auction. However, the auditor disagreed and concluded that the food should have been given directly to the colonial prisoners, as that was their biggest concern during captivity. Despite the disorganization and corruption within the aid organizations, overall, they substantially improved conditions for the colonial prisoners.

Colonial Humanitarianism

Both powers saw the colonial prisoners as an element for either stability or chaos on their return home. Germany felt it could benefit from chaos and anti-French feeling in the colonies. It used the threat of further controls and more German inspectors on the ground if the Vichy regime was unable to maintain control over North Africa. The French naturally wanted to reconsolidate their control, faced with Spanish and Italian claims to parts of Morocco and Tunisia, and to avoid an increased German presence in the colonies. French political motivations behind the humanitarian mobilization appeared quickly: improving conditions for the colonial prisoners in France would translate into future obedience and support from loyal subjects cognizant of French efforts on their behalf. Representing the largest proportion of colonial prisoners, and hailing from strategic positions in the Mediterranean, North African prisoners were targeted for propaganda and relief efforts. Germany's interest in the French bases in North Africa, though waning, persisted until the Allied invasion of North Africa in late 1942. As for France, North Africa, especially Algeria, continued to hold a special place in its heart. Algeria was not technically a colony but was composed of three French departments and had been part of France longer than the Savoy.

Reestablishing the connections between the colonial prisoners and their families became a priority for the Vichy government and its humanitarian network. After a year of captivity, Besson reported that the lack of news from home had had a devastating effect on the physical and mental health of "our protégés."[56] External and internal factors hindered the colonial prisoners' ability to correspond with their families. The British blockade, lack of French ships, and continuing war impeded prisoners' letters. Additionally, many prisoners and their families had been denied an education under French colonial rule and needed assistance corresponding. In March 1941 Scapini asked Abetz to create an official secretariat, run by an officer and a "native NCO" in the camps, specifically to help illiterate North African prisoners with their letters.[57] There is no trace of an official office having been established. Instead, prisoners depended on their literate comrades to write letters and help with administrative procedures.

Difficulties persisted, forcing the CCAPG to think creatively about correspondence. One idea was a postcard scheme in which colonial prisoners could write fewer than fifteen words on a card. The message was sent to Vichy, not the colonies, and broadcast to the empire via the shortwave radio show *Voice of France*.[58] Responses were sent back via Vichy, ensuring that even the most intimate moments of the colonial prisoners' lives passed through French control. Connecting colonial prisoners with their families obviously improved morale greatly, but the difficulties continued.[59] Some prisoners hailed from remote areas of the colonies or did not have a postal address. The individual relief agencies played an essential role in reestablishing communication with home or, failing that, creating new connections with countrymen in France. Amitiés africaines distributed postcards to colonial prisoners for their exact names and addresses so they might be properly identified.[60] The Amicale des annamites de Paris wanted Indochinese prisoners to receive letters even though communication with Indochina was limited by the Japanese occupation. Tran-Huu-Phong wrote an open letter to the Indochinese prisoners introducing a new section of the Amicale that could visit them in the hospital, organize penpals, and provide a hostel in Paris after their release.[61]

The relief effort for the colonial prisoners of war blended two typically distinct types of humanitarianism: alchemic and emergency humanitarianism. Strong political aims motivated the different types of humanitarian relief for the colonial prisoners and cannot be dissociated from the theoretical debate on humanitarianism. The distinctions between alchemic and emergency humanitarianism reveal the complicated and multifaceted motivations driving aid for the colonial prisoners. Alchemic humanitarianism, based on science and the Enlightenment reasoning, rather than religious motivation, was concerned with improving the root causes of suffering. As Michael Barnett argues, it was inherently paternalistic, believing that solving crisis situations created by "childlike" populations required external, often European, intervention.[62]

Paternalism was such a defining characteristic of both the French colonial tradition and the Vichy regime that it is important to unpick the various ways in which this paternalism affected and colored the colonial prisoners' experiences of captivity. To do so, the other face of humanitarianism, emergency or international humanitarianism, requires an introduction.

Emergency humanitarianism got a later start than alchemic humanitarianism. Some historians date its beginning to Henry Dunant's *A Memory of Solferino*, the subsequent founding of the International Committee of the Red Cross (ICRC), and the Geneva Conventions to regulate warfare at the end of the nineteenth century.[63] Others imagine a continuity of humanitarian and human rights practices connecting the Magna Carta (1215), the French Declaration of the Rights of Man (1789), and growing notions of self-determination in the early twentieth century.[64] The turning point in humanitarianism concerning the colonial prisoners' experiences was the codification of international law, especially regarding the rights of combatants and the growing definition of noncombatants.

The colonial prisoners' suffering was a direct result of the European war in which they fought. Consequently, their captivity was governed by the laws of war, which would not be the case if it had been a colonial conflict, and the infrastructure used to relieve that suffering was one of emergency relief agencies: the Red Cross, the ICRC, and the Vichy government. The French response to suffering colonial subjects was certainly rooted in the French history of colonialism and its associated paternalism, which in turn was connected to a desire to spread the values of the French Enlightenment abroad. The vocabulary used by different French actors is remarkably consistent: "naive" colonial soldiers would not survive the physical and mental rigors of German captivity without French intervention. Yet the relief efforts for the colonial soldiers reflected both colonial humanitarianism and emergency intervention. During the era of colonial humanitarianism, relief agencies depended on religious orders, private donations, and charities, but the Second World War marked a shift toward greater reliance on the state.[65] This is clearly reflected in how aid for the colonial prisoners was organized, combining support from individual actors and government donations.

The defeat and occupation turned France into a "zone of suffering," which required Pétain's paternal guidance to fix. Despite the context of war and captivity, the French imagined aid for the colonial prisoners within a framework of colonial humanitarianism with its accompanying paternalism. The expansion of this paternalism to metropolitan France was in reaction to the defeat, but it did not significantly change the colonial prisoners' lived experiences. As Barnett argues, paternalism and the development of colonial humanitarianism were tightly connected, as evidenced in the French "civilizing mission," the British "white man's burden," and the American "manifest destiny," all based on racist assumptions of a hierarchy of races.[66] Paternalism was so deeply imbued throughout the French Empire and the colonial military experience that it had framed most aspects of the colonial prisoners' prewar lives under French rule.

Humanitarian relief to the colonial prisoners was about more than ensuring timely deliveries of rice or books; it was designed to reinforce and strengthen ties to France. Through donations of material goods, food, and warm clothes, the French publicly, but concretely, improved the colonial prisoners' physical conditions. Moral aid had a subtler and more important mission. The first vital step was to counteract German propaganda in the camps. Next, it sought to create an association between French relief efforts and positive feelings of home via deliveries of traditional foods, letters from family, and religious celebrations. Furthermore, supplying the camps with food from the colonies confirmed that the Vichy government still controlled the empire despite de Gaulle's growing influence and claims by German guards that Germany controlled North Africa. Prisoners received foods based on their cultural and culinary traditions. North African prisoners received couscous, while the Indochinese and Madagascan prisoners received rice.[67] Ten tons of kola nuts were delivered to Senegalese prisoners. Kola nuts, caffeinated and bitter nuts that one chews, had a ceremonial role in presentations to leaders or chiefs across West Africa. Wherever possible, the French tried to make these deliveries a permanent feature of the colonial prisoners' captivity.[68]

As months turned into years, the prisoners were entreated to use their lengthening captivity as an opportunity for self-improvement. Pétain encouraged the idea that the men could return home, after a period of suffering and hardship, improved and ready to start rebuilding France. Until that time, the National Revolution encouraged each part of French society to undertake appropriate leisure activities to improve the nation's moral character. Prisoners' families were also invited to participate in this moral retraining, with the renewal of the patriarchal family as a key step in moving beyond the "corruption" and "individualism" of the Third Republic, blamed for

France's defeat.[69] The colonial prisoners were given a helping role in France's future as idealized colonial subjects who should demonstrate their gratitude for benevolent French rule through their obedience, loyalty, and discipline.

In the first year alone, the CCAPG sent carefully selected games, "traditional" musical instruments, phonographs with Arabic music, and books for "natives and illiterates."[70] The YMCA sent 135,000 books in nine languages.[71] Colonial prisoners were encouraged to attend French classes or traditional craft workshops organized in the camps.[72] Paul B. Anderson and Auguste Senaud, representing the YMCA, were surprised when Senegalese and North African prisoners at Le Mans Camp fervently requested books and literature. They estimated that perhaps half of the North African prisoners were literate.[73] Overall, leisure activities, even without thought of moral improvement, greatly improved morale in the camps. Colonial prisoners expressed their gratitude, and requested additional items, in thank-you letters to the relief agencies. Reflecting the paternalism of the time, Bonko Hambrié, a prisoner from West Africa, wrote to thank Pétain "for the favors that France has generously given to its African children prisoners in captivity with their brothers from the metropole."[74] The relief agencies did have a sincere desire to improve the conditions of the prisoners' daily lives, but that motivation sprang from a belief that colonial men could be improved through contact with the white French. The National Revolution imagined clearly defined, but never equal, roles for everyone under the French flag.

Gender and Paternalism

To fulfill its promise of redemption for France, the National Revolution created strictly segregated spaces and roles for everyone living under French rule. As Pétain explained, "A people is a hierarchy of families."[75] Vichy paternalism built on a long-standing imperial tradition of infantilizing the colonial subjects. Indeed, this view filtered into Vichy's gender and colonial politics, as well as the political motivations of its humanitarian aid for the colonial prisoners.

This restructuring and redefinition of the family greatly affected the colonial prisoners' experiences of captivity. Sometimes France itself was personified, as in Hambrié's letter to Pétain: "Without France's benevolent attention, we do not know what severe treatments would be inflicted on us natives. But now our good mother, watching over her children, knew how to soften yesterday's enemies and manage to pamper us through the mesh of the barbed wire."[76] Behind the image of mother France were real women attempting to survive the German occupation and sometimes help others do the same. While a few formidable women, like Weygand and Noguès, coordinated major relief efforts in North Africa, it was the local French women who had the greatest impact on the colonial prisoners during their captivity. The women who drove the French Red Cross trucks or inspected camps on behalf of local relief agencies brought a personal touch to impersonal group deliveries. Sometimes these women had access to spaces, such as the colonial prisoners' work groups, denied to male Vichy officials.[77]

Even though their captivity was strictly regulated, colonial prisoners interacted with French women more often than they had in the racialized colonies. Through the interactions between colonial prisoners and French women, the lines between Vichy-sponsored humanitarian aid and unregulated, spontaneous, bottom-up assistance blurred. Vichy's conservative gendered politics established clear rules for men, women, and sex. The ultimate role for a woman was that of a mother. As Miranda Pollard dissects expertly, creating the distinction between maternal women and paternal men went far beyond simple morality; it was an inherent characteristic of the Vichy regime's autocratic and gendered politics and its vision for a new France.[78] Pollard argues that the defeat emasculated France, whose sons were now German captives, while the victorious Germans were in France with French women. Forcing women into maternal boxes was a way to regain control and repair the damage done by the Third Republic's "decadence."[79] The colonial prisoners, despite being men in captivity like the white prisoners, were not accorded the right to be "paternal men"; instead, they were to remain children of the empire. By placing the French women in the colonial prisoners' orbit on a maternal pedestal, the French authorities hoped the women would not be viewed as objects of sexual desire.

Sexual policies for colonial soldiers were problematic and imbued with stereotypes. The French authorities actively discouraged relationships between French women and colonial prisoners, fearing this would place white women in an inferior position to people of color.[80] The French censored letters from Madagascan prisoners with photographs of their "white wives," who were described as "easier" than the French women in the colonies.[81] Unsurprisingly, some German guards held similarly negative views of colonial soldiers interacting too closely with French women, as seen through the suspicious death of the young prisoner Tayeb because he was suspected of having an affair with a French milkmaid.[82] Although the Scapini Mission requested an inquiry into Tayeb's murder, that does not suggest it condoned the relationship. It is unclear what, if anything, happened to the woman and why exactly the German guards killed Tayeb. Was it an attempt to redeem the milkmaid's honor, an expression of sexual jealousy, or a mundane act of violence against a colonial prisoner? More likely it was a warning to other colonial prisoners to remain appropriately detached from women while in captivity. Yet interactions between the colonial prisoners and French women continued.

Many schoolchildren and women were encouraged to "adopt" a colonial prisoner and as "godparents" send parcels and correspondence; that children were allowed to sponsor adult men from the colonies further reinforced French infantilization of the colonial populations. Acting as a godmother was meant to give young French women outlets for their "natural maternal instincts," while creating important ties between the colonial soldiers and France. Camp doctor Jean-Pierre Prost described how meetings between colonial prisoners at Epinal and their godmothers were arranged: "We sent the [godsons] for medical visits in Haxo on prearranged days, and along the road to the hospital [the godmothers] had all the time they needed to meet a Samba Diouf or a Santa Traoré transformed into Jean Jacques or Jean Louis (those were the fashionable first names) and who were very impressed with their recent promotion to an apostle and proud to have a godmother who sends them, from time to time, a parcel or a letter."[83] As Léopold Senghor explained, the godmothers were "the best propagandists for France."[84] The godmothers walked a line between state-sponsored aid and individual actions to help the colonial prisoners. They were given the same financial and material assistance that white families received to send packages for their family members in Germany.[85] While the government subsidized the costs and provided much of what was included in the parcels, it could not control the friendships that formed between the colonial prisoners and the godmothers. The French decided that the benefits to the colonial prisoners' morale outweighed the risks of relationships crossing the line.

Furthermore, the colonial prisoners were pushed into imagined traditional roles that the white aid workers, German guards, or Vichy administrators believed they should occupy. After visiting a number of camps throughout occupied France, Senaud and Anderson of the YMCA concluded that the "native soldiers should be encouraged to express their desire to receive certain materials (raffia, wood, clay, etc.) that would allow them to either individually or collectively to engage in useful occupations."[86] The colonial prisoners had the agency to request materials and activities to ease the boredom of captivity, as evidenced in the numerous requests for sporting equipment, games, musical instruments, and books. However, this desire for "native" crafts and sculptures was external, not from the colonial prisoners, which reveals much about how these men were viewed. The German guards thought the YMCA's suggestion was excellent and decided to sell the "African statues" to raise money for the camp. The German High Command concurred that the artisan work would be good for the colonial prisoners, since they could not "devote their time only to reading, and harmful idleness [was] likely to lead to unfortunate attitudes."[87] In another case, a prisoner requested a flute, and Anderson and Senaud suggested providing bamboo so the colonial prisoners could make "native" flutes. These assumed traditional roles were "safe" and "useful," allowing the westerners to view colonial prisoners as an extension of a mythologized colonialization and not as individuals capable of defining their own leisure.

The popularity of these "native crafts" resulted in the colonial prisoners being used to generate public interest in their captivity and raise funds on their behalf. The CCAPG sponsored a public auction in 1942 to raise money for the colonial prisoners by selling their art in raffia, leather, wood, or clay. Andlauer, head of the Overseas Section, argued that this would "draw attention to our native prisoners, to the sacrifices they have made, and demonstrate their attachment to our country and the bonds that unite our overseas territories to France."[88] This "native" art was popular among the French, reflecting a wider image of the colonies as raw and unsophisticated.

One sale, spanning only three neighborhoods, raised approximately three million francs for the colonial prisoners.[89] The popularity of these sales probably had more to do with the population's support of prisoners of war in general, rather than an increased attachment to the empire. Nevertheless, the two issues remained intertwined.

The colonial prisoners provided a personification of Vichy's imperial goals and a way to bridge the gap in the public mind between a symbolic vision of the empire and a real belief in its importance. Even at the zenith of French imperialism in 1930–31, much of France remained uninterested in the empire, a trend that continued under the Vichy regime. Since the empire was key to the regime's postwar goals, it became increasingly urgent to change popular attitudes. Paul Marion, secretary of state for information, declared in 1942, "We have only imperial territories, we do not yet have an imperial soul [but] we will also be Europe's imperial educators, since we know how to keep and defend our empire. We will become pioneers who will lay down powerful bridges, our bridges, between this continent and Africa."[90] Without the empire, France had little of value to offer the new Europe. With the empire, Marion argued, France had resources and hope for a new France.[91] For the Vichy regime, the empire was a pillar of French independence and future greatness, juxtaposed with the increasingly difficult German occupation. The fates of the colonial prisoners, willingly or not, became part of that.

Despite the Vichy regime's substantial humanitarian work on behalf of the colonial prisoners, it feared the aid might set a dangerous precedent that would lead the colonial subjects to believe they were owed something, even as small as food deliveries. In the Ardennes, Bonnaud reported that the colonial prisoners had become accustomed to chocolate, couscous, rice, sugar, kola nuts, and dates. They allegedly assumed it was "a normal ration owed to them and that they could claim it as such. The German guards helped reinforce this view by pointing out the merits of their claims, and often joining the prisoners in complaining . . . if there were delays or reductions in the quantities distributed."[92] Any hints of similar entitlement were considered outright disobedience and blamed on the Germans. In Beaulieu-sur-Oudon (Mayenne), five colonial prisoners in a work group held a morning-long hunger strike to complain about their food. The short length of their hunger strike notwithstanding, their demands were seen as excessive, and they were disparaged for their "arrogance."[93]

The French feared that any complaint about their contributions, not about the German captors, was a slippery slope to outright rebellion. This fear was greater than the actual risk but was not totally unjustified. The potential for subversion of Vichy's authority was real. The French reaction to these deliberate yet minor acts of disobedience sprang directly from the new political and moral landscape created by the Vichy regime, accurately described by Pollard as ultraconservative and moralistic, praising sacrifice and duty, and condemning individualism as inherently unpatriotic and antisocial.[94] Colonial prisoners who demanded change or complained that efforts on their behalf were insufficient were seen to be demonstrating individualistic tendencies, which went against the "common good" as defined by a racist, patriarchal, and paternalistic state. The politics behind the aid to the colonial prisoners were aimed at reinforcing the imperial status quo, wherein a benevolent father improved conditions for grateful subjects. However, in the Frontstalags, as in the colonies, the men were actual people with diverse experiences, expectations, desires, and plans for the future, not simply idealized recipients of French colonial humanitarianism. Likewise, the risks some French took to help the colonial prisoners suggest that helping individuals from the colonies, itself a form of resistance and solidarity, was more appealing than supporting Vichy's imperial goals.

Escapes and Bottom-Up Assistance

The Vichy regime's imperial policies rested on the need to create a personal attachment for French men to their empire and to reinforce gratitude and loyalty toward France among its colonial subjects. However, as white citizens responded to Vichy's calls to help the colonial prisoners, the government lost some of its control over how that assistance was provided. Escape reports and postcaptivity debriefings all mention how the French civilians helped the colonial prisoners throughout their captivity. Despite the success of these individual efforts, the French state preferred that all humanitarian aid go through official French missions to ensure it included the "correct message."[95] French officials worried that unregulated, bottom-up assistance could create uncomfortable situations; for example, smuggling food to the colonial prisoners was tolerated, but helping them escape was murkier.

Escape from captivity was an individual choice that could have huge political implications because of the intertwined French and German relations. Articles 47–53 of the 1929 Geneva Convention dealt with prisoner escapes and limited disciplinary measures if a prisoner was caught before rejoining his army. Generally, it was assumed that prisoners had the right to attempt escape if they so chose.[96] Controversially, the Vichy regime, informally at first and then officially, advised prisoners not to escape. As early as October 1940 an article in *Le Petit Vésulien* condemned the "selfish escapes," warning that if they did not cease, work groups would be confined to the Frontstalag.[97] Neither warnings nor laws prevented motivated prisoners from escaping nor civilians from assisting. Helping prisoners escape was punishable by arrest or even deportation.[98] In Germany, rewards of twenty reichsmarks were offered to civilians who helped the police or camp authorities capture escaped prisoners.[99] French prefects were dragged into a legal and ethical quagmire when they were expected to locate escaped prisoners and report back to tribunes held in the Frontstalag.[100] After the French general Henri Giraud escaped from captivity in Germany in 1942, Scapini officially asked prisoners to stop escaping.[101]

Despite the official opposition, escaped prisoners provided valuable information and insights on conditions in France and Germany. According to French officials in the colonies, "Our best propagandists . . . are the escaped tirailleurs, who all emphasize the kindness shown them by the metropolitan French and blame [Germany] for the beatings and brutality they suffered during captivity."[102] Instead, an informal system of plausible deniability was exploited by officials sympathetic to the would-be evaders. For example, after three Tunisian prisoners escaped from Joux-la-Ville, the mayor dutifully filed a police report and answered questions about the prisoners' escape. The prisoners had waited until they were paid for the month's work, then left without mentioning their intentions to the mayor. The mayor swore he knew neither why they ran nor the direction they took. Luckily for the mayor and the prisoners' employer, they had left on a Sunday, when they were under the German guards' supervision.[103] Despite the restrictions and the dangerous consequences for helping colonial prisoners escape, civilian aid in many forms was found across metropolitan France.

French men and women risked their own safety to help individuals, regardless of origin, escape from the enemy. Escape reports from the colonial prisoners recounted exciting tales of hardship and sacrifice, while unanimously applauding this solidarity from below. Using established routes, Resistance networks moved colonial prisoners from the camps to the free zone.[104] Still, attempting to escape was dangerous. One North African prisoner who got caught in the barbed wire was killed outside Epinal. Abdoulaye Maiga and ten other prisoners tried to leave together, but a guard fired on them through the barbed wire. They dispersed into the nearby woods, and only four met up later that night. French peasants cared for them over the four-day trip to the demarcation line. Once across, they continued on to Rivesaltes and Provence.[105]

As colonial prisoners were housed by race, those who chose to escape often did so with their fellow countrymen. The first prisoners to escape from Epinal were white French and North Africans. This gave the sub-Saharan Africans a reputation for dependability, which they soon exploited with a succession of successful escapes. Lucien Aïtounaboua's departure from Epinal on November 23 launched other colonial prisoners into the escape network. Some prisoners preferred to remain in captivity and engage in the lucrative business of selling civilian clothes. Gnimagnon warned that while many civilians appeared willing to help, some would expose the escapees' plans.[106] Yet without the support of local populations, colonial prisoners found it difficult to navigate an unfamiliar countryside. Senghor reported that few prisoners escaped in the Gironde, as the camps were surrounded by complex systems of barbed wire and the civilians were indifferent to the colonial prisoners.[107]

For a successful escape, creativity was as essential as good directions and civilian clothes. Colonial prisoners could not blend in with the civilian population as the white prisoners did. Instead, they sought advantages where they could. Albin Bancilon hid in plain sight on a French farm, pretending to be the farmer's servant.[108] Mohamed Ben Ali took a risky but simple approach: carrying only a bucket and dressed in civilian clothes, he walked across France pretending to be a North African civilian worker.[109] French civilians provided directions and assistance to colonial prisoners to compensate for their lack of local knowledge. Mohamed Ben Mohamed Ben El Habib walked all night, following directions provided by several Frenchmen. When he arrived in a village, he met a farmer who was a former P O W and *mutilé de guerre* (disabled veteran) from the previous war. The farmer gave Mohamed Ben El Habib food and civilian clothes and advised him to walk during the day to avoid German patrols.[110]

Men, women, and children all helped feed, shelter, and clothe escaping colonial prisoners, in some cases even giving them money.[111] The journey to the unoccupied zone was long and could be terrifying. Prisoners risked being recaptured, getting lost, and running out of food and water. It took Mohamed Ben Brahim and Mohamed Ben Ali nine days to get from their camp to the unoccupied zone. They swam across the Loire and Cher Rivers to reach the French post in Lury (Cher) on September 13, 1940.[112] Georges Brabant ferried three North African colonial prisoners who could not swim across the Doub on his small boat.[113] All the colonial prisoners who escaped praised the generosity and assistance found among the French civilians.[114]

Resistance networks, like that in Vesoul or Epinal, created opportunities and facilitated escape for prisoners who asked for assistance. Gnimagnon first learned of the escape networks in Chaumont (Haute-Marne) but felt the one at Epinal, which assisted with massive daytime escapes, notably from the work groups charged with installing the barbed wire, was the best organized.[115] The prisoners destroyed the barbed wire and absconded through the sewers and underground tunnels that opened just outside the camps. Pierre Choffel, military leader of the Resistance in Vesoul, kept detailed records during the occupation and in 1956 summarized their activities during the war. Choffel was also the locksmith for the Frontstalag, which gave the Resistance a rather large advantage over the camp guards.[116] According to Choffel, the installation of the Frontstalag in Vesoul in 1940 prompted some "patriots" to meet and discuss plans to help the prisoners escape. From that meeting, an entire network grew. Drivers from the Citroën factory organized transportation. A large number of women, named Lasnier, Weber, Elvire

Meyer, Walter, Choffel, Rigolot, Depoulain, and Larcher, helped finding clandestine accommodations. Mme. de Beauchaine found food. During the first eighteen months of activity, over four hundred prisoners were released, hidden, and secreted out of Vesoul. Two members, Petit and Choffel, were arrested and sent to prison, but still the network persisted. Many in Vesoul, most notably the police commissioner, Jean Lhorte, were complicit in the escapes. Once out of the camp, colonial prisoners were given false papers and food and were moved away quickly.[117]

In the early days at Vesoul, there was a certain complicity between the Resistance and the German camp commander Lieutenant Boehm, who felt the prisoners were only doing their duty in escaping. This did not last; by the end of 1940 Boehm had been replaced by Wagner because too many prisoners had escaped. After Boehm's replacement, the German guards were more vigilant, and the escapees more creative.[118] In December 1940 a prisoner escaped from a work group composed of four men while Pierre Choffel happened to be nearby. The German guard accused Choffel of facilitating the escape, complaining that he could not return to the camp with only three prisoners. Choffel offered to find a decoy prisoner, and the guard accepted. A medical officer working with the Red Cross agreed to help. Removing his Red Cross armband, he accompanied the guard back to the camp, pretending to be a POW. The guard was seen returning with four prisoners, and nothing out of the ordinary was noted. Later that day, the medical worker simply put on his Red Cross armband and walked out of the camp. The escape was not reported until the next morning, leaving Choffel and the guard in the clear.[119]

Escaping from captivity took patience, effort, and daring. Prisoners took time to study the different possibilities. Lt. Gregoire Pische from Martinique, serving in the 1st Régiment de Zouaves, was initially taken to two different oflags in Germany before returning to France with other colonial prisoners. During his first week at Charleville, he studied the different options for escape, including identifying which civilians might help him. Pische and Second Lieutenant Bougherera hid in the infirmary toilets after lights out, waiting until 1:30 a.m., just after the change in German guards. They slipped out of the infirmary through a small nest of barbed wire, and crawling on their stomachs, they entered the German officers' barracks. Still slithering along the ground, they sneaked out through the exterior wire only one hundred meters from the sentinel post. Pische and Bougherera traveled together for two days, finally separating at Chauny. Pische continued on to Paris and from there to Bordeaux, Dax, and finally to the demobilization center in Pau. By August 1941 Pische was reassigned to the 6th Régiment de tirailleurs marocains in Casablanca.[120]

It took Michel Gnimagnon over a month of planning and several abortive attempts before he was able to escape. He wrote a long and dramatic report of his escape from a work assignment:

> I managed to get through the barbed wire. I stayed hidden on the ground and from that position I climbed the rampart. When I hurtled down the slope and reached the private path, I followed the landmarks that I had previously chosen—a group of pine trees approximately two hundred meters from the path. That is where my guide was waiting. Upon seeing my signal, he replied with another signal (owl cries). I joined him. It was 7:35 p.m. We took a detour, sodden by the recent snow, muddy in certain places, and after three-quarters of an hour's walk we reached the route de Domèvre, which, as I knew, was not covered by patrols at night. We increased our pace, and at 8:30 p.m. we arrived at Messen's Maison Forestière, from where I informed Mrs. Bruand that I had arrived; she lived one kilometer from there, about three hundred meters from the canal de l'est (roughly). My former guide, whose job was just to bring me here, took his leave. I arrived at Mrs. Bruand's at 9:00 p.m. She welcomed me warmly. I spent the night there, and the next day I prepared to leave Epinal. She gave me victuals for the road (bread, cheese, hard-boiled eggs, cake, apples). At 10:00 p.m, Mrs. Bruand's young friend Mr. Georges, who is most probably linked to the intelligence service and who saw to many escapes, collected me at the house. We both left by bicycle. Disguised as I was, I did not raise suspicions when we passed in front of the German post that was along our route; I was lucky, since the guard who was at the post would have certainly recognized and arrested me had he turned his flashlight on us, his favorite activity.[121]

Eventually, Gnimagnon was hidden aboard a train for Marseilles, where he caught bronchitis from the cold. He finally made it to the camp for colonial soldiers in Fréjus.[122]

The Eboué brothers likewise had several close calls before managing to leave captivity. Henry and Robert Eboué first planned to escape hidden in a delivery truck, but at the last minute, the driver backed out in fear. Later, they tried to get assigned to a work group, but that was denied once the camp authorities realized they were Félix Eboué's sons. At Charleville, Henry had his own room near a stairway leading to the basement. He moved the piano from the theater into his room and created his own "refuge" within the camp. From the basement, Eboué and other prisoners calculated that they would be able to dig a tunnel connecting into the sewer system and a pipe leading out of the camp. It took two months of digging to complete the tunnel, during which time Henry warned his brother to be discreet around his "Jewish friends," who allegedly were always trying to flatter the "boches" in exchange for favors. The night before the escape, someone informed the guards, and Robert was forced to destroy papers, maps, and photographs linked to the escape. After this new setback, Henry started on a new plan with a Mrs. Pascalini, who arranged to get Robert, Henry, and their sister, Ginette, out of occupied France and to the external resistance.[123]

Henry decided not to inform Robert of the plan, to ensure that he would not accidentally reveal it. However, Robert was also making his own solo plan to escape. Henry and Robert had family and friends in France, especially among the civilians around their camp, and their father was well-connected. Robert managed to escape, and Henry was released for medical reasons. Both were demobilized in France, another peculiarity of their experience, after which they joined another underground network, which smuggled them to Spain. Here they were surprised to find Ginette, who had escaped France on foot.[124]

Crossing the demarcation line was the most dangerous and crucial part of the colonial prisoners' journey. Article 2 of the armistice agreement created the demarcation line to protect German interests. It started on the Franco-Swiss border and covered over 750 miles through Dôle, Chalons-sur-Saône, Digoin, Paray-le-Monial, Moulins, Vierzon, Angoulême, Mont-de-Marsan, and Saint-Jean-Pied-de-Port on the Spanish border. Escaped prisoners who crossed the demarcation line before November 1942 were technically free from captivity and could then be sent home and demobilized. The French initially understood that the demarcation line would be an administrative marker between occupied and unoccupied zones. Instead, it acted as a closed border. Secret organizations and motivated individuals took charge of moving those without the requisite paperwork across the line. Escaped prisoner Hassen-Ladjimi explained how one crossing worked:

> They each take their turn with those who passed through, feeding them, hiding them, giving them supplies for the next day and often money. At the demarcation line another organization exists. I crossed at a farm that had purposely installed a millstone along the border. While two women acted as lookouts, a child brought the prisoner thirty meters along the road where the track was made in such a way that it was always camouflaged, and all the difficult parts are fitted with a ladder or holes in the fences. A dozen prisoners took this route every day. The day before, two Senegalese, armed and in uniform, had crossed.[125]

One smuggler created a path through a sewer under a canal to get people across.[126] Two brothers in a village near Dôle (Jura) collected the signatures of four hundred prisoners they helped sneak across the line.[127]

Once across the demarcation line, colonial prisoners had to decide whether to report to the French authorities. Shelters for North African prisoners provided beds and enough money to continue to Fréjus or Marseilles. Some escapees were repatriated to their home countries before the Vichy regime lost access to the empire. After November 1942 former prisoners were placed in French-run camps in the southeast: Rivesaltes for North Africans and Fréjus for everyone else. Additionally, after November 1942 prisoners were no longer considered free once they crossed the demarcation line; instead, they could be sent back to their camps if caught. Similarly, former prisoners who had remained in Vichy-run camps in the southern zone were now increasingly sent to work for the German authorities in conditions quite similar to their captivity.

Nevertheless, colonial prisoners continued to escape throughout the war at slightly higher rates than white prisoners (see table 2): 6.7 percent of the colonial prisoners escaped compared with less than 5 percent of white prisoners.[128] Several factors explain the difference. As seen, the colonial prisoners profited from the help provided by the Resistance networks and local population. From their work, they had access to French francs to buy food or train tickets, whereas prisoners in Germany were paid in *Lagergeld*, money valid only in the camps. Colonial prisoners had shorter distances to cover to reach freedom than prisoners in Germany. Even when white prisoners were able to escape from camps in Germany, they had great difficulties reaching France. In one case, three French prisoners escaped and remained free for three months without managing to leave Germany.[129] Perhaps a final consideration is that in support of their propaganda campaign in North Africa, the German authorities allowed an unknown number of North African prisoners to escape (in fact, the number of North Africans who escaped was higher than that for other colonies). According to data from the German High Command, approximately 2,481 North African prisoners had escaped from the Frontstalags by March 31, 1942.[130]

Table 2. Percentage of colonial prisoners who escaped

Colony	Percentage who escaped
Algeria	9.1% (9.5% if two recaptured are included)
Tunisia	7.5%
Morocco	6%
Senegal	5.7%
Madagascar	3.7%
Guinea	3.7%
Côte d'Ivoire	2.9%
Indochina	4.2%
French Equatorial Africa (AEF)	50% (one of the two prisoners from AEF escaped)

SOURCE: Based on the ICRC capture cards at the Bureau des archives des victimes des conflits contemporains, Caen, France.

For the Scapini Mission and the DSPG, helping colonial prisoners was as much a political as a philanthropic cause, a guarantee of future obedience. During the first two years of the occupation, the colonial prisoners' potential as an influencing force in the colonies outweighed their numerical importance compared with the 1.5 million white prisoners. Between the armistice and December 31, 1941, of the total aid from the DSPG, the Frontstalags received 26 percent of the food donations, 14 percent of the tobacco, and 20 percent of the articles of clothing.[131] Even considering the number of white prisoners still in France in the summer and fall of 1940, the colonial prisoners received a disproportionate amount of French aid compared with prisoners in Germany. French humanitarian aid objectively improved the physical conditions for colonial prisoners, while it also reduced German expenditure for their upkeep. As the occupation and captivity continued, colonial prisoners became increasing disillusioned with their situation. All the packages and goodwill could not compensate for being left in the Frontstalags after the white prisoners were released in the spring of 1941. The paternalism that accompanied the humanitarian efforts was often offset by interactions colonial prisoners had with individual French men and women, especially those who put themselves in danger to help the prisoners escape. Worse for the Vichy regime, the bottom-up aid had led many colonial prisoners to believe that formal hierarchies between colonizer and colonized were crumbling, or at least that the lines were blurring.

The Allied landings in North Africa marked a turning point in the war but condemned the colonial prisoners to three more years in France under increasingly strained conditions. Deliveries from the colonies, which had been slowed by the British blockade, were now stopped completely. Overall, the structure and type of aid continued post-November 1942, but the actors changed slightly. The DSPG took over for the North African charities, which were no longer able to supply the colonial prisoners' packages and group deliveries.[132] The press continued to generate interest around the colonial prisoners but now framed it within the context of the lost empire: "The dramatic events that cost us the loss of our colonial lands drew attention to the plight of our prisoners of war from the empire.... [A]ll precautions have been taken to ensure that our native colonial prisoners receive Christmas packages and the regular monthly package. . . . These shipments have not slowed down, but unfortunately the occupation of the colonies by the Anglo-Americans is an extremely hard blow to obtaining colonial products, which are so enjoyed by our native soldiers."[133]

Schoolchildren were still encouraged to "adopt" colonial prisoners and send them parcels and letters.[134] Replacing the supremacy of the French Red Cross, the ICRC was asked to help colonial prisoners with administrative formalities, such as sending military allowances to family members, as the Vichy government could no longer communicate with the colonies.[135] While the humanitarian efforts for the colonial prisoners continued, the underlying political motivation had changed dramatically.

7

HOSTAGES TO MISFORTUNE
Politics and Colonial Prisoners of War

Life in the Frontstalags could at times feel quite divorced from the wider context of the Second World War. Nevertheless, it was this broader framework, shaped by political negotiations, military victories, and regime change, that defined the importance placed on the colonial prisoners' captivity. That importance was defined not by their humanity, something rarely noted by the two powers, but rather by how the colonial prisoners as a group could fulfill French imperial goals or German war aims. Previous chapters have explored Franco-German negotiations over the colonial prisoners' everyday lives in captivity: their food, work, clothing, and homes. This chapter zooms out and offers a wider view of the colonial prisoners within the spectrum of collaboration, imperial rivalry, and international relations between 1940 and 1944. It shows how initial French eagerness and commitment to the colonial prisoners were surpassed by the all-important goal of getting the white prisoners home from Germany. This reinforces the argument that Vichy protection of the colonial prisoners was a paradox when placed within the larger context of the regime's priorities and actions.

As the occupation advanced, it became increasingly obvious to the French population that white prisoners in Germany were not returning as quickly as promised. Ninety thousand white prisoners were repatriated in 1940, 193,000 in 1941, and 75,000 in 1942. However, in 1943 almost one million men remained in Germany. The Vichy regime sought new concessions from the Germans, who were even less willing to consider Vichy's propositions. At the same time, the loss of the empire and German total occupation of France negated much of the colonial prisoners' value in Franco-German negotiations. From the German perspective, the labor power of the colonial prisoners (an important consideration from the start) was now their only value.

In the weeks after the fall of France in 1940, German victory over Great Britain seemed inevitable. The pending end of the war meant many in France believed that final peace terms were forthcoming and France should prepare for its postwar role. Unsurprisingly, France and Germany had different goals and plans for the future. Germany's immediate focus was winning the war, and for that it needed men, labor, supplies, cash, and influence over French industry. France had to remain stable and neutral so that Germany could use as few resources and personnel as possible in occupying the country. Victory, occupation, and the 1.8 million French prisoners gave Germany a measure of control and influence over the French. However, by resigning itself to total German victory in Europe, the Vichy regime set itself on a protectionist path that underestimated its potential to resist German demands, even as a defeated country. France held certain bargaining chips, including neutrality, collaboration, and the empire. The fate of the colonial prisoners of war was inextricably entangled with the political negotiations over the future of France and the role of the French Empire in it.

Pétain, Collaboration, and the POW Question

On October 30, 1940, one week after meeting Hitler in Montoire, Pétain outlined his plan for the future of France to the French people in an eight-minute radio address. He explained that his meeting with Hitler, between victor and vanquished, was the first step toward France's rebirth. A renewal that, Pétain elaborated, was possible only because of the French population's hard work and dignity, the colonial chiefs' energy, and the indigenous populations' loyalty.[1] Pétain announced that he had chosen the "path of collaboration" to protect ten centuries of French unity and give France an active role in rebuilding Europe. The Vichy regime's early political legitimacy was based on the promise that France could rebuild after such a defeat, that the prisoners would return home, and that the empire would remain French. Pétain hoped that collaboration would bring those promises to fruition and warned the French people that they must be sincere and peaceful if they were to improve conditions for the prisoners, reduce the occupation costs, and increase the fluidity of the demarcation line. The key point in Pétain's speech was his insistence that this was a French decision.[2]

Pétain had a vision and plan for the future of France that would not wait: get the prisoners back, rebuild economically and spiritually, and keep control of the empire. As seen, the Geneva Convention provided a level of protection for France and its prisoners. As the occupation and war continued into 1942 and German victory seemed less certain, Pétain could have chosen a multitude of paths, but instead he and his supporters remained illogically wedded to the idea, even when faced with proof to the contrary, that collaboration would benefit France in both the short and long term. Collaboration as a political tool brought increasingly diminishing returns for the French.

The colonial prisoners were caught up in this prolonged diplomatic game. The political negotiations over the colonial prisoners' fate reveals a longer perspective of how the empire fit into France's vision for the future and what the Vichy regime could actually obtain from Germany. The French believed that influencing the colonial prisoners and keeping their allegiance was a powerful guarantee of future loyalty from a small but influential portion of the indigenous populations. From the signature of the armistice, the Vichy regime enthusiastically attempted to regain control over the colonial prisoners by requesting their release or relocation south. However, a major miscalculation, which was common to most colonizers, was to equate direct control with actual influence. As we saw through the colonial prisoners' work, the French accepted considerable financial responsibility in exchange for little real authority.

The Germans quickly understood French interest in their colonial prisoners and conceded only enough to let the French believe in their good faith in collaboration. Even so, and despite their status as colonial subjects (and a few citizens), the colonial prisoners were not merely pawns in the Franco-German political negotiations. They had limited means to influence their conditions of captivity, which in turn influenced political negotiations, but they used them effectively. Many of the colonial prisoners shared three basic desires: to have decent conditions in captivity, to be treated fairly with regard to release, and most important, to return home. They had the agency to take a range of actions to protest their situation. Complaints and official manifestations were the most effective, especially as the French worried they would bring their discontent back home. During camp visits, prisoners' representatives, often an NCO or other respected colonial prisoner, met French and international inspectors. Literate prisoners had the ability to write to Scapini or the Red Cross. Illiterate prisoners could push for change by refusing to work or complaining to civilians about conditions in the camps. However, they knew that these kinds of protests put them at greater risk for a violent overreaction than writing letters. Finally, the colonial prisoners could exploit French fears of disloyalty or even give their allegiance to the Germans in hopes of better conditions and quicker release.

When peace did not come, both the French and Germans were forced to refine their political priorities, which affected the colonial prisoners' experiences. Over time, French labor for the German war effort became a more important consideration than the neutrality of the French Empire. The uneasy balance achieved during the first two years was shattered during the winter of 1942–43, with the Allied landings in North Africa, German invasion of the southern zone, and Battles of Stalingrad and El Alamein. German victory was no longer ensured, which might have shifted negotiating power in favor of the Vichy regime had Pétain not persisted in remaining neutral at any cost. The most significant external event for the colonial prisoners during their captivity was the Vichy regime's loss of the empire. When the colonial prisoners could no longer return home, their political weight was diluted further, and they were incorporated into the Germans' overall labor strategy.

Colonies in Collaboration

The French defeat in 1940 presented the first major possibilities for colonial expansion since the European powers divided Africa among them at the 1884 Berlin conference. Instability and defeat in the French metropole and division between Free French and Vichy colonies fed Spanish, Italian, and German colonial designs. France and Spain had been colonial rivals in the Americas since the sixteenth century; now their focus moved to Morocco. Fascist Italy dreamed of a new Roman empire beyond Libya and Abyssinia.[3]

Legally, the empire remained French, as the Franco-German armistice laid no claim to the overseas territories. In the immediate aftermath of their victory, the Germans benefited more from a neutral French Empire under Vichy's control than they would through Axis territorial demands, which might push the French military leaders across North Africa and the Middle East into resistance and rebellion. The lack of a direct German threat to the integrity of the French Empire had been a major factor in persuading the colonial leaders to support the armistice.[4] Yet the armistice agreement was not enough to protect Vichy's empire from internal and external threats.

Germany's interest in gaining a new colonial empire or reclaiming its colonies lost after the First World War had grown in the years preceding the Second World War. The German press ran articles designed to incite instability and discredit the French and British Empires. The *Deutsche Bergwerkszeitung* criticized them "as plutocratic exploitations of the 'natives,'" while the *Deutsche Allgemeine Zeitung* ran a "tendentious survey of French Morocco and Spanish Morocco aimed at exacerbating French and Spanish rivalry in the country."[5] Scapini had even suggested creating a European empire controlled by the Germans, but maintaining French administration in the standing French colonies, in exchange for real collaboration.[6] Anglo-Gaullist attacks on the French Empire in July and September 1940 enhanced anti-British feeling in the metropole and spurred the Vichy regime's efforts to defend the empire.

The French feared that the indigenous populations' susceptibility to propaganda would turn them from their duty and weaken imperial defenses. In October 1940 Pétain sent Maxime Weyand, *délégué général du gouvernement en Afrique*, on a propaganda tour of the African territories following on the heels of several major losses, and one victory, for the Vichy regime: the British had sunk the French fleet in Algeria in July, and Chad, the French Congo, Ubangi-Shari, Cameroon, Gabon, and some territories in India and the Pacific declared loyalty to Charles de Gaulle in August. Yet when faced with Anglo-Gaullist forces off the coast of Dakar in September 1940, instead of surrendering or joining de Gaulle, Pierre Boisson's Vichy forces fought back and successfully repelled the attack. Pétain gave Weygand detailed instructions to shore up support among European and indigenous communities:

France must be vigilant, stand ready to repel any aggression and control any hint of dissidence. We must regain control of French West Africa by bringing the civilian and military authorities to a sense of unequivocal loyalty to the marshal's government, his politics, and the New Order that he instituted, by reminding them of the fundamental notion of obedience to the powers of the state, [and] emphasize this action by improving the economic activity of the various territories in order to mitigate the effects of the blockade and thus improve the lives of settlers and indigenous populations.[7]

The same approach as that for the colonial prisoners was used to keep the allegiance of the indigenous and settler populations: preach loyalty and obedience while improving conditions.

However, negotiations with Germany hindered French plans. French commitment to collaboration undermined its negotiating position, while the German Armistice Commission consistently demonstrated that Vichy's concerns were not its priority. Arguing that France was practically at war with Germany's enemy, the United Kingdom, Vichy officials, including Huntziger and Foreign Minister Paul Baudouin, had unsuccessfully tried to entice Germany into a peace settlement via a summit meeting.[8] The German High Command remained courteous and attentive to the French delegation but rarely implemented resolutions taken in Wiesbaden, preferring to claim ignorance of agreements.[9] For example, by November 1940 it had still not acted on an August decision on conditional liberations for POWs.[10] The illusion of fair negotiations was just that. The German interlocutors pretended to make generous concessions on small details but never compromised on principles, even when required by international law.[11] Despite the efforts of Pétain, Scapini, and Laval, the Germans never considered the Vichy regime as an equal partner.

North Africa's strategic importance made it a battleground for Franco-German relations. Germany's targeted and lasting radio propaganda tried to incite the North African populations to revolt against the French.[12] This coincided with repeated warnings that Germany remained skeptical that the Vichy government could maintain control over North Africa.[13] Using the threat of conflict as an excuse, Germany threatened that armistice inspectors would be sent to Morocco to ensure stability. Direct control of Morocco or even North Africa was not a German priority, especially after the Russian campaign began in the summer of 1941. Rather, the Germans wanted to have eyes on the ground and to obtain concessions from the Vichy government in North Africa, such as use of military bases. Putting the French on the defensive strengthened the German negotiating position.

While Pétain and his circle of advisors appeared unwavering in their belief in German good faith in collaboration, the members of the French delegation to the armistice commission saw matters differently. As a note for the French armistice delegation explained, "Germany has tried to under-take what might be called 'the blackmail of inspection' and let us hope it will mitigate its decisions if we allow German inspections in French North Africa."[14] The threat of German intervention in North Africa was real and could potentially fuel instability in the region, further subverting the Vichy regime's control. While the armistice agreement did not require the French to allow German inspectors in the colonies, almost all negotiations were intertwined. The French War Ministry feared that refusing the inspections would provoke the Germans to reject subsequent French requests. In this case, the Vichy regime need German permission to move military goods held in depots under Italian control to reinforce its defense of West Africa.[15] Paul-André Doyen, member of the French Armistice Delegation, explained to Carl-Heinrich von Stülpnagel, head of the M B F, that France would allow the inspections to dispel suspicions about French motivations. Yet Doyen requested that the German inspectors take care to mitigate the "undesirable" difficulties arising from their presence in Morocco by humoring the local populations' "sensitivities."[16]

Considering that the French had only "pacified" Morocco after the Rif War in 1927, the real risks of allowing greater German influence seem dispropor-tionate to the potential advantages. Indeed, British propaganda promoted the idea that the Germans had come to Morocco to "stir up the natives and arm them against France."[17] At this stage, the damage was done: the Germans had expanded their presence in North Africa and the British had exploited it for their propaganda aims. The only avenue left to the French was formal protest. Doyen complained to Oskar Vogl, the new head of the German Armistice Commission, "The French government has pledged to defend the integrity of our African possessions and maintain internal order. It does not accept, under the pretext of inspections, that the German Commission of Casablanca brings to Morocco an activity hostile to France."[18]

Still, Germany continued to expand its influence throughout Vichy's empire. Eventually, the French were providing Germany with lists of merchandise, manifests, and ships' movements from North Africa to the other colonies and the United States.[19] By July 1942 the German Armistice Commission was overseeing French maritime traffic and requiring "very heavy concessions in exchange for the authorization of certain movements."[20] The armistice agreement had placed no restrictions on French trade, and Germany had no legal basis to require it. For the Vichy regime, these compromises remained subordinate to the ultimate priority of bringing the prisoners home. The fatal flaw of the Vichy regime, from Laval's first government in 1940 onward, was its continued belief that collaboration was the tool to obtain what it wanted. Instead, the French received less and less in return for greater and greater concessions, and worse for the regime, the people noticed.

De Gaulle and the Free French represented a constant menace for the Vichy regime, and attacks on the Levant in 1941 lent support to Vichy's requests to release more prisoners for imperial defense. In July 1941 interim president of the French armistice delegation, Frix Michelier, explained to Vogl that the French Empire was a great source of soldiers, "but these men are worth little without a strong, specialized, and quality European supervision. In addition, the slowness of their training does not make them usable for a year, and the substantial reinforcements needed could be achieved by the release of our educated native reserves that are currently in prisoner-of-war camps."[21] Having more trained and disciplined troops in the colonies would amount to a triple advantage for Vichy: it would remove the colonial prisoners from German influence, increase stability in the colonies, and potentially lead to the release of white officers and NCOs to supervise the colonial soldiers. The French also assumed, probably correctly, that the colonial prisoners' loyalty to France would be better preserved if France obtained their release quickly.

Ultimately, and setting a precedent for similar requests, the colonial prisoners were not released. Worse, one repatriated high-ranking former European prisoner sent to Syria nearly caused a diplomatic incident. Gen. Joseph de Verdilhac had been released from captivity because of mental illness and was subsequently assigned to an important military post in Syria. Scapini feared that the Germans would assume he was a "malingerer" or that the French government had no intention of actually resisting in Syria.[22] After the loss of Syria to the Anglo-French forces in July 1941, Darlan, who was notoriously anti-British, tried to push the French into military collaboration with Germany. He suggested normalizing diplomatic relations between the two countries by replacing the armistice agreement, but only if Germany formally recognized France's prewar colonial borders in the event that imperial defense lead to war against the Allies. This shows Darlan's desire for closer collaboration with Germany but also a fear that promises made in the armistice agreement might not survive until peace. However, German focus had shifted from the Mediterranean to the eastern front, and the armistice remained in place.[23]

In political speeches and the press, the Vichy regime connected the prisoners' release to collaboration, which showcased the French negotiators' success and German generosity. In reality, negotiations stagnated when the French consistently bent to German pressure. As time went on, the French in the metropole started to express doubts about their government. In April 1942 the sous-prefect of Libourne, André Giberton, while reporting on public opinion, noted, "We hope for the prisoners' return; that is the question that preoccupies every Frenchman, and, if results could be obtained, the government would strengthen its position in public opinion. We also believe the government's efforts will contribute to loosen the grip of the occupation and improve supplies for the country."[24] The next month he reported that his constituents were worried about the future of the nation, and having counted on the prisoners' return and a relaxation of the demarcation line, neither of which had happened, many feared that the current government under Pierre Laval was not as capable as previous ones.[25] Publicly, difficulties in negotiations were never blamed on the German authorities; rather, individual responsibility was emphasized.

The collaborationist paper *Je suis partout* published Scapini's warning: "The problem of releasing prisoners is primarily a political problem. It depends on continuing negotiations between the French Government and the Government of the Reich. It depends especially on the attitude of France—and not only government but also the attitude of the population. . . . The main obstacle to the release of prisoners is Gaullism."[26] The message was clear: supporting the Resistance or de Gaulle would keep your prisoners in Germany. Blame lay not with the Scapini Mission, Pétain, or Laval, and not with an inflexible German government, but with shadowy enemies bent on destroying the new era of collaboration.

As far as colonial prisoners specifically were concerned, Vichy showed a pattern of concession and compromise regarding the empire that affected their status in negotiations. Behind requests for the release of the colonial prisoners was the careful consideration of the internal political consequences and opportunities for useful propaganda. Vichy policy from the beginning favored the return of white prisoners and removing colonial prisoners as a target for German propaganda. Despite German claims in June 1940 that France would be treated as a courageous enemy, the political negotiations showed far less respect for the Vichy regime's positions. As the next chapter demonstrates, the Germans sought to encourage nationalist ideas among North Africans at a time when France's sovereignty and imperial unity were questionable. While Vichy strove for concessions, the rewards, especially concerning the empire, often caused conflict. The German authorities used the internal political situation in France and the empire to reward French "good behavior" with prisoner releases.

North Africa's potential and strategic importance influenced German policy toward North African prisoners, which in turn weakened the French position with the prisoners from sub-Saharan Africa. The most well-known example happened after General Weygand was removed from power in 1941. As a reward for "newfound stability" in North Africa, credited to Weygand's departure, the Germans promised to release ten thousand colonial prisoners.[27] Pleased with the opportunity to have over 10 percent of its colonial prisoners released, the Vichy authorities requested that sixty-two hundred North Africans and thirty-eight hundred West Africans be selected. Instead, the German authorities exclusively released North African prisoners who could work in mining and agriculture.[28] This was the single largest release of colonial prisoners during the Second World War and came on the heels of the liberation of the remaining white prisoners from the Frontstalags that spring. After these releases, "a painful uneasiness [was] born among prisoners of color. This feeling has not been eased by measures taken on behalf of veterans or parents of four minor children as these special provisions have hardly affected them."[29]

Rather than interpret this as a failure vis-à-vis the Black prisoners, some members of the French armistice delegation felt this release proved that the economic arguments had worked. Having had one success, they suggested requesting that an additional six thousand colonial prisoners be released. Other members feared that might confuse the issue with the original ten thousand North African prisoners. In the end, the second request was removed from official correspondence with the Germans.[30] There were no subsequent attempts to get the additional six thousand colonial prisoners released. By February 1942 the repatriation of the ten thousand North African prisoners had been completed, and the Germans indicated that this would be the last mass release of colonial prisoners.[31]

Collaboration without Colonies

The Allied landings in French North Africa transformed the situation in France and the colonies. On November 8, 1942, Anglo-American forces landed in Algiers, Oran, and Casablanca. Secret negotiations between American diplomat Robert Murphy and French officers willing to bring the North African armies over to the Allied side had set the stage for the landings. However, as Robert Paxton describes in his elegant prose, "Hypnotized by the dread consequences of an Allied commando raid in the Empire, conditioned to neutrality in a stalemate war, schooled like all officers to fire back when fired upon, the officers fought back."[32] Ultimately, the Vichy defense was short-lived; Noguès ordered the Moroccan forces to stop fighting on November 10. Fighting between Axis and Allied forces did continue in Tunisia until May 1943. Darlan, who happened to be in North Africa because his son was sick, became high commissioner of the French state and pretended to be following secret orders from Pétain to help ease the transition.[33] He was assassinated a month later, on December 24.

In France, on November 11, 1942, the German authorities invaded the unoccupied zone, destroying any remaining illusions of French sovereignty. The French scuttled their own fleet at Toulon to keep it from falling into German hands, and the Armistice Army was forcibly dissolved on November 27. The Vichy regime was left without an army, a fleet, or an empire, everything the armistice had purported to protect.[34] By the end of the month the remaining colonies, including French West Africa under Pierre Boisson, joined the Allied cause. Conditions in the metropole continued to worsen. The deportation of Jews to death camps had already begun in July, as had food rationing. This could have been a defining moment for the Vichy regime; instead, Pétain recommitted to collaboration.

The Allied landings shifted some public opinion in France. In Libourne, the news was greeted with restrained excitement, and those who a few months earlier were committed to collaboration now hoped for an American victory.[35] Willfully blind to the true nature of the Nazi regime and Vichy's own complicity, Pétain clung to the notion that Vichy was neutral and that there was valor in its neutrality. For many, these harshening conditions and the risks of social revolution accompanying an Allied liberation made neutrality even more appealing. Pétain and Laval increasingly pushed for a compromise peace between Allies and Axis to be facilitated by the French.[36] With Germany occupying all of France, relations between the governments moved to a new footing. The loss of the empire changed the political landscape entirely. Externally, with the Battles of El Alamein and Stalingrad, the balance of the war had shifted against the Axis, forcing Germany to mount a total mobilization of the economy. This double change of context dramatically affected the colonial prisoners as a political issue.

Colonial Prisoners in the German War Economy

The absolute primacy of labor for the German war effort meant any further negotiations would turn on increasing productivity. This led to the forced conscription of French workers to be sent to Germany and a desire to release Frontstalag guards to supervise Soviet prisoners on the eastern front.[37] The Scapini Mission had thought this might be an opportunity to obtain the release of the remaining thirty-eight thousand colonial prisoners as "a guarantee of influence . . . among the indigenous peoples who have so many times reaffirmed their loyalty through their words and their acts."[38] The French slowly recognized that the colonial prisoners still in captivity were increasingly unhappy. While the Vichy regime continued to act as though it had political and internal sovereignty, that was simply no longer the case, especially in regard to the colonial prisoners. The Vichy regime would not have been able to effectively resist outright German demands to convert the colonial prisoners into civilian laborers. However, and this remains a key point in the historiography of Vichy, the regime never attempted to resist or refuse German demands. Instead, Pierre Laval's second government (1942–44/45) moved into full-scale collaborationism.

Germany's interest now shifted. German losses and remobilization for total war—not the empire—set the new political terms during the winter of 1942–43. Already in early 1942 Germany pushed to improve productivity; this became vital after the defeat at Stalingrad. In February 1942 Albert Speer was given control of the German war economy as minister of armaments and war production. After Fritz Todt's death, he took over the Todt Organization, which had used colonial labor to build extensive military defense structures like the Atlantic Wall. Speer centralized and organized the economy, bringing it up to the standards required for total war. Production increased despite the Allied bombings. To mirror the boost in industrial productivity, Paul Joseph Goebbels, Reich minister of propaganda, gave his famous "total war" speech in February 1943. Germans civilians were assured that total war equaled the fastest war and that sacrifices at home would benefit the soldiers at the front, motivating them to continue a war that was rapidly turning against them. In reality, conditions continued to deteriorate, especially with food rations decreasing dramatically in 1943.[39]

Pressure also increased on the occupied territories, and France was not spared. Under Pierre Laval, Vichy moved into its period of greatest collaboration with the Germans. Already in June 1942, in what was known as the *relève* (relief or replacement), the Germans demanded that 250,000 French workers, including 150,000 skilled workers, be sent to work in Germany. In exchange for every three workers, the Germans offered to release one French prisoner.[40] Its initial success was due to a misunderstanding: many French joined believing "their" prisoners would be released. The relève was the most notorious attempt to use POWs as a bargaining tool with the French public, and it failed. By the end of the summer only 60,000 French workers had gone to Germany; many young French men preferred to join the Resistance instead. As the German war effort increased, their dependence on French labor did as well. In February 1943 Laval introduced the Service du travail obligatoire (compulsory work service), which forcibly sent young men to work in Germany. Over 600,000 men left for Germany between June 1942 and August 1943. No former colonial prisoners were forced into the Service du travail obligatoire, unlike white colonial settlers present in France.[41] By September 1943 Laval and Speer signed an agreement integrating a number of French industries directly into the German economy. The Todt Organization also increased its dependence on POW and forced laborers recruited from the occupied countries. This included released colonial prisoners who had not been repatriated before November 1942.[42] By the end of 1944, 1.4 million laborers worked on the Todt projects in deplorable conditions.

The colonial prisoners were now a political issue in this new context of direct economic collaboration. Already a minority among French prisoners, the colonial prisoners saw their importance further diluted by the need for a massive increase in laborers. They were increasingly viewed as ready-organized work groups. Worse for the colonial prisoners, there were no way home. Even if they escaped or were released for ill health, they were stuck in metropolitan France, as travel between the metropole and the colonies was now impossible.

Faced with difficulties recruiting the French to work in Germany after 1943, the Germans became increasingly dependent on colonial prisoner labor.[43] So they tempted the French with something they had sought since June 1940: direct control over the colonial prisoners. Refusing once again to release the colonial prisoners, the Germans suggested an experimental change of guards. The colonial prisoners could work under French custodial staff, who in turn would report to the German authorities. As a reward, after work hours the colonial prisoners would be free to walk into the local villages to buy extra food.[44] This unorthodox idea that the French guard their own colonial prisoners had in fact been Laval's.[45] As Pétain's government had continually demonstrated its commitment to stability under collaboration, there was little risk for the Germans that it would abuse this opportunity by encouraging resistance. Scapini had protested against converting colonial prisoners into a colonial civilian labor force in semimilitarized formations. However, his protest was not on moral grounds, but rather due to the potential inconveniences in switching German guards for French ones.

The question of the colonial prisoners' guards in the latter half of the war exemplifies the thinking among Vichy leaders. For many in Vichy, there remained a blind, fervent, and totally unrealistic hope that France might still benefit from German demands, in this case by requesting the release of white prisoners with colonial experience to guard the colonial prisoners. The idea that the French would guard their own colonial soldiers as they worked for the German war effort, while their families in the colonies were once again at war with Germany, was not considered problematic—or at least, not problematic enough to push back against the lethargy of neutrality that led the Vichy regime into greater and greater crimes. The French were confident in their right and duty to lead the colonial prisoners, and that outweighed other concerns.

Also present in France during this period were a significant number of colonial subjects. Some were soldiers or ex-prisoners waiting to go home; others were civilian workers who had lived in France before the war or arrived shortly after its outbreak. As conditions in France got more chaotic, these groups intermingled with the remaining 36,751 colonial prisoners still in captivity, composed of 6,007 Moroccans, 4,550 Tunisians, 12,584 Algerians, 8,823 Senegalese, 2,212 Madagascan, 2,055 Indochinese, and 520 West Indians.[46] In June 1943 German records counted 212 white officers, 4 "colored" officers, 422 white NCOs, 633 "colored" NCOs, and 15,335 indigenous men working in France.[47] This appears to correspond to another German record of 16,197 colonial soldiers working for the German military in France in 1943: 8,118 Madagascans, 6,257 Indochinese, 1,641 West Africans, and 181 "creoles."[48] French records confirm that there were approximately 16,000 colonial soldiers, of whom 4,004 worked for the Ministry for Work, 4,992 directly for the German authorities, and 4,537 for the *commissaires régionaux militaires* (regional military commissioners), while 2,484 were in rehabilitation centers.[49] Potentially 53,000 men from the French Empire were available to work as the French and Germans prepared a trial run for the new guard system. In the end, only 10 percent would have French guards. Several camps, led by the French captain La Touche in Nancy, took part in the experiment. La Touche oversaw a team of white officers, ranging in rank from officer cadets to captains with the occasional indigenous NCO.[50] Once constituted, these groups of colonial prisoners and workers were placed at the German authorities' disposition.[51]

Despite the initial French reservations about guarding the colonial prisoners, they saw two potential opportunities: employment for white officers who had been released from duty when the Armistice Army was dissolved and a means to get white prisoners who had experience with colonial troops released from Germany for guard duty.[52] The French and German authorities disagreed on exactly what the French role was to be. According to the Germans, it was a simple switch of nationalities, with all responsibilities remaining the same, including the requirement to prevent escapes and imprison disobedient soldiers.[53] The French feared reprisals against their officers if the colonial prisoners escaped and felt that the new guards should merely ensure that the prisoners worked correctly.

These new pressures for productivity affected how the colonial prisoners worked. Previously, they had traveled to work together with German guards, which had limited their working hours. Now they were organized on shift work. In one steel mill, three teams of colonial prisoners worked around the clock. Consequently, kitchen staff was also organized to provide meals for each shift separately. Working on different shifts throughout the day and night destroyed any sense of community that had previously existed. Work was strenuous, and the steel mill burned and destroyed the colonial prisoners' clothes and shoes.[54] Conditions in France were deteriorating quickly, and the colonial prisoners were no longer sheltered from the war.

Although technically the French were responsible for the colonial prisoners, the German authorities continued to impose their decisions. Crucially, they refused to release white prisoners with colonial experience, something the

French believed was essential to lead indigenous soldiers effectively. Instead, the Germans chose the guards, sometimes selecting civilians with no colonial experience. Commandant Daveau, a French official responsible for the colonial prisoners in their new status, believed the civilian supervisors were unsatisfactory and that the colonial prisoners' complaints were because the French staff did not support and help them as they expected French soldiers would have done. To support this, Daveau argued that colonial prisoners at Nancy, Vesoul, and Chartres had welcomed the French guards because of their colonial experience.[55] While previously Vichy concessions to the Germans had worked in the colonial prisoners' favor, once the possibility arose of bringing white prisoners home, one of Pétain's earliest promises, this was no longer the case. Having removed the colonial prisoners from direct German influence, the French authorities felt they could focus their diplomatic efforts elsewhere. Considering the general deterioration throughout France and Germany, even without the change in guards, the colonial prisoners suffered more during the final years of captivity, with harder work under more difficult conditions. The important difference was that some were guarded by the French. Blurring the lines between captor and prisoner was a tremendously shortsighted decision in terms of future relations with the colonies. Although only six thousand colonial prisoners experienced the French guards, the impact of this decision left a much larger legacy in the experiences and memories of the colonial prisoners.[56]

As seen, during the first few years of occupation, Vichy had attempted to mask collaboration from the colonial prisoners and colonial populations, fearing that the nuances of its relations with the Germans would confuse loyalties and make colonial prisoners more susceptible to German propaganda. The realities of collaboration became clear to the colonial prisoners when their transfer to French guards did not equal liberation from captivity. To mitigate the colonial prisoners' frustration, in a tradition long used in the colonies to shore up support for French rule, the Scapini Mission sought the cooperation of respected indigenous officers. Capt. Ahmed Rafa in Frontstalag 153 in Orléans recalled, "I was solicited by the German authorities, represented on this occasion by a battalion chief from Scapini's services, in order to convince my Algerian compatriots to agree to accept command of the POW camps that would become North African labor camps (this would have contributed to freeing all the German guards, who would then be sent to combat units). Having refused his proposition, he responded that I understood nothing and would regret it later." Rafa was categorical in his condemnation of the Scapini Mission, which he described as "mere German emissaries."[57]

There were legitimate fears of the colonial prisoners' reaction to this peculiar situation, but the possibility of gaining the release of experienced officers who supposedly "understood" the French way to manage colonial subjects outweighed the risks for many in the Vichy regime. On the contrary, Col. Henri Dantan-Merlin, who reported extensively on the change in guards, believed that such an abnormal situation placed the French guards in an awkward and potentially dangerous position of responsibility. He astutely wondered whether "there is reason to fear that the natives will, in little time, realize that their former officers have simply become their jailers? Is there not reason to fear that this realization might have grave consequences for the future and that French prestige will suffer from it?"[58] Prestige was, of course, directly connected to continued French rule of the empire, demonstrating the widespread belief that France would retain control over its empire after the war.

German priorities dominated, and no white officers were released to guard the colonial prisoners. By October 1943 most of the one thousand French supervisors were officers or senior employees of the Armistice Army.[59] The French could not control the choice of guards and had showed the Germans that they would do no more than protest. The program expanded with the insatiable German demand for labor. By the end of 1943 five thousand colonial prisoners were divided into smaller work groups under French supervision and custody.[60] The French chose to believe that the colonial prisoners were generally pleased to be under French guard. The change in guards and increased pressure from the German war effort created some unusual situations. In the Landes, a mayor was given control of the local colonial POW camp when the company of German guards was removed.[61] In Orleans, NCOs on captivity leave supervised colonial prisoners who had been converted into civilian workers in German factories.[62]

For many colonial prisoners in agriculture and forestry, work continued much as it had between 1940 and 1942. The major shift was in the numbers working directly for the Germans: 3,751 for the Todt Organization, approximately 1,200 for the armed forces, including in chemical factories, and 5,450 as workers in the former occupied zone.[63] By 1944 the system was well integrated throughout France, with two different kinds of work groups: semifree and free. In the former, the prisoners had a German guard but were free to move about outside work hours and on Sunday. In the latter, a French NCO was solely responsible for the prisoners.[64] Even the free work groups were only nominally free, and prisoners remained under the ultimate control of the Frontstalag commanders.

Camp commanders often treated the guards as menial subordinates, which they felt undermined their attempts to regain the "confidence and affection of our former tirailleurs."[65] German reports glossed over any potential problems and claimed the colonial prisoners maintained excellent attitudes and discipline and were uninterested in politics. A German end-of-year report from 1943 on "colored units" in France claimed, "Both natives and white leaders came to their tasks willingly. No case of conflict has been recorded. The conduct of the officers has been entirely loyal, and the natives' work has been satisfactory."[66] Despite previous efforts to avoid discussing collaboration with the colonized peoples, the "loyalty of the French NCOs" to Germany could not have gone unnoticed by the colonial soldiers. Yet the Scapini Mission simply recorded that the colonial prisoners complained about the lower quality and quantity of food.[67]

The colonial prisoners did benefit in a limited way from the change in guards. As noted, some were given limited freedom to visit local towns when not working. The unsupervised contact with civilians and workers worried the French authorities now more than ever as popular attitudes slowly moved against the regime. The Vichy regime's fear of resistance in general, and from its colonial subjects particularly, motivated the supervising officers to limit the colonial prisoners' contact with the population. Worse still was the fear that French workers and their "insidious propaganda" might incite the colonial prisoners to protest. Now the colonial prisoners, still earning only ten francs a day as in the Frontstalags, worked side by side with white workers earning ten francs an hour.[68] The prisoners' salary was much higher than that paid to workers in the colonies, reflecting the hierarchy of importance given to laborers. In French Equatorial Africa, workers were paid two francs per day, while porters earned six francs per day while building thousands of kilometers of roads to connect the Free French to the British colonies.[69] In response to complaints, Daveau studied the possibilities of a daily bonus of six, eight, or twelve francs, depending on productivity.[70] Even with this potential bonus, the colonial prisoners were grossly underpaid compared with the civilian workers. This highlights a fundamental hesitation across the colonial empires to quantify what the colonized "deserved" to be paid. Linking a bonus to productivity stratified the men into deserving and undeserving, unlike a salary that would be paid to all workers.

This decision to change guards marked a fundamental shift in how colonial prisoners were treated in France, and its significance has marked the historical literature. Armelle Mabon asserts that using the French to guard the colonial prisoners was the origin of their disillusion with France because of their "betrayal" during captivity.[71] More likely, the change in the guards was one event that shaped the experiences of colonial prisoners and formed part of their growing disillusionment with Vichy and France. Scheck has demonstrated that while some of the colonial prisoners did appreciate the freedoms under the new regime, more complained about corrupt practices and the racism of the old-school colonial officers.[72] Fundamentally, the source of many former prisoners' frustration was the inequality of their status as compared with white prisoners or workers. Both the arrival of the French staff and "liberation" from captivity should have equaled freedom, as it did for white prisoners. Instead, the colonial prisoners were required to work in similar conditions as before.[73] The colonial prisoners also lost a degree of separation from the German war effort in this new arrangement. Now the French were supporting the increasingly thorough integration of the colonial prisoners into the German war economy.

Despite the inherently problematic nature of French guards, combined with the disproportionate salaries between white and indigenous workers, the French expected the colonial prisoners to demonstrate the loyalty and obedience "worthy" of a colonial soldier. However, these men had already survived years of captivity, with material conditions in France steadily worsening. With the loss of the empire, they were now also deprived of contact with their families. If their work remained the same, it was now their former officers who punished them for trying to escape, not the Germans. Any expression of discontent was met with French accusations that the colonial prisoners were parroting German propaganda rather than with a recognition of its legitimacy. Underlying French attitudes did not radically change during the winter of 1942–43, but combined with the increased integration of the colonial prisoners into the German war effort, the impact of these attitudes on the colonial prisoners was amplified.

By 1944 Germany had become increasingly suspicious of France and feared that the French planned to surrender the remaining thirty thousand colonial prisoners to the Allies.[74] When the Allies did land in Normandy on June 6, 1944, the German authorities recalled colonial prisoners to the Frontstalags, leaving the French with no one to guard. In some cases, the guards were also detained for several hours and allowed to leave.[75] Without the legal framework provided by the Geneva Convention or even the armistice agreement, the French staff were in unmapped territory. Some were technically on captivity leave and thus subject to recall by the German authorities at any time. Yet despite the renewed fighting, the French guards did not return to captivity; instead, they were placed under the remit of the Ministry of Colonies and Commandant Daveau.[76] At Charleville, the NCOs and officers were told they remained free but were under the authority of Captain Bouzigues.[77] In Vesoul, the NCOs were released after their workers were reinterned in the camp. No information was available from Bordeaux. Some, like thirty-five Moroccan prisoners in Nancy, took advantage of the confusion to escape. The French captain Boutier and his assistant traveled through the department and recaptured all but two of them.[78] That members of the French Army actively recaptured escaped prisoners and returned them to the detaining power while the Allies were liberating France shows the perverse nature of the arrangement instituted after November 1942.

Whereas the Vichy regime's legitimacy had initially been anchored to protecting the prisoners and the French Empire, by 1944 it was doing neither.

The empire had been lost, while the colonial prisoners, with the Vichy regime's assistance, were fully integrated into German war production in France. Despite ample proof between 1940 and 1942 that its tactics were not working, Vichy granted ever-greater concessions to maintain German interest in negotiations. During the first half of the occupation, colonial prisoners benefited from being a serious political stake in the regime's relationship with the German occupiers. The French attempted to ensure their repatriation or improve their conditions. Yet many colonial prisoners were further disillusioned about the empire after witnessing the massive French defeat, closely interacting with the French population while in the Frontstalags, and experiencing a lifetime of racist imperial rule. Constantly concerned that the Germans might exacerbate this situation with anti-French propaganda, the Scapini Mission redoubled its efforts to obtain the colonial prisoners' release. As this proved impossible, the Vichy government and aid groups tried to improve their conditions. All this yielded some benefits, not just for the ten thousand North Africans or First World War veterans who were released as a result of Scapini's negotiations, but also for colonial prisoners in their continued captivity. If colonial prisoners had been of no political concern to Vichy, fewer efforts to improve conditions in the Frontstalags would have been made, and such benefits would have been forgone.

Taking financial and eventually legal responsibility for colonial prisoners began gradually but culminated in 1943. The next logical step was responsibility for guarding the colonial prisoners, but under German military control and with no real power to make decisions. The French saw this as an opportunity to negotiate for the release of white prisoners with colonial experience, but it cut no ice with the Germans. By the end of the German occupation, the Vichy regime had little real control, and the colonial prisoners were left to the vicissitudes of war and liberation, which was a process barely different from their experience of being made captive in 1940.

8

COLONIAL PRISONERS
UNDER THE INFLUENCE

German and French Propaganda

By the Second World War the use of propaganda to influence public opinion to maintain morale, justify participation in the war, and vilify the enemy was widespread. The presence of eighty-five thousand colonial prisoners in France provided a rare opportunity to cultivate favor and influence among a diverse group of men destined to return home to the colonies. For Germany, the colonial prisoners represented a small part of their greater North African propaganda strategy to undermine French and British rule in this strategically important region. For the Vichy regime, close control of colonial prisoners, who might prove a disturbing element for future French colonial rule because they had experienced the defeat and collaboration, now became vital. Still, for the French, inviting the colonial prisoners into a political discussion felt unwise, as it might incite demands at a time when French imperial rule was threatened. Capitalizing on French vulnerability, the Germans encouraged nationalist discussions. The Vichy regime needed to be seen as the legitimate French government of both metropolitan France and the empire. However, competing claims on the colonies, from Gaullists in Francophone Africa or the Japanese in Indochina, forced the Vichy regime to bargain for colonial loyalties.[1] With an increase in anticolonial resistance during the interwar period, the French used surveillance and repression in the colonies and metropole to ensure the people subject to their colonial rule toed the line.[2]

After the defeat, Vichy officials felt that having "two Frances" left the colonies vulnerable to nationalist or pro-German views, which might spread unchecked. Faced with a diminished international status, territorial losses in the metropole, and the absence of 1.5 million prisoners, the Vichy regime needed to demonstrate strength and control, particularly in regard to the colonial empire. French fear of German propaganda was paramount and reasonable, leading the Vichy regime to try to control the flow of information to colonial prisoners, notably through a propaganda campaign to counteract that of the Germans.

The white French public was invited to reflect on the causes of the defeat and the hope collaboration provided for France's rebirth. Of course, they had to perform mental gymnastics to accept the new situation of German dominance. They had, unlike the populations of the colonies, witnessed the defeat and the collapse of France. Many had a visceral reaction to it and were happy to allow Pétain to lead them out of "Republican decadence" and back to "traditional French values." Overseas, the French struggled with how to justify the defeat and the abrupt change in allies to the colonized populations, who they felt were incapable of comprehending. Unfortunately for the French, the most effective propaganda was tied to military victories. As Harold Lasswell argued in 1927, retreat and humiliation spread seeds of discord and defeatism.[3] This gave Germany an immediate advantage. Colonial prisoners could compare the well-organized German military machine that invaded France in six short weeks with the disorganized French retreat. When necessary, the French explained that the defeat had been a material one, compounded by French overextension protecting its allies.

German propaganda had fewer constraints. It made promises it had no intention of keeping and focused on populations with strong regional or national identities that it felt could be exploited: Bretons, Alsatians, Lorraines, and North African Muslims. Germany championed nationalist movements and encouraged revolt in the British and French colonies, while, as the previous chapter demonstrated, threatening the Vichy government with intervention if it could not maintain stability in North Africa. Both powers exploited Islam to gain influence over colonial prisoners, drawing on a long prehistory of French and German contests over Islam, especially during the First World War. In the end, what actually influenced the colonial prisoners' captivity experience had little to do with religion.

Imperial Considerations

Naturally, German propaganda was directly connected to its developing war aims. Hitler wanted access to French ports in North Africa for the war against Great Britain and Senegalese submarine ports in anticipation of war with the United States.[4] North Africa and the Middle East were strategically important to both the Allies and the Axis, and control over French North Africa could (and would) shift the balance of war. German propaganda abounded with contradictions. As the only major European country without an empire, Germany presented itself as an anti-imperialist power without explaining what had happened to its colonies. Visions of the Reich's eventual victory and takeover of North Africa were reflected in the chatter and bravado from guards who told colonial prisoners that North Africa would require Germany's help to free it from the French yoke, that Germany would rule North Africa, or that North African Muslims would get self-determination after the war.[5] In Epinal, the German commander discussed the events in Iraq with the North African prisoners, evoking the "English" subjugation of their brothers in the "Orient" and promising German material assistance in their struggle against foreign dominance.[6] Overall, German propaganda cultivated the interests of Moroccan, Algerian, and Tunisian prisoners and showed Germany as an attractive alternative ruler.[7] It focused less on prisoners from other parts of the French Empire.

German interest in North Africa and Islam demonstrated Nazi willingness to temporarily suspend racialized beliefs in a pragmatic deployment of religious hatred. Jeffrey Herf has shown how the Nazi regime sought an alliance with North African and Middle Eastern revolutionaries and Islamists by fusing Nazi ideology with Koranic scripture through a mutual hatred of Judaism.[8] Under Wilhelm Melchers, head of the Oriental Department in the Foreign Ministry, and Kurt Munzel, head of the Department of Radio Policy, two radio shows, *Berlin in Arabic* and the *Voice of Free Arabism*, made daily broadcasts to North Africa between 1939 and 1944. Muslim listeners were urged to revolt against colonial powers and sometimes to kill Jews.[9] The German authorities established a Maghreb Propaganda Bureau in occupied France staffed by Algerians, Tunisians, and Moroccans, often from active independence groups, sometimes releasing nationalists the French had imprisoned.[10] The bureau also coordinated the radio broadcasts and publications transmitted to colonial prisoners in the Frontstalags, frequently parroting the Berlin broadcasts.[11] From July 1942 the German broadcaster Jakob Mar led a popular radio show with music and culture from the French Empire. Mar's broadcasts, while focused on French imperial duty and the need for industrialization throughout "our empire," began to set the stage for future German claims to the French Empire.[12] Surprisingly, antisemitism only rarely appeared in the propaganda for North African prisoners and was never the main focus.

Intelligence briefings and monthly reports detailed the Vichy regime's growing concern over Germany's interest in the French colonies.[13] In September 1940 Germany attempted to reopen its consulates throughout the French Empire. The French Ministry of Foreign Affairs opposed this resumption of diplomatic relations, as it would spread German influence and personnel throughout the colonies with few benefits for the French. Instead, flipping the usual German response, the French suggested that the question be studied after the war.[14] The French correctly assumed that if Germany had more access to the empire, it would encourage anti-French sentiment and divisions. Yet this remains one of the only instances where the Vichy regime refused the Germans access to French colonies.

While it was impossible to hide the magnitude of defeat from the colonial soldiers in France, the French tried to mitigate its importance for the indigenous populations in the empire. In Sudan (Mali), Lieutenant Colonel Duboin concluded that "since the natives are ignorant of the geography and the consequences of the armistice, and since nothing has changed in their lives, the armistice was, for the majority of them, a news item that they have already forgotten."[15] Not all colonial administrators were as confident as Duboin, and the French began immediate efforts to shore up prestige and showcase French power in their colonies. Following a tour of the colonies, Maxime Weygand warned against concessions to Germany or Italy regarding naval or air bases in Africa, since the Africans still considered both the enemy. He feared that such allowances would undermine "native" trust in their leaders and might provoke the indigenous populations to take actions that would endanger imperial unity.[16] Pétain's first speech to the empire in

September 1940 reiterated that France remained united despite the defeat and occupation. The emphasis on French unity was not merely rhetorical; several days earlier French Equatorial Africa had rallied to de Gaulle, and Pétain wanted to ensure no other colonies followed suit. He reminded listeners in the empire, "The first duty, today, is to obey. The second is to help the government in its task, without second thoughts, without hesitation. To the call of the fatherland, the empire, this jewel in the French crown will respond."[17]

Obedience was a pillar of the National Revolution, but its roots went deeper into French imperialism. All imperial powers considered obedience to be the greatest quality for colonial subjects. This was especially true when France was under threat. In shifting focus away from the defeat and toward renewal, the Vichy regime incorporated the colonial subjects in its task, even if their role was to be a passive one. Pétain's paternalistic call for obedience was echoed in the secretary of state for the colonies' instructions to the colonial governors. Charles Platon explained that to maintain its world status, French propaganda must persuade the overseas populations to obey in the spirit of unity and national discipline.[18]

The National Revolution's paternalism and emphasis on work and obedience resounded with the values that Pierre Boisson hoped to spread in French West Africa. As Ruth Ginio argues, the Vichy regime used the colonies to implement practices that would have had difficulty gaining acceptance in Republican France.[19] Colonial governors relied on influential European and indigenous leaders, officials, and religious figures to maintain unity and cultivate loyalty to the Vichy regime.[20] Vichy propaganda for French West Africa had two main goals. The first was to guarantee African obedience through the promotion of an official interpretation of events and censorship of other narratives. The second was to promote Pétain's National Revolution, whose conservative values were deemed better suited to the colonies than republican ones had been.[21] Individualized propaganda was tailored for each colony and included praise for French colonial leaders, reminders of the technological advances provided by France, and visions for the empire's crucial role in France's postwar future.

Maintaining French prestige in the colonies was increasingly difficult as Germany, the Free French, and the British sought to undermine Vichy authority whenever possible. Signs of *V* for victory with the *Croix de Lorraine* had "mysteriously" begun to appear in cities in France, and Platon warned colonial governors to watch for similar infiltrations of British propaganda.[22] The Egyptian press, influenced by London, and several other Arabic newspapers printed a series of articles in the summer of 1940 rationalizing that the French populations actually opposed the Vichy government.[23] All these efforts sowed hints of discord, making it harder for the Vichy regime to control the local populations, which was exactly the point.

Sometimes the language of the Vichy regime caused issues in the colonial context. Antoine Félix Giacobbi, governor of French Guinea, complained to Boisson that emphasizing collaboration with Germany might be misconstrued by "the natives to whom we have spoken so negatively about Germany (commentaries on *Mein Kampf*, Seydou Nourou Tall's propaganda tour, etc.)."[24] Tall was a popular and influential leader in Senegal and the grandson of a great religious and military leader, El Hadj Oumar Tall. He had helped recruitment drives at the outbreak of war and regularly preached obedience and loyalty to God and France, which allegedly resonated particularly well with the rural populations.[25] Bearing in mind the extensive anti-German discourse during the military recruitment and Phony War, Giacobbi suggested that propaganda texts designed for the indigenous populations focus on France's future and how its relations with Great Britain had changed, rather than attempt to explain why France was now allied with Nazi Germany. The governor of Senegal, Jean Paul Parisot, also worried that the sarcastic headlines in the monthly bulletin would affect the "less-evolved" masses, who he believed took the written word literally.[26] The real problem was not that the indigenous populations did not understand the defeat, but rather that they understood it too well, hence the emphasis on obedience. The colonial populations had received dogmatic and one-dimensional descriptions of Germany because France actively suppressed political discussion and activism.

However, sometimes French actions betrayed an attention to colonial sensibilities that went beyond the usual maintenance of the status quo. Bibi Traoré, a prisoner from French Sudan, had written to the commander of the French administration in Goumbou, claiming payment for a steer that a visiting French delegation had eaten fifteen years previously.[27] Despite proof that the animal had been purchased at the time, Traoré's claim was forwarded through the colonial administration to increasingly higher-ranked officials, eventually reaching Pierre Boisson and Georges Scapini. Boisson's rationale for escalating the letter to the secretary of state for colonies revealed, precisely because of the inconsequentiality of the incident, the fundamental issue at stake—loyalty to the empire from its colonized subjects:

> The case is of minor importance and does not exceed, in itself, the territorial scope of the *cercle*. But I felt obligated to inform you since Bibi Traoré intends to write to the ambassador of France, Scapini. I also believe it is necessary to inform the applicant that the request has been studied and make him understand why it is unfounded. While they suffer the rigors of captivity, during which they may be tempted to stray from us, our native prisoners need to be imbued, by any means, with the certainty that we do not neglect their interests.[28]

Although acknowledging that Traoré's complaint had no basis, Boisson believed in the importance of showing Traoré that his claim had been heard, especially if he intended to inform Scapini. Duty required the French to take care of their "loyal native soldiers," but sometimes duty was also a calculated political decision at a time when France desperately needed its subjects' loyalty.

A Captive Audience

Colonial prisoners were a concentrated group, in a peculiar position, whose environmental conditions could easily be manipulated. They were neither like most of the French, who, initially at least, actively welcomed the armistice, nor like the colonial populations who had not lived the defeat. They were the exception. They had experienced the defeat and its consequences, but sooner or later they would go home. They were thus a critical group in terms of negotiating what the defeat might mean in the empire. For the French, the colonial prisoners were to be symbols of, not participants in, colonial unity, while white prisoners were expected to contribute actively to collaboration. For example, colonial prisoners received portraits of Pétain in their parcels but were not encouraged to join the Cercles Pétain common among French POWs in Germany. The Cercles Pétain were political groups committed to promoting the National Revolution through discussions and conferences concentrating on Pétain as a leader. In 1941 the prefect of the Vosges praised returning French prisoners as "wholeheartedly collabora-tionist" despite having been treated well by the Germans.[29] Yet the French were uneasy when colonial prisoners expressed similarly positive opinions about the Germans, preferring colonial prisoners to associate captivity with German brutality.

French officials were divided on the most effective means to reach and influence the colonial prisoners in German captivity. The Vichy regime had fifteen minister-secretaries of state for radio and eight for information between 1940 and 1944.[30] Hoang Van Co, chief of the imperial section of the Ministry of Propaganda, passionately believed that propaganda was an essential political question that could prevent the colonial prisoners from moral and intellectual collapse. He coordinated the French propaganda efforts for approximately forty thousand Indochinese, Madagascan, and Senegalese soldiers and workers in the unoccupied zone.[31] Two bilingual publications (one French and Vietnamese, the other French and Malagasy) attempted to bring this imperial propaganda to both the colonial prisoners and civilian workers.[32] In May 1942 Van Co wrote to Paul Creyssel, director of Vichy's propaganda service, criticizing the lack of a clear mission and complaining that current propaganda efforts preferred to deal with imme-diate issues facing colonial subjects in France, like food and heating, while ignoring the larger issue of imperial loyalty. He accurately stressed, "If ever there was a time when France must rally all her willing colonial subjects, rich or poor, to her cause, it's when the empire's integrity is threatened."[33]

The Vichy regime wanted short-term solutions to alleviate suffering while the colonial prisoners remained under German control, but nothing more. Previously, "loyalty to France" had been enough, but that had changed when colonial governors began choosing sides between Pétain and de Gaulle, sug-gesting the colonized might also consider choosing their leaders. To prevent that, the Vichy regime went to great lengths to remind its prisoners that the French Empire remained united and under French control. Propaganda and messages of solidarity during captivity were never designed to imply fundamental changes to their status as colonial subjects.

German propaganda directed toward colonial prisoners was less extreme than that for North Africa and took a two-pronged approach. First, propaganda aimed for the Frontstalag population could be quite generic, using Arabic-speaking officers and evoking German military prowess. Second, a more targeted approach brought motivated colonial prisoners together, often in Germany, for special training and attention, after which they were reintegrated among the prisoner population or released to North Africa to spread pro-German propaganda. While some were certainly true believers, others welcomed the associated benefits, such as better food, increased freedoms, and even early release. David Motadel suggests that the German desire to encourage Muslims to revolt was a consequence of military losses, and not based on long-term strategy, and that it was only after the German military engagement in North Africa in 1941 that the North African prisoners in France were viewed as politically important.[34] On the contrary, the potential significance of the colonial prisoners in Germany's occupation of France was established as early as the summer of 1940. However, Motadel is correct in noting 1941 as the turning point in incorporating North African prisoners into a broad propaganda strategy.

By 1942 Vichy's Section des affaires musulmanes also confirmed that the Germans had a coherent propaganda system for Muslims.[35] Using German and Muslim agents, it encouraged Muslims of different socioeconomic backgrounds from the Maghreb to the Middle East, and non-Muslims in Asia, to rise against their colonial powers. In this way the Nazis built in a far more radical form on a long-standing German championing of Islam. They highlighted, and sometimes invented, similarities between National Socialism and Islam, while fueling existing Muslim frustrations over the higher status and citizenship given to Algerian Jews.[36] This exploitation of religious tensions was another means of encouraging anti-French sentiment and redirecting some of the frustrations of captivity toward the French colonial regime.

German propaganda argued that the French were too cowardly to fight, hence the use of colonial troops in 1940. This, the Germans claimed, gave the colonial prisoners the right to demand equal rights for equal service, reopening claims from the previous generation of colonial veterans of the Great War.[37] In June 1940 the colonial prisoners witnessed white soldiers slipping into civilian crowds to avoided capture, while they could not. In a conscious attack on discrimination within the French military ranks, German guards liberally promoted North African prisoners and distributed "stripes."[38] Elsewhere, camp guards mocked and criticized the North African participation in French wars. Deliberate lies were told in an effort to discourage escapes. Camp authorities informed colonial prisoners that Germany occupied Tunisia, Morocco, and Algeria, so any prisoner who escaped would simply be returned to the Frontstalags.[39] The French fear that pro-German NCOs would become dangerous propagandists and influence other prisoners, who would then shape opinions at home, motivated much of the humanitarian action for colonial prisoners.

Both Germany and Vichy exploited propaganda methods designed for a combined literate and illiterate population. North Africa's strategic position in the war effort made its colonial prisoners particularly valuable targets of propaganda. After release from captivity, trained North African propagandists could intervene in areas inaccessible to Europeans, such as the *cafés* and *bains maures* (Moorish cafés and baths), markets, and other informal meeting places, to spread either pro- or anti-French opinions.[40] The Germans promoted and encouraged political discussions among North African prisoners. Captain Lölhöffel from the Bordeaux chapter of the MBF's propaganda section even invited nationalist students to speak to the North African prisoners and organize aid for them while in the camps.[41] Articles distributed in the camps equating the colonial prisoners' duty as Muslims with the call for independence reflected themes presented by Kurt Munzel's Orient Office broadcast on December 3, 1940, which reminded listeners that a good Muslim obeys God's law and fights against those who oppress Muslims—in other words, the French.[42]

These kinds of political discussions were not explicitly extended to the West African, Madagascan, or Indochinese prisoners, but some ideas crossed national lines. There is little evidence of German propaganda efforts toward Indochinese prisoners, presumably because they were far removed from

Germany's theater of operations. The French, on the other hand, searched for NCOs who spoke Malagasy or Vietnamese to "remind" soldiers and prisoners from Madagascar and Indochina that they were "excellent soldiers" and to provide them with professional training.[43] Propaganda for West African prisoners differed from that for the North Africans, and as Scheck argues, it was short-lived and often backfired, increasing the other prisoners' hostility toward their captors and not toward France.[44] Michele Gnimagnon remembered that at Chaumont, the Germans distributed cigarettes in hopes of obtaining information on the colonies, their resources, and soldiers' motivation for fighting against Germany. However, he believed that most of the information provided by the West African prisoners was false.[45]

German officers who spoke Arabic went on tours of the Frontstalags, often accompanied by North African prisoner agents. Dressed as civilians, these "agents" circulated freely, listening to everything in the camps and in town.[46] At Mont-de-Marsan, a German officer interrogated Moroccan prisoners in Arabic and recorded their addresses to visit them after the war.[47] This officer may have been Lieutenant Krebs, the chief German propaganda officer, who was an active presence throughout the Frontstalags and appeared regularly in captivity and intelligence reports. Krebs was fluent in Arabic and had an impressive knowledge of North Africa and the local leaders and customs. He traveled between the camps in France and Germany, interviewing colonial soldiers about their parents, homes, and ways of life, while promoting nationalists like Habib Bourguiba from Tunisia in an attempt to influence North Africans and motivate prisoners to continue their oral propaganda in the southern zone.[48] French intelligence was justifiably worried about Krebs.[49] In Berlin, he took colonial prisoners from Stalag III-A on tours of the city. His propaganda was simple and presented in Arabic. He would warn the colonial prisoners not to escape, arguing that conditions in the camps were better than those in North Africa, where they would return to tedious military service.[50]

Krebs's visit to the Frontstalags coincided with increased German propaganda efforts and publications. At Saint-Médard, a newsletter allegedly published by colonial prisoners, *Doumia jdida* (New world), was distributed with illustrations and photographs revealing German strength and its support of Muslim prisoners.[51] Literate prisoners were encouraged to read the articles, which played on their legitimate fears of finding work to exacerbate religious tensions. One article claimed that after "fifteen years of service, [the North African soldiers] receive a pension of 4 francs 50 per day and a job sweeping in the Jewish quarter, where the French mock him."[52] The strength of these arguments combined some truth—colonial pensions were lower than white pensions—with emotional fears that despite their sacrifice for France, the Muslim prisoners would remain in an inferior position to North African Jews.

Multiple articles blamed France for the continued captivity of the Moroccan prisoners, ignoring the fact that Germany was in fact the detaining power. The focus on Moroccan prisoners is unusual, as most propaganda targeted Algerian and Tunisian prisoners. Because of Spanish interests in Morocco, the Germans kept propaganda for Moroccan prisoners lighter and avoided outward support for independence.[53] *La Voix du prisonnier*, another free Arabic-language publication distributed to colonial prisoners, described why Germany treated the Moroccan prisoners so well: "We are convinced that the Moroccans did not fight voluntarily, but were forced to fight us, and thus are innocent prisoners. If France had left them alone and had not led them to war, they would currently be enjoying a quiet life in their country. Germany is aware of this situation and is also sympathetic to the small nations that are under French and English subjugation, which is why Moroccan prisoners get better treatment." The anonymous author, ostensibly a Moroccan prisoner, concluded that all Muslim prisoners must acknowledge the great leaders of Germany because of their good treatment during captivity.[54] While clearly German propaganda, these articles may well have been written, or at least influenced, by pro-German prisoners who spent time in special training camps. French intelligence firmly believed that these newspapers would encourage political opposition against France.[55]

Spy Training Camps

Immediately after the armistice, and as it had done in the First World War, Germany targeted educated prisoners in an attempt to influence the North African populations. Literate prisoners and those with religious education were removed from the general Frontstalag population and sent to special training camps in France and Germany.[56] Stalag VII-A had a section built for North African prisoners, but the most important camp was Stalag III-A, Luckenwalde, near Berlin, where Abwehr members taught the prisoners of all nationalities covert spy craft.[57] As in the Frontstalags, prisoners were separated by country and then by region. North African prisoners had comfortable lodgings and abundant food.[58] French reports estimated between three hundred and five hundred North African prisoners were at Stalag III-A.[59] However, Scheck argues that the number was much higher: between one thousand and two thousand North Africans.[60] The discrepancy may have been because groups of North African prisoners came to the camp in succession.

The camp was used to re-create an idealized North Africa centered on Islam. The mosque had a minaret flying the German and "Arab" flags and a generous space for ablutions and prayers. On Fridays, the Muslim holy day, ceremonies were held with military honors presented to the flags. These ceremonies were filmed on special occasions or during camp inspections. Everything was carefully constructed to showcase German appreciation for Islam and to demonstrate that under German rule, Islam would maintain a significant and legitimate role in North Africa—unlike in Algeria, where Muslims had to renounce their religion to take up French citizenship. A chosen few were introduced to North African deserters and nationalists living in Berlin, with whom they discussed the radio and press, held conferences, and even visited the cinema.[61]

During their stay in Germany, Muslim prisoners met frequently with German officers familiar with North Africa. Former prisoners reported that every Monday they were visited by two German officers, one speaking French and the other Moroccan-Arabic and Berber. Several Moroccan prisoners remembered having met one of these officers in 1932 in Fez, where he was an "itinerant pharmacist" pretending to be a Turkish Muslim. This officer explained that since France was a defeated and unimportant nation, the Germans would settle in Morocco after the war, expelling the French and dethroning the Francophile sultan, who had forced them to fight for France. He concluded by promising that "all Jews would be stripped of their belongings and returned to the miserable life they had before the protectorate." He also promised a bonus and better treatment for prisoners who succeeded in discovering the soldiers and officers in the camps who hid their Jewish origins.[62] Perhaps the Germans felt that this officer's connection to Fez and previous relationships with some prisoners might overcome the previous difficulties they had recruiting Moroccan prisoners to the German cause.

Once their training was completed, the new spies, armed with films and brochures, were temporarily reintegrated into the Frontstalags. From there, they were released as ill or allowed to escape.[63] A few remained to teach German officers Arabic.[64] Before leaving, the new spies were meant to disseminate anti-French ideas among the prisoner population and provide the Germans with any information on the French administration in North Africa. French intelligence knew that some spies went directly from a training camp in Angers to North Africa on missions.[65] German propaganda was designed to maximize distrust of the Vichy regime in the empire. Multiple French sources confirmed that the pro-German propaganda spreading in North Africa was the work of "natives indoctrinated in metropolitan [France] and Europeans who have 'bet' on German victory."[66] One colonial prisoner confessed that he was among one hundred prisoners who had been allowed to escape to the free zone to spread pro-German propaganda among Muslims.[67]

Allowing prisoners to "escape" or releasing them for illness was one way to move the spies back to North Africa. Training or influencing colonial prisoners was only half of the German project. The goal was to encourage uprisings to coincide with German military advances in North Africa. To do so, Germany used different actors in France and the colonies. An Algerian named Mekari ran a café maure in Clermont-Ferrand, which he transformed into a backroom spy center channeling propaganda to North Africa.[68] Even white prisoners with knowledge of North Africa were targeted.[69] The French knew that the German Armistice Commission, which had an important presence in North Africa, was contacting former colonial prisoners, which reinforced Vichy's decision to keep tabs on them.[70] French intelligence also suspected Germany of using private companies to solicit information on electrical installations throughout West Africa in order to set up a clandestine radio network.[71]

Without knowing who was a German spy and who was legitimately sick or had escaped, military officials invested time and resources in interviewing and following their colonial soldiers. There were several interrogation centers to interview repatriated colonial prisoners, the most important of which was in Clermont-Ferrand. From these interviews, the French maintained lists of "suspicious" colonial prisoners and "German orientalists," which they shared with the authorities in North Africa.[72] The French monitored German propaganda in the metropole and in the colonies, expending massive manpower and resources to fight back effectively. One French agent, Officer Nardin, was charged with evaluating the potential efficacy of propaganda emanating from Stalag III-A. Nardin was particularly concerned with the German officer who had spent time in Fez. While he doubted this man's influence over the colonial prisoners generally, he feared that the preexisting relationships with certain Muslims might negatively influence the local populations.[73] Indeed, a former colonial prisoner, Lahssen Ben Bouchta Ben X, reported that this man had visited Angoulême. Following that visit, Ben Bouchta was released with 180 other North African veterans of the First World War.[74] The French dreaded allowing such propaganda into the colonies, where it might find fertile ground, which was exactly what German propaganda was designed to do.

On rare occasions, the French delegation at Wiesbaden lodged official complaints about Germany's anti-French behavior. In complaining about Stalag III-A, the delegation acknowledged that the German authorities could explain away the presence of imams, mosques, and traditional clothing as simple measures to improve the North African prisoners' experience but felt that the deliberate anti-French tendencies in the newspaper *Alhilal* were unacceptable.[75] The French delegation diplomatically suggested that such a publication must have slipped the camp authorities' attention and requested that *Alhilal* and any similar papers be forbidden and remaining copies confiscated.[76] French protests were ignored, and German propaganda continued on.

Mobilization of Religion

Neither French nor German propaganda was revolutionary in its arguments, but both exploited knowledge of colonial cultures and religions to create potentially effective messages. As seen, German propaganda toward North Africa was organized and detailed, and it drew on a long history of deploying Islam to its cause. During the First World War, Germany had used the call for jihad to motivate its East African troops and the Arab corps.[77] The Second Reich also courted Ottoman Turkey in attempt to foster a revolt against the British and French Empires. During the interwar period, France had tried to reconcile its protection and even advocacy of Islam with its colonial interests in West and North Africa, where access to citizenship was blocked for most Muslims under French rule.[78] Both powers sought to increase their influence over the colonial prisoners by addressing their religious faith. Religious imagery dominated the German texts distributed to colonial prisoners, while the French focused on facilitating religious practices.

The French provided sweets, fruit, food, and tobacco so that Muslim prisoners, hailing mostly from West and North Africa, could celebrate their religious holidays while in captivity.[79] General Andlauer, head of the overseas section of the Comité central d'assistance aux prisonniers de guerre en captivité, explained to the French departmental delegates how Ramadan and Eid Seghir were celebrated and their importance for Muslim prisoners. Helping the colonial prisoners practice their religion, Andlauer condescendingly argued, demonstrated France's solicitude and tolerance and allowed the colonial prisoners "to feel all the love we have for them and all the interest that we show them to soften the hard times of this captivity of which they do not always understand the necessity and duration."[80] Humanitarian organizations in the colonies sent packages for Eid and Christmas.[81] By January 1941 Muslim prisoners could attend religious services.[82] French support for religious activities encompassed most religious faiths. Catholicism had played an important role in French colonialism and was facilitated in camp life. Catholic prisoners at Montargis were lucky to have a priest among them, who said mass daily.[83] But elsewhere, at the guard's discretion, Catholics were allowed to attend mass in the local church. One priest requested Scapini's help in obtaining permission for all Catholic prisoners working for Ostland to attend Sunday mass.[84]

While German support of Muslim prisoners was mostly rhetorical or limited to select prisoners, the French tried to provide all the colonial prisoners with the necessary means to practice their religions.[85] The French Red Cross provided one Koran per camp, but as they were unable to purchase prayer beads, prisoners were given wooden beads to string themselves.[86] Separate cooking facilities to accommodate religious or cultural preferences were common. The Muslims at Chanzy had their own cook and separate food, even though only a dozen celebrated Ramadan.[87] In camps with only one kitchen, alternatives to pork were provided for Muslim prisoners.[88] In Orléans, nothing official was organized for Muslim prisoners, but some men gathered together for their daily prayers.[89] The Germans also allowed greater religious freedoms when it coincided with their propaganda goals. For example, in March 1942 Germany, motivated by sanitary concerns, decided that prisoners were no longer allowed to wear beards.[90] By June the German High Command had reversed the decision and allowed beards for religious reasons.[91]

The effectiveness of religion as a vehicle for propaganda relied on the individual religious leaders within the camps, giving the Germans a distinct advantage, as they controlled access to the prisoners. Both the Germans and French used religious leaders to ensure the "correct messages" reached colonial prisoners during services. The Germans recruited a number of explicitly anti-French religious students and imams.[92] At Luçon, imams loyal to Germany led the prayer sessions, reminding the "North Africans that they live under the domination of a foreign race."[93] Sometimes the guards joined the prisoners at prayer.

To counteract their influence, the French wanted access to the Frontstalags for the "right" sort of Muslims. The Institut Musulman de Paris, whose mosque was a gift to the North African veterans of the First World War, was asked to nominate three imams from North Africa to visit the North African prisoners.[94] This was a public relations failure for the Vichy regime; it paid for one imam's visit, but the French press gave the German High Command credit for the positive initiative bringing religious support to the Muslim prisoners.[95] Worse, the Germans never actually allowed the French imam into the camps. Instead, he visited sick colonial prisoners in Parisian hospitals and was eventually sent to minister to Tunisian ex-prisoners in the southern zone.[96] Despite the setbacks, the French asked that a West African religious leader be authorized to visit the camps.[97] While much of West and North Africa shared Islam as a religion, their practices were and remain quite different. The French hoped an imam from one of the powerful Senegalese brotherhoods might stop anti-French feelings from permeating the camps.

The search for the Senegalese imam exemplifies how religion became a tool in the propaganda battle between Germany and Vichy and reveals how little officials actually understood about Islam. Before receiving German approval, the authorities in Senegal and France immediately began to argue over whom to send. In February 1941 the German Armistice Commission announced that Prince Aliou Kane (also known as Mamdou Kane or Alioune Kane), a West African imam, had been authorized to visit the Frontstalags.[98] Before the defeat, Georges Mandel, minister of colonies, had given Kane an official role as a leader to the African soldiers. After the French defeat, he ran a small charity bringing assistance to Senegalese prisoners and their families, Oeuvre d'assistance aux prisonniers sénégalais et leurs familles. His exact role during the occupation is unclear, but he was well liked by some West African prisoners. Benefiting from German authorization to circulate and generous donations of food, gasoline, and chocolate from French prefects, Kane had unprecedented access to the colonial prisoners.[99] While the YMCA reported that his visits were greatly appreciated, the French were worried about his increasing influence and dubious loyalties.[100]

In typical fashion, the Vichy authorities chose to avoid direct conflict with the German authorities and continued to search for an alternate imam who spoke one of the major West African languages and belonged to a Senegalese brotherhood.[101] Boisson's choice was Seydou Nourou Tall, who continued to publicly offer support for the French. In June 1941 Tall reminded returning soldiers of their duties toward God and the French: "Behave correctly toward the French. Their politics and treatment of us are superior to all other treatments and politics. Before their arrival in our home, wars between tribes existed: homicide, looting, violence, and oppression were rampant. When Allah brought them to us, their arrival brought peace. We ask Allah to grant them peace, as their peace is our own.... Know that it is God himself (his name be exalted) that made the French superior to us."[102] While Platon and Boisson agreed that Tall was appropriately influential, Platon believed he was too important to leave Senegal. However, Boisson's fear that Kane's charity was being used by the Germans to gather intelligence persuaded Platon to request permission for Tall to visit the colonial prisoners.[103] Unsurprisingly, the Germans denied the request, and Kane continued in his somewhat ambiguous role.

Kane's story starts with the confusing and descends into the ridiculous. He introduced himself as Grand Marabout Prince Mamadou Aliou Kane, but his real name was Alphonse William Kane, and he was most likely Catholic.[104] Kane was unapologetically and publicly grateful to the Germans for their generous welcome and respect, unlike the French, who, Kane argued, were cold and had done everything possible to hinder his work for the African prisoners.[105] Since quiet attempts to distance Kane from the colonial prisoners had failed, the French authorities arrested him on suspicion of being a German agent and stealing supplies for the colonial prisoners. His arrest and trial revealed many existing racial tensions in France. One former colonial prisoner, Saliou N'Doye, rushed to Kane's defense and wrote to the judge: "My imprisoned countrymen and I owe only thanks and gratitude to the Marabout Prince Aliou Mamadou Kane for the great morale and material support he gave us with total devotion and lack of self-interest. . . . He is our only benefactor. One must be noble to risk one's life and suffer from cold and hunger only to bring us relief. The person who claimed he solicited money in the camp and that he sold us sand or took our savings is an infamous villain and a liar."[106]

N'Doye need not have worried about Kane suffering from the cold, as Kane claimed to have 450,000 francs and 1,450 dollars in gold hidden in his apartment. Kane was a brilliant and provocative writer with a great number of supporters of different backgrounds. After his arrest, Kane wrote to the prefect of Loiret, claiming innocence and suggesting that his success in helping the colonial prisoners had kindled jealousy. Kane explained, with hints of paranoia, that his legal advisor and former classmate was blackmailing him, had stolen his money, and seduced his secretary.[107]

Kane's trial was followed with great interest in the press. *Paris-Soir* used the occasion to mock Mandel with the headline "Mandel turns Conman into Great *Marabout!*"[108] Kane's lawyer argued that he should not be convicted because "blacks are big children who do not understand our complex and cruel politics. There are frequent pitfalls, and even the most experienced navigators can run aground." Naturally, the lawyer's racist arguments, which were published in the press, did not sit well with many. Boisson was adamant in a letter to Darlan that "it seems highly inappropriate to represent so lightly, at the helm of a public prosecutor and under the eyes of the occupying authorities, the quality of ties that unite our black army to France. It also seems equally inappropriate to treat such a seasoned crook, who was perfectly aware of his actions, with such indulgence. [He] was hardly a naive native, as I believe the article reported with glee, but a dishonest individual who shamelessly exploited his fellow countrymen." Boisson did not object to the inherently racist idea that "natives" were children; rather, he objected to the idea that Kane could be judged naive and innocent. Furthermore, he felt the references to indigenous soldiers who "died for us without ever having understood anything" were particularly misplaced.[109] Nevertheless, the court accepted the lawyer's argument, and Kane paid only a small fine. The verdict took French paternalism to an extreme and uncomfortable conclusion: if colonial subjects were not considered fully adult, then they could not be responsible for their actions.

Whether Kane was a thief or a great comfort to the Senegalese prisoners, or both, it is interesting to note that N'Doye considered him the sole person to help the Senegalese prisoners in captivity. This marked a huge failure for the French, confirming that the considerable French humanitarian mobilization could not defeat German propaganda, precisely because the Germans controlled access to the colonial prisoners. This realization also influenced how the French, from Vichy to the provisional government, overreacted to colonial soldiers' demands after the war, fearing they were a result of German propaganda. Some West African prisoners, who had not been the focus of German propaganda efforts and remained solidly behind France, felt that their champion had been unfairly accused and removed. Furthermore, the French press published a judicial decision that revealed the ugly truth about the way in which many white French viewed the people subject to colonial rule.

Consequences of Propaganda

By forcing Vichy to question the loyalty of its colonial prisoners, Germany effectively undermined what it had criticized for decades: French pride in its colonial troops. One ex-prisoner, Mohamed Ben Amar, was arrested for "making comments potentially diminishing our prestige in the native's eyes by glorifying German strength."[110] This accusation reveals how the intelligence services interpreted any praise of Germany as an attack on France. Prestige was such a malleable concept that to protect it, the police and military claimed far-reaching powers over the indigenous populations. Surveillance of suspected colonial subjects did not begin with the Vichy regime; colonial administrators had been following and watching the indigenous populations since the early days of colonial expansion. Prompted by a constant fear of armed uprising, the French used surveillance to keep informed on how their soldiers were reintegrating into civilian life. Sometimes the information gathered was timely and accurate. For example, Vichy placed Warrant Officer Boukahri under surveillance in Tunisia after he allegedly recruited forty spies for North Africa.[111] Shortly afterward, forty "sick" colonial prisoners were released from the POW camp Germinian.[112]

Reacting against this double threat—radio broadcasts to North Africa and the influence of returning colonial prisoners—the Vichy authorities severely punished those caught spreading anti-French ideas in North Africa and the colonies. Ahmed Ben Hadj Ali, a career soldier with the 3rd Spahis released from captivity as a First World War veteran, was caught distributing anti-French pamphlets in Meknès. He was arrested and imprisoned for "endangering the external security of the state."[113] Ben Bouchta was also arrested after distributing German articles. Former prisoner El Hachemi Ben Moussa was arrested and sent to prison for declaring at Tedders, Morocco, that "the French are dogs. The Germans are much better than them. Wait until they arrive; then the rich will be like the poor and the poor like the rich."[114] In the Ivory Coast, a returned tirailleur refused to participate in the rubber harvest, violent and exhausting work, saying, "The French can't count on me; they brought me to fight in a country that isn't mine, and I owe my return to my country and my family to the English. If the English ask me to work for them, I will." He was promptly arrested. Boisson felt that the incident was an isolated one, but it showed that the French could not control the information that former soldiers and prisoners received.[115]

An anonymous source in Senegal alleged that the local population was unduly influenced by two recently repatriated colonial prisoners who claimed that the Germans were not racist, had treated them like equals, spoke their language, and ate the same food.[116] After a short investigation, it became clear that none of the accusations were true. The two former colonial prisoners remained outwardly loyal to France. One had been released from captivity immediately. The other, Bari Diop, had been a prisoner in Epinal, where he was treated correctly. Nevertheless, he decided to escape in the middle of winter and reported being "intensely grateful to the French civilians who looked after him completely after his escape and without whom he would never have been able to cross into the free zone."[117]

While some prisoners accepted the benefits that accompanied dueling French and German propaganda efforts, few became true converts. Even if, as Scheck argues, an important minority of prisoners accepted German anti-French propaganda, more were purely interested in the associated material benefits.[118] Accepting early release did not automatically make one a "true believer." Some "spies" reported directly to the French authorities once free, which confirmed French suspicions that targeted prisoners were being surreptitiously released. North African colonial prisoners near Bordeaux refused the offers of early release.[119] Capt. Ahmed Rafa explained that because he actively counteracted the anti-French propaganda, he and six others were the only ones among fifty colonial officers not released early.[120] If Rafa is correct in his calculations, only 14 percent of the officers in his camp chose to remain in captivity as a matter of principle. Rafa was clearly an exceptional officer who took his duty to the military and France quite seriously, and he may have joined the Resistance after his release. In January 1940 his military review had described him as an "*évolué* in the good sense of the term and perfectly devoted."[121] In 1950 he was named a *chevalier de la legion d'honneur*.

Placing the colonial prisoners within a binary of loyal or disloyal actively flattened French understanding of how captivity affected the colonial prisoners and sometimes led to overreactions at the hint of complaint. For most colonial prisoners, refusing to accept German propaganda did not necessarily mean acceptance, or love, of French colonial rule. There was a broad spectrum of political views, from those of active spies to those of men like Rafa who would spend their career in the French military. Most colonial prisoners understood the realities of life under colonial domination and believed that silence on political questions was the best means to survive and return home.

Generally, recruiting colonial prisoners for military roles was largely unsuccessful. At Quimper, German officers tried, and failed, to convince North African prisoners that because of "improved Franco-German relations, they could fight for the French cause in the ranks of the soldiers of the Reich."[122] Even without all the details of collaboration, few colonial prisoners were willing to fight for Germany. At Charleville, they categorically refused to fight against Russia and Great Britain.[123] There were a few exceptions: several hundred colonial prisoners volunteered to fight with the anti-Bolshevik league or the Phalange africaine in North Africa. Seven Moroccans joined the German Army.[124] According to French intelligence, this impressed the Moroccan population of Dakar, who felt that having one of their own leading the Moroccan volunteers on the Russian front made Germany a protector of Islam.[125] These recruitment attempts were designed to showcase the multinational nature of the German Army, which, as David Motadel demonstrates, recruited tens of thousands of Muslims into the Wehrmacht and Waffen ss.[126]

French fear of German propaganda was tied to the level of French control in each colony. This manifested in a belief that prisoners of "certain races" were more vulnerable than others. As with many stereotypes, there was no consensus on which race was at the greatest risk. French doctor Jean Guérin's observations show his prejudices. He claimed that the North Africans were prone to lying and laziness, promoting resistance through inertia, whereas the Malagasy passively obeyed and were often used as workers. Guérin reckoned that "the loyalty of the Senegalese and the Malagasy appeared intact. However, the North Africans, who were targeted by discreet German propaganda and having characters that tend towards protest, often underestimate the French government's interest in them."[127] Others believed that as a professional army, the Moroccans were least likely to be swayed. Martin Thomas explains that Algerians living in France before the war and Berber Kabylie intellectuals, as well as Tunisian conscripts, were likely to accept anti-French propaganda.[128] In a rare demonstration of anti-French feeling, Nguyen-Van-Lai, an Indochinese civilian worker, publicly claimed that Indochina was better under Japanese rule.[129] Very few colonial prisoners were convinced by vague promises of independence under German rule, but morale issues influenced their opinions on France.

The effect of German propaganda in the colonies was equally underwhelming. The indigenous populations remained generally indifferent to German propaganda or, at best, reluctantly neutral toward France.[130] In Tangiers, indigenous agents working for Germany were accused of attempting to organize, without much success, a pro-German and anti-Bolshevik demonstration to coincide with German entry into Moscow.[131] In Algeria, a French report declared in August 1941 that the rural indigenous populations were indifferent to the form of government but remained loyal to the marshal. The report confirmed that many Algerians regarded Germany as a strong country and supported it against the Russians and that they followed the measures taken against the Jews with interest.[132] Again, this was not unlike a strong current of French opinion at the time. Boisson argued that anti-French propaganda in French West Africa was largely ineffective and that the colonial administration actively counteracted any acts of denigration, concluding that the most effective neutralization of German propaganda would be done directly in the Frontstalags.[133]

Some colonial prisoners felt they had not been actively targeted by German propaganda. This is hardly surprising, as colonial prisoners would have been quite careful about how they presented German propaganda to the French authorities to avoid becoming targets of suspicion themselves.[134] Makan Traoré and Mamadou Koné reported only one clumsy attempt to influence them, when guards claimed that after the war the Germans would come to Africa and become their chiefs.[135] A group of seventy North African prisoners repatriated in May 1941 claimed no knowledge of German propaganda.[136] A July 1941 report noted that overall, interviews with released colonial prisoners reassured the French that "German propaganda ha[d] not deeply touched the mass of North African prisoners." The report explained, "Most of those who return remember the abuse of which they were victims, the harsh treatment that was imposed upon them and the acts of cruelty they witnessed. They are unanimous in praising the kindness of the French doctors and effectiveness of relief efforts by the Red Cross. Overall, the repatriated North Africans, the Moroccans in particular, display good spirits, and their morale does not appear to have suffered much from the hardships endured during their captivity."[137]

One escaped prisoner said that German propaganda had used a literary Arabic that most prisoners could not understand. In his opinion, efforts to convert Moroccan prisoners were in vain, and the "Senegalese community remains tightly sealed against them and completely hostile. . . . On the other hand, the discreet propaganda carried out by the French Red Cross in the camp (distribution of two highly appreciated weekly meals of couscous) has had the best effect."[138] By mid-1942 Louis Koeltz, commander of the 19th Military Region (Algeria and Tunisia), reported to the governor of Algeria that the German propaganda efforts were not as effective as previously feared.[139]

Despite believing that German propaganda had generally failed in its aims, the French continued to use the specter of propaganda as the catchall explanation for any conflicts with its colonized populations. However, much of the colonial prisoners' discontent was due to the difficulties of captivity, rather than to German propaganda. Letters from Toucouleur and Foulah prisoners (two of the ethnic groups in Senegal) revealed that they were suffering in captivity and wondering when they would be released.[140] In language often reserved for white prisoners, they were described as reacting stoically to their plight: "The colonial prisoners in France naturally wish to return home but bear their captivity with courage."[141] Characterizing colonial prisoners as bravely enduring the difficulties of captivity served two purposes: it equated complaints with cowardice and imposed a sense of unity, through loyalty, on a diverse population.

Visibly different types of treatment, especially between civilian workers and colonial prisoners, shaped opinions more effectively than propaganda could. North African civilian workers in the occupied zone earned between 130 and 150 francs per day, compared with 10 francs for prisoners. In fact, much of the civilian workers' praise of Germany to other North Africans in France and Algeria was sincere and spontaneous.[142] The French were unable to limit the recruitment of North African workers or influence their pay rates, nor were they willing to increase salaries in the colonies to prevent colonial subjects from working for the Germans. Instead, the French fought to keep prisoners and workers apart. As seen in the previous chapter, even when colonial prisoners were converted to labor units working directly for the Germans, they retained the normal prisoner salary. Anyone, regardless of nationality and without exposure to propaganda, would wonder why one worker was paid ten times more than another. Legitimate complaints about salaries, or later the demobilization bonuses, were regularly conflated with German propaganda, as that was easier than making systemic changes.

Both the French and the Germans understood the implications of a sustained propaganda campaign aimed at the colonial prisoners generally and North Africans specifically. It went beyond cultivating the opinions of a relatively limited population; it was another arena where Germany could showcase the unequal power dynamic. In the spring of 1942 the German authorities asked permission to bring 250 Senegalese prisoners to Italy to make a film. François Darlan, de facto head of the Vichy government as Pétain's trusted advisor, felt that using colonial prisoners as extras in a propaganda film benefited the occupying authorities to the prisoners' detriment, but he feared that if they refused permission, Germany would only force the issue without listening to their concerns.[143] The French were aware of their own limitations and again hoped that cooperation would minimize the impact on the colonial prisoners while safeguarding French prestige. In attempting to hide its impotence from the colonial prisoners, the Vichy regime took the risk that the colonial prisoners would begin to question why the French government seemed to actively participate in German efforts, which played directly into German propaganda aims. Eventually, Darlan gave his permission and pushed Scapini to request continued Geneva Convention protection and that the prisoners be accompanied by someone familiar with Senegalese troops who could protect them, if necessary, from racism in a population unfamiliar with Africans. Darlan, while sincere in his desire to protect the colonial prisoners from Italian and German racism, was, like many French leaders at the time, less self-reflective on his own racial views.

The colonial prisoners were caught between conflicting German and French imperial aims. The Vichy authorities dreamed of colonial expansion to compensate for territorial losses in metropolitan France but never received concrete assurances from Germany that the empire would remain intact after the war. Germany, in turn, hid promises made to Italy and Spain from France. In the meantime, the colonial prisoners became one of the main arenas for competing French and German propaganda efforts. Unable to open a consular network throughout the French Empire, the Germans focused their energies on the colonial subjects under their direct control. Tensions grew because the French feared German influence over the colonial prisoners but lacked the political clout to stop it. Instead, the French mobilized humanitarian aid to the colonial prisoners as part of a concerted effort to keep their allegiance. For the Vichy regime, propaganda was a political question and concern. French intervention on the colonial prisoners' behalf was driven by the fear of politicized colonial prisoners returning to their home colonies. On a material level, the colonial prisoners benefited from this fear, which translated into interest in their care. However, the consequences of this French assumption that politically aware colonial prisoners spelled the beginning of the French downfall in the colonies would be seen the violent repressions of the first signs of "disloyalty."

German and French propaganda efforts targeting the colonial prisoners were part of a larger web connecting internal and external concerns, war and postwar aims, imperial goals, and how each power viewed its country's future. The Germans hoped to encourage and harness chaos in the French and British colonies in their struggle to conquer North Africa and the Middle East. They used emotions, revolt, desires for independence, and calls to God, and they mobilized students and religious leaders to encourage political thought and nationalist debates. For the French, successful propaganda would result in stability, obedience, loyalty, and recognition that France was the superior European power. The defeat damaged French prestige and confidence, increasing worries about potential German influence on the colonial soldiers. The colonial prisoners had seen material proof that the white French leaders could be defeated in Europe and divided in the colonies. To regain prestige and ensure continued control, the French needed to present strength in another way—and not just to the colonial prisoners but also to the French in the metropole, to show them that there was strength and hope in collaboration but only weakness and division in resistance.

For the colonial prisoners, rejecting German propaganda and remaining outwardly loyal to France was not the same as supporting French colonialism. Many colonial soldiers believed they were doing their duty by resisting overt German efforts to influence them while they were in captivity. This did not mean they supported every aspect of the French colonial regime or that they would not protest unfair treatment once back under French rule. Knowledge of the colonial prisoners' real thoughts and feelings on captivity, propaganda, France, and Germany are missing from the primary sources, which are often intelligence briefings or reports given to French officers. Even so, it was clear that as captivity continued, the colonial prisoners became increasing disillusioned with their situation. The colonial prisoners' opinions were as nuanced and varied as the men themselves. As they lingered in France, their frustration with the lack of change grew. This can be seen clearly in the colonial prisoners' reactions to repatriation and release. Legitimate concerns like delayed repatriation, fear of unemployment, and problems with demobilization bonuses and pensions were much more damaging to colonial loyalties than German propaganda.

9

THE LONG ROAD HOME, 1940–1945
Repatriation and Reintegration

As soon as a prisoner was captured, he began to wonder when he could return home. Some prisoners were released after diplomatic negotiations between the Vichy and German governments or because they were sick or injured. Others actively sought a way out by feigning illnesses or escaping. Released white prisoners were demobilized in France and, after three days of administrative formalities, were returned to their families. For the colonial prisoners, leaving the Frontstalags was the first of many steps in their long road home. Upon arrival in the unoccupied zone, the now former colonial prisoners were sent to Vichy-run camps until they could be repatriated to their colonies of origin. This was ostensibly to maintain discipline and counteract any residual German propaganda. They were almost always demobilized in the colonies. During the first half of the war, transportation could be found more or less regularly, depending on the British blockade and available ships. After the Allied landings in North Africa in November 1942, colonial POWs lingered in the southern zone camps or were sent back to work for the Germans, until the maritime routes were reopened in 1944. This division between pre– and post–November 1942 marked a fundamental change in how prisoners were received once back in the colonies. In the early period, returning prisoners were generally greeted with a celebration and debriefing before being quickly dispersed to their villages. While many of the policies for reintegration, and even the French staff, remained in place, the international and local contexts to which colonial prisoners returned changed dramatically between 1942 and 1945.

The stress of captivity, frustration at delays, and anger over the unfair payment systems were all exacerbated by long land and sea voyages back to the colonies. Discrepancies between how the colonial prisoners imagined their return home and the realities of returning to French colonial rule led in some cases to clashes between colonial authorities and former prisoners. By routinely overestimating the colonial prisoners' susceptibility to German propaganda and politicizing even the smallest legitimate requests, the French reacted as though the former prisoners were constantly on the edge of revolt. The drawn-out processes of homecoming throughout the Second World War became one of the many roots of postwar conflict. A few violent incidents were noted under the Vichy regime, but the most dissatisfaction, understandably, came from colonial prisoners repatriated in 1944 and 1945 after four or five years of captivity and internment, the last two without news from home.

During their captivity, the colonial prisoners were nourished on Vichy rhetoric that accompanied food parcels and deliveries, emphasizing imperial unity and celebrating their sacrifices in defense of the motherland. They received packages, spent time with white civilians, and most importantly, were allowed to complain about conditions, other prisoners, even sometimes the French. The relaxation of some previously impenetrable boundaries led some colonial prisoners to believe that France was changing and that the distances between colonized and colonizer were decreasing. The limits of that solidarity became clear when the colonial prisoners were released back under French control. Rhetoric and the Vichy's regime's decreasing autonomy could not protect the colonial prisoners from the worsening conditions in France and increased pressures from Germany's total-war economy. Yet hope returned with 1944. It became clear that the Vichy regime would not survive the impending German defeat. Roosevelt's "Four Freedoms" speech of January 1944, building on ideas in the 1941 Atlantic Charter, suggested that a new era of self-determination was imminent. The Brazzaville Conference, hosted by de Gaulle, showed that France would not be left behind; de Gaulle praised the colonies' contribution to the victory and promised reform in return. The world had transformed dramatically while the colonial soldiers were prisoners, yet once home, the French colonial administration appeared as inflexible to change as ever.

Leaving the Frontstalags

Release from captivity was a complex administrative process: first the German authorities decided which prisoners were eligible, then transportation to the southern zone was organized, and only then could arrangements for repatriation be made. Because of fuel shortages, prisoners usually traveled by train to the southern zone. Once they had crossed the demarcation line, they were officially back under French control. As prisoners made their way home, they moved between the legal jurisdictions of several different offices. While they were in captivity, the MBF, German High Command, and camp commanders decided how the colonial prisoners would live and work. Once prisoners were in the southern zone, the French general staff took over, specifically its First and Fourth Offices.[1] The First Office organized logistics behind the prisoners' repatriation, allocated tasks, and set the budget for personnel and material goods. More importantly for the prisoners, the First Office set the rules for captivity leave, demobilization, and how different kinds of prisoners could be discharged. The Fourth Office concentrated on transportation and organizing convoys. Once the prisoners were back in the colonies, they were passed to the local administrations. In North Africa, the residents general in Tunisia and Morocco and the governor general of Algeria, along with the Commissariat au reclassement, helped former prisoners reintegrate into civilian life and, when possible, find work.[2]

The French considered the transition out of captivity to be a determining moment in ensuring the mental stability and loyalty of the colonial and white prisoners alike. In the summer of 1941 detailed instructions for their reintegration were issued:

> If the prisoner, still mentally numb, is welcomed warmly, he will discover, with love, the new face of France. Poorly received upon arrival and neglected in the first weeks home, he will choose a spiritual and moral path unfavorable to the new society. This is extremely important. It is essential he avoid cumbersome administrative formalities. It is appropriate to clothe him, feed him, pay him, and guide the individual, as early as possible, to his new existence. What has been said is broadly applicable

to native North Africans and colonials, with the difference that their repatriation to their country of origin is required as soon as possible.[3]

Unfortunately, the colonial prisoners did not escape the "cumbersome administrative formalities," and the new face of France was actually the old conservative, imperial one. Colonial prisoners received a warm welcome, often with coffee and cigarettes; underwent a preliminary medical visit; and were reintroduced to the strong military discipline typically imposed on the colonial troops.

In March 1941 a triage center was opened near Limoges to welcome returning prisoners who had been released individually or in large groups. The Limoges center greeted returning prisoners; facilitated medical exams, including a chest X-ray to detect tuberculosis; and separated prisoners needing immediate hospitalization. The healthy prisoners were sent to a regrouping center, where they generally spent two or three days. These temporary shelters prepared prisoners for the next stage of the journey by separating the colonial prisoners by destination, supplying military or civilian clothes, paying an advance on their salary (two hundred francs for a soldier on a daily wage), and providing rations for the next stage of their trip.[4] One center processed approximately three thousand repatriated prisoners during its first three months of operation. Still under the jurisdiction of the French military, white officers who had been released from captivity to fight against the Free French in the Levant (Syria and Lebanon) escorted the colonial prisoners from triage to new camps.[5] After the loss of Syria and Lebanon to the Allies, the Germans required these officers to remain in the unoccupied zone.

By providing shelter and guidance for their readjustment to postcaptivity life, a paternalistic Vichy government hoped to reorient the colonial prisoners to their "proper role" in French society, a role that was subservient to that of returning white prisoners. At the same time, the French press praised the welcome parties for colonial prisoners, where mulled wine, biscuits, chocolate, and cigarettes were provided as a sign of Vichy's continued commitment to the French Empire.[6] Sick colonial prisoners received a similar welcome, although they usually arrived in the southern zone in smaller groups. Sometimes religious or military figures presided over these formalities, where hot food and cigarettes were distributed as colonial prisoners listened to military music designed to impress and evoke pride in French military prowess.[7]

The general principle of welcoming returning prisoners held for both white and colonial prisoners, but with different aims. The Vichy government wanted to prove to the white prisoners that France had changed, that the failings leading to the defeat and their capture had been fixed. For the colonial prisoners, the French took a different tack. Darlan, for example, believed that refreshments and speeches missed the point. Rather, he argued, "it is essential that these men are informed, as soon as they enter France, of the marshal's work, his politics, and his government's actions and that they do not feel they have arrived in a country where they will find indiscipline and slackness."[8] Darlan wanted the colonial prisoners to understand that their sacrifice had already been recognized and sufficiently rewarded during their captivity through Pétain's efforts on their behalf. In turn, they were expected to respond with loyalty and, more importantly, discipline. Sending the white prisoners home quickly demonstrated government and military support for French families, one of the pillars of the National Revolution. Since the colonial prisoners could not immediately return home, the French used this period to reiterate the "healthy" opinions expected of colonial subjects.

All of the Vichy regime's actions toward returning colonial prisoners reflected the mentality of a government conforming to an imperial status quo. When the colonial prisoners eventually arrived in the colonies, they were dispatched to their villages as soon as possible, not out of concern for their families, but rather to avoid the potential spread of anti-French ideas and avoid conflicts in the urban centers.[9] The French felt that individuals were easier to control and reintegrate into their prewar roles. As seen, this fear of "native uprisings" had a long prehistory in the empire and had been a contributing factor to the decision by French military leaders in North Africa to follow Pétain and not de Gaulle.[10] Now this fear was compounded by the return of trained colonial soldiers whose experiences in France had removed more of their illusions about the colonial power. Many French leaders felt the solution was to prove that France remained a strong imperial power and expected the colonial prisoners to respond accordingly. Readjustment and reeducation began as soon as the colonial prisoners arrived in the southern zone.

Under the layers of bureaucracy was a complicated system designed to maintain the colonial prisoners' attachment to France while limiting their freedom of movement. A major difference between white and indigenous soldiers was the right to be demobilized in France. Following the tradition established after the First World War, colonial soldiers had to be demobilized in their colonies of origin.[11] Colonial prisoners who had French citizenship and had lived in France before the war did have the right to be demobilized in France. However, exercising that right proved challenging. After escaping from captivity, Robert Eboué made his way to Fréjus, where the French refused to demobilize him despite his citizenship and long-time residence in France. Robert left Fréjus discreetly and went to Lyons, known to be a center for the French Resistance, where he was eventually demobilized.[12]

In 1942 Vichy used a Third Republic law to allow hospitalized white prisoners to be demobilized in situ.[13] These prisoners were allowed to remain in military hospitals but were considered free of their military obligations. The colonial prisoners were never given similar rights. In March 1942 an exception was granted for North African prisoners who had lived in France before the war and could not be immediately repatriated. Instead, they were demobilized at the Centre démobilisateur de Montferrand (Puy-de-Dôme). After demobilization, they were required to report to a center in Sainte-Foy-lès-Lyon (Rhône) until they could obtain individual work contracts. Most of the North African prisoners released before November 1942 were sent home to North Africa, including the majority of the ten thousand released by the German authorities in 1942.[14] Only the sick prisoners remained in France.

Obtaining transportation to the colonies was the next challenge. Usually, colonial soldiers traveled by sea from southern France to one of the port cities in Northern Africa, such as Oran, Port-Lyautey, or Casablanca. Oumar Diallo took the sea route to Algeria, then traveled overland from Oran to Casablanca. From Casablanca, he was given one month's leave before returning to his military service in Thiès, Senegal.[15] It is unclear whether the French arranged travel for Diallo or whether he was required to make his own way to Thiès, a distance of seventeen hundred miles. Tirailleur Aba Mame had a simpler experience: repatriated on the hospital boat *Canada*, he arrived in Dakar on January 2, 1942, and was sent to the infirmary in Thiaroye, where he remained until invalided out of the army.[16] The *Canada* continued to travel between France and the African colonies. In September 1942 it was carrying sick prisoners to Madagascar. Both the Direction des troupes coloniales and the colonial ministry wanted to delay the ship's departure because of the risk of a British attack on Madagascar, but the Admiralty insisted, and the ship left.[17] As predicted, the British attacked Madagascar in May 1942, but they did not occupy the island until November. It is unclear what happened to the colonial prisoners on the *Canada*.

Prisoner transportation was affected by the external political and rapidly changing military situations. Factors outside of the Vichy regime's control—the Allied blockade, lack of available ships, and changing military loyalties—all determined when the colonial prisoners could return home. Understandably, many prisoners directed their frustrations at the French for the worsening conditions in which they waited for an increasingly delayed voyage home.

Home at Last

Arriving back in the colonies after months, even years, of absence was an important moment for the colonial prisoners. They could begin the slow healing process and look forward to a new civilian life—a life where, because of their military sacrifices, they hoped they would get good jobs in the colonial administration and be able to better provide for their families. The soldiers had traveled abroad, experienced war and captivity, maybe even managed a daring escape. Some were healthy, others sick, still others broken by battle and imprisonment in ways their families had difficulties understanding. They had lived with the French, eaten at their tables, made friends. Now they were home. Yet instead of being returned to their families with payments and gratitude for services rendered, they found that their homecoming became an integral part of the French campaign to reassert dominance and control over the colonies.

Colonial administrators used the prisoners' arrival home as an opportunity to prove the defeat had not changed the empire. In North Africa, Gen.

Paul Beynet preferred that the prestigious Armée d'Afrique welcome the prisoners home to showcase a strong and intact French army and hide the reductions in numbers imposed by the armistice.[18] This display of strength was one of many acts of counterpropaganda specifically targeting residual German propaganda and the loss of French prestige. Throughout North Africa, returning prisoners were greeted in similar ways. In Sétif, Algeria, the sous-prefect Lauvel, Colonel Schwartz, and the mayor of Bordj Catoni hosted a reception for three hundred returning colonial prisoners. Together they laid a wreath on the Monument aux morts. The solemn ceremony ended with a parade led by the former prisoners to the local hall, where traditional couscous and coffee sponsored by the governor general were served. At the end of the party, the colonial prisoners were given fabric to make new clothes.[19] It was important for the colonial prisoners to return home from war well clothed. Many believed they had fought for an important cause and wanted to return home looking as though it had mattered. When colonial soldiers arrived in Algeria in uniform, they were given military clothes, a greatcoat, underclothes, and a pair of work boots.[20] The gift of cloth was in direct response to complaints that colonial prisoners had had been forced to exchange their comfortable warm uniforms for cheaper clothes.[21]

The first few days after the colonial prisoners' return to the colonies followed a similar pattern to those after their arrival in the unoccupied zone. The former prisoners were moved through centers designed to process their administrative status and assess their physical and mental health. They were reinterviewed about their captivity experiences. These interviews were mainly to learn about German propaganda and gather intelligence on the Frontstalags. However, they were also a place for colonial prisoners to air specific grievances about captivity or its aftermath. In August 1941 the POW service in Algiers interviewed thirty-eight hundred escaped or repatriated colonial prisoners.[22] Eventually, the former prisoners were demobilized, and travel arrangements were made to send them the rest of the way home.[23] For prisoners without families or in need of more support, the Direction du travail au gouvernement général in Algeria ran a welcome center for returning colonial prisoners. It had only fifty beds and showers, but the kitchen was capable of serving one thousand meals. The center was designed to help the colonial prisoners reintegrate and provide a subtle means of monitoring their morale.

Repatriation to the colonies was the moment for the Vichy regime to assess the impact of captivity on the former colonial prisoners. The French had been discreetly supervising the return of colonial soldiers from June 1940. Colonial governors gathered reports from the local administrators on the mental status of returned soldiers, their "character," and their readjustment to civilian life. In Morocco in October 1940 the returning soldiers appeared tired but loyal to France: "Their spirit of simple and fatalistic men makes it difficult for them to understand such a rapid and brutal defeat."[24] The French used these reports to gather information on captivity, especially in the early months, when the Scapini Mission had little information on their prisoners. Later the administrators were asked to assess the returned colonial prisoners' attitudes and potential demands they might make on the French government. These reports could be quite detailed, even when the colonial prisoners had not remained in captivity long.[25] For example, the governor of the Ivory Coast reported at length that former prisoner Touré Vamoutari led a quiet life and appeared to be a devoted and conscientious civil servant. His only friend, Amara Touré, worked for customs. Vamoutari avoided political discussions, and his morality and behavior were irreproachable.[26] Most reports confirmed that the former colonial prisoners' behavior and actions conveyed their continued loyalty to France.

Any anti-French action was quickly suppressed and isolated. Soldiers who grumbled or had small complaints were separated and sent home quickly.[27] Duboin in Sudan (Mali) reported differences in attitude between the soldiers from Goa (Mali) and those from Dahomey (Benin). Allegedly, the soldiers from Goa behaved perfectly and were excited to return home to their families. They discussed, without bitterness or complaints, the battles they had fought. However, those from Dahomey had "different mindsets," which forced, or allowed, Duboin to crack down on the ringleaders.[28] In Algeria, similar reports recorded how the former colonial prisoners reintegrated. In Bou-Saada, they returned to their old lives, "safely" dispersed throughout the population without negative consequences.[29] Most Algerian prisoners had been released because they were farmers or miners or because of ill health. Outwardly, their morale generally seemed high, and their loyalty and fidelity did not appear affected by captivity.[30]

Most returning prisoners were preoccupied with practical concerns rather than "disloyalty." Quite a few prisoners returned to Tablat, Algeria, in early 1942. They were in good spirits and appeared to be loyal. However, the local French administrator reported "a certain brevity in their responses to questions asked about the camp authorities' behavior toward them. This attitude does not appear to respond to orders, but rather [displays] a desire to forget a period of physical and mental suffering."[31] Reintegration into the colonial system was designed to reduce the potential for conflicts. These reports reassured the Vichy regime that its subjects remained loyal to France. In reality, they tell us very little about how the former colonial prisoners felt about their return to life after the war.

Practically, and officially, the former colonial prisoners reacted positively to French efforts to facilitate their reintegration into civilian life. The governor general of Algeria recognized in early 1942 that the conditions to which the colonial prisoners returned were harder than those before their mobilization: "[This] difficult economic situation and lack of clothing especially provoke their disappointment and a particularly sharp discontent, since they were assured of benevolence and a special concern." He warned against blaming the former prisoners' reactions on German propaganda but admitted that the increased numbers of returning prisoners forced the administration to be vigilant. By acknowledging the legitimate reasons behind the former colonial prisoners' malaise, he was able to effectively fight it, in the short term, by doubling their allocations of food and clothing during their first two months home. Additionally, the returning soldiers were given either a job or a loan of seeds to start an agricultural project.[32]

Two months later, the prefect of Alger noted that the former prisoners in his region were generally happy with the small amounts of cash and extra supplies provided. They felt that the assistance had helped them bear the current difficulties, which they found easier than captivity. The overarching goal was to refocus the colonial prisoners' attention away from France and back on local matters and everyday struggles; rapidly dispersing the former prisoners to their villages and maintaining a close eye on them were key. The prefect acknowledged that the employment problems facing other areas had not yet affected his prisoners, who were mostly farmers who had retaken control of their small or medium-size farms.[33]

Finding work was a major concern for returning soldiers, many of whom believed that their military service entitled them to jobs within the French administration after the war. Legal measures did protect jobs for returning soldiers; the June 30, 1941, law even required companies to hire more returned soldiers than the number of employees they had lost to the war effort.[34] Administrative jobs were rare, and many soldiers did not want the physical labor offered, preferring instead to wait for a more prestigious job, which would never materialize.[35] In Algeria, only a few returning POWs obtained artisanal work.[36] A French administrator complained that returning prisoners "systematically refused all job offers for manual workers or laborers." He explained, "We are trying to make them understand that the 'jobs' that they want are limited and it is in their best interest to accept what they are offered."[37] Aware that the limited number of jobs available in the colonial administration could not satisfy the demand, 1941 guidelines stated that former prisoners should be sent home immediately to wait for work.[38]

Differing expectations led to frustrations for both colonial prisoners and employers. Reserving jobs for returning soldiers was also fraught in other countries, including the United Kingdom and Ireland. However, in the colonies, officials bristled at any hint of entitlement. The governor general of Algeria warned that former prisoners felt that they deserved prestigious positions, such as foreman or rural policeman, and were often disappointed. He thought that the problem lay with the demobilization centers, which had led colonial prisoners to believe the local authorities owed them a good job with benefits.[39] As seen, the French authorities were generally nervous when the colonial prisoners specifically, or colonial subjects more generally, felt they were "owed" anything. The French were aware of the colonial soldiers' expectations and found them exaggerated—but did that reaction reflect disrespect for "simple native soldiers" or a lack of funds, or a combination of both?

Instead, new villages on arable land were created to accommodate returning soldiers and their families. In North Africa, to facilitate reintegration into colonial civilian society, returning prisoners were given parcels of collective or state-owned land, which allowed them to immediately return to work.[40] With an indigenous population of over six million Muslims and a settler population of under one million, these efforts were also a means of distancing the indigenous populations from urban centers. If no collective land was available, authorities were told to purchase lots for the returning prisoners. Former prisoners also received an advance to permit them to survive on their new land until the next harvest. By July 1941 over fifteen hundred families had been placed on these allotments.[41] A year later houses were under construction on lots ranging from seventy to two hundred hectares. The goal was to create a model hamlet where a dozen families, equipped with the necessary tools for tilling and for livestock, would live and work. This "return to the land" was one of the backbones of the Vichy regime. The National Revolution praised the agrarian lifestyle and the moral stock of the peasants. In some ways these developments responded to local needs, like creating more irrigated land.[42]

The life of a farmer was full of challenges, which the French authorities hoped might distract the former prisoners from other claims. The creation of idealized villages ensured that the veterans owed the French for their new houses and lands, while facilitating French surveillance of the former soldiers and breaking down the cohesion of the indigenous populations, something the French felt was particularly important in Algeria, where the minority white settlers lived in fear of an uprising against the harsh racist exploitation of the indigenous populations. These "generous gifts" from France were designed to bind the soldiers, literally and figuratively, to their lands of origin. The new clothes and traditional food were meant to further distance them from their experiences in the metropole and reinforce local and cultural ties.

Having implemented welcome lunches, given gifts of land and cloth, and provided a few jobs, the French colonial authorities felt that they had made a considerable effort to help the colonial prisoners reintegrate. Yet many colonial prisoners believed that they had been promised more. Explicit criticism of the French remained rare, but was most likely to occur when soldiers were unable to return home. This was the case for soldiers from French Equatorial Africa after August 1940, when Felix Eboué declared his support for de Gaulle. Platon feared that if these men were sent home, they would reenlist (either voluntarily or forcibly) with the Free French and be used against Vichy forces elsewhere in the empire. Unsurprisingly, the soldiers were unhappy to find themselves doing forced labor in Morocco instead of being sent home to their families.[43] The soldiers allegedly caused great problems in Morocco, so Boisson suggested sending them to the Sudan, which had a similar climate to their home country. The question of climate hid the real benefit for the French: moving them to an isolated area would avoid their "infecting" the populations in French West Africa with their negative attitude. Here again, signs of discontent were attributed to outside influence, not to potentially legitimate grievances.

Despite the difficulties and frustrations, repatriations between 1940 and 1942 were overwhelmingly peaceful. A revolt in Kindia, Guinea, on November 28, 1940, was a notable exception. Seventy-five miles from the coast, Kindia was an important stop on the Conakry-Kankan railway and a meeting point of four major roads. The newly arrived soldiers had received only five hundred francs of their demobilization bonus, and that payment had been split in two. Frustrated by the lack of transparency regarding their demobilization bonus, four hundred demobilized soldiers and former prisoners revolted. During the protest, several white soldiers were wounded. In response, one of the protesting soldiers was killed and others imprisoned.[44] The governor of Guinea's initial report recognized that lack of payment had inspired the Kindia revolt. Understanding the roots of this protest and why it had turned violent could have been an important lesson for the French for future repatriations. Instead, the governor changed his official interpretation of the protest and blamed it on Communist and Gaullist propaganda.[45] The protest in Kindia indicated that returning soldiers believed that payment was an issue important enough to spark a potentially violent protest.

The Liberation of France

By 1943 the Free French and Allies had control of North Africa, and Boisson had finally rallied French West Africa to their cause. The Vichy regime had lost its empire, and the remaining thirty-seven thousand colonial prisoners had no hope of returning home until the war was over, as maritime channels between metropolitan France and the colonies were closed.[46] In the empire, change was promised. At the beginning of 1944 de Gaulle, Felix Eboué, and René Pleven (leading members of the external Resistance) and the colonial governors and administrators gathered in Brazzaville, birthplace of the Free French, to plan for the future of the French Empire. The Brazzaville Conference planned to "give" Africans their "deserved place" in the French Empire.[47] Participants imagined practical solutions to improve economic development, health, and education for the native populations. Reclaiming French grandeur, this conference promised a new future for the French Empire based on its critical role during the war.

The final years of captivity were the hardest. Rationing throughout France increased. Forced recruitment for German labor needs increased. After the D-day landings on June 6, 1944, conditions degraded significantly for the colonial prisoners. Active fighting returned to France as the Allies slowly liberated the country. Fearing that the remaining prisoners would be integrated into the advancing Allied armies, the Germans forcibly brought between ten thousand and thirteen thousand colonial prisoners to Germany. This retreat was the most dangerous time for colonial prisoners since their capture in 1940. Conditions continued to deteriorate as they moved east: camps were overcrowded, supplies were limited, and they were forced to do dangerous war work under Allied attack.[48] Eleven colonial prisoners were killed and fifty-three were wounded when Dungen (Rhineland) was bombed on October 30, 1944.[49] The wounded were hospitalized in Germany.

Paris was liberated on August 25, 1944. The provisional government replaced the Vichy regime and two weeks later declared all laws passed under Vichy illegal and void. Many of these colonial prisoners did not return to France until the end of 1944. Another 38 colonial prisoners who had escaped in Belgium were not moved from Brussels to Lille until September 1944.[50] The Colonial Service recorded that 252 colonial prisoners remained in Germany until December 1944.[51] Conditions were not much better in France, and Myron Echenberg accurately describes 1944–45 as the "winter of the colonial prisoners' greatest discontent" because of a lack of food, clothing, and housing and the severe military discipline.[52] The last colonial prisoners in Germany returned to France in 1945. Twenty-two Moroccans were liberated from the Russian Front in April 1945, but the final group of colonial prisoners to return to France were those working for the Todt Organization on the Channel Islands.[53] The islands were not liberated until May 9, 1945, having been cut off from Britain for five years. By this stage, the colonial prisoners had endured five years in captivity, either as German prisoners or in semimilitarized work groups guarded by French officers.

The liberation of France significantly changed the context in which the colonial prisoners were considered. A unified and liberated France, with its empire behind it, was victorious, and Germany was the enemy once again. The colonial prisoners as a group never regained the political weight they had in the early years of the Vichy regime. On the contrary, colonial administrators, whether Vichy holdouts or early supporters of de Gaulle, pushed for a return to "colonial normalcy," where France did not bargain for its subjects' loyalty. Still, the provisional government felt it was potentially dangerous to repatriate colonial prisoners with low morale due to German propaganda and exacerbated by "Vichy's incompetence": "It follows that under these conditions the morale of the North Africans suffered, and they remain resentful toward France, having been abandoned after giving their health for its service, which will certainly hurt French interests on their return to Africa. It is desirable to get these seriously ill or disabled prisoners packages like the ones they received in captivity; the *médecin-colonel* in each hospital in the southern zone could provide a list. Amitiés africaines was only able, on one occasion, to provide them with biscuits and a little jam."[54]

The provisional government's solution was to provide better parcels for the former colonial prisoners, which was the exact same action the Scapini Mission had taken. This text clearly acknowledged that these former colonial prisoners were justified in their frustration with France, especially considering how the Vichy regime had treated them after release and before repatriation. The provisional government, as the Vichy regime had done, blamed the previous government for the current difficulties. Despite the acknowledgment that the colonial prisoners might be resentful, unsurprisingly, no significant policy changes ensued. The treatment of colonial soldiers did not change under the new government; instead, work and close supervision were presented as antidotes to frustration and criticism.[55]

After the chaos of the liberation, a number of colonial prisoners were in irregular situations. Some had not reported to the *centres de libération* after leaving captivity and had gotten jobs instead. In 1945 civilian and military authorities were tasked with finding and regrouping the missing colonial prisoners, some of whom were living with civilians, while others had joined the Resistance. In September 1944 Gen. Roger Noiret enacted a temporary demobilization for North Africans who were resident in metropolitan France before September 1, 1939, and had housing and work. This was similar to Vichy's law of March 1942, and it gave the centers charged with liberation and demobilization time to conduct thorough investigations to confirm the former prisoners' identities. Once the colonial prisoners' situations were regularized, they were sent to demobilization centers for medical visits. Here they each also received a provisional demobilization document and an advance of two hundred francs.[56] Formalities were finalized in the colonies.

Repatriation in 1944 and Beyond

Repatriations in 1944 included soldiers who had fought for the Free French, as well as the prisoners captured in 1940. Many civil servants in the colonies remained in place throughout the war. The two demobilizations took place in dramatically different contexts. Before 1942 the prisoners and the empire remained pillars of the Vichy regime and symbols of France's enduring future. In 1944–45 prisoners, white and colonial, were not a priority, as the provisional government struggled with practical matters like feeding France.[57] While many factors certainly contributed to the returning colonial prisoners' protests, financial ones were the most important and the most likely to turn violent.

In 1944 the soldiers' financial concerns and desire to return home were paramount, but without the threat of German or Allied propaganda forcing the French to "cultivate loyalty" among prisoners, reimposing discipline took precedent. Complaints about the demobilization bonus were rampant and not limited to colonial soldiers. An editorial published in *Femme de prisonniers* criticized the fact that the bonus of 1,000 francs had not increased since 1940, despite the dramatic increases in the cost of living during the occupation.[58] White soldiers who had spent five years captivity would receive 2,758 francs, plus the *prime d'accueil* (welcome bonus) of 1,000 francs and the demobilization bonus of 1,000 francs. In addition to that 4,758 francs, each white prisoner received one month of paid holiday based on the average salary in his department.[59] On the other end of the spectrum, many colonial prisoners had difficulty ascertaining how much they were actually owed. Either intentionally or as a result of the chaos of postwar France, the French government misled colonial soldiers about their payments and their financial rights.

Colonial soldiers faced a trifecta of challenges to ensure proper payment: competing financial priorities for the provisional government, logistical issues surrounding sending cash to the colonies, and racist assumptions about their spending habits. African soldiers usually were forced to wait to receive the balance of their payments in the colonies, as the French wanted to prevent them from "wasting" their money on gifts.[60] Once they arrived in the port cities of the empire, many soldiers were informed that the balance would actually be paid in their hometowns or villages. They were expected to return home, often overland, with only a vague promise of payment. Worse, the colonial administrators inland were not given the funds required for the payments.[61]

In this common scenario, soldiers had been told in France that they would receive payment upon arrival in Senegal. In Senegal, they were told they would be paid in their village, which could be hundreds or thousands of miles away. When they finally arrived home, the soldiers were still not paid. There, they had no recourse but to wait and hope, knowing they had been misled. Many of the colonial soldiers were the sons or nephews of First World War veterans. They had experienced the postwar payment process once before. After 1918 the families of soldiers who received the designation *Mort pour la France* were entitled to an additional death benefit. This right was limited to French citizens, a small minority of the quarter million indigenous soldiers who fought for France during the First World War.[62] Even the payment rules for pensions were complicated, and many First World War veterans were disenfranchised. As a result, many of the returning soldiers in 1944 had inherited a sense of distrust in France's commitment to paying the colonial soldiers.[63]

For the French, paying the colonial soldiers, many of whom had large amounts of cash already, was simply not a priority.[64] Some soldiers had over eighty thousand French francs, mostly earned working and sometimes supplemented by selling their cigarettes, chocolate, and American uniforms on the black market. Despite proof to the contrary, the colonial authorities assumed they had stolen the money and in some cases confiscated it. When demobilization bonuses were paid, the amount was significantly less than the soldiers expected. Finally, the exchange rate between French and West African francs had changed with the devaluation of the French franc, decreasing the value of their bonuses.[65]

The colonial prisoners were owed their bonuses regardless of assumed spending habits or the amount of money saved during captivity. However, France and the colonies were financially stretched, and metropolitan needs were given precedence. The decision to delay payment for a marginalized group with limited rights was representative of the violence inherent in the forced use of colonial soldiers. Soldiers were exhausted from captivity and war, and the legacy of the First World War loomed large as their payments were repeatedly delayed.

Keeping the colonial prisoners in France was expensive; as much as possible, the government prioritized their return to the colonies.[66] Repatriations began in the autumn of 1944. Between November 1944 and April 1945 almost 10,000 men returned to French West Africa, among them 3,261 former prisoners and 6,334 from the armies in North Africa.[67] Captivity had taken its toll. The men were tired of being separated from their families and perhaps tired of equal suffering for unequal pay. Anger and protest seemed unavoidable. In October a group of 500 colonial soldiers awaiting repatriation via Great Britain raided bakeries in Cherbourg because they felt their rations were too low. Then, fearing a French trick when the ship to take them to Britain was too small for everyone, they rebelled. Their "indiscipline" continued in Liverpool, where the African NCOs tried to force their way into an officers' mess.[68] As Scheck vividly describes, colonial soldiers "left a trail of drunken and disorderly behavior, theft, harassment and rapes."[69] The French were losing control over their colonial soldiers. The tipping point was reached near Dakar.

On December 1, 1944, colonial prisoners and soldiers revolted at the Thiaroye barracks in Senegal. This group of soldiers had been growing more and more frustrated at their conditions and general treatment since leaving France. Three hundred soldiers had refused to embark because they had received none of the payments owed to them. While the other soldiers received a portion of their payment, the protesters were arrested; six were shot and the ship left without the others. Despite the small payment, the soldiers concerns persisted. At Casablanca, the same events occurred. This time the numbers of protesters grew to 420, as fears that they would not be paid increased.[70] These men were also left behind. The remaining 1,300 men arrived in Dakar on the ss *Circassia* on November 21, and according to the colonial authorities, in Senegal the trouble began immediately. Discipline was nonexistent, and the officers no longer had control. The ship was left dirty, and the soldiers refused to remain in barracks and wandered the streets of Dakar armed with bayonets and cash. Several French women were reportedly molested by the soldiers.[71] Some soldiers smuggled their arms ashore and refused to be demobilized until their indemnities were paid.[72]

After attempts by the French to reimpose order without conceding on the payment, the protestors took a French officer hostage. Thus began one of the most famous massacres in French colonial history, immortalized in Ousmane Sembène's 1988 film, *Le Camp de Thiaroye*. The Senegalese soldiers refused to surrender their arms. In return, the French officers ordered their men, who included other colonial soldiers, to fire on the protesters. Twenty-two men died immediately, and forty-seven were injured. The death toll subsequently increased to thirty-five. The British consul in Accra reported to the Foreign Office that the "ringleaders were marched through Dakar under armed guard yesterday afternoon and taken to army prison. All French troops [were] confined to Barracks last night."[73] The protest and violent aftermath of what is known as the Thiaroye Massacre immediately sent shockwaves throughout the French and British colonies.[74]

The official report written in Senegal attributed the events in Thiaroye to a series of bad decisions and measures taken in metropolitan France. Furthermore, it claimed that blame could not be placed on the authorities in the colony, who were forced to make difficult and dangerous choices.[75] While the report was obviously attempting to protect those who had decided to fire on the colonial soldiers, there was truth in the accusation. The colonial soldiers had arrived in Senegal already angry, disillusioned with French leadership, and legitimately worried that they would not be paid. Their comrades had been arrested or abandoned in France and Morocco for demanding their still outstanding payments.[76] Refusing to obey orders and locking a French officer up until they were heard seemed like a necessary escalation.

For officials in France, it was absurd to blame a massacre in the colonies on the metropole. Henri Laurentie, director of political affairs, felt the official report confirmed that "most of the *inspecteurs des colonies*, after having spontaneously failed at their national duty in 1940, remain incapable in 1945 of fulfilling the smallest demands of their professional duty."[77] The soldiers' revolt became a point of contention between those who had supported de Gaulle from the beginning and those who only joined post–November 1942. At no time were the soldiers' demands for payment considered legitimate or even understood as the reason for their protest. Instead, it was blamed on propaganda and "its disastrous effects on the mentality of the native ex-prisoners."[78] Propaganda was a tidy explanation that exonerated the French from any wrongdoing and placed responsibility on those who, because of the fortunes of war, were once again France's enemy.

Thiaroye threw a harsh light on the growing tensions between the paternalistic colonial rhetoric of solidarity and the realities of demobilizing colonial prisoners who had developed a justifiable sense of entitlement. It served as a radical reminder that the former colonial prisoners were not mere symbols of imperial solidarity whose needs could be surpassed by newer priorities. The protest forced the French to confront their racialized stereotypes of the "loyal and childlike" West African soldiers who needed only their white officers' love.[79] Instead of deep introspection and reevaluation of the premises of colonial conscription, the French report on Thiaroye concluded unsurprisingly, "Far from their country and separated from their officers for five years, successively subjected to captivity then freedom that did not often assuage the discipline, sometimes chosen as insidious propaganda instruments, often abusively spoiled, the Senegalese ex-prisoners suffer from the turmoil that follows troubled times and particularly affects crude natures."[80]

The idea that colonial prisoners had been "abusively spoiled" certainly contributed to the repressive measures taken in response to events seen to challenge the colonial regime. The French, under Vichy and the provisional government, repeatedly showed their reluctance to acknowledge that colonial prisoners had reasonable complaints, fearing that doing so might create "unfortunate precedents" whereby colonial subjects might feel they could make demands on the French government. At a time when the colonies began to demand recognition for their contribution to the victory, the French encouraged a return to the repressive practices of the conquest era, hoping "the results of this path will be positive and will see our protégés fully realize, again, the greatness and the civilizing power of France."[81] Many colonial prisoners felt they had experienced enough of French civilizing power and were ready to return home paid in full. Only later would some push for change.

Despite refusing to acknowledge any wrongdoing, the French improved the payment system after Thiaroye. In February 1945, 350 former colonial prisoners returned to Dakar. Generally, their "behavior" had been good during the trip, with the exception of one official report. Boisson credited their smooth transition home to payments made in the metropole and firm discipline en route.[82] Seeing the impact of early payments, the Ministry of Colonies was urged to pay colonial prisoners before they embarked. When news of payments reached Casablanca, the "behavior" of the 523 former colonial prisoners already headed for Dakar improved substantially. Four days later, they were on their way home.[83]

Even prisoners not paid in France were affected by the greater transparency. Former prisoners repatriated on the *Faucon* and the *Montaigne* arrived in Dakar on March 2, 1945, without incident during the trip or after arrival. Over four million West African francs were paid to reimburse the former prisoners' saving accounts opened during captivity and fulfilled their end-of-captivity payments.[84] Another 877 colonial prisoners voyaged without major incidents on the *Providence*, *Marrakech*, *Dunkerque*, and *Schiaffino*, with only a few soldiers punished for drunkenness while docked at Casablanca.[85] Information was spreading among the colonial soldiers, and they knew their rights. However, unlike in captivity, they no longer had the

International Committee of the Red Cross or other humanitarian groups validating their concerns. The colonial soldiers had felt their only recourse was violence. Those who protested at Thiaroye were punished severely, but their actions prompted positive change for those coming after. Only in June 1947 was general amnesty announced for Thiaroye. Five men had already died in prison.

While the financial question was clearly the catalyst, other factors also motivated the former prisoners to protest at Thiaroye. Indiscipline began on the ship and can be attributed to a combination of the difficulties of captivity, the hypermasculinity of the French Army and POW regime, distrust over decisions made in the colonies versus those made in France, and the prisoners' real fear that they would not be paid properly. Scheck adds two more points: first, the difficult transition from relative freedom at the end of captivity to strict discipline before repatriation created much resentment; and second, some of these men were torn away from French women with whom they had relationships and sometimes a child.[86] Despite holding up imperial loyalty as the backbone of the French Empire, the French routinely underestimated the soldiers' commitment to and pride in their service. That led to their misinterpreting the returning colonial soldiers' demands that the payment schedule, biased as it was against them, be enforced properly as signs of a general revolt.

More globally, the massacre at Thiaroye revealed the underlying issues and tensions bubbling under the surface of the colonial regime. The lack of experienced NCOs exacerbated the financial situation, and the soldiers' mistrust that the situation would be fixed contributed to the frustration generally and Thiaroye specifically.[87] NCOs were a key element in the military structure, serving as the linchpin between the men below and the hierarchy above. Without these trusted elements, and with the legacies of the First World War looming, the colonial soldiers were left alone to deal with the increasing discipline and discriminatory payments. Gregory Mann correctly concludes that Thiaroye was neither an isolated event nor characteristic of the colonial prisoners' repatriation.[88] Thiaroye came to symbolize the transformation that the Second World War wrought on Franco-imperial relations, the roots of which began during the colonial prisoners' captivity. As Myron Echenberg argues, French officials did not recognize that captivity had changed and united the African prisoners.[89] The unity Echenberg evokes was not simply with France, but rather it was the beginning of collective consciousness that captivity specifically, and military service for France generally, had meant something and that the colonial soldiers deserved more than a return to the harsh reality of forced labor and minimal rights. Popular opinion in France remained at best paternalistic and more often self-centered, hence the surprise when colonial populations started demanding change.[90]

To these arguments, one must add another complicating factor: the evaporation of solidarity that appeared for the colonial POWs during their captivity and the return to the harsh reality of life in the French colonies. Any hope for change that had been sparked by Vichy rhetoric and seemingly confirmed by the Brazzaville Conference had once again been quashed by violent reactionary efforts to reassert control over the indigenous populations. The colonies had fought for France during the war, some had even continued fighting after the armistice, but at the end of the day, very little changed for them. France had changed during the Second World War, but the colonial and military hierarchies had not, and the real repercussions of the war were to come slowly, beginning in Algeria.

Another, larger, more consequential event deserves a place in the discussion of postwar violence, even though it did not directly involve former colonial prisoners. On May 8, 1945, while the Allies were celebrating victory in Europe, a fairly moderate nationalist parade of five thousand in Sétif, Algeria, degenerated when the French military police fired on those carrying anticolonial signs. The Algerian population responded with violent attacks on European settlers. The violence continued into the evening, and approximately one hundred Europeans were attacked and killed horrifically. Tensions in Algeria were already high. The local population was severely malnourished as a result of famine conditions dating from 1944. The French response to the Algerian violence was completely out of proportion. Racism, fear, and hysteria prompted the French civilians to take up arms and kill, essentially at random, thousands of Algerians. Violent repression continued for ten days, pitting the colonial infantry (including West African and Moroccan soldiers), navy, and air force against unarmed Algerian civilians. This was an organized act of state-sponsored terror designed to bring the nationalists to heel and was widely photographed by the French.

In Guelma, events unfolded in a slightly different manner. There was a demonstration on May 8 as well, but unlike in Sétif, the aftermath was relatively calm. Using the nationalist violence in Sétif as an excuse, the French settlers in Guelma, led by the sous-prefect André Achiary, organized an extralegal militia.[91] Joined by police and soldiers, they waged an illegal purge on the Algerian civilians. Guelma was a small subprefecture, and the French knew the Algerians they were killing. This continued until the minister of the interior arrived at end of June. It was a methodical use of violence to break the nationalist movement in the region.

At first participants denied reports of the violence, as they hid behind rumors of a conspiracy by colonists, fascists, nationalists, or Americans.[92] Later arguments explained that the violence had resulted from a combination of fear and hatred.[93] Now the events at Sétif and Guelma are widely considered a turning point in Franco-Algerian relations, and for many, they mark the point of no return leading to the Algerian War. The episode speaks to the mood and tensions throughout the French Empire. It highlights the fear the white settlers had of the indigenous populations and the idea that any change might bring about their downfall. Instead, this inflexibility directly contradicted what the Brazzaville Conference hoped to do, and it would eventually bring down the entire colonial system in Algeria, but not before a bloody, cruel, and devastating war for independence.

The long-term repercussions of Thiaroye and Sétif were to come slowly. Both colonial and white prisoners suffered the consequences of a rhetoric-filled captivity. White prisoners also felt that their suffering entitled them to a significant role in postwar political and social life, and they were disillusioned to find that the country had survived without them.[94] Colonial prisoners witnessed reactionary efforts to reassert control over them replace the rhetoric of solidarity from the Vichy years. Frustration began almost immediately after their release from captivity, during which colonial prisoners had generally positive interactions with the French civilians, as they now had to engage with a large and conservative French bureaucracy limited by the constraints of an ongoing war. This was compounded by the lack of freedom after liberation.

The lucky ones were repatriated quickly. They experienced the best efforts of the Vichy colonial administrations, receiving fanfares, couscous, and (limited) assistance in finding housing and work. Even then, the compensation for war service was inadequate, and the Vichy administrators in the colonies remained suspicious of the colonial prisoners and tried to ensure that they brought only pro-French attitudes home. Already the discrepancies in postcaptivity expectations appeared. Some returning colonial prisoners believed they would be given important jobs and consequently resisted the return to manual labor. Others, through their contact with civilians, inflated by the years of rhetoric, believed racial hierarchies were softening. They had worked and eaten, and sometimes even lived, alongside the French. On the other hand, many white officials shared Darlan's belief that supporting the colonial prisoners during their captivity was recognition enough for their service and sacrifice.

The reactionary colonial regime remained in place throughout the Vichy regime and under the provisional government. If anything, the events in France reinforced a desire among imperial officials to preserve the status quo. Whereas there was an utter change of view with regard to the French POWs, the provisional government (and postwar governments) maintained and strengthened Vichy views of colonial prisoners and the empire in general. The two waves of demobilization took place in dramatically different contexts. Hints of change were viewed as the result of dangerous German propaganda and as something to be quashed. Coming home, after five years of combat and then captivity, brought many of the tensions of imprisonment and the contradictions between French principle and prejudice to a head. This route home was, for some, the end of the war and the start of the long road toward decolonization.

CONCLUSIONS

The colonial prisoners interned in France during the Second World War were a small minority among the millions of prisoners of war in western Europe. As individuals, they carried their personal experiences of war, suffering, and captivity home with them, shaping their future relations with France. As a group, their experiences help us understand war captivity, Vichy collaboration, the decline of French imperialism, shifts in global humanitarianism, and the enduring impact of racialized views on medicine, labor, and migration. By providing an in-depth social, military, and political history of the colonial prisoners, this book has highlighted the voices of an exile community of colonial citizens and subjects caught between competing French and German goals.

The Second World War was not the first, nor would it be the last, time that France brought its colonial subjects and citizens abroad for battle. Indeed, as this book has shown, the long history of European war shaped much of what the eighty-five thousand colonial prisoners of war experienced. The legacies of the First World War dominated the German occupation of France, with Hitler insisting that the armistice agreement be signed in the same train carriage in Compiègne where the Germans had signed their armistice in 1918. While there was a tendency in the early scholarship to treat the Vichy regime as a dark period outside "normal" French and republican history, the experiences of the colonial prisoners show how entangled the Vichy period was with the longer history of the Third, Fourth, and Fifth Republics. The everyday experiences of the colonial prisoners in captivity reveal these continuities of racial politics, imperial goals, paternalism, and labor policy.

Much of the previous historiography of colonial prisoners incorrectly emphasized their neglect under the Vichy regime, focusing on the influence that French and German racism had on their captivity, which resulted in harsher conditions than those for white prisoners.[1] This is true if one looks exclusively at the beginning and end of captivity. Colonial prisoners were at risk of being killed outright in June 1940, and they were not the priority for the provisional government in 1945. The brief and intense fighting in May and June 1940 brought into sharp focus the differences between French and German racial ideologies. To keep the colonial soldiers from surrendering prematurely, French officers warned them that the Germans viewed African soldiers as "savages" and would not accept their surrender. The warnings worked, and many colonial soldiers felt they had fought harder and longer than the white soldiers, a belief that was later fanned by German propaganda. The drawn-out fighting, rumors of illegal warfare, and Nazi racism created a quagmire, and some German soldiers massacred hundreds of African soldiers along the front or, less frequently, between capture and arrival at a temporary camp. Surprisingly, these massacres were limited in time and scope, and the attitude of individual German soldiers toward the captured colonial soldiers rapidly changed from shock to curiosity.

Often the crucial stage of their captivity is overlooked: from their arrival in a permanent camp until November 1942, the colonial prisoners' captivity was characterized more often by boredom and loneliness than by fear and violence. Conditions in France, and thus the Frontstalags, were more comfortable than those in Germany or the eastern occupied territories. By examining how the colonial prisoners lived and adapted to life in German captivity, this book has shown how racist ideologies were deployed or suspended in service of war aims or in hopes of postwar greatness.

A wealth of historical literature has examined the fall of France and its impact on French institutions and psyche. In giving France the "gift of himself," Pétain tried to redirect French anxiety about the future into confidence in him, the father of the French nation. He argued that French rebirth would come from real repentance for the decadence of the Third Republic. Pétain immediately drew the French people into a new order, a national revolution, which would atone for the past and signal the dawn of new French greatness. With the inclusion of the colonial prisoners in the narrative of Vichy and the National Revolution, our understanding of Pétain's goals are broadened. While France appeared to be a nation falling back on introspection and redemption, the Vichy regime had no intention of remaining isolated in defeat. Everyone had a role to play under the National Revolution: white prisoners were the cornerstone of the new France, having given up their freedom in the defense of France; women were mothers; the indigenous peoples were loyal and obedient; and together, France could rebuild as an imperial, and thus important, nation.

The gender roles imposed by the National Revolution have been brilliantly examined by historians Hannah Diamond, Sarah Fishman, and Miranda Pollard. By looking at the official, paternalistic, discourse on the colonial prisoners, this book unpicks many of the intersections between Vichy's gendered, imperial, and racialized policies. In the end, both captivity and the Vichy regime ended, but their legacies continued to affect how France saw its role in the world and, in many ways, how it reacted to the different populations under its hegemony.

This book strengthens the existing scholarship on the Vichy regime in the empire by determining that during a limited period, the regime managed to protect the colonial prisoners from a far more difficult captivity than if they had been interned in Germany. However, it is important to stress that the Vichy regime was "benevolent" toward the colonial prisoners because it had an interest in being that way. The protection of the colonial prisoners during their internment in occupied France must be understood in the wider history of Vichy's racism in the colonies and utter inability, or even desire, to protect Jews from the final solution.[2] It is doubtful that the Vichy regime would have spontaneously shielded the colonial prisoners if the empire had not been a means to maintain sovereignty and reclaim greatness. Racism returned as the guiding principle concerning the colonial prisoners' treatment once they left the framework of captivity. Indeed, protecting the colonial prisoners was a self-serving decision upheld at various levels of the Vichy government and colonial office to ensure French interests would be sustained once the colonial prisoners returned home.

By bringing new source material and an innovative approach to bear, this book is a significant departure from the previous literature on Vichy collaboration, German racism, and the captivity experiences.[3] As such, it settles the debate over the degree of material hardship and political protections or vulnerability the colonial prisoners experienced by looking in detail at their experiences during the period when the Vichy regime enjoyed real (if limited) power and by assessing the degree of interest displayed by the Vichy regime in these particular colonial subjects.

The main focus of this book is the period from June 1940 to November 1942, although it is by no means confined to this time frame. This focus allows for an in-depth thematic analysis of the experiences of captivity, including camp structures, labor, food, interactions with civilians, health, and escape, across a relatively stable time period during which the French regime still had legitimacy and limited power. This critical period is often glossed-over in favor of "big events" like the massacres in 1940 or 1945. While those events cannot be dissociated from the experiences of captivity, they did not, for most colonial prisoners, define them. This new perspective changes the paradigm of colonial prisoners' experiences of captivity. However, the war did not end in November 1942. The single biggest external event for the colonial prisoners was Vichy's loss of the empire and thus the loss of their political significance.

While the Vichy regime did protect the colonial prisoners, that protection was limited in scope and time. Once colonial prisoners came under direct French authority, in the occupied zone or with French officers as guards, the advantages evaporated and the French reestablished strict discipline and reimposed racial hierarchies. Paternalism, one of the factors that pushed the French to help the colonial prisoners during their captivity, also ensured that this assistance would never imply equal rights. Instead, the French assumed that soldiers, be they French or colonial, were doing their duty for France and nothing more. Of course, white French soldiers received greater financial and political compensation for their duty. Colonial subjects were considered as children, placing the French, and especially the officers, in a fatherlike role. Many French believed that having a superior "civilization" imposed civic obligations toward their subjects, including elevating them to a similar level of civilization. Vichy's actions for colonial prisoners were not unselfish but were based on both political ideology and a sense of responsibility, which was used to justify colonial domination. The Scapini Mission and other French authorities assumed that the colonial prisoners would respond to the efforts made on their behalf with obedience and appreciation.

Because of the efforts to mobilize aid, and despite Nazi and French racism, the colonial prisoners fared better while in the Frontstalags than in the southern zone. The German authorities took advantage of collaboration, and the Scapini Mission's search for greater contact with the colonial prisoners, by transferring financial responsibility for the colonial prisoners to the French. This meant French towns and prefectures were building work camps and feeding colonial prisoners in their area. Extra comforts were sent to remind the colonial prisoners that the French had not forgotten their sacrifices. The Vichy regime's negotiations on the colonial prisoners' behalf were designed to remove them from German influence and restore them firmly under French rule. Ideally, this meant repatriation. In reality, many remained in the southern zone of France under French control, which changed French priorities, as these prisoners were no longer in direct danger from German propaganda. The French authorities wanted an immediate return to the discipline of the colonial army. Any protest at this reduction in freedom and importance was attributed to the residual German propaganda. The French seemed shocked that colonial prisoners had not recognized the efforts made on their behalf, and many prisoners were confused to witness this evaporation of solidarity. This discrepancy between the rhetoric of imperial unanimity and the reality of an unchanged colonial system exacerbated the returning colonial prisoners' complaints. Continued delays in repatriation and lack of payment at the end of the war left many former prisoners feeling they had been abandoned and used by the French government, which is reflected in the popular memory and historiography of their captivity.

It would be an error to claim that the Vichy regime collaborated to protect the colonial prisoners; rather, as this book argues, it was a fortuitous combination of having the colonial prisoners in France, the Vichy regime's imperial project, and its edification of POWs. Caught within its own rhetoric of a unified empire, the Scapini Mission had to ensure that the colonial prisoners were not neglected. Unexpectedly, they held a privileged and contradictory position within Franco-German negotiations. While the Vichy regime strongly prioritized the return of the white prisoners, it could not afford to isolate the colonial prisoners completely. Instead, they became caught up in the Vichy regime's rhetoric of imperial solidarity and the prisoners' redemptive suffering. Scattered across the occupied zone in large camps, the Frontstalags, and in small work groups on local farms and civil projects, the colonial prisoners became visible symbols of the Vichy regime's imperial goals. Their importance became immediately clear to the French, who saw them as tools for shaping how the defeat would be portrayed in the colonies after their return home. The specter of German propaganda, and fears that the colonial prisoners would stray from their duty, increased the importance of maintaining their loyalty.

By examining French and German propaganda aimed at the colonial prisoners, this book contributes to the rich scholarship on the National Revolution, notably the work of Ruth Ginio on Vichy propaganda in French West Africa, which establishes that reactionary Vichy thinking "fit" the colonial context more comfortably than did the Third Republican values of liberty, equality, and fraternity.[4] This book shows that Ginio's argument can be applied throughout the empire. Through the colonial prisoners, we see a consistent policy of racial and social hierarchies designed to control every aspect of society. The Vichy regime sought to control and mobilize the everyday lives of the French in the metropole in ways similar to its imperial rule over the indigenous populations. Even within its overarching imperial goals, wartime practicalities and emotional attachments influenced how the French responded to the different colonial prisoners. North Africa was, and remained until 1962, the jewel of the French Empire. Its importance was reflected both in French efforts to keep the North African prisoners' allegiance and in German attempts to lead them to revolt or inspire nationalism. While prisoners remained in captivity, French counterpropaganda highlighted the long ties that bound the colonies and France, as well as the efforts by Pétain's government and the Scapini Mission to improve their conditions of captivity.

Colonial captivity challenged the rhetoric and realities of empire. Many historians have critically examined the contradictions between republican ideas and French imperial expansion between 1871 and 1940, but the Vichy regime never claimed to be egalitarian or free. Nevertheless, it repeatedly and earnestly called its colonial prisoners to demonstrate solidarity with and commitment to France. In many ways, during the colonial prisoners' captivity, boundaries blurred between prisoners of the empire and men and women of the metropole. The philanthropic mobilization of aid for colonial prisoners reflected the importance of the French Empire to the Vichy regime's postwar plans and helps refute claims of French neglect. Efforts to protect the colonial prisoners stemmed from the political importance that the empire, and thus the colonial prisoners, represented. The Vichy regime struggled to reinforce its imperial identity and maintain the loyalty of its subjects while other influences—the Free French, the Japanese in Indochina, or even the Germans in North Africa—threatened the empire. This book has argued that these repeated calls for solidarity and praise for the colonial prisoners' sacrifices were designed to reinforce feelings of loyalty and obedience among the colonial prisoners, while creating a "benevolent" image of French imperialism in which white citizens cared for colonial prisoners during their time of need. The French hoped that supplying vital goods, such as food and clothing, to the colonial prisoners would prove their continued dependence on France and thus confirm France's right to rule.

The experiences of the colonial prisoners—as men under military captivity and recipients of substantial philanthropic aid—reveal the multidimensional nature of humanitarianism in the twentieth century. This book contributes to the history of global humanitarianism by exposing the different and competing motivations behind French aid for the colonial prisoners. Both France and Germany had signed the Geneva Convention of 1929, establishing the legal boundaries for the treatment of prisoners of war and providing official channels for food aid and material support. The Vichy regime co-opted the support and organizational network of the French Red Cross, allowing for greater state control over the humanitarian efforts. The ties between political goals and humanitarian aid reified under the Vichy regime would flourish in the postwar period. As France tried to redefine its ties to the colonies, at Brazzaville in 1944 and then through the French Union, one constant remained: France connected aid and support to its continued influence abroad. The idea that the French had a responsibility to help their colonial subjects in German captivity, and the right to determine the form that aid would take, would continue through the postcolonial period. By studying the captivity of the colonial soldiers and the politics surrounding the Vichy regime's desire to "support" them through captivity, one sees the roots of international development aid in what many call the neocolonial period. Indeed, many of the politics surrounding aspects of the colonial prisoners' captivity tied into larger questions within the French Empire.

The prism of colonial prisoner labor contributes not only to our understanding of POW work but also to the larger question of forced labor in the colonies. Many of the colonial prisoners would have been familiar with the different forms of obligatory labor common in the French colonies. Even as soldiers, they would have worked in different, often physical, jobs. The rules that governed their captivity experience and assumptions that affected their treatment reflected the colonial prisoners' dual status as POWs, protected by international law, and colonial subjects with little independent legal standing. On the one hand, work reinforced the colonial prisoners' "otherness"; some French and Germans seemed reluctant to apply French labor law to the colonial captives and assumed they were "inherently lazy." Many of the paternalistic and racist assumptions about colonial prisoners grew out of the preconceived notions of work ethic and productivity in the colonies. These ideas had allowed forced labor to continue in the colonies despite its inherent contradiction with Third Republic values and let it thrive in both Free French and Vichy colonies. On the other hand, work also drew the colonial prisoners together with white civilians, giving them the opportunity to create relationships, even friendships, or start planning an escape.

The camaraderie and solidarity that existed between French civilians and colonial prisoners in the early years was slowly replaced by more isolated and strenuous work, under increasingly difficult and dangerous situations. Over time, public support for the colonial prisoners as a labor force faded with the ever-increasing financial burdens, as paid labor remained rare on the small family farms that dominated the French countryside. Under the Vichy regime, as seen through the different jobs the colonial prisoners were forced to do, the French became increasingly involved in the German war effort. In the later years of the occupation, many colonial prisoners worked directly for Ostland, on building the Atlantic Wall with the Todt Organization, or in munitions factories. What remained consistent was the French assumption that the imposition of work was necessary and good for colonial subjects.

While this book rejects the thesis that French racism led to "neglect," it is clear that racism and racialized ideas shaped the colonial prisoners' experiences of captivity. Brutality was a part of life for many prisoners of war, and the colonial prisoners did not escape that. They reported being hit or mistreated and even witnessing murder in the camps. Most prisoners reported that the colonial prisoners were more likely to be victims of violent overreactions than the white prisoners were. Yet here again, captivity in France rather than Germany proved to their advantage, as the French were quickly made aware of the colonial prisoners' deaths. While the French could not stop the Germans from hurting the colonial prisoners, they could protest officially and unofficially and hold funerals for the dead. The colonial prisoners could report incidents to the International Committee of the Red Cross, something they could no longer do when faced with racial violence back in the colonies.

The way violence was reported, by the prisoners themselves and by French officials and civilians, suggests that incidents remained rare enough to shock. This book has shown that overall, there was not a culture of brutality in the Frontstalags. Many colonial prisoners reported that discipline could be overwhelming, especially at the beginning of captivity, but as routines were set in place, an equilibrium was found. On small work groups, guards were friendly and sometimes relaxed.[5] Overall, ill health was much more dangerous for colonial prisoners than the limited number of violent guards in the camps. The colonial prisoners were living in close quarters, with less-than-ideal sanitary conditions, in a climate that was often much colder than home. The fear of "native" diseases prompted the Germans' generous release policies for potentially sick prisoners, as well as systematic testing for tuberculosis, which was not accorded to white prisoners in Germany. The statistical findings, specifically data on the colonial prisoners' health, go against the grain of much of the previous scholarship. Mental health and illness among colonial prisoners remains an area open for exciting new research.

The impact of the French racialized views can be clearly seen in the choice of who should assume leadership positions for the colonial prisoners. One of the themes that appeared regularly in the negotiations between the French and the Germans, and later in the struggles to reintegrate former colonial soldiers, was the need for officers and NCOs who "knew" how to work with the colonial troops. Indeed, the French Army had developed detailed training manuals during the interwar period to teach white officers about the different cultures of the empire and how best to lead them toward French civilization. This growing interest in ethnography remained firmly grounded in stereotypes and racism. The Scapini Mission viewed Marcel Bonnaud's prewar experience with the colonial troops as an advantage for a camp inspector. Certainly, his knowledge of colonial medicine and access to sick prisoners gave weight to his commentaries. However, that experience did not necessarily make him an ally for the colonial prisoners, working in their best interests; instead, he was a proponent of what the French believed those interests should be. "Knowing" colonial soldiers did not imply a deep cultural understanding, but rather the old notions of infantilization and accompanying paternalism. This was a key method for the French to maintain control and limit the colonial prisoners' exposure to new or different ideas.

The consequences of the colonial soldiers' return were felt in the dissension and discontent that continued to grow throughout the French Empire in the decades following the Second World War. The paternalism of the Vichy years never entirely faded and continued to influence relations between France and its colonies. Even before the war was over, it was clear that the imperial contributions, from the colonial prisoners or the African soldiers fighting with the Free French, would not bring about significant change to the French imperial regime. Open frustration once captivity had ended, combined with the French government's lack of recognition for their contributions, fueled grievances. These complaints turned into violent reactions at Thiaroye when the French officers refused to give the colonial prisoners what they were owed. Veterans and former prisoners, with extremely active membership groups, were often at the forefront of these movements. During captivity, colonial prisoners had gained increased political awareness and recognition of French fallibility. The Vichy regime's actions toward and for the colonial prisoners during their time in German captivity showed that France intended to continue to rule the colonies after the war. Suppressing nationalist discourse and limiting interactions among prisoners from different colonies demonstrated French fear that the hint of discontent could spread across the empire. These were not the actions of a country moving toward decolonization.

At the war's end, the colonial soldiers were expected to uphold the image of imperial loyalty and behave accordingly. War had changed them, but to their disappointment and shock, it had not fundamentally changed the colonial regime to which they returned. Both France and Britain struggled to get their colonial soldiers home and reintegrate them into civilian life. For a variety of reasons, the repatriation of colonial soldiers was often accompanied by incidents of violence or insurrection. Revolts, protests, strikes, and rebellions occurred in various forms during and after the Second World War. Some, like the strike of Mauritian soldiers in Madagascar in 1943, had limited international consequences, but those found guilty were punished harshly, with up to fifteen years in prison. Other affairs, like Thiaroye and Sétif, had repercussions that spread throughout the colonies or marked the beginning of a bloody war for independence. After five years of brutal warfare, the end of the Second World War should have brought peace and stability; instead, for thousands of African soldiers, it ushered in a new era of colonial violence. Career colonial soldiers found themselves shipped off to fight for colonial oppression in Indochina and Algeria.[6] Faced with colonies' demands for recognition for their contribution to the victory, the colonial governments instead encouraged a return to the repressive practices of the conquest era, in what John Lonsdale and Anthony Low famously termed "the second colonial occupation."[7]

Ostensibly, these measures were designed to remind the subjects of the glory and prestige of the colonial conquest.[8] In reality, France and Britain were attempting to reestablish their places in a postwar world, one that increasingly called for domination of imperial markets and resources. At the same time, international movements, with establishment of the United Nations, the Universal Declaration of Human Rights, and organizations like UNESCO, provided a platform for resistance.

The former colonial prisoners saw their experiences in captivity and war echoed in the diverse experiences of other peoples from across the colonial empires, prompting some to join trade unions or political parties on their return home. While most prisoners were forced to wait for repatriation to make these decisions, Henry, Robert, and Ginette Eboué chose to flee France, crossing the Pyrenees on foot to join the external resistance. Having paid sixty thousand francs to a guide, Ginette left Marseille for Perpignan on October 5, 1941, accompanied by a young Spanish woman, Candida Del Castillo, who had escaped from a French internment camp for foreigners. Henry and Robert traveled separately, following a less expensive but riskier route, planning to meet Ginette in Lisbon. At the Franco-Spanish border, Ginette and Candida met their guides and began walking through the night. In darkness, they navigated fields, climbed over barriers, and crossed streams, trying to avoid falling into crevasses. They walked for hours, stopping only briefly to rest and eat some cold chicken and dried sausages that the guide provided. Eventually, they joined a 4:00 a.m. train for Barcelona.[9]

They narrowly escaped arrest, thanks to Candida's judicious flirting with a train conductor who had asked for their papers, which they obviously did not have. Having safely distracted the conductor, they hid in a Spanish woman's home until the British Embassy opened on Monday morning. At first the consular employee refused to help Ginette, until she explained who she was. With great surprise, the consul general received Ginette and made plans to inform her parents, Eugénie Tell and Felix Eboué, that she had escaped to Spain. In a fortuitous coincidence, Henry and Robert arrived at the consulate the same day. After three weeks hidden indoors, they left for Madrid, traveling on newly issued British passports. Finally, on November 30 at 4:00 p.m., they sailed for French Equatorial Africa. After almost two years apart, they were reunited with their mother at Boma, Congo, and their father the next day in Brazzaville.[10]

For Ginette, arrival in Brazzaville was only the beginning of her work challenging undemocratic rule. From there she joined the women's branch of the external resistance. While this choice was inspired by her politically active family, her later role in anticolonial movements through a twenty-year career at UNESCO was not inherited, as her father held very conservative views on empire and civilization.[11] Like Ginette, some colonial prisoners returned home changed and unable to accept a continuation of the imperial status quo. Ginette's first husband, Léopold Senghor, went into politics after the war, trying to shape the new French constitution to create a union where the colonies had real influence. Although we know little about Ginette's life, we know far more about her than the rank-and-file colonial prisoners who lived through the Second World War.

The task moving forward is to reconstruct the different postwar paths they took. For many soldiers, the war did not end in 1945; it lived on through their demobilization and reintegration into their families and civilian lives or redeployment in colonial wars. Their challenge after the trauma of captivity was to rebuild their lives, still under colonial rule. In 1940 they had given their freedom for France, but their own emancipation escaped them. In 1944 they had celebrated France's liberation, but they returned home underpaid. Like Paris, the colonial soldiers had been outraged, some martyred and others broken, but unlike Paris, they were not yet liberated.

NOTES

tourist office for the general government of Algeria)

OKW	Oberkommando der Wehrmacht (German High Command)
PG	Prisonnier de guerre
PTT	Postes, télégraphes et téléphones
RAA	Régiments d'artillerie antiaérienne
RIC	Régiment d'infanterie colonial
RICMS	Régiment d'infanterie coloniale mixte sénégalais
RTA	Régiment de tirailleurs algériens
RTM	Régiment de tirailleurs marocains
SDPG	Service diplomatique des prisonniers de guerre
SHD	Service Historique de la Défense
TOAFN	Theatre d'operations afrique francaise du nord

INTRODUCTION

1. Ginette Eboué, captivity report, Dossier "Félix Eboué," AOL, 7–8. All translations are my own. I would like to thank Géraud Létang for sharing the files for Ginette, Henry, and Robert Eboué.

2. Henry Eboué, captivity report, Dossier "Félix Eboué," AOL, 9.

3. Ginette Eboué, captivity report, 10; Henry Eboué, captivity report, 11.

4. Ginette Eboué, captivity report, 8.

5. Henry Eboué, captivity report, 7.

6. Ginio, *French Colonialism Unmasked*, xiv.

7. Scheck, *Hitler's African Victims*, 58.

8. For an excellent discussion on race and empire in France, see Peabody and Stovall, *Color of Liberty*.

9. Vourkoutiotis, *Prisoners of War*, 35.

10. Scapini to Tiepelmann, 16 December 1940, SHD, 2P66.

11. Thomas, "Vichy Government," 663.

12. Anzahl der Kriegsgefangen weisse und farbige Frz. in Frankreich, 1 March 1941, AN, F/9/2959.

13. Note for Mr. Lucas regarding meeting with Captain Roussane, 27 November 1941, AN, AJ/41/2053; Dupuy, analysis of reports on the Frontstalags from 1 October [1941] to 1 April 1942, SHD, 2P63.

14. Approximations concerning prisoners from Algeria, the colonies, protectorates, and countries under mandate for General Andlauer, 5 May 1941, AN, F/9/2351. This total was calculated by adding statistics from each department sent to Andlauer. Variations are due to different racial categories used by each department.

15. Lawler, *Soldiers of Misfortune*, 93.

16. Calculations based on the ICRC capture cards at the BAVCC, Caen.

17. Dupuy, Analysis of Dr. Bonnard's reports from 1 October [1941] to 1 April 1942, 13 July 1942, SHD, 2P78; Mabon and Cuttier, "La singulière captivité," 138.

18. Scheck, *French Colonial Soldiers*, 27.

19. See publication of the full text of Senghor's captivity report that Scheck found and identified in *Jeune Afrique* 51, no. 2637 (July 24, 2011): 25–30, AN, F9, 2345. During my first month of PhD research I came across a copy of the same captivity report in the French military archives as Compte-rendu de captivité établi par un prisonnier indigène récemment libéré (Captivity report written by a recently released prisoner), 7 July 1942, SHD, 2P70, without realizing its significance and naively hoping it would be one of many such reports. All credit to the identification of its author lies with Raffael Scheck.

20. Scheck, *French Colonial Soldiers*, 98.

21. Robert Eboué, captivity report, Dossier "Félix Eboué," AOL, 3.

22. Cooper and Stoler, *Tensions of Empire*, 4.

23. For Australian prisoners of war, see Twomey, *The Battle Within*; Beaumont, Grant, and Pegram, *Beyond Surrender*; Monteath, "Australian POWs in German Captivity in the Second World War." For important early reading on POWs see Moore and Fedororwich, *Prisoners of War*. For the conditions and political negotiations over POWs, see MacKenzie, *Colditz Myth* and "Treatment of Prisoners of War"; Vourkoutiotis, *Prisoners of War*; Wylie, *Barbed Wire Diplomacy*. French historian Yves Durand's work remains the reference for scholarship on French POWs during the Second World War, but it mentions the colonial prisoners only in passing. See Durand, *La Captivité*. Finally, Clare Makepeace's monograph is particularly interesting for her examination of mental health in the camps, something missing from much of the scholarship. See Makepeace, *Captives of War*.

24. Jones, *Violence against Prisoners*.

25. Marc Michel is the eminent French scholar on colonial soldiers. See Michel, *Les Africains*. While Michel concentrates on the military contribution of Africa and Africans during the First World War, historians Richard Fogarty, Allison Fell, Nina Wardleworth, and Dónal Hassett all tackle questions of race and representations of colonial soldiers in Third Republic France. See Fogarty, *Race and War*; Fell and Wardleworth, "Colour of War Memory"; Hassett, *Mobilizing Memory*. While many historians' works are on colonial soldiers in the twentieth century, captivity remains a small part of the stories they tell. Fogarty's more recent work, examining North African POWs during the Great War, is a welcome addition to the scholarship on colonial captivity. See Fogarty, "Out of North Africa," 1–20.

26. Works by Ruth Ginio and Eric Jennings demonstrate both Vichy and Free French racism in the colonies. See Ginio, *French Colonialism Unmasked* and *French Army*; Jennings, *Vichy in the Tropics* and *Free French Africa*.

27. French sociologist Armelle Mabon has publicly criticized the French government for obscuring the truth and ignoring the colonial prisoners' memory in an impassioned treatment of the subject. By concentrating on French-language sources almost exclusively, Mabon has missed much of the previous scholarship on Thiaroye specifically and colonial prisoners generally. See Mabon, *Prisonniers de guerre "indigènes."*

28. Fishman, *We Will Wait*; Fishman, "Grand Delusions"; Pollard, *Reign of Virtue.*

29. See Lawler, *Soldiers of Misfortune*; Thomas, "Vichy Government," 658; Mabon and Cuttier, "La Singulière captivité," 142; Mabon, *Prisonniers de guerre "indigènes"*; Fargettas, *Les Tirailleurs sénégalais.*

30. Scheck, *French Colonial Soldiers.*

31. Gregory Mann's monograph expertly examines the role of West African veterans of both world wars in shaping the French colonies throughout the twentieth century. His arguments are particularly strong when examining the impact of war on veterans and the social context to which many colonial soldiers returned. See Mann, *Native Sons*. Myron Echenberg has one chapter on captivity, but his critical argument is that the French authorities disregarded a fundamental change in its colonial soldiers, who united through captivity and felt that they had fought better than the French in 1940 and thus deserved to be treated fairly after the war. See Echenberg, *Colonial Conscripts.*

32. Note on the role of the CRF in assisting POWs, 6 November 1941, SHD, 2P67; see also, Besson, note for Direction général de l'administration de la guerre et du contrôle, 12 November 1941, SHD, 2P66; Jugnet, note regarding the POW service, 6 May 1941, SHD, 9R36.

33. Soon after the war, André Siegfried established the theory of a good Vichy following Pétain and a bad Vichy under Pierre Laval's influence. See Azéma, "Vichy et la mémoire," 26; Siegfried, *De la IIIe à la IVe Republique*. This theory sought to reconcile Pétain, the immensely popular war hero of Verdun, with the dark history of Vichy. Taking up an argument used by Pétain at his trial, the historian Robert Aron established in the 1950s the "shield metaphor," based on unpublished records from the High Court trials, to explain that Pétain's decisions, albeit difficult ones to make, acted as a shield protecting France "from worse" at the hands of the Germans. See Aron, *Histoire de Vichy*. Until the 1960s French scholarship continued to focus on the French Resistance and avoided more difficult topics like collaboration. In a revolutionary move, using German archives, Henri Michel ventured the thesis that the French had sought collaboration with the Germans to avoid some of the constraints from the armistice. See Michel, *Vichy* and "La révolution nationale." Using American, German, and French sources, Paxton disproved the "shield metaphor," instead arguing that Pétain and other Vichy officials had acted

voluntarily and deliberately in hopes of a better place in Hitler's Europe. The strength of Paxton's arguments lay in his insistence that choices made between 1940 and 1944 were French ones and had not been imposed by the Germans. See Paxton, *Vichy France*, xv. While Paxton receives much of the historical credit, many of his arguments were published by the German historian Eberhard Jäckel in 1966 and translated into French in 1968. See Jäckel, *Frankreich in Hitlers Europa*.

1. GENESIS

1. Echenberg, *Colonial Conscripts*, 27.
2. Echenberg, *Colonial Conscripts*, 35.
3. Huré, *L'Armee d'Afrique*, 2.
4. Michel, *Les Africains*, 16.
5. Michel, *Les Africains*, 16.
6. Fogarty, *Race and War*, 44.
7. Clayton, *France, Soldiers and Africa*, 6.
8. Sharp, *French Army*, 116.
9. Clayton, *France, Soldiers and Africa*, 6–7.
10. Clayton, *France, Soldiers and Africa*, 7.
11. Echenberg, *Colonial Conscripts*, 31.
12. Michel, *Les Africains*, 81–82.
13. Pedroncini, *Histoire militaire*, 298; Thobie et al., *Histoire*, 78.
14. Echenberg, *Colonial Conscripts*, 33; Crowder, *Colonial West Africa*, 110.
15. Thobie et al., *Histoire*, 76.
16. Jennings, "Remembering 'Other' Losses," 10.
17. Deroo and Champeaux, "Panorama des Troupes coloniales," 73.
18. Fogarty, *Race and War*, 42–43.
19. Note, Comité d'aide et d'assistance coloniale, 1914–1915, BDIC, O Pièce 14168.
20. Michel, *Les Africains*, 35.
21. Michel, *Les Africains*, 29, 111.
22. Echenberg, *Colonial Conscripts*, 31.
23. Echenberg, *Colonial Conscripts*, 32.
24. Thobie et al., *Histoire*, 77.
25. Crowder, *Colonial West Africa*, 111.
26. Crowder, *Colonial West Africa*, 113.
27. Michel, *Les Africains*, 49.
28. "We have seen that during the war as many Negroes as possible were recruited, to be used as cannon-fodder. They recruited so many that the French governors refused to go on recruiting because they were afraid the people would revolt. But since it was necessary to recruit at all costs, they sought out an outstanding Negro, heaped

honours upon him and made him Commissioner General and representative of the French Republic in Africa. They had him accompanied everywhere he went by French officers and decorated Negroes." Senghor, "Negro's Fight for Freedom."

29. Jones, *Violence against Prisoners*, 74.

30. Fogarty, *Race and War*, 85.

31. Echenberg, *Colonial Conscripts*, 33.

32. Abbal, *Soldats oubliés*, 57.

33. Huré, *L'Armee d'Afrique*, 296.

34. Lunn, "Les Races guerrières," 525.

35. Lunn, "Les Races guerrières," 529; Echenberg, *Colonial Conscripts*, 530–31.

36. *Histoire et épopée*, 327.

37. *Manuel troupes*, 2:342, BDIC, S 11562.

38. Jones, *Violence against Prisoners*, 136.

39. Meynier, *L'Algérie révélée*, 434–35.

40. Gayme, *Les Prisonniers de guerre*, 56; Abbal, *Soldats oubliés*, 57.

41. Jones, *Violence against Prisoners*, 134.

42. Lüsebrink, "Les Troupes coloniales," 74.

43. Abbal, *Soldats oubliés*, 57–58.

44. Jones, *Violence against Prisoners*, 136.

45. Nelson, "'Black Horror,'" 611; *Manuel officiers*, 2:342.

46. Nelson, "'Black Horror,'" 613.

47. Roos, "Women's Rights, Nationalist Anxiety," 477.

48. Interpellation of May 19, 1920, Document No. 2995 in Verhandlungen der verfassungsgebenden Deutschen Nationalversammlung, Stenographische Berichte, Session 1919/20, vol. 343, 3407, cited in Roos, "Women's Rights, Nationalist Anxiety," 474.

49. Roos, "Women's Rights, Nationalist Anxiety," 495; 498.

50. General Brissaud-Desmaillet, "Ordres generals d'opérations, 3e partie, 127th Division," 3 May 1919, SHD, 15 H136.

51. La Gorce, *L'Empire écartelé*, 10.

52. Evans, "Culture and Empire," 2, 10.

53. Ginio, *French Colonialism Unmasked*, 26.

54. *Manuel officiers*, 3:14, BDIC, S Pièce 8551.

55. *Manuel troupes*, 2:46; see also *Histoire et épopée*, 327–28.

56. *Manuel officiers*, 1:9, BDIC, S Pièce 8551.

57. General Langlois, *Manuel officiers*, 2:11, BDIC, S Pièce 8551.

58. *Manuel officiers*, 2:339.

59. *Manuel officiers*, 1:9.

60. *Manuel troupes*, 1:36, BDIC, S 11562; Fogarty, *Race and War*, 98, 100.

61. *Manuel troupes*, 1:101.

62. Roux, *L'Appel de l'Afrique*, 71.

63. *Manuel officiers*, 2:16.

64. Doze, *Le Général Mazillier*, 141.

65. *Manuel troupes*, 1:8.

66. *Manuel officiers*, 2:16, 25.

67. *Manuel officiers*, 3:11.

68. *Manuel officiers*, 1:9.

69. *Manuel troupes*, 2:226.

70. *Manuel troupes*, 1:36.

71. *Manuel troupes*, 2:36.

72. *Manuel officiers*, 3:20.

73. *Manuel troupes*, 1:36.

74. Fogarty, *Race and War*, 2.

75. Girardet, *L'Idée coloniale*, 117.

76. La Gorce, *L'Empire écartelé*, 9.

77. Blaise Diagne, *L'Effort colonial dans le monde* (Sud-Ouest Economique, 31 August 1931), 743, BDIC, Q 16314; Krooth, *Arms & Empire*, 95.

78. Paul Reynaud, "L'Empire français," in *L'Effort colonial*, 687, BDIC, Q 16314.

79. Charbonneau, *Les Contingents coloniaux*.

80. Jean Odin, "La Plus grande France," in *L'Effort colonial*, 745, BDIC, Q 16314.

81. Lebovics, *True France*, 55, 70.

82. Aldcroft, *From Versailles to Wall Street*, 178–81.

83. Krooth, *Arms & Empire*, 95.

84. Hitler, *Mein Kampf*, 589.

85. Commission général de l'information, summary of intelligence on German propaganda from the press 16 January to 29 February, 31 March 1940, SHD, 27N68; http://dresden-postkolonial.de/kolonialausstellungen.

86. Michael Wilson, "Camp for German Military Prisoners," 4 March 1940, SHD, 27N36.

87. Summary of German radio broadcasts, 18 July 1940, SHD, 31N123.

88. Adolf Hitler, speech, 6 October 1939, SHD, 27N68.

89. Jackson, *France*, 94.

90. Lawler, *Soldiers of Misfortune*, 31.

91. Luguern, "Ni civil ni militaire," 185.

92. Governor of French Guinea to Léon Cayla, 16 September 1939, ANS, 2D5.

93. Letter for directeur du service des informations from Direction des affaires politiques et administrative, 22 September 1939, ANS, 2D5.

94. Fogarty, *Race and War*, 2.

95. Crowder, *Colonial West Africa*, 107.

96. *Manuel troupes*, 2:48.

97. Abdou N'Diaye to chef de la Brigade des recherches à Saint-Louis, 15 September 1939, ANS, 2D5.

98. Directeur des affaires politiques et administratives to directeur des services des informations, 16 September 1939, ANS, 2D5.

99. Abdou N'Diaye to chef de la Brigade des recherches à Saint-Louis, 15 September 1939 ANS, 2D5.

100. Clayton, *France, Soldiers and Africa*, 121–22.

101. Rives and Dietrich, *Héros méconnus*, 121.

102. Jones, *Violence against Prisoners*, 123.

103. Perisse, note for the Direction des services du personnel et du materiel de l'administration centrale, 25 March 1940, SHD, 7N2480.

104. Michael Wilson, "Camp for German Military Prisoners," 4 March 1940, SHD, 27N36.

105. Ministre de l'information, summary of intelligence on German propaganda in the press 1 March–1 April 1940, 15 May 1940, SHD, 27N68.

106. Chef d'Etat Major to General Gamelin, 2 January 1940, SHD, 27N68.

107. General d'armée Georges, note for the army, 19 February 1940, SHD, 27N68.

108. Commandant Gibou, postal control for 53rd RIC, 3 May 1940, SHD, 34N1081.

109. Cayla to the governors of Senegal, Mauritanie, and governor administrator of Dakar, 2 May 1940, ANS, 2D5.

110. Desanti to Cayla, 31 May 1940, ANS, 2D5.

111. Echenberg, *Colonial Conscripts*, 92.

112. Colonel Gauche, daily summary of military postal censorship, 7 June 1940, SHD, 27N70.

113. Daily summary of military postal censorship from 30 May 1940, 31 May 1940, SHD, 27N70.

114. Daily summary of military postal censorship from 16–19 May 1940, 20 May 1940, SHD, 27N70.

115. Captain Pilet, extracts from report of 21 RIC, 2e Bataillon du 53 RICMS, 11 September 1940, SHD, 34N1081.

116. Daily summary of military postal censorship from 29 May 1940, 30 May 1940, SHD, 27N70.

117. Bloch, *L'Etrange défaite*, 65–66.

118. Summary of the first reports from the censor of the troops' reaction to the announcement of a large enemy offensive, 16 May 1940, SHD, 27N70; see also Sous-Lieutenant Gilbert, combat report for the 7th company of the 53 RICMS, 5–7 June 1940, SHD,

34N1081; daily summary of military postal censorship from 26 May 1940, 27 May 1940, SHD, 27N70.

119. Daily summary of military postal censorship from 26 May 1940, 27 May 1940, SHD, 27N70.

120. Sous-Lieutenant Gilbert, combat report for the 7th company of the 53 RICMS, 5–7 June 1940, SHD, 34N1081; see also Colonel Gauche, daily summary of military postal censorship, 7 June 1940, SHD, 27N70.

121. Information from an occasional native informant, 17 September 1941, ANS, 2D23/28.

122. Deroo and Champeaux, *La Force noire*, 174.

123. Sous-Lieutenant Maurice Chatelard, summary of command report for 4th section of the 9th Company of 53 RIC, 25 November 1940, SHD, 34N1081; Sous-Lieutenant Gilbert, combat report for the 7th Company of the 53 RICMS, 5–7 June 1940, SHD, 34N1081.

124. MacKenzie, *Colditz Myth*, 37; Scheck, *Hitler's African Victims*, 22.

125. Sergeant Langenfeld, report 10th RTM, n.d., SHD, 2P88.

126. Colonel Bouriand, report on 19 June 1940's combat, 28 June 1940, SHD, 34N1098.

127. Levavasseur to the governor of the Sudan, 7 May 1941, ANS, 2D23/28.

128. Edouard, interview of Dibor Cissé, 17 April 1941, ANS, 2D23/28.

129. Intelligence forwarded to the Direction des affaires politiques et administratives and sûreté générale, 22 August 1941, ANS, 2D23/28.

130. Lawler, *Soldiers of Misfortune*, 95.

131. 28e RICMS, information briefing, 10 July 1940, SHD, 14P46.

132. Sergent d'activité Hassen-Ladjimi, escape report, 30 September 1940, SHD, 14P16

133. Caporal-chef Leonanci, escape report, n.d., SHD, 14P17; see also Scheck, *Hitler's African Victims*, 24; Lawler, *Soldiers of Misfortune*, 96.

134. MacKenzie, *Colditz Myth*, 36.

135. Chief of the 12th Section of the Affaires politiques et administration to Boisson, 18 March 1941, ANS, 2D23/28.

136. Scheck, *Hitler's African Victims*, 25.

137. Chief of the 12th Section of the Affaires politiques et administration to Boisson, 18 March 1941, ANS, 2D23/28.

138. Scheck, *Hitler's African Victims*, 58.

139. Hull, *Absolute Destruction*, 145–46.

140. Joseph Julien Dache, witness statement, n.d., AN, 72/AJ/291; see also Paul Mansire, report on captivity, June 1940–January 1941, AN, 72/AJ/291.

141. Hitler, *Mein Kampf*, 384–85.

142. Scheck, *Hitler's African Victims*, 118.

143. Streit, "Prisonniers de guerre allies," 31–32.

2. PHASE ONE

1. Ageron, "Vichy," 122.
2. Azéma, *From Munich*, 42.
3. de Gaulle, Speech on the BBC, 18 June 1940.
4. Note from LaCarniere, president of the Comité départemental d'accueil et d'entr'aide de la L. F. C. de l'Isère, SHD, 2P82; see also Paxton, *Vichy France*, 15.
5. Report on situation of the French armies at the time of the armistice request, n.d., SHD, 27NII.
6. Thomas, *French Empire at War*, 39.
7. Thomas, *French Empire at War*, 39–43.
8. Thomas, *French Empire at War*, 43.
9. State of negotiations, subcommittee for POWs, 8 October 1940, AN, AJ/41/1835.
10. Clayton, *France, Soldiers and Africa*, 125.
11. Suret-Canale, *French Colonialism*, 464; Betts, *France and Decolonialism*, 51.
12. Jennings, *Free French Africa*, 17.
13. Jennings, *Free French Africa*, 176.
14. Thomas, *French Empire at War*, 70.
15. Ginio, *French Colonialism Unmasked*, xiv.
16. Thomas, *French Empire at War*, 40.
17. Report regarding the prisoners' return, 15 September 1941, SHD, 2P82.
18. Fishman, *We Will Wait*, xii.
19. Note regarding POWs, 22 December 1941, AN, AJ/41/2053; Jackson, *France*, 509.
20. Note for the cabinet of the secretary of state for war, 4 October [1940?], SHD, 2P79; "Faces of Prisoners" from Stalag VII-C in Silesia [1942?], AN, F/41/273.
21. Pétain's message to prisoners, 9 October 1940, quoted in Durand, *La Captivité*, 311.
22. Paxton, *Vichy France*, 69.
23. Report regarding the prisoners' return, 15 September 1941, SHD, 2P82.
24. *Paris-Midi*, 12 June 1941, SHD, 2P79.
25. Brochure, *Un an de travail*, 17 June 1941, SHD, 2P82.
26. Chauvin, note for the CAA, 8 September 1940, AN, AJ/41/1834.
27. Articles on politics or Franco-German relations required prior German approval; see AN, F/9/2007, Scapini to the ministers and secretaries of state, 12 November 1941.
28. *Je suis partout*, 25 October 1941.
29. *L'Oeuvre*, 12 August 1942, AN, F1a/3653.
30. Brochure, *L'Empire, notre meilleur chance, retour sur le passé*, n.d., AN, F/41/273.
31. *La France socialiste*, 28 August 1942, AN, F1a/3653; see also *Inter-France*, "Les Délais d'achèvement," n.d., AN, F1a/3653.
32. Jackson, *France*, 129.
33. Darlan, report on Franco-British relations, 31 May 1941, SHD, 2P82.

34. Barnett, *Empire of Humanity*, 99–101, 104.

35. Palmieri, "How Warfare Has Evolved," 986.

36. Barnett, *Empire of Humanity*, 104.

37. Hoffmann, "Introduction," 7.

38. Jones, *Violence against Prisoners*, 126–28.

39. Jones, *Violence against Prisoners*, 132.

40. Palmieri, "How Warfare Has Evolved," 992.

41. Vourkoutiotis, *Prisoners of War*, 28.

42. Huntziger, note for the minister of defense, Nationale direction des services de l'armée, 22 July 1940, AN, AJ/41/1834.

43. Mieliecki, CAA to DFCAA, 26 July 1940, AN, AJ/41/1834.

44. Mieliecki, CAA to DFCAA, 1 August 1940, AN, F/9/2001.

45. Letter to president of the CCAPG, 2 December 1940, AD Vienne, 1J746; Frebault to Bigard, copied to Scapini, 6 December 1941, AN, F/9/2351.

46. Chauvin, note for the sous-commission des prisonners de guerre, 17 September 1940, AN, F/9/2002.

47. Convention Relative to the Treatment of Prisoners of War, Articles 8 and 77.

48. French POW camps in Eure et Loir, 20 August 1940, AD Eure et Loir, 1W101; *Le Petit Vésulien*, 9 September 1940, AD Vesoul, 1PJ32.

49. PTT, note for the regional, departmental and ambulant line directors, 8 October 1940, AN, F/9/2829.

50. Bigard to Diemer, 9 November 1940, AN, F/9/2959; Huntziger to von Stülpnagel, president of the CAA, 16 July [1940?], AJ/41/1834.

51. OKW collective releases, no. 2, 7 July 1941, BA-MA, RW6/270.

52. Humbert, note for DSA POW section, 13 November 1940, AN, AJ/41/1834.

53. Wylie, "1929 Prisoner of War Convention," 101.

54. Wylie, *Barbed Wire Diplomacy*, 7.

55. Scheck, "Prisoner of War Question," 375.

56. CRF, Paris automobile section, 21 September 1941, SHD, 1P33.

57. Humbert, note for DSA POW section, 13 November 1940, AN, AJ/41/1834.

58. Durand, *La Captivité*, 315.

59. Scheck, *French Colonial Soldiers*, 69.

60. D. A. Davis to Madame Huntziger, 21 February 1941, SHD, 2P66.

61. Vourkoutiotis, *Prisoners of War*, 29–30.

62. For examples, see Scheck, *French Colonial Soldiers*, 54, 63, 65, 85–86.

63. State of negotiations, subcommittee for POWs, 8 October 1940, AN, AJ/41/1835.

64. Jeanmot, *Les Prisonniers de guerre*, AN, 72 AJ/291.

65. Durand, *La Captivité*, 312.

66. Paxton, *Vichy France*, 72.

67. Durand, *La Captivité*, 317.
68. Scheck, *French Colonial Soldiers*, 68.
69. Chauvin, note for the CAA, 9 September 1940, AN, AJ/41/1834.
70. Scheck, "Prisoner of War Question," 367, 369.
71. Wiesbaden, summary of meeting between Chauvin and Von Rosenberg, 14 September 1940, AN, AJ/41/1835.
72. DFCAA summary activity from 14 to 17 September 1940, 18 September 1940, AN, AJ/41/1835.
73. Besson to Scapini, 5 December 1940, SHD, 2P66.
74. Humbert, note for the DSA, 13 December 1940, AN, AJ/41/1834.
75. Scheck, *French Colonial Soldiers*, 75.
76. Scapini to Tiepelmann, note concerning colored troops, 16 December 1940, SHD, 2P66.
77. Prost, report on captivity and escape, n.d., SHD, 14P46.
78. Scheck, *French Colonial Soldiers*, 89.
79. Scapini to Abetz, 10 December 1941, AN, F/9/2007.
80. Poussart, meeting with Scapini's services, 6 June [1941?], AN, AJ/41/2053.
81. State of negotiations, subcommittee for POWs, 8 October 1940, AN, AJ/41/1835.
82. Durand, *La Captivité*, 111.
83. Report of the DFCAA's activities 17–23 November, 25 November 1940, AN, AJ/41/1835.
84. Subcommittee for POWs, 1 December 1940, AN, AJ/41/1835.
85. Scheck, "Prisoner of War Question," 369.
86. Jackson, *France*, 233.
87. Doyen to Scapini, 21 January 1941, AN, F/9/2007; Annex IV questions du cadre de la Convention de Genève traitées par le SDPG, n.d., AN, F/9/2007; Annex V questions hors du cadre de la Convention de Genève traitées par le SDPG, n.d., AN, F/9/2007.
88. Summary, 17 April 1942, SHD, 2P64.
89. Oelsner-Wolner to the prefect of Gironde, 30 November 1940, AD Gironde, 45W15.
90. C. Stupley to Dr. Bonnaud, 15 November 1941, AN, F/9/2351.
91. Memo from Boisson to governors of Senegal, Mauritania, circumscriptions of Dakar and its dependences, Sudan, Guinea, Ivory Coast, Dahomey, Niger, and the commissioner of Togo, 27 January 1941, ANS, 2D24. 28.
92. Scheck, *French Colonial Soldiers*, 62, 75.
93. Mamadou Kane to his cousin, 8 December 1940, ANOM, IAFFPOL/639.
94. Platon to Boisson, 19 January 1941, ANOM, IAFFPOL/639.
95. Moussa Baccouche to the president of the Red Cross Alger, 8 September 1941, AN, F/9/2351.

96. Summary of meeting regarding POWs, 17 October 1941, SHD, 2P64.

97. Secretary of State for War, summary of meeting regarding POWs, 31 July 1941, SHD, 2P64; Note 1388, 22 December 1941; AN, AJ/41/2053.

98. Leonanci, escape report, n.d., SHD, 14P17; for similar accounts, see Captain Debayeux to the chef d'escadron commanding the IV/64e RAA, 10 October 1940, SHD, 14P31; Ahmed Ben Mohamed, escape report, 11 September 1940, SHD, 14P17; Hassen-Ladjimi, escape report, 30 September 1940, SHD, 14P16, Pasquier, escape report, 30 August 1940, SHD, 14P16; Manuel Aldeguer, captivity report, 4 November 1940, SHD, 14P16.

99. Chedorge, escape report, 2 November 1940, SHD, 14P17; Report on soldiers who escaped from POW camps, 7 November 1940, SHD, 14P17.

100. Robert Paris and François Sanchez, escape report, n.d., SHD, 14P17.

101. De Peralo, escape from Epinal, 27 September 1940, SHD, 14P46.

102. Hassen-Ladjimi, escape report, 30 September 1940, SHD, 14P16; Paris and Sanchez, escape report, n.d., SHD, 14P17; Robert Chedorge, escape report, 2 November 1940, SHD, 14P17.

103. Lieutenant de Peralo, escape from Epinal, 27 September 1940, SHD, 14P46; Lieutenant Bon, excerpt from report, n.d., SHD, 14P17.

104. T. E. Bonne to général directeur des Troupes coloniales, 23 September 1944, SHD, 34N1081.

105. Vourkoutiotis, *Prisoners of War*, 31.

106. Scheck, *French Colonial Soldiers*, 36.

107. Proposition de citation à l'ordre du régiment, Bancilon Albin, du 27e Régiment de Tirailleurs algériens, 1 August 1940, SHD, 14P16; Debayeux to the chef d'escadron commanding the IV/64e RAA, 10 October 1940, SHD, 14P31.

108. Lieutenant Colonel Nardin, special native office report, 2 November 1940, SHD, 14P31.

109. Debayeux to the chef d'escadron commanding the IV/64e RAA, 10 October 1940, SHD, 14P31; A. Belkacem, escape report, 28 October 1940, SHD, 14P16.

110. Pasquier, escape report, 30 August 1940, SHD, 14P16.

111. Debayeux to the chef d'escadron commanding the IV/64e RAA, 10 October 1940, SHD, 14P31.

112. Lavavasseur to the governor of the Sudan, 7 May 1941, ANS, 2D23.

113. Mohamed Ben Mohamed Ben El Habib, escape report, 29 August 1941, SHD, 14P17.

114. Debayeux to the chef d'escadron commanding the IV/64e RAA, 10 October 1940, SHD, 14P31.

115. Pasquier, escape report, 30 August 1940, SHD, 14P16.

116. For more on German inspiration for physical buffer zones, see Bernhard, "Borrowing from Mussolini," 631.

117. MacKenzie, *Colditz Myth*, 266.

118. Lawler, *Soldiers of Misfortune*, 104.

119. Vourkoutiotis, *Prisoners of War*, 38.

120. Waltzog, *Les Principaux accords*. This is a French translation of *Recht der Landkriegsführung* (1942), where he quotes and explains the Geneva Convention.

121. Pasquier, escape report, 30 August 1940; SHD, 14P31, Debayeux to the chef d'escadron commanding the IV/64e RAA, 10 October 1940, SHD, 14P16.

122. Scapini to Koeltz, 20 March 1941, SHD, 2P65.

123. Captain Rafa, report on his activities during his captivity, 10 July 1948, SHD, 1K908.

124. OKW, special report on POWs, no. 5, 10 October 1941, BA-MA, RW6/270.

125. Captain Larroque, escape report, 12 July 1940, SHD, 14P46; see also Warrant Officer Fillet, report on capture by the Germans, detention, and escape, n.d., SHD, 14P17.

126. Jeanmot, *Les Prisonniers de guerre*, AN, 72 AJ/291.

127. Ferrières, *Jean Cavaillés*, AN, 72AJ/1965.

128. Scheck, *French Colonial Soldiers*, 125.

129. Thomas, "Vichy Government," 663.

130. Telegramme from Cercle Segou to governor of the Sudan, 19 January 1941, ANS, 2D23.

131. General François to commander in chief of the TOAFN, 10 July 1940, SHD, 3H253.

132. Paris and Sanchez, escape report, n.d., SHD, 14P17.

133. Lallemant, report on the POW camps in the region of Montdidier, 6 May 1941, AD Somme, 48W70.

134. Le Féloch, captivity report, 26 February 1942, SHD, 34N5.

135. Marti and de Morsier, ICRC, visit to Frontstalag 195 Onesse-Laharie, 13 June 1941, AN, F/9/2351.

136. De la Laurencie to prefect of Charente, 30 September 1940, AD Charente, 1W37.

137. Paul B. Anderson and August Senaud, report on Airvault, 23 January 1941, AN, F/9/2351.

138. Vourkoutiotis, *Prisoners of War*, 50.

139. Durand, *La Vie quotidienne*, 51–52.

140. Report from the city engineer, "Alimentation hydraulique et assainissement d'un camp de prisonniers sur les terrains du Polo," 18 October 1940, AD Pyrénées-Atlantiques, Bayonne E Dépôt Bayonne 1W14.

141. Prefect of Charente to Le Calloc'h, inspecteur du travail, 10 October 1940, AD Charente, 1W37.

142. Le Calloc'h to prefect of Charente, 12 October 1940, AD Charente, 1W37.

143. Kommandant Frontstalag 184 to prefect of Charente, 15 November 1940, AD Charente, 1W37.

144. Prefect of Charente to ingénieur en chef des ponts et chaussées, 18 November 1940, AD Charente, 1W37.

145. Convention Relative to the Treatment of Prisoners of War, Article 4.

146. Von Ploetz to prefect of the Charente, 18 December 1940, AD Charente, 1W37.

147. Letter from l'intendant près du chef de district de l'Administration militaire de Bordeaux, 19 March 1941, AD Charente, 1W37.

148. J. Brunet, note for the prefects, 4 October 1941, AD Somme, 26W401.

149. Mayor of Voves to prefect of Eure et Loir, September 1940, AD Eure et Loir, 1W101.

3. EVERYDAY LIFE IN CAPTIVITY

1. Durand, *La Captivité*, 59.

2. Thomas, "Les Prisonniers coloniaux," 114.

3. Frontstalags in France, 1 March 1941, AN, F/9/2959; Analysis of inspectors' reports from POW camps in occupied France, 15 April 1941, SHD, 2P78.

4. Scheck, *French Colonial Soldiers*, 69, 24; Thomas, "Le Gouvernment de Vichy," 327.

5. Jean Schmidt, monthly report, 1 February 1942, AN, F/9/2351.

6. Le Gouest, summary of inspection reports from POW camps, n.d. (camp visited 12 June 1941), SHD, 2P78.

7. Scheck, *French Colonial Soldiers*, 62.

8. MacKenzie, *Colditz Myth*, 280; OKW special report, no. 2, 7 July 1941, BA-MA, RW6/270.

9. Wylie, *Barbed Wire Diplomacy*, 171.

10. René Scapini, visit to Frontstalag 153, 28 March 1941, SHD, 2P78; René Scapini, inspection report of Frontstalag 153, 12 June 1941, SHD, 2P78.

11. "Service de l'aide aux prisonniers de guerre: Une oeuvre humanitaire," *La Gazette de Lausanne*, 21 January 1941, AN, F/41/266.

12. Paul Anderson and Auguste Senaud, report of YMCA visits to POW camps in occupied France, 6 April 1941, AN, F/9/2351.

13. Lawler, *Soldiers of Misfortune*, 112.

14. Mrs Henri Dehau, observations from various POW camps, n.d. (attached to a protocol dated 4 November 1941), SHD, 2P65.

15. Convention Relative to the Treatment of Prisoners of War, Article 10.

16. Captivity report written by a recently released prisoner, 7 July 1942, SHD, 2P70.

17. Mohamed Ben Ali, capture and escape report, 7 November 1940, SHD, 14P17.

18. T. C. le Féloch, captivity report, 26 February 1942, SHD, 34N5.

19. Haeusler to prefect of Vienne, 13 May 1941, AD Vienne, 1566W2.

20. Taittinger to prefect of Loire Inférieure, 22 July 1940, AD Loire Atlantique, 1690W127.
21. Captivity report written by a recently released prisoner, 7 July 1942, SHD, 2P70. Senghor has identified the camp commander as Lieutenant Bayle; however, Scheck asserts that Senghor is probably referring to Lieutenant Bayle; see Sheck, *French Colonial Soldiers,* 110.
22. Anderson and Senaud, report on camp visits in occupied France, Montargis, 20 January 1941, AN, F/9/2351.
23. Anderson and Senaud, report of YMCA visits to POW camps in occupied France, 6 April 1941, AN, F/9/2351.
24. Marti and de Morsier, ICRC visit to Frontstalag 195, Onesse-Laharie, 13 June 1941, AN, F/9/2351.
25. Paul B. Anderson and August Senaud, report on camp visits in occupied France, Airvault, 23 January 1941, AN, F/9/2351.
26. Michel Gnimagnon, captivity report, 7 February 1941, SHD, 14P4.
27. Captivity report written by a recently released prisoner, 7 July 1942, SHD, 2P7.
28. For more examples, see Anderson and Senaud, report on camp visits in occupied France, Airvault, 23 January 1941, AN, F/9/2351; Bigard, DSPG mission to Savenay, n.d., AN, F/9/2963; Bigard, DSPG mission to Troyes, 6 January 1941, AN, F/9/2963; Bonnaud, visit to Frontstalag 124 Joigny, 19 March 1941, SHD, 2P78; Georges Scapini and Jean Desbons, summary of visit to Frontstalag 195, 10 April 1941, SHD, 2P78.
29. Prefect of Loiret, note regarding POWs in the department, 6 February 1941, AD Loiret, 11R14; camp inspection report for Rennes, 23 January 1941, AN, F/9/2963; Anderson and Senaud, report on camp visits in occupied France, Orléans, 21 January, 4 February 1941, AN, F/9/2351.
30. DSPG, report on the camp of Chalôns sur Marne, 6 January 1941, AN, F/9/2963.
31. Anderson and Senaud, report on camp visits in occupied France, Montargis, 20 January 1941, AN, F/9/2351.
32. Lieutenant de Peralo, escape report, 27 September 1940, SHD, 14P46.
33. Faure, report on information provided by escaped prisoner Marcel Guillet, 20 January 1941, SHD, 2P88.
34. ICRC, report on Joigny, 18 June 1941, AN, F/9/2351; Vourkoutiotis, *Prisoners of War,* 54.
35. Henry Eboué, captivity report, 10.
36. Debayeux to chef d'escadron, 10 October 1940, SHD, 14P3.
37. Analysis of inspectors' reports from POW camps in occupied France, 15 April 1941, SHD, 2P78.
38. Jean Detroyat, report of visit to Frontstalag 121 Epinal, 27 March 1941, SHD, 2P78.
39. André Paul Sadon to secretary of state for home affairs, 10 Octobre 1941, SHD, 2P78.

40. Analysis of inspectors' reports from POW camps in occupied France, n.d. (camp visited 22 May 1941), SHD, 2P78; Le Gouest, summary of inspection reports from POW camps, n.d. (camp visited 12 June 1941) SHD, 2P78.

41. YMCA, report on visits to POW camps, 11 April 1941, AN, F/9/2351.

42. Scheck, *French Colonial Soldiers*, 240.

43. Anderson and Senaud, report on camp visits in occupied France, Montargis, 20 January 1941, AN, F/9/2351.

44. CRF, Automobile section of Bordeaux, report on camp visits in the Landes, 15 October 1941, AN, F/9/2351.

45. Bigard, DSPG mission to St Medard, 6–10 January 1941, AN, F/9/2963.

46. Lallemant, report on the situation of POW camps, 6 Mai 1941, AD Somme, 48W70; see also ICRC, visit to St. Martin d'Orney, 13 June 1941, AN, F/9/2351.

47. Scheck, *French Colonial Soldiers*, 232.

48. CRF, Automobile section of Bordeaux, report on camp visits in the Landes, 15 October 1941, AN, F/9/2351.

49. Prefect of the Loiret, note regarding POWs in the Loiret, 6 February 1941, AD Loiret, 11R14.

50. CCAPG to prefect of Haute Saône, 7 December 1940, AD Haute Saône, 63J33.

51. L. Bonnaud-Delamare to prefect of the Ardennes, 21 January 1942, AD Ardennes, 1W146.

52. René Scapini, visit to Frontstalag 153, 28 March 1941, SHD, 2P78.

53. Jean Detroyat, report of visit to Frontstalag 121 Epinal, 27 March 1941, SHD, 2P78; see also CRF, automobile section of Bordeaux, report on camp visits in the Landes, 15 October 1941, AN, F/9/2351.

54. Verdier to Huntziger, 26 April 1941, SHD, 2P78.

55. Ageron, "Vichy," 131.

56. Anderson and Senaud, report of YMCA visits to POW camps in occupied France, 6 April 1941, AN, F/9/2351.

57. Captivity report written by a recently released prisoner, 7 July 1942, SHD, 2P70.

58. Bigard, DSPG mission to Troyes, 9–10 January 1941, AN, F/9/2963.

59. Schimmer and de Morsier, ICRC visit to Frontstalag 195, 28 October 1942, AN, F/9/2351.

60. ICRC, report on Joigny, 18 June 1941, AN, F/9/2351; for more examples, see Local delegate to the president of the CCAPG, 23 March 1941, AD Haute Saône, 63J33; Anderson and Senaud, report of YMCA visits to POW camps in occupied France, 6 April 1941, AN, F/9/2351.

61. Anderson and Senaud, report of YMCA visits to POW camps in occupied France, 6 April 1941, AN, F/9/2351; Marti and de Morsier, ICRC visit to Frontstalag 195 Onesse-Laharie, 13 June 1941, AN, F/9/2351.

62. ICRC, report on Joigny, 18 June 1941, AN, F/9/2351.

63. Schirmer and de Morsier, ICRC visit to Frontstalag 141 Vesoul, 12 November 1942, AN, F/9/2351

64. Jean Guérin, report of captivity and release, 22 December 1941, SHD, 34N1081.

65. Scheck, *French Colonial Soldiers*, 92.

66. Guerin, report of captivity and release, 22 December 1941, SHD, 34N1081.

67. Mabon, *Prisonniers de guerre "indigènes,"* 56.

68. Schirmer and de Morsier, ICRC visit to Frontstalag 141 Vesoul, 12 November 1942, AN, F/9/2351.

69. Convention Relative to the Treatment of Prisoners of War, Article 43.

70. Bigard, DSPG, subsection in Paris, n.d., AD Marne, Châlons-en-Champagne, 5Z783.

71. Bouret to Popelain, April 1942, AD Marne, Reims, 6W R819.

72. Mrs Henri Dehau, observations from various POW camps, n.d. (attached to a protocol dated 4 November 1941), SHD, 2P65.

73. Anderson and Senaud, report of YMCA visits to POW camps in occupied France, 4 February 1941, AN, F/9/2351,

74. Anderson and Senaud, report on camp visits in occupied France, Orléans, 21 January 1941; Montargis, 20 January 1941, AN, F/9/2351,

75. Schirmer and de Morsier, ICRC camp visit, Rennes, 5 November 1942l AN, F/9/2351,

76. Letter from the department delegate to the director [director of what is not indicated], 17 June 1942, AD Marne, Reims, 6W R819.

77. MacKenzie, *Colditz Myth*, 128.

78. El Mouldi Benhassen to president of the CRF, forwarded to Scapini, 17 May 1942, AN, F/9/2351.

79. Préfecture d'Oran, Centre d'information de d'etudes, 6 February 1942, ANOM, Alg GGA ICM-73.

80. Bonko Hambrié to Pétain, n.d. (response dated 11 August 1941), AN, F/9/2351.

81. Bonnard to sous-direction des prisonniers de guerre, 20 June 1941, AN, F/9/2351.

82. Robert Eboué and Henry Eboué, captivity reports.

83. ICRC, visit to Mont de Marsan, 13 June 1941, AN, F/9/2351; for more examples, see Captivity report written by a recently released prisoner, 7 July 1942, 2, SHD, 2P70; Gnimagnon, captivity report, 7 February 1941, SHD, 14P46; Report on escapes from POW camps, subdivision of Taza, 4 November 1940, SHD, 14P17; Le Féloch, captivity report, 26 February 1942, SHD, 34N5.

84. Guerin, liberation report, 22 December 1941, SHD, 34N1081.

85. Prost, report on captivity and escape, n.d., SHD, 14P46.

86. Scheck, *French Colonial Soldiers*, 262.

87. Mabon, *Prisonniers de guerre "indigènes,"* 56.

88. Jean Brelivet, captivity report, 22 July 1941, SHD, 2P88; Roger Dabin to secretary general of the committee for captivity stories, 14 August 1958, AN, 72/AJ/291.

89. Schirmer and de Morsier, ICRC visit to Vesoul, 12 November 1942, AN, F/9/2351.

90. Jean Morane to president CCAPG, 17 February 1941, AD Loiret, 11R14.

91. Prost, report on captivity and escape, n.d., SHD, 14P46.

92. G. Chenard to Andlauer, 10 December 1941, AN, F/9/2351.

93. Scheck, *French Colonial Soldiers*, 80.

94. Remarks on three camps, Onesse-Laharie, St-Medard, and Bayonne-Anglet, and their Arbietskommandos, n.d., AN, F/9/2351.

95. Dupuy, analysis of all reports on the Frontstalags from 1 October [1941] to 1 April 1942, SHD, 2P63.

96. See Cooper, *Citizenship*.

97. See *Manuel officiers*; *Manuel troupes*.

98. Inspector general des services administratifs, note for conseiller d'etat section général pour l'administration sous-direction des affaires indigènes, 20 May 1942; AN, F/1a/4526.

99. Herf, *Nazi Propaganda*, 2–3.

100. Bigard to chief of OKW in France, 5 January 1941, AN, F/2959.

101. Major commander in chief of the German Army in France to Bigard, 27 January 1941, AN, F/2959.

102. CCAPG Section d'outre-mer, minutes from 24 November 1941 meeting, 28 November 1941, SHD, 2P67.

103. Mayor of Voves to prefect of Eure et Loir, September 1940, AD Eure et Loir, 1W101.

104. Jean Carcy, report on the interrogation of a released prisoner, 17 June 1941, ANS, 2D23.

105. Henry Eboué, captivity report, 6.

106. Mme. Lyautey to CCAPG, 25 October 1940, AN, F/9/2959.

107. Translation and commentary of Mme. Lyautey's letter to CCAPG, 1 November 1940, AN, F/9/2959.

108. Jean Brelivet, captivity report, 22 July 1941, SHD, 2P88.

109. Gnimagnon, captivity report, 7 February 1941, SHD, 14P46.

110. Barker, *Behind Barbed Wire*, 78.

111. Gnimagnon, captivity report, 7 February 1941, SHD, 14P46.

4. OCCUPYING THEIR TIME

1. Ginio, *French Colonialism Unmasked*, 76; Fall, "Le travail forcé," 2.

2. Ginio, *French Colonialism Unmasked*, 77.

3. Fargettas, *Les Tirailleurs sénégalais*, 251; Ginio, *French Colonialism Unmasked*, 77.

4. Cooper, *Decolonisation and African Society*, 18.

5. Jones, *Violence against Prisoners*, 127; Convention (IV) respecting the Laws and Customs of War on Land and Its Annex, Article 6; Convention Relative to the Treatment of Prisoners of War, Article 31.

6. Jones, *Violence against Prisoners*, 128–29.

7. Convention Relative to the Treatment of Prisoners of War, Article 31.

8. Billig, "Le Rôle des prisonniers," 61.

9. Besson to US Ambassador to France, 1 October 1940, AN, F/9/2828.

10. Scheck, *French Colonial Soldiers*, 183–85.

11. Boehme, CAA to DFCAA, 31 August 1940, AN, AJ/41/1834.

12. Doyen to von Stülpnagel, 14 January 1941, AN, F/9/2002; see also Humbert, note for the CAA, 3 December 1940, AN, F/9/2002.

13. Meeting between Dupuy and Scapini, 14 March 1941, SHD, 2P63.

14. Scapini, *Mission sans gloire*, 155.

15. Scheck, *French Colonial Soldiers*, 168.

16. Gutschmidt to Joseph Bourgeois, 7 July 1940, AD Yonne, 1W643.

17. Paxton, *Vichy France*, 209.

18. Scheck, *French Colonial Soldiers*, 171.

19. Hassen-Ladjimi, escape report, 28 September 1940, SHD, 14P16.

20. Michel Gnimagnon, captivity report, 7 February 1941, SHD, 14P46.

21. Ducrot to prefect of Eure et Loir, 24 August 1940, AD Eure et Loir, 1W2; Directeur des services agricoles to prefect of Eure et Loir, 27 August 1940, AD Eure et Loir, 1W2.

22. Henry Eboué, captivity report, 5.

23. Caporal Amar Belkacem, captivity report, 28 October 1940, SHD, 14P16.

24. Jean-Pierre Prost, captivity report, n.d. (escaped 24 December 1940), SHD, 14P46.

25. François, *La Guerre*, 304–5.

26. André Paul Sadon, monthly report, May 1941, AD Nièvre, 137W 126.

27. Scheck, *French Colonial Soldiers*, 170.

28. Durand, *La Captivité*, 117.

29. Sadon to Scapini, 18 July 1941, AD Nièvre, 137W 126.

30. Scheck, "French Colonial Soldiers," 430.

31. Brault, notes on a mission to the Eastern Region, Overseas Section, 27 October–9 November 1941, AN, F/9/2351.

32. Prefect of the Ardennes to the sous-prefects and mayors, 21 January 1941, AD Ardennes, 1W145.

33. Billig, "Le Rôle des prisonniers," 56.

34. Scheck, *French Colonial Soldiers*, 174–75.

35. Scheck, *French Colonial Soldiers*, 175.

36. Use of prisoners in the following camps: Latille, Vouzailles, Vouille, Neuville, Mirebeau, Scorbe-Clairevaux, n.d., AD Vienne, 1566w2; see also Engineer in chief to local engineers, 13 November 1941, AD Marne, Châlons en Champagne, 7w s598.

37. Based on the ICRC capture cards at the BAVCC, Caen.

38. Letter to the prefect from the mayor of Ballots, 18 September 1941, AD Mayenne, 227w6; Arrête du maire, 4 November 1941, AD Mayenne, 227w6; Ingénieur de l'arrondissement to M. le Colonel Desseault, délégué aux PG, 8 January 1942, AD Mayenne, 227w6.

39. Mairie de Changé to préfet de la Mayenne, 24 March 1941, AD Mayenne, 227w6.

40. Prefect of Yonne, memo to mayors of Yonne, 23 June 1941, AD Yonne, 1w655.

41. Captivity report, Michel Gnimagnon, 7 February 1941, SHD, 14P46.

42. ICRC camp inspection, Joigny, 18 June 1941, AN, F/9/2351.

43. Mayor of Nitry to prefect of the Yonne, 23 May 1941, AD Yonne, 1w643.

44. Approximations concerning prisoners from Algeria, the colonies, protectorates, and countries under mandate for General Andlauer, 5 May 1941. This total was calculated by adding statistics from each department sent to Andlauer. Variations are due to different racial categories, AN, F/9/2351.

45. Fogarty, *Race and War*, 64.

46. ICRC camp inspection, Vesoul, Drs. Schirmer et de Morsier, 12 November 1942, AN, F/9/2351; Vialet, note for Colonel Reichel, 8 March 1943, AN, AJ/41/2230.

47. Résumé des rapports d'inspection de camps de prisonniers de guerre par les délégués de M. Scapini, Inspection Frontstalag 232 Dr. Bonnaud, 8 January 1942, SHD, 2P69; Préfet de la Haute Saône to Maurice Cousin, 9 June 1941, AD Haute Saône, 62J 32; Commandant P. de Perthuis à M. le Préfet de la Nièvre, 3 July 1942; AD Nièvre, 999w 1924, AD Nièvre, 108w67; Commandant P. de Perthuis, to Monsieur le Contrôleur de l'Armée, sous-directeur du service des prisonniers de guerre, 1 September 1942, AD Nièvre, 999w 1924.

48. Captivity report, Michel Gnimagnon, 7 February 1941, SHD, 14P46.

49. ICRC camp inspection, Vesoul, Drs. Schirmer et de Morsier, 12 November 1942, AN, F/9/2351.

50. Captivity report, Michel Gnimagnon, 7 February 1941, SHD, 14P46.

51. Commandant Dupuy, Synthèse des résumés de rapports d'inspection de camps de prisonniers, inspection Frontstalag 141 Vesoul, René Scapini, 13 May 1941, SHD, 2P78.

52. Henry Eboué, captivity report, 5.

53. Henry Eboué, captivity report, 6–7.

54. Henry Eboué, captivity report, 7.

55. Henry Eboué, captivity report, 9.

56. Henry Eboué, captivity report, 9.

57. Maurice Vincent to prefect of Yonne, 15 March 1941, AD Yonne, 1W655; see also mayors of Ambrières, Chantigné, Signé et Saint Loup du Gass to the commandant in charge of POW services, n.d., AD Mayenne, 227W22.

58. Prefect of the Yonne to directeur des services agricoles, 27 May 1941, AD Yonne, 1W655.

59. Dr. Heerdt to prefect of the Gironde, 22 April 1941, AD Gironde, 45W15.

60. French forestry department inspector to prefect of the Yonne, 24 May 1941, AD Yonne, 1W655.

61. Lieutenant-Colonel Laub, poster, "*Consignes pour les prisonniers aidant aux travaux des champs,*" n.d., AD Haute Saône, 27W63.

62. Prefect of the Somme to the mayors of the department, 20 February 1941, AD Somme, 49W27.

63. Prefect of the Loiret, note on POWs in Loiret, 21 February 1941, AD Loiret, 11R14.

64. L. Bonnaud-Delamare to prefect of the Ardennes, 21 January 1942, AD Ardennes, 1W146 see also Letter to General Massiet, Amitiés africaines, 29 May 1941, AD Vienne, 1J746.

65. Scheck, *French Colonial Soldiers*, 101.

66. Georges Scapini, speech on POWs, 15 October 1941, AN, 72/AJ/1840.

67. Commune of Beaulieu-sur-Oudon to the prefect of Mayenne, 11 June 1941, AD Mayenne, 227W6.

68. Prefect of the Loiret to the mayors of the department, 5 May 1941, AD Loiret, 11R14.

69. Prefect of the Yonne to sous-prefect of Avallon, 21 April 1942, AD Yonne, 1W655.

70. Prefect of the Yonne to mayor of St-Martin-des-Champs, 3 June [1941?], AD Yonne, 1W655.

71. Blank contract, Frontstalag 194, AD Marne, Châlons en Champagne, 7W S5989.

72. Contract between the German Reich represented by the chief of the military administration in Bordeaux and the chief of the French forestry department at Bordeaux, n.d., AD Yonne, 1W652.

73. R. P. Picourt to prefect of Yonne, 17 May 1941, AD Yonne, 1W643.

74. Wildermuth to French forestry department inspector, 7 June 1941, AD Yonne, 1W655.

75. Prefect of the Yonne to French forestry department inspector, 30 May 1941, AD Yonne, 1W655.

76. Pearson, "'Age of Wood,'" 781.

77. Scheck, *French Colonial Soldiers*, 176.

78. Prefect of Yonne to Feldkommandanteur 509, 4 June 1941, AD Yonne, 1W655.

79. Feldkommandanteur 509 to prefect of Yonne, 10 June 1941, AD Yonne, 1W655.

80. Scheck, *French Colonial Soldiers*, 179.

81. Letter from directeur départemental du ravitaillement général to Mauice Cousin, 27 December 1941, AD Haute-Saône, 63J33.

82. Letter to Maurice Cousin from Frontstalag 141, 20 October 1941, AD Haute-Saône, 63J33.

83. Scheck, *French Colonial Soldiers*, 178.

84. Captivity report written by a recently released prisoner, SHD, 2P70.

85. Commandant Dupuy, Synthèse des résumés de rapports d'inspection de camps de prisonniers, inspection Frontstalag 141 Vesoul, René Scapini, 13 May 1941, SHD, 2P78.

86. ICRC camp inspection, Frontstalag 184A Mont-de-Marsan (Landes), 13 June 1941, AN, F/9/2351.

87. Dr. Marti and Dr, de Morsier, ICRC visit to FS 195 Onesse-Laharie (Landes), 13 June 1941, AN, F/9/2351.

88. Letter Maire de Labouheyre to préfet des Landes, 11 April 1942, AD Landes, RS1.

89. Pontenx-les-Forges to préfet des Landes, 13 March 1942, AD Landes, RS1.

90. Lawler, *Soldiers of Misfortune*, 112.

91. Ginio, *French Colonialism Unmasked*, 77.

92. Ginio, *French Colonialism Unmasked*, 82–83.

93. Jennings, "Extraction and Labor," 200, 202.

94. Jennings, "Extraction and Labor," 203.

95. Ulrich to prefect of Yonne, 2 April 1942, AD Yonne, 1W655; see also Wildermuth to prefect of the Yonne, 4 August 1941, AD Yonne, 1W644; Hassen-Ladjimi, escape report, 28 September 1940, SHD, 14P16.

96. French forestry department inspector to prefect of the Yonne, 24 May 1941, AD Yonne, 1W655.

97. Michel Verneaux, minister of agriculture report, 15 May 1941, AD Yonne, 1W655.

98. Schimmer and de Morsier, ICRC visit to Frontstalag 195, 28 October 1942, AN, F/9/2351.

99. Mayor of Ballots to the prefect of the Mayenne, 18 September 1941, AD Mayenne, 227W6.

100. Jean Brunet to the prefects, 12 May 1941, AD Ardennes, 1W145; see also prefect of the Yonne to mayor of Gisy-les-Nobles, 28 February 1942, AD Yonne, 1W655; sous-prefect Avallon to prefect of the Yonne, 15 March 1941, AD Yonne, 1W655.

101. Directeur des services agricoles to prefect of the Yonne, 27 February 1942, AD Yonne, 1W655.

102. Feldkommandantur to directeur des services agricoles, 6 October 1941, AD Yonne, 1W652.

103. Prefect of the Yonne to Feldkommandantur 509, 3 December 1941, AD Yonne, 1W652.

104. Direction des services agricoles, list of POW camps, 14 April 1942, AD Yonne, 1W655.

105. Mayor of Ballots to the prefect of Mayenne, 2 April 1942, AD Mayenne, 227W6.

106. Secretary of state for finance to prefect of the Somme, 5 August 1942, AD Somme, 26W401.

107. Chef de l'administation militare régionale to prefect of Gironde, 26 August 1941, AD Gironde, 45W15.

108. Prefect of the Somme to the mayors of the department, 20 February 1941, AD Somme, 49W27

109. Mayor of Bléneau to prefect of the Yonne, 31 May 1941, AD Yonne, 1W655.

110. Prefect of Yonne to mayor of Chatel Gérard, 17 April 1941, AD Yonne, 1W655.

111. Kratzenberg to prefect of the Marne, 14 January 1942, AD Marne, Reims, 6W R819.

112. Prefect of Gironde to mayors of Gironde and Dordogne in occupied zone, 16 December 1940, AD Gironde, 45W15; see also prefect of the Marne to Popelin, 19 January 1942, AD Marne, Reims, 6W R819.

113. Mayor of Changé to the prefect of Mayenne, 4 July 1941, AD Mayenne, 227W6.

114. Mayor of Bais to special commissioner at the prefecture, 1 April 1941, AD Mayenne, 227W6.

115. Huntziger to Amiral de la Flotte, 23 May 1941, SHD, 7NN2022.

116. Stabazahlmeiter und Dienstatellenleiter FS 124 to prefect of the Yonne, 30 May 1941, AD Yonne, 1W655; Dr. Richelmann to prefect of the Yonne, 17 June 1941, AD Yonne, 1W655.

117. Dr. Richelmann to prefect of the Yonne, 5 April 1941, AD Yonne, 1W643; for more examples, see Prefect of the Yonne to mayor of Saint-Fargeau, 25 October 1941, AD Yonne, 1W655; Sous-prefect Avallon to prefect of the Yonne, 15 March 1941, AD Yonne, 1W655; Order from the director of the prisoners stationed in Couptrain, 20 May 1941, AD Mayenne, 227W6.

118. Worms and Co. to the directeur du ravitaillement général, n.d., AD Loire Atlantique, 1690W127.

119. Durand, *La Captivité*, 114.

120. Scheck, *French Colonial Soldiers*, 175.

121. Mabon, *Prisonniers de guerre "indigènes,"* 87.

122. Gnimagnon Escape report, 7 February 1941, SHD, 14P46.

123. Convention Relative to the Treatment of Prisoners of War, Article 28.

124. Mabon, *Prisonniers de guerre "indigènes,"* 65.

125. Engineer in Chief Poitiers to engineers in the sous-divisions, 23 April 1941, AD Vienne, 1566W2.

126. ICRC, visit to Mont-de-Marsan, 13 June 1941, AN, F/9/2351.

127. Prefect of the Yonne to mayor of Dixmont, 13 June [1941?], AD Yonne, 1W655; Prefect of the Yonne to mayor of Arges, 2 June 1941, AD Yonne, 1W655.

128. Stabazahlmeiter und Dienstatellenleiter FS 124 to prefect of the Yonne, 29 May 1941, AD Yonne, 1W655.

129. Georges Scapini and Jean Desbons, summary of visit to Frontstalag 195, 10 April 1941, SHD, 2P78; Durand, *La Captivité*, 60.

130. Scheck, *French Coloial Soldiers*, 172.

131. Michel Gnimagnon, captivity report, 7 February 1941, SHD, 14P46.

132. Stabazahlmeiter und Dienstatellenleiter FS 124 to prefect of the Yonne, 4 June 1941, AD Yonne, 1W655; see also Mayor of Vézelay to prefect of the Yonne, 11 June 1941, AD Yonne, 1W655; Prefect of the Yonne to mayor of Coutarnoux, 3 June 1941, AD Yonne, 1W655; Mabon, *Prisonniers de guerre "indigènes,"* 64.

133. Chauvin, note for the CAA, 25 August 1940, AN, F/9/2002.

134. Mayor of Nitry to prefect of the Yonne, 23 May 1941, AD Yonne, 1W643.

135. Mayor of Selle-Craonnaise to Bussière, 22 March 1941, AD Mayenne, 227W6.

136. Mayor of Chatelain to the prefect of Mayenne, n.d., AD Mayenne, 227W6.

137. Letter from sous-prefect of Sens to prefect, n.d., AD Yonne, 1W652.

138. J. F. Bussiere to Kraaz, 26 March 1941, AD Mayenne, 227W22.

139. Prefect of the Yonne to sous-prefect of Avallon, 21 April 1942, AD Yonne, 1W655.

140. Mayor of Saint-Agnan to the sous-prefect of Yonne, 20 May 1941, AD Yonne, 1W652.

141. Mayor of Cossé to the prefect of Mayenne, 21 March 1941, AD Mayenne, 227W6.

142. Sadon to Scapini, 9 August 1941, AD Nièvre, 137W127; Sadon, monthly report, 4 November 1941, AD Nièvre, 137W128; prefect of the Yonne to commandant of Frontstalag 124, 29 September 1941, AD Yonne, 1W644.

143. Prefect of Yonne to the mayors of Joux la Ville, Sacy and Brimault, 2 May 1941, AD Yonne, 1W652; for more examples, see Mayor of Fourgerolles-du-Plessis to Jacques-Félix Bussière, 18 March 1941, AD Mayenne, 227W6; Mayor of Fromentières to Bussière, 24 March 1941, AD Mayenne, 227W6; Mayor of Gesvres to Bussière, 18 March 1941, AD Mayenne, 227W6.

144. French forestry department inspector to prefect of the Yonne, 24 May 1941, AD Yonne, 1W655.

145. Mabon, *Prisonniers de guerre "indigènes,"* 65.

146. Inspector for the French forestry department to prefect of the Yonne, 17 June 1941, AD Yonne, 1W655.

147. Billig, "Le Rôle des prisonniers," 58.

148. Mayor Pont sur Yonne to mayor de Gisy les Nobles, 16 June 1942, AD Yonne, 1W655

149. Prefect of the Yonne to the Feldkommandantur 745, 27 June 1942, AD Yonne, 1W644; see also Commune of Beaulieu-sur-Oudon to the prefect of Mayenne, 11 June 1941, AD Mayenne, 227W6.

150. Scheck, *French Colonial Soldiers*, 169.

151. Ginio, *French Colonialism Unmasked*, 5.

152. Paxton, *Vichy France*, 144.

5. MALADIES AND MISTREATMENT

1. MacKenzie, "Treatment of Prisoners," 490.

2. Hoffmann, "Introduction," 14, 18; Paulmann, "Humanity," 294–95.

3. MacKenzie, *Colditz Myth*, 109; Dower, *War without Mercy*, 11.

4. Wallace, "Welcome Guests?," 957.

5. Paul Anderson and Auguste Senaud, report of YMCA visits to POW camps in occupied France, 6 April 1941, AN, F/9/2351.

6. Michel Gnimagnon, captivity report, 7 February 1941, SHD, 14P46.

7. Scheck, *French Colonial Soldiers*, 94.

8. Sergeant Jacques Boyer, addendum to escape report, 15 April 1941, SHD, 34N1081.

9. Scheck, *French Colonial Soldiers*, 108.

10. Durand, *La Vie quotidienne*, 230.

11. CRF, report on camp visits in the Landes, 15 October 1941, AN, F/9/2351.

12. Telegram, P. Chasseriaud and H. Dechamps to Boisson, 24 May 1941, ANS, 2D23/28; see also Beraud to the Governor of Senegal, 28 May 1941, ANS, 2D23/28.

13. Gnimagnon, captivity report, 7 February 1941, SHD, 14P46.

14. Warrant Officer Fillet, report on his capture by the Germans, detention and escape, n.d., SHD, 14P17.

15. Creuse to the governor of Senegal, 13 September 1941, ANS, 2D23/28.

16. Paul Mansire, captivity report, June 1940 to January 1941, AN, 72/AJ/291.

17. Information from a recently escaped Muslim soldier from Douar Key, August 1943, AN, F/1a/3780; General Vergez to général d'armée, ministry secretary of state for war, 7 October 1940, SHD, 3H257.

18. Information from an occasional native informant, 17 September 1941, ANS, 2D23/28.

19. Prefect of the Meuse to Scapini, 6 May 1942, AN, F/9/2351.

20. Medical report, n.d., SHD, 2P72.

21. De Brinon to the chef du gouvernement, DSA, 25 October 1942, SHD, 2P72.

22. Besson to Scapini, 18 September 1942, AN, F/9/2351.

23. Faure, report based on information from the escaped prisoner Marcel Guillet, 20 January 1941, SHD, 2P88.

24. Schirmer and Morsier, ICRC, visit to work camp Saucats at Frontstalag 221, 26 October 1942, AN, F/9/2351.

25. Gnimagnon, captivity report, 7 February 1941, SHD, 14P46.

26. Scheck, *French Colonial Soldiers*, 104; 106.

27. Wylie, *Barbed Wire Diplomacy*, 178.

28. Information from a recently escaped Muslim soldier from Douar Key, August 1943, AN, F/1a/3780.

29. Durand, *La Vie quotidienne*, 228–29.

30. MacKenzie, "Treatment of Prisoners," 499.

31. Jean Guérin, liberation report, 22 December 1941, SHD, 34N1081.

32. Besson to Scapini, 12 May 1942, SHD, 2P72.

33. Dupuis, note for the DSPG, 4 November 1942, SHD, 2P72.

34. Scheck, *French Colonial Soldiers*, 109.

35. AN, F/1a/3650, prefect of the Meuse to Scapini, 10 April 1942.

36. AN, F/9/2351, Mission Brault in the Eastern Region, 27 October to 9 November 1941.

37. Lawler, *Soldiers of Misfortune*, 104.

38. Correa, "O 'combate,'" 69, 86.

39. Chef de l'administration militaire régionale Bordeaux to prefect of Gironde, 22 November 1940, AD Gironde, 45W82.

40. Scheck, *French Colonial Soldiers*, 249–51.

41. Ngalamulume, "Keeping the City," 186.

42. Ngalamulume, "Keeping the City," 191.

43. Thomas, "Vichy Government," 682.

44. Fogarty and Osborne, "Constructions and Functions," 216–18.

45. Berlan and Thévenin, *Médecins et société*, 143.

46. Marti and De Morsier, ICRC visit to Epinal, n.d., AN, F/9/2351.

47. Bonnaud, Camp visit, 21 April 1941, AN, F/9/2351; report on Ambroise POW camp, 23 January 1941, AN, F/9/2963; DSPG, report on Chalons sur Marne POW camp, 6 January 1941, AN, F/9/2963; DSPG, report on Angoulême POW camp, 13–15 January 1941, AN, F/9/2963.

48. DSPG, report on the Bayonne-Anglet POW camp, 23 January 1941, AN, F/9/2351.

49. Cohen, "Malaria and French Imperialism," 23, 26.

50. Thomas, "Vichy Government," 683.

51. CCPPG, intelligence on Stalag VII-A, 20 July 1940, SHD, 31N123.

52. DSPG, report on the Bayonne-Anglet POW camp, 23 January 1941, AN, F/9/2351; see also Marti and De Morsier, ICRC visit to Epinal, n.d., AN, F/9/2351; Lawler, *Soldiers of Misfortune*, 111.

53. CCPPG, intelligence on Stalag VII-A, 20 July 1940, SHD, 31N123.

54. Guérin, liberation report, 22 December 1941, SHD, 34N1081.

55. ICRC, visit to Montargis, 18 June 1941, AN, F/9/2351; Madame Duhau, "Quelques suggestions au sujet des camps de prisonniers indigènes présentées," 26 May 1941, AN, F/9/2351.

56. Marti and Morsier, ICRC, visit to Frontstalag 161, Nancy, 25 June 1941, AN, F/9/2351.

57. Bigard, report of Camp Dijon-Longvie, 6 January 1941; AN, F/9/2963.

58. Anderson and Senaud YMCA, visit to Frontstalags, 4 February 1941; AN, F/9/2351.

59. DSPG, report on the Bayonne-Anglet POW camp, 23 January 1941, AN, F/9/2351; Guérin, liberation report, 22 December 1941, SHD, 34N1081.

60. Scheck, *French Colonial Soldiers*, 245.

61. Report on Airvault POW camp, 30 December 1940, AN, F/9/2963.

62. Report on Airvault POW camp, 23 January 1941, AN, F/9/2963.

63. Bigard, reports on La Roche sur Yon and Le Mans, 6 January 1941, AN, F/9/2963.

64. Guérin, liberation report, 22 December 1941, SHD, 34N1081.

65. Echenberg, *Colonial Conscripts*, 97; Lawler, *Soldiers of Misfortune*, 113.

66. Scheck, *French Colonial Soldiers*, 246.

67. Makepeace, "Going 'Round the Bend,'" 1483.

68. Convention Relative to the Treatment of Prisoners of War, Annex, Section 2, Special Principles for Direct Repatriation or Accommodation in a Neutral Country.

69. Makepeace, "Going 'Round the Bend,'" 1484.

70. Database from ICRC capture cards at the BAVCC, Caen.

71. Liste de l'hopital psychiatrique de Fleury Les Auchais, n.d., AN, F/9/3816.

72. René Scapini, visit to hospital at Orléans, 8 January 1943, AN, F/9/2351.

73. Guillaume, *Du Désespoire au salut*, 180.

74. Echenberg, *Colonial Conscripts*, 152.

75. Lacaze, *La Guerre européenne*, cited in Michel, *Les Africains*, 199.

76. Fogarty and Osborne, "Constructions and Functions," 222.

77. Thomas, "Le Gouvernment de Vichy," 328.

78. Besson to Scapini, 5 December 1940, SHD, 2P66.

79. SDPG, report on Angoulême POW camp, 3 February 1941, AN, F/9/2963.

80. YMCA report on visits to POW camps, 11 April 1941, AN, F/9/2351.

81. Le Gouest, summary of POWs, 5 September 1941, SHD, 2P64.

82. Vaillaud, Rivet, Bonnot, Bonelli, Roussanne, Le Gouest, Dupuy, Buzenac, summary for prisoners, 17 October 1941, SHD, 2P64.

83. Huntziger to Scapini, 24 March 1941, SHD, 2P74.

84. Besson, DSPG summary of activities 2–15 December 1940, 23 December 1940, SHD, 2P66; Scapini to Tiepelmann, note concerning the colored troops, 16 December 1940, SHD, 2P66.

85. Colored colonial units in France, 1 October 1943, BA-MA, RW34/77.

86. Schirmer and Morsier, visit to Frontstalag 153, 22 October 1942, AN, F/9/2351.

87. CRF, report on the systematic X-raying of prisoners in Montargis camp, 15–22 April 1941, SHD, 2P74.

88. Scapini, *Mission sans gloire*, 73.

89. Martin and de Morsier, ICRC, visit to Luçon, 29 May 1941, AN, F/9/2351.

90. Cochrane, "Tuberculosis," 656–57.

91. Durand, *La Vie quotidienne*, 169–70.

92. MacKenzie, *Colditz Myth*, 172.

93. Cochrane, "Tuberculosis," 657.

94. MacKenzie, *Colditz Myth*, 172.

95. Durand, *La Vie quotidienne*, 135.

96. Bonnaud, report of visits, 21 April 1941, AN, F/9/2351; Scheck, *French Colonial Soldiers*, 244.

97. Bonnaurd to Vernes, 27 May 1941, AN, F/9/2351.

98. Scheck, *French Colonial Soldiers*, 244.

99. CRF, report on systematic X-rays at Montargis POW camp, n.d., SHD, 2P74.

100. Schirmer and Morsier, visit to Frontstalag 153, 22 October 1942, AN, F/9/2351.

101. CRF, results of systematic X-rays done in the Frontstalags 1 January–10 February 1942, AN, F/9/2351.

102. Daniels, "Tuberculosis in Europe," 1065.

103. Dantan-Merlin, summary of inspection reports for Frontstalag 132, 19 June [1941?], SHD, 2P78; DSPG, activities 2–15 December 1940, 26 December 1940, SHD, 2P66.

104. Scheck, *French Colonial Soldiers*, 202.

105. CRF, statistics of tuberculosis cases found at Montargis, 15–22 April 1941, SHD, 2P74; CRF, statistics of tuberculosis cases found at Le Mans, 29–30 May 1941, SHD, 2P74.

106. CRF, statistics of tuberculosis cases found at Chartres, 19–23 May 1941; Bourges, 24 April–2 May 1941; Châteaudun, 23–27 May 1941, SHD, 2P74.

107. CRF, statistics of tuberculosis cases found at Nonant-le-Pin, 23 May 1941, SHD, 2P74.

108. Calculations based on the ICRC capture cards at the BAVCC, Caen.

109. Mabon, *Prisonniers de guerre "indigènes,"* 106; Letters from Fribourg-Blanc to Bonnaud, 13 May, 24 October 1942, AN, F/9/2351.

110. Durand, *La Vie quotidienne*, 169.

111. Dr. Louis Bazy, "L'Aspect medico-social du retour du prisonnier," n.d., SHD, 2P67.

112. Crozat to secrétaire d'etat à la guerre, Direction des troupes coloniales, 8 February 1943, SHD, 3P84.

113. Creuse to the governor of Senegal, 13 September 1941, ANS, 2D23/28.

114. ICRC visit to Montargis, 18 June 1941, AN, F/9/2351.

115. Mallet to Scapini, 3 June 1941, SHD, 2P74.

116. Mabon, *Prisonniers de guerre "indigènes,"* 59.

117. Wender, note on repatriated North Africans undergoing treatment in Marseilles, 27 April 1942, ANOM, ALg GGA 1CM/73.

118. Schirmer and Morsier, visit to Frontstalag 153, 22 October 1942, AN, F/9/2351.

119. Echenberg, *Colonial Conscripts*, 97.

120. Echenberg, *Colonial Conscripts*, 97.

121. Crozat to secrétaire d'etat à la guerre, Direction des troupes coloniales, 8 February 1943, SHD, 3P84.

122. Paquin to général chef de l'état-major de l'armée, 1 November 1941, SHD, 2P85.

123. Paul Lecourt, report for Commandant Le Gouest, 14 May 1943, SHD, 2P85.

124. Report for Commandant Fauée, commissariat général aux prisonniers de guerre rapatriés, 1 April 1943, SHD, 2P85.

125. Wender, note on repatriated North Africans undergoing treatment in Marseilles," 27 April 1942, ANOM, ALg GGA 1CM/73.

126. Thomas, "Vichy Government," 684.

127. Gaston Joseph to secretary of state for foreign affaires, 14 November 1942, ANOM, FM 1 AFFPOL/833.

128. Martin and de Morsier, visit to Lucon, 29 May 1941, AN, F/9/2351.

129. Colored colonial units in France, 1 October 1943, BA-MA, RW34/77.

130. Note, 1st Group de Divisions militaires, 1 Bureau et SA, 20 February 1941, SHD, 3P82.

131. Telegramme, Troupes coloniales guerre royat to organe liquidateur, 23 February 1943, SHD, 3P84; Valette, note for the Section militaire de liaison, 4 March 1943, SHD, 3P84.

132. Coudraux, Number of patients at Fréjus hospital by year and by race, 5 February 1943, SHD, 3P84.

133. Telegramme, Détachement militaire de liaison Avignon to Section militaire liaison Vichy, 9 March 1943, SHD, 3P84.

134. Cochet, *Les Exclus*, 18; Durand, *La Captivité*, 214. The 3.4 percent is from calculations based on the ICRC capture cards at the BAVCC, Caen.

135. Scheck, *French Colonial Soldiers*, 10.

136. Moore, "Treatment of Prisoners," 116.

137. Calculations based on the ICRC capture cards at the BAVCC, Caen.

138. Durand, *La Captivité*, 215.

139. Calculations based on the ICRC capture cards at the BAVCC, Caen.

140. Scheck, *French Colonial Soldiers*, 29.

141. Scheck, *French Colonial Soldiers*, 202.

142. Fogarty and Osborne, "Constructions and Functions," 223.

143. Moore, "Treatment of Prisoners," 116.

6. HELPING "OUR" PRISONERS

1. Section Bibliothèque et Jeux, Report of activity during its first year, October 1940 to October 1941, SHD, 2P67.

2. Barnett, *Empire of Humanity*, 135–37.

3. Roger Dabin to the secretaire general de la communication d'histoire de la captivité, 14 August 1958, AN, 72/AJ/291.

4. Gnimagon, captivity report, 7 February 1941, SHD, 14P46.
5. Prost, escape report, n.d., SHD, 14P46.
6. CCAPG, founding and goals, 16 December 1941, SHD, 2P67.
7. Convention Relative to the Treatment of Prisoners of War, Article 78.
8. DSPG, *Le Service des prisonniers*, SHD, 9R37.
9. Besson, note pour la direction général de l'administration de la guerre et du contrôle, 12 November 1941, SHD, 2P66.
10. President of the CRF to the Darlan, 17 April 1942, SHD, 2P67; Note on the role of the CRF in assisting POWs, 6 November 1941, SHD, 2P67; see also Besson, note for direction général de l'administration de la guerre et du contrôle, 12 November 1941, SHD, 2P67; Jugnet, note regarding the POW service, 6 May 1941, SHD, 9R36.
11. Barnett, *Empire of Humanity*, 137.
12. *Le Service des prisonniers*, SHD, 9R37; Huntziger, note for the organizations taking care of POWs, 30 May 1941, SHD, 9R36.
13. Note for the CAA, 4 August [1940?], AN, AJ/41/1839.
14. CCAPG, Marne delegation, 5 June 1942, AD Marne, Reims, 6W R819.
15. Léon Noel, Mandate for the CCAPG, 22 July 1940, SHD, 2P67; *Le Service des prisonniers*, SHD, 9R37.
16. CCAPG, founding and goals, 16 December 1941, SHD, 2P67; see also CCAPG, report, 1 January 1942, AN, F/1a/3650.
17. Governor general of Algeria to Darlan, 4 June 1941, SHD, 1P89.
18. Report Comité d'aide et d'assistance coloniale 1914–1915, 10, BDIC, O Pièce 14168.
19. CCAPG, founding and goals, 16 December 1941, SHD, 2P67.
20. Recham, *Les Musulmans algériens*, 89.
21. *Le Figaro*, 23 July [1941?], AN, 72/AJ/1840.
22. Huré, report on Amitiés africaines, 19 November 1941, SHD, 2P67.
23. For proposed distribution of funding, see Cullen to the contrôleur de l'armée, 12 June 1942, AN, F/9/2964; Cosbard to the secretary of state for the colonies, 22 June 1942, AN, F/9/2964.
24. AFIP, "La Sollicitude de la Tunisie à l'égard des prisonniers musulmans," 28 November [1941?], AN, 72/AJ/1840; AFIP, "Un Don de M. Pucheu aux prisonniers de guerre musulmans," 19 October [1941?], AN, 72/AJ/1840.
25. Dupuy to Madame Weygand, n.d., SHD, 2P67.
26. CCAPG, report, 1 January 1942, AN, F/1a/3650.
27. *Le Service des prisonniers*, SHD, 9R37.
28. DSPG, instructions for organizations in North Africa for collective relief of colonial prisoners, including their identification and informing the families, [February or March 1942?], SHD, 2P68.
29. CCAPG, minutes, 13 January 1942, AN, F/9/2959.

30. Bouret to Popelain, n.d., AD Marne, Reims, 6W R819.
31. Bonnaud to Salle, minister of colonies, 16 July 1941, AN, F/9/2351.
32. S. Kieuty to Dr. Bonnaud, 10 January 1942, AN, F/9/2351.
33. Lawler, *Soldiers of Misfortune*, 107.
34. Paulmann, "Humanity," 291–92.
35. DSPG, instructions for organizations in North Africa for collective relief of colonial prisoners, [1942?], SHD, 2P68.
36. Service des prisonniers de guerre, end of the year report for 1941, 27 January 1942, SHD, 9R37; *Le Service des prisonniers*, SHD, 9R37.
37. Besson to the general delegate of the CRF, 2 December 1940, SHD, 2P66.
38. CCAPG, Overseas Section, 24 November 1941 minutes, 28 November 1941, SHD, 2P69.
39. Verbal note to the Militärbefehlshaber in France, 12 August 1941, AN, F/9/2351.
40. Convention Relative to the Treatment of Prisoners of War, Article 33; Response to 12 August note to the Militärbefehlshaber in France, 20 August 1941, AN, F/9/2351.
41. Report, use of subsidies given to the organizing committee for the "Semaine de la France d'outre-mer 1941," n.d., AN, F/41/85.
42. L. Audisio, Ministry of the interieur, Affaires algeriennes, 9 February 1942, AN, F/1a/3650.
43. Anonymous to the president of the Red Cross, 1 December 1941, forwarded to Scapini 16 December 1941, AN, F/9/2351.
44. Scheck, *French Colonial Soldiers*, 153.
45. Until 1944 the Germans did not generally remove Jewish prisoners from Western armies, including soldiers in the British armies with Palestinian nationality. See Moore, "Treatment of Prisoners," 115.
46. Paul Gibson to Noirot, 29 October 1941, AN, F/9/2351; Report, use of subsidies given to the organizing committee for the "Semaine de la France d'outre-mer 1941," n.d., AN, F/41/85; Captivity report written by a recently released prisoner, SHD, 2P70.
47. Letter from A. Robert of the French Red Cross in Moulins to the French Red Cross in Paris, 14 February 1941, AN, F/9/2351; letter from Dr. Bonnaud to the Bureau d'inspection des camps, 20 June 1941, AN, F/9/2351.
48. Henry Eboué, captivity report, 9.
49. Captivity report written by a recently released prisoner, SHD, 2P70.
50. Frebault to Bigard, 6 December 1941, forwarded to Scapini 19 December 1941, AN, F/9/2351; OKW, special report no. 4, 1 September 1941, BA-MA, RW6/270.
51. Bigard to secretary of state for colonies, 11 April 1942, AN, F/9/2964.
52. Law number 782, 12 August 1942, AN, 72/AJ/1840.

53. Honnorat to the director du contrôle et du contentieux, 22 May 1942, SHD, 9P38; Report on Amitiés africaines, particularly the Lyons branch, 17 November 1942, SHD, 9R8; Report on the CCAPG's agreement for blankets, 21 July 1941, SHD, 9R36.

54. For the full details of audits, see H. Lemery to Honnorat, 26 July 1943; F. Vezia to Honnorat, 26 July 1943; Bouge to Honnorat, 26 July 1943; Huré to Honnorat, 28 July 1943; Benoit to Honnorat, 28 July 1943; Henri Peltier to Honnorat, 5 August 1943; Honnorat to F. Vezia, 8 September 1943, SHD, 9R36. See also note for the conseilleur d'etat, secretaire general par l'administration, sous-direction des affaires algériennes, 20 May 1942, AN, F/1a/4526.

55. Report on Amitiés africaines, particularly the Lyons branch, 17 November 1942, SHD, 9R8.

56. Besson, note for direction général de l'administration de la guerre et du contrôle, 12 November 1941, SHD, 2P66.

57. Scapini to Abetz, 10 March 1941, AN, F/9/2959.

58. Andlauer, memo to the sous-délégués d'outre-mer, 7 April 1942, AN, F/9/2351.

59. L. Audisio, Ministry of the interieur, Affaires algeriennes, 9 February 1942, AN, F/1a/3650.

60. Besson, note for the sous-direction du Service des prisonniers de guerre, 28 January 1941, AN, F/9/2959.

61. Tran-Huu-Phong to Annamite prisoners of war, 1 April 1942, AD Marne, Reims, 6W R819.

62. Barnett, *Empire of Humanity*, 57.

63. Barnett, *Empire of Humanity*, 99.

64. Ferris, *Politics of Protection*, 40–41; see also Geyer, "Humanitarianism and Human Rights," 34.

65. Barnett, *Empire of Humanity*, 155.

66. Barnett, *Empire of Humanity*, 82.

67. DPSG, summary of activities, 2–15 December 1940, 26 December 1940, SHD, 2P66.

68. Besson, summary of the DSPG's activities, 1–16 March 1941, 1 April 1941, SHD, 2P66; summary of the DSPG's activities, 17 March–6 April 1941, 26 April 1941, SHD, 2P66.

69. Fishman, *We Will Wait*, xviii, 42–43.

70. Section bibliothèque et jeux, report of activity during its first year, October 1940–October 1941, SHD, 2P67.

71. "Service de l'aide aux prisonniers de guerre," *La Gazette de Lausanne*, 21 January 1941, AN, F/41/266.

72. CCAPG, report, 1 January 1942; SHD, 2P67, CCAPG, founding and goals, 16 December 1941, AN, F/1a/3650.

73. Rapport sur la visite aux camps de prisonniers de guerre en France occupée, Paul B. Anderson et Auguste Senaud, YMCA, 4 February 1941, AN, F/9/2351.

74. Bonko Hambrié to Pétain, n.d. (response dated 11 August 1941), AN, F/9/2351.

75. Fishman, *We Will Wait*, 42.

76. Bonko Hambrié to Pétain, n.d. (response dated 11 August 1941), AN, F/9/2351.

77. Bonnaud to Commandant Jalluzot, 15 December 1941, AN, F/9/2351

78. Pollard, *Reign of Virtue*, 42, 45.

79. Pollard, *Reign of Virtue*, 45.

80. Mabon, *Prisonniers de guerre "indigènes,"* 94–95.

81. Service des contrôles techniques des colonies, secretary of state for colonies, 5 November 1941, ANOM, FM 1 AFFPOL/929/Bis.

82. Besson to Scapini, 18 September 1942, AN, F/9/2351.

83. Prost, escape report n.d., SHD, 14P46.

84. Captivity report written by a recently released prisoner, SHD, 2P70.

85. Andlauer to the sous-délégués d'outre-mer aux associations marraines, 27 April 1942, AN, F/9/2351.

86. Rapport sur la visite aux camps de prisonniers de guerre en France occupée, Paul B. Anderson et Auguste Senaud, YMCA, 4 February 1941, AN, F/9/2351.

87. Röhrig, note on making art and other objects in POW camps, 31 December 1941, SHD, 2P77.

88. Andlauer, memo to CCAPG Overseas Section, 12 November 1942, AN, F/9/2352.

89. Note, Ministry of the interieur, Affaires algeriennes, 10 March 1942, AN, F/1a/3653.

90. Paul Marion, speech in Toulouse, 24 January 1942, AN, F/41/305.

91. Paul Marion, speech in Toulouse, 24 January 1942, AN, F/41/305; Report for the inspector of finance, 4 March 1942, AN, F/41/273.

92. L. Bonnaud to contrôleur de l'armée sous-directeur de Service des prisonniers de guerre, 19 August 1942, AD Ardennes, 1W146.

93. Commune of Beaulieu-sur-Oudon to prefect of Mayenne, 11 June 1941, AD Mayenne, 227W6.

94. Pollard, *Reign of Virtue*, 42.

95. Secretary of state for national education and youth to the prefects, rectors, and academy inspectors, 2 April 1941, AD Loiret, 11R14.

96. Durand, *La Captivité*, 324.

97. *Le Petit Vésulien*, 22 October 1940.

98. Journal de marche du "Mouvement Lorraine" de la Haute-Saône, 28 September 1940, AD Haute-Saône, 9J10.

99. Gez Breyer Oberstlt, OKW, Az 2f 24 Kriegsgef. I, 16 June 1941, BA-MA, RW6/270.

100. Tribunal de la Feldkommandantur 529 to prefect of Gironde, 14 December 1940, AD Gironde, 45W82.

101. Bories-Sawala, "Les Prisonniers français," 97.

102. Political and economic information bulletin, 9–15 March 1941, SHD, 3H159.

103. Procès-Verbal, 6 October 1941, AD Yonne, 1W652.

104. Jean Pierre Prost, escape report, SHD, 14P46.

105. Levavasseur to governor of Sudan, 7 May 1941, ANS, 2D23/28.

106. Gnimagnon, captivity report, 7 February 1941, SHD, 14P46.

107. Captivity report written by a recently released prisoner, SHD, 2P70.

108. Nussard, recommend Albin Bancilon for commendation, 1 August 1940, SHD, 14P16.

109. Mohamed Ben Ali, escape report, translated by Ould Yahoui, 7 November 1940, SHD, 14P17.

110. Sergeant Mohamed Ben Mohamed Ben El Habib, escape report, 29 August 1941, SHD, 14P17.

111. Aomar Ben Mohamed Ben Aissa, information provided after his escape, n.d., SHD, 14P17.

112. Mohamed Ben Ali, escape report, translated by Ould Yahoui, 7 November 1940, SHD, 14P17.

113. Mohamed Ben Ali, escape report, translated by Ould Yahoui, 7 November 1940, SHD, 14P17.

114. For more examples, see Mohamed Ben Mohamed Ben El Habib, escape report as told to Lieutenant Charpentier, 29 August 1941, SHD, 14P17; Salah Allag, escape report, n.d., SHD, 14P16.

115. Gnimagnon, captivity report, 7 February 1941, SHD, 14P46.

116. Journal de marche du "Mouvement Lorraine" de la Haute-Saône, 28 September 1940, AD Haute-Saône, 9J10.

117. Pierre Choffel, isolated resistance: escapes from Stalag 141, 22 June 1956, AD Haute-Saône, 9J10.

118. Journal de marche du "Mouvement Lorraine" de la Haute-Saône, 2 November 1940, AD Haute-Saône, 9J10.

119. Journal de marche du "Mouvement Lorraine" de la Haute-Saône, 20 December 1940, AD Haute-Saône, 9J10.

120. Pische, captivity report, 16 August 1941, SHD, 14P16.

121. Michel Gnimagnon, captivity report, 21 January 1941, SHD, 14P16.

122. Michel Gnimagnon, captivity report, 21 January 1941, SHD, 14P16.

123. Henry Eboué, captivity report, 6, 10, 11.

124. Robert Eboué, captivity report, 7–8; Henry Eboué, captivity report, 11–12.

125. Hassen-Ladjimi, escape report, 28 September 1940, SHD, 14P16.

126. Pische, captivity report, 16 August 1941, SHD, 14P16.

127. De Peralo, captivity and escape report, n.d., SHD, 14P16.

128. For the colonial prisoners, calculations based on the ICRC capture cards at the BAVCC, Caen; for the white prisoners, see Durand, *La Vie quotiedienne*, 107.

129. Durand, *La Vie quotiedienne*, 108.

130. Dupuy, analysis of full report of the Frontstalags, 1 October [1941] to 1 April 1942, SHD, 2P63.

131. *Le Service des prisonniers*, SHD, 9R37.

132. Bigard to the secrétaire general de la delegation du gouvernement français dans les territoires occupés, 23 November 1942, AN, F/9/2964.

133. *Le Petit Parisien*, 16 December 1942, SHD, 2P54.

134. Adoption of prisoners by Ecole mixte à deux classes de Souain, 1 February 1943, AD Marne, Reims, 6W R810.

135. Verdier to secretary of state for colonies, 16 December 1942, ANOM, IAFFPOL/639.

7. HOSTAGES TO MISFORTUNE

1. Pétain, "Le lancement."

2. Paxton, *Vichy France*, xv, 1.

3. Bernhard, "Borrowing from Mussolini," 620.

4. Thomas, *French Empire at War*, 39–40.

5. Summary of intelligence on German propaganda from 1 December 1939 to 15 January 1940, 15 February 1940, SHD, 27N68.

6. Scheck, "Prisoner of War Question," 373.

7. Pétain, mission instructions for General Weygand, 5 October 1940, SHD, 1P89.

8. Paxton, *Vichy France*, 61.

9. Subcommittee for POWs, state of negotiations, 8 October 1940, AN, AJ/41/1835.

10. Subcommittee for POWs, state of negotiations, 3–9 November 1940, AN, AJ/41/1835.

11. Subcommittee for POWs, state of negotiations, 19–25 January 1941, AN, AJ/41/1835.

12. Herf, *Nazi Propaganda*, 9; 11.

13. Note for the DSA, 14 March 1941, AN, AJ/41/1788.

14. Note for the DSA, 14 March 1941, AN, AJ/41/1788.

15. Parisot to secretary of state for war, 6 November 1941, AN, AJ/41/1788.

16. Doyen to von Stülpnagel, 24 January 1941, AN, AJ/41/1788.

17. Doyen to Vogl, 22 March 1941, AN, AJ/41/1788.

18. Doyen to Vogl, 22 March 1941, AN, AJ/41/1788.

19. Darlan to president of the CAA for economy, 20 March 1942, AN, AJ/41/2081.

20. DFCAA to the French Admiralty, 24 July 1942, AN, AJ/41/2081.

21. Michelier to Vogl, 22 July 1941, AN, AJ/41/2081.

22. Scapini to Darlan, 17 December 1941, SHD, 2P82.

23. Paxton, *Vichy France*, 122.

24. A. Giberton, sous-prefect of Libourne, monthly report for 25 March–25 April 1942, 25 April 1942, AD Gironde, 61W5.

25. Giberton, monthly report, 29 May 1942, AN, AJ/41/1835.

26. *Je suis partout*, 25 October 1941.

27. Vogl to Beynet, 24 November 1941, AN, AJ/41/2081.

28. Secretary of state for the colonies to the secretary of state for foreign affairs, 14 November 1942, ANOM, FM/IAFFPOL/833.

29. Secretary of state for the colonies to the secretary of state for foreign affairs, 14 November 1942, ANOM, FM/IAFFPOL/833.

30. Note for DSA, release of prisoners for the North African economy, 2 December 1941, AN, AJ/41/2053.

31. Summary of POW meetings, 9 February 1942, SHD, 2P64.

32. Paxton, *Parades and Politics*, 342.

33. Paxton, *Vichy France*, 282.

34. Kedward, *Occupied France*, 281.

35. Giberton, monthly report, November 1942, AD Gironde, 61W5.

36. Paxton, *Vichy France*, 287–88.

37. Scheck, *French Colonial Soldiers*, 116. Here Scheck corrects the commonly held belief reflected in the French primary sources that the German Frontstalags' guards were sent to fight on the eastern front. Most were too old or physically unsuitable to fight and were used as guards. After 1944 the military situation was so desperate that even these men were recruited into fighting units.

38. Secretary of state for the colonies to the secretary of state for foreign affairs, 14 November 1942, ANOM, FM/IAFFPOL/833; SDPG, information bulletin, 6 March 1943, AN, AJ/41/2053.

39. Durand, *La Vie quotidienne*, 125.

40. Jackson, *France*, 220.

41. Thomas, "Vichy Government," 667.

42. Scheck, *French Colonial Soldiers*, 188.

43. Giberton, monthly report, 30 July 1942, AD Gironde, 61W5.

44. Fourquet, note for Direction des troupes coloniales, bureau technique, 29 March 1943, SHD, 3P84.

45. Le Gouest, L'Encadrement des prisonniers indigènes des Frontstalags par des Français, 25 August 1943, SHD, 2P64.

46. Effectifs approximatifs des indigènes nord-africains et des indigènes coloniaux stationnés dans la métropole (prisonniers de guerre, main d'œuvre), 23 July 1943, SHD, 2P78.

47. Special report no. 3, Kontrollinspektion der DWStK, 5 June 1943, BA-MA, RW34/77.

48. Kontrollinspektion der DWStK, Einheiten farbiger Kolonialsoldaten in Frankreich Stand vom 1/9/43, 5 October 1943, BA-MA, RW 34/78.

49. Effectifs approximatifs des indigènes nord-africains et des indigènes coloniaux stationnés dans la métropole (prisonniers de guerre, main d'œuvre), 23 July 1943, SHD, 2P78.

50. Daveau to secretaire général à la defense terrestre, 7 July 1943, SHD, 3P84.

51. Special report no. 3, Kontrollinspektion der DWStK, 5 June 1943, BA-MA, RW34/77.

52. Scheck, *French Colonial Soldiers*, 119.

53. Mabon, *Prisonniers de guerre "indigènes,"* 140.

54. Daveau to secretaire général à la defense terrestre, 7 July 1943, SHD, 3P84.

55. Daveau, Note for the direction du personnel militaire, 11 November 1943, SHD, 3P84.

56. Scheck, *French Colonial Soldiers*, 116.

57. Ahmed Ben Rabah Rafa, report on his activities during captivity, 10 July 1948, SHD, 1K908.

58. Dantan-Merlin, report on the inspection of Frontstalag 194 Nancy, 16–20 February 1943, SHD, 2P78.

59. Units of colored colonial soldiers in France, 1 October 1943, BA-MA, RW34/77.

60. Daveau, note for services liquidateurs de la défense terrestre, 30 November 1943, SHD, 3P84.

61. Prefect des Landes to commander of Frontstalag 222, 17 February 1944, AD Landes, RS88.

62. Le Gouest, prisoners working in the occupied zone, 30 April 1943, SHD, 2P64.

63. Sarrat, note for le général de corps d'armée, 4 March 1943, SHD, 3P84; Units of colored colonial soldiers in France, 1 October 1943, BA-MA, RW34/77.

64. Commissaire régional à la liberation des prisonniers de guerre d'amiens to secretaire d'Etat à la Defense Paris, 6 March 1944, SHD, 3P84.

65. Commissaire régional à la liberation des prisonniers de guerre d'amiens to secretary of state for defence Paris, 6 March 1944, SHD, 3P84.

66. Units of colored colonial soldiers in France, 1 October 1943, BA-MA, RW34/77.

67. SDPG, note for the "camp inspection" service, 8 December 1943, AN, F/9/2351.

68. Daveau to Secretaire général à la Defense terrestre, 7 July 1943, SHD, 3P84.

69. Jennings, "Extraction and Labor," 214.

70. Daveau, note, 20 December 1943, SHD, 2P78.

71. Mabon, *Prisonniers de guerre "indigènes,"* 152.

72. Scheck, "French Colonial Soldiers," 442

73. Daveau, note, 20 December 1943, SHD, 2P78.

74. Scheck, *French Colonial Soldiers*, 167–68.

75. Dupuy, note for the Cabinet, situation in the Frontstalags, 22 June 1944, SHD, 3P84.

76. Dupuy, note for the Cabinet, situation in the Frontstalags, 22 June 1944, SHD, 3P84.

77. Report on the state of native workers in the northern zone, Secretary of State for Colonies, 13 June 1944, SHD, 3P84.

78. Report on the state of native workers in the northern zone, Secretary of State for Colonies, 13 June 1944, SHD, 3P84.

8. PRISONERS UNDER THE INFLUENCE

1. Ginio, *French Colonialism Unmasked*, xiv.

2. See, for example, Aissaoui, "Exile"; Boittin, *Colonial Metropolis*; Goebel, "Spokesmen, Spies, and Spouses"; Lawrence, *Imperial Rule*.

3. Lasswell, *Propaganda Technique*, 189.

4. Scheck, *French Colonial Soldiers*, 134.

5. Herf, *Nazi Propaganda*, 61; Note, intelligence on German propaganda for North African prisoners, 23 August 1941, SHD, 1P200; Intelligence from an escaped prisoner, Centre de rassemblement de Marseille, 30 July 1941, SHD, 1P200.

6. Note, intelligence on German propaganda for North African prisoners, 26 July 1941, SHD, 1P200.

7. Inspecteur de Police Spéciale Martin to the commissaire spécial chef de service, 19 July 1941, SHD, 1P200.

8. Herf, *Nazi Propaganda*, 3.

9. Herf, *Nazi Propaganda*, 9, 11.

10. Thomas, "Vichy Government," 670; Scheck, *French Colonial Soldiers*, 135.

11. Mabon, *Prisonniers de guerre "indigènes,"* 155.

12. Ageron, "Vichy," 130–31.

13. For regular intelligence reports on German propaganda for North Africa, see SHD, 1P200.

14. Ministre des affaires etrangères, note for the ministre de la défense nationale, 9 September 1940, ANOM, 1AFFPOL/363.

15. Duboin, excerpt from Sudan's annual political report for 1940, 31 January 1941, ANS, 17G174.

16. Weygand to Pétain, 10 November 1940, SHD, 1P89.

17. Leméry, direction des affaires politiques, 4 September 1940, ANOM, 1AFFPOL/355.

18. Telegram, Platon to Dakar, Hanoi, Tamanarive, Fort de France, Djibouti, Saint-Denis, 3 November [1940?], ANOM, 1AFFPOL/355.

19. Ginio, *French Colonialism Unmasked*, xv.

20. Boisson, Memo to governors and commissioners of AOF, November 1940, ANS, 2D3.

21. Ginio, "Marshal Pétain," 295.

22. Telegram to Platon, n.d. (probably 1940 or 1941, when Platon was secrétaire d'etat aux colonies), ANOM, 1AFFPOL/355.

23. Press review and Muslim questions, 2e Bureau, Colonies, June–July 1940, ANOM, IAFFPOL/363.

24. Giacobbi à Boisson, 27 November 1940, ANS, 2D3/14.

25. Ginio, "Marshal Pétain," 307.

26. Parisot to Boisson, 21 November 1940, ANS, 2D3/14.

27. Cercle Goumbou to governor of Sudan, 15 October 1941, ANS, 2D23/28.

28. Boisson to secretary of state for colonies, POWs service, 7 November 1941, ANS, 2D23/28.

29. Cabinet of the prefect of the Vosges, report, 2 June 1941, AD Vosges, 3W2.

30. Paxton, *Vichy France*, 200.

31. Michel Favre, report on imperial propaganda, 9 March 1944, AN, F/41/279.

32. Ageron, "Vichy," 128.

33. Hoang Van Co to Paul Creyssel, 11 May 1942, AN, F/41/279.

34. Motadel, *Islam*, 2, 78.

35. Section des Affaires Musulmanes, Germany's Islamic policy, 20 July 1942, ANOM, IAFFPOL/363.

36. Herf, *Nazi Propaganda*, 36; Scheck, *French Colonial Soldiers*, 138.

37. Barret, Troisième Bureau, note, 25 July 1941, SHD, 2P82.

38. Intelligence from occasional but sincere source, 25 November 1940, ANOM, IAFFPOL/920.

39. Note, intelligence on German propaganda for North African prisoners, 21 July 1941, SHD, 1P200.

40. Note on Germanophile propaganda in Algeria, 15 February 1941, SHD, 1P200.

41. Scheck, *French Colonial Soldiers*, 142.

42. Succinct analysis of *La Voix du prisonnier*, 1 July 1941, SHD, 1P133; Herf, *Nazi Propaganda*, 44.

43. Richert, Service des Prisonniers de guerre, Propagande auprès des tirailleurs Malgaches et Annamites, 20 March 1941, ANOM, IAFFPOL/920.

44. Scheck, "French Colonial Soldiers," 428; Scheck, *French Colonial Soldiers*, 154.

45. Gnimagnon, captivity report, 21 January 1941, SHD, 14P46.

46. Note, intelligence on German propaganda for North African prisoners, 28 June 1941, SHD, 1P200.

47. DSA to DSPG, note, intelligence on German propaganda for North African prisoners, 9 August 1941, SHD, 1P200.

48. De Bourget to DSA, Algiers, n.d., SHD, 1P200.

49. Intelligence on Stalag III-A Luckenwald, 22 July [1941?], SHD, 1P200.

50. Note, intelligence on German propaganda for North African prisoners, 23 August 1941, SHD, 1P200.

51. DSA to DSPG, note, intelligence on German propaganda for North African prisoners, 9 August 1941, SHD, 1P200.

52. Rivet, DSPG report, 23 July 1941, SHD, 2P66.

53. Scheck, *French Colonial Soldiers*, 153.

54. Succinct analysis of *La Voix du prisonnier*, 1 July 1941, SHD, 1P133.

55. Capitaine chef du BMA 15 to capitaine chef du centre interrogatoire des militaires nord africaines camp de Ste. Marthe, 6 October 1941, SHD, 7NN2022.

56. Note, intelligence on German propaganda for North African prisoners, 15 April 1941, SHD, 1P200.

57. CCPPG, report on the French prisoners in Germany, occupied France, and Switzerland, 18 August 1940, SHD, 31N123; Thomas, "Vichy Government," 671.

58. Note, intelligence on German propaganda for North African prisoners, 6 September 1941, SHD, 1P200.

59. Note, intelligence on German propaganda for North African prisoners, 15 April 1941, SHD, 1P200; intelligence on Stalag III-A Luckenwald, 22 July [1941?]; SHD, 1P200.

60. Scheck, *French Colonial Soldiers*, 139.

61. Herf confirms the existence of Germanophile Arab exiles in Berlin. Herf, *Nazi Propaganda*, 3.

62. Nardin, special native office report, 2 November 1940, SHD, 14P31.

63. Thomas, "Vichy Government," 671; Intelligence on Stalag III-A Luckenwalde, 22 July [1941?], SHD, 1P200.

64. Note, intelligence on German propaganda for North African prisoners, 20 June 1941, SHD, 1P200.

65. Secret intelligence for 10.000, 5 March 1941, SHD, 7NN2022.

66. German propaganda for North African POWs, February 1941–January 1942, SHD, 1P200.

67. French general resident in Morocco, bulletin of political findings, 2–8 August 1941, ANS, 2D23.

68. Secret intelligence for 1.300, 27 February 1941, SHD, 7NN2022.

69. Intelligence, excerpt of Henri Macker's letter to his family, 17 December 1941, SHD, 7NN2022.

70. De Bourget to DSA, Algiers n.d., SHD, 1P200.

71. Nemo to secrétaire d'etat aux colonies, 6 July 1942, SHD, 7NN2281.

72. Capitaine chef du BMA 15 to capitaine chef du centre interrogatoire des militaires nord africaines camp de Ste. Marthe, 6 October 1941, SHD, 7NN 2022.

73. Nardin, special native office report, 2 November 1940, SHD, 14P31.

74. Dody, report on Lanssen Ben Bouchta Ben X, 4 November 1941, SHD, 7NN2666. The prisoner's name is spelled inconsistently in the source, alternately Lanssen and Lahssen Ben Bouchta.

75. Bourget, note for the DFCAA, 22 August 1941, SHD, 1P200.

76. Michelier to Vogl, 29 August 1941, SHD, 1P200.

77. There is a wealth of literature on French and German contests over religion during the First World War. See, for example, Maghraoui, "'Grande Guerre Sainte'"; Fogarty, *Race and War*; McMeekin, *Berlin-Baghdad Express*; Zürcher, Buskens, and Lüdke, *Jihad and Islam*.

78. Ginio, *French Colonialism Unmasked*, 138.

79. Louis Morand, CCAPG, role of the Comité de l'Afrique du Nord, 16 October 1941, SHD, 2P67.

80. Andlauer, memo to CCAPG departmental delegates, 27 September 1941, AD Marne, Reims, 6WR819.

81. Chef des services du Comité Algérien to Popelin, 9 December 1941, AD Marne, Reims, 6W R819; Bouret to Popelin, n.d., AD Marne, Reims, 6W R819.

82. Anderson and Senaud, visit to POW camps in occupied France, 20 January 1941, AN, F/9/2351.

83. Anderson and Senaud, visit to POW camps in occupied France, 20 January 1941, AN, F/9/2351.

84. Father Collin to R. Mérillon, forwarded from Mérillon to Scapini, 2 October 1942, AN, F/9/2351.

85. Andlauer to the departmental delegates, 18 March 1942, AN, F/9/2351.

86. S. Kieuty of OFALAC to Bonnaud, 15 September 1942, AN, F/9/2351.

87. YMCA, report of camp visits, 1–10 April 1941, AN, F/9/2351.

88. YMCA, visit to Vesoul, 7 April 1941, AN, F/9/2351.

89. Anderson and Senaud, visit to POW camps in occupied France, 20 January 1941, AN, F/9/2351.

90. Vourkoutratis, *Prisoners of War*, 62.

91. OKW, Az 13 Chef Kriegsgef. Gr. St. 26 June 1942, BA-MA, RW6/270.

92. Scheck, *French Colonial Soldiers*, 148.

93. Note, intelligence on German propaganda for North African prisoners, 16 May 1941, SHD, 1P200.

94. Bigard, note for the DSPG, 18 September 1941, AN, F/9/2959.

95. Secretary of state for the interior to secretary of state for war, 26 August 1941, AN, F/9/2959; AFIP, 24 May 1941, AN, 72/AJ/1840.

96. Bonnaud to Bigard, 29 May 1942, AN, F/9/2959; Bigard, Note for the DSPG, 19 June 1942, AN, F/9/2959.

97. Doyen to Von Stüpnagel, 14 January 1941, AN, F/2/2002.

98. Boehme to DFCAA, 4 February 1941, ANOM, IAFFPOL/920/bis.

99. Boisson to secretary of state for colonies, 15 March 1941, ANS, 2D23; Bigard, police report, 8 March 1941, AD Loiret, 138W 26009; Director of ravitaillment general to Mamadou Kane, 24 January 1941, AD Loiret, 138W 26009.

100. Anderson and Senaud, report of YMCA visits to POW camps in occupied France, 4 February 1941, AN, F/9/2351.

101. Platon to Boisson, 13 September 1941, ANOM, IAFFPOL/920/bis.

102. Translation of El Hadj Seydou Nourou Tall's advice to all Muslims, especially returning tirailleurs, 25 June 1941, ANS, 2D29.

103. Platon to Boisson, n.d., ANOM, IAFFPOL/920/bis.

104. Intelligence report, Dakar, 16 March 1942, ANS, 17G110 17.

105. Ailoune Mamadou Kane to Estarèllas, 20 January 1941, SHD, 7NN 2031.

106. Saliou N'Doye to the judge for Mamadou Kane's case, 9 February 1942, AD Loiret, 138W26009.

107. Mamdou Kane to prefect of Loiret, 9 February 1942, AD Loiret, 138W26009.

108. Ginio, *French Colonialism Unmasked*, 131.

109. Boisson to contre-amiral, secretary of state for colonies, 21 August 1941, ANS, 17 G 110/17.

110. Laroubine to général de corps d'armée, secrétaire d'etat à la guerre, Service de la justice militaire à Chamalieres, 22 July 1942, SHD, 7NN2664.

111. Interrogation of Brahim Ben Seghir Ben Mohammed, 13 April 1941, SHD, 1P200.

112. Note, intelligence on German propaganda for North African prisoners, 15 April 1941, SHD, 1P200.

113. Note, intelligence on German propaganda for North African prisoners, 15 April 1941, SHD, 1P200.

114. Summary of arrest, 12 November 1941, SHD, 7NN 2666.

115. Boisson to secretary of state for colonies, n.d., ANOM, IAFFPOL/920.

116. Intelligence, 29 April 1941, ANS, 2D23/28.

117. A. Beraud to govenor of Senegal, 28 May 1941, ANS, 2D23/28.

118. Scheck, *French Colonial Soldiers*, 144.

119. Intelligence note on German propaganda for North African prisoners, 15 April 1941, SHD, 1P200.

120. Rafa, report on his activities during captivity, 10 July 1948, SHD, 1K908.

121. Rafa, report card from 13th RTA, 10 January 1940, SHD, 1K908.

122. Note, intelligence on German propaganda for North African prisoners, 20 June 1941, SHD, 1P200.

123. Note, intelligence on German propaganda for North African prisoners, 6 September 1941, SHD, 1P200.

124. Note, intelligence on German propaganda for North African prisoners, 15 April 1941, SHD, 1P200.
125. Confidential native informant, intelligence, 23 July 1941, ANS, 2D23/28.
126. Motadel, *Islam*, 1.
127. Jean Guérin, release report, 22 December 1941, SHD, 34N1081.
128. Thomas, "Vichy Government," 671.
129. Laitard to commander of MOI camp, Marseilles, 31 July 1941, ANOM, IAFFPOL/920.
130. Unsigned letter for Professor Berthier, 16 May 1941, SHD, 2P82.
131. Zone de Tanger, information bulletin, 17–23 October 1941, ANS, 2D23.
132. Roubard, report on life in Algeria during August 1941, 30 August 1941, SHD, 7NN2022.
133. Boisson to secretary of state for colonies, 15 March 1941, ANS, 2D23/28.
134. Scheck, *French Colonial Soldiers*, 148.
135. Telegram, Magendie to gouvernor in Loulouba, 19 November 1941, ANS, 2D23/28.
136. Note, intelligence on German propaganda for North African prisoners, 23 May 1941, SHD, 1P200.
137. Note, intelligence on German propaganda for North African prisoners, 21 July 1941, SHD, 1P200.
138. Report, escaped prisoner from Frontstalag 184 for the DSA, 1 July 1941, SHD, 1P200.
139. Koeltz to the gouveneur eneral d'Algérie, 14 March 1942, ANOM, Alg GGA 1CM/73.
140. Note summarizing the principal intelligence gathered from the AOF postal censor, January 1941, ANOM, IAFFPOL/929.
141. Service des contrôles techniques des colonies, secrétaire d'etat aux colonies, 13 September 1941, ANOM, IAFFPOL/929.
142. Note on German Islamic propaganda in Paris, 9 August 1941, ANOM, IAFFPOL/363.
143. Darlan to Scapini, 26 February 1942, SHD, 2P77.

9. THE LONG ROAD HOME

1. Chef du 1er Bureau, note for cabinet du ministère, 10 September 1941, SHD, 2P66.
2. Summary of 27 February 1942 meeting on POWs, 2 March 1942, SHD, 2P64.
3. Barret, note, 25 July 1941, SHD, 2P82.
4. Report, Palais Centre sanitaire de reception et de triage, 29 June 1941, SHD, 9R37.
5. Bourget, note to DFA from DSA, 23 December 1943, AN, AJ/41/796.
6. *Le Matin*, 3 January 1942, AN, F/9/2929.
7. Service d'accueil et d'information auprès des prisonniers de guerre, 19 January 1943, SHD, 2P82.
8. Darlan to secretaries of state for war and information, Scapini, president de la commission du retour des prisonniers, 25 June 1941, SHD, 2P82.

9. Dupuy, analysis of all reports on the Frontstalags from 1 October [1941] to 1 April 1942, SHD, 2P63.

10. Thomas, *French Empire at War*, 39.

11. Michel, *Les Africains*, 197.

12. Robert Eboué, captivity report, 6–7.

13. Salland, memo, Service de liberation des prisonniers de guerre, de documentation, et de placement des militaries de carrière, 22 May 1942, AN, F/9/2007.

14. Vialet, note for Colonel Reichel, native units stationed in France, 8 March 1943, AN, AJ/41/2230.

15. Creuse to the govenor of Senegal, 13 September 1941, ANS, 2D23.28.

16. Direction du cabinet oeuvres d'assistance to secretary of state for colonies, n.d., ANS, 2D25.28.

17. Le Gouest, memo for Bureau 5/CAB, 19 September 1942, SHD, 2P63.

18. General Beynet, service note, 17 July 1941, ANOM, Alg GGA/ICM/73.

19. Lauvel to prefect of Constantine, 27 May 1942, ANOM, Alg GGA/ICM/73.

20. Koeltz to governor general of Algeria, 14 March 1942, ANOM, Alg GGA/ICM/73.

21. Centre d'information et d'etudes, Oran, 14 February 1942, ANOM, Alg GGA/ICM/73; see also Captivity report written by a recently released prisoner, SHD, 2P70.

22. POW service in Algiers, activity report, 1–31 August 1941, ANOM, Alg GGA/ICM/73.

23. Secretary of state for home affairs to secretary of state for war, 27 November 1941, AN, F/9/2828.

24. General Vergez to EMA 2e Bureau, [Oct. 1940], SHD, 3H257.

25. Governor of Sudan to Boisson, 16 May 1941, ANS, 2D23/28.

26. Governor of Ivory Coast to Boisson, 24 May 1941, ANS, 2D23/28.

27. Telegram Amirauté française to colonies, 14 November [1940 or 1941?], ANOM, IAFFPOL/636.

28. Duboin, excerpt from the annual political report for 1940, 31 January 1941, ANS, 17G174.

29. Administrateur de la Commune mixte de Bou-Saada, from weekly report, 21 February 1942, ANOM, Alg GGA/ICM/73.

30. Administrateur de la Commune mixte de Berrouaghia, excerpt from weekly report, 24 January 1942, ANOM, Alg GGA/ICM/73.

31. Administrateur de la Commune mixte de Tablat, excerpt from weekly report, 24 January 1942, ANOM, Alg GGA/ICM/73.

32. Governor general of Algeria to the prefect of affaires musulmanes, 4 February 1942, ANOM, Alg GGA/ICM/73.

33. Prefect of Alger to governor general of Algeria, 27 April 1942, ANOM, Alg GGA/ICM/73.

34. Secretary of state for home affairs to secretary of state for war, 27 November 1941, AN, F/9/2828.

35. Political and economic information bulletin, 5–11 January 1941, SHD, 3H159.

36. Administrateur de la Commune mixte de Bou-Saada, from weekly report, 21 February 1942, ANOM, Alg GGA/ICM/73.

37. Political and economic information bulletin, 5–11 January 1941, SHD, 3H159.

38. Recasement des prisonniers de guerre musulmans to governor of Algeria, residents general of Morocco and Tunisia, 1 April 1941, SHD, 1P133.

39. Koeltz to the généraux commandant les divisions territoriales: d'Alger, Oran, Constantine, 18 May 1942, ANOM, Alg GGA ICM/73.

40. Recasement des prisonniers de guerre musulmans to governor of Algeria, residents general of Morocco and Tunisia, 1 April 1941, SHD, 1P133.

41. Political and economic information bulletin, 19–25 July 1941, SHD, 3H159.

42. Résident général de France au Maroc, political information bulletin, 30 January–5 February 1942, SHD, 3H159.

43. Telegram Boisson to colonies, 28 October 1941, ANOM, IAFFPOL/636.

44. Fargettas, *Les Tirailleurs sénégalais*, 255.

45. Ginio, *French Colonialism Unmasked*, 126.

46. Le Gouest, Numbers in the Frontstalags on 30 November 1942, 9 January 1943, SHD, 2P64; SDPG, information bulletin, 6 March 1943, AN, AJ/41/2053; approximate numbers of natives and North Africans stationed in the *métropole*, 23 July 1943, SHD, 1P33.

47. Jennings, *Free French Africa*, 250.

48. Scheck, *French Colonial Soldiers*, 293, 295–96.

49. Directeur des réfugiés to directeur du fichier central, Ministère des PG, 4 March 1945, BAVCC, 22P3026. Raffael Scheck argues that this town is most likely Düngenheim. Scheck, *French Colonial Soldiers*, 294–302.

50. List of escaped prisoners who passed through CRF in Brussels in September 1944, BAVCC, 22P3046.

51. Colonial Service, list of French native colonial soldiers currently located in Germany, 7 December 1944, BAVCC, 22P3046.

52. Echenberg, *Colonial Conscripts*, 99.

53. Ministère des prisonniers de guerre, déportés et réfugiés to délégation Ministère prisonniers Casablanca, 6 April 45 BAVCC, 22P3046; Scheck, *French Colonial Soldiers*, 302.

54. Provisional government of the French Republic, repatriating the North African troops to France, 21 May 1944, AN, F/1a/3780.

55. Noiret to the commanders of the military regions, 8 September 1944, SHD, 9P8.

56. Noiret to the commanders of the military regions, 8 September 1944, SHD, 9P8.

57. Fargettas, *Les Tirailleurs sénégalais*, 264.

58. "Ce n'est pas une aumone, c'est un du," *Femme de prisonniers,* AN, F/41/226.

59. Gayme, *Les Prisonniers de guerre*, 42–43.

60. Michel, *Les Africains*, 201.

61. Lawler, *Soldiers of Misfortune*, 198.

62. JO AOF, 8 May, 5 June, 18 October, 8 November 1919 in Michel, *Les Africains*, 201.

63. Mann, *Native Sons*, 115.

64. Echenberg, *Colonial Conscripts*, 101; Lawler, *Soldiers of Misfortune*, 199.

65. Lawler, *Soldiers of Misfortune*, 199, 198.

66. Gayme, *Les Prisonniers de guerre*, 196.

67. De Boisboissel to ministre de la guerre, Direction des troupes coloniales, 29 March 1945, SHD, 5H16.

68. Scheck, *French Colonial Soldiers*, 255; Lawler, *Soldiers of Misfortune*, 197.

69. Scheck, *French Colonial Soldiers*, 255.

70. Scheck, *French Colonial Soldiers*, 253.

71. Telegram from British Consulate General Dakar to principal secretary of state for foreign affairs, Foreign Office, London, n.d., Kew, FO/371/42267.

72. Telegram from Consul General Meiklereid, Dakar to Foreign Office, 2 December 1944, Kew, FO/371/42267.

73. Telegram from Consul General Meiklereid, Dakar to Foreign Office, 2 December 1944, Kew, FO/371/42267.

74. De Boisboissel to ministre des colonies, Direction des affaires militaires, 21 December 1944, SHD, 5H16.

75. Merat, detailed report on the events at Thiaroye, 14 February 1944, SHD, 5H16.

76. Scheck, *French Colonial Soldiers*, 253–55.

77. Laurentie, note for M. le Ministre, 31 March 1945, SHD, 5H16.

78. De Boisboissel to Pierre Charles Counarie, 14 December 1944, SHD, 5H16.

79. General Langlois, *Manuel officiers*, 2:16, 9, BDIC, S Pièce 8551.

80. De Perier, appendix to report on the events at Thiaroye, n.d., SHD, 5H16.

81. Digo for the absent governor general to Minister des colonies, 22 December 1944, SHD, 5H16.

82. De Boisboissel, report, 8 February 1945, SHD, 5H16.

83. Telegramme Boisseau to colonies Paris, 25 February 1945, SHD, 5H16.

84. De Boisboissel to ministre de la guerre, Direction des troupes coloniales, 14 March 1945, SHD, 5H16.

85. De Boisboissel to ministre de la guerre, Direction des troupes coloniales, 29 March 1945, SHD, 5H16.

86. Scheck, *French Colonial Soldiers*, 251, 254–55.

87. Deroo and Champeaux, *La Force noire*, 201.

88. Mann, *Native Sons*, 117.
89. Echenberg, *Colonial Conscripts*, 103.
90. Ageron, "Vichy," 131–32.
91. Peyroulou, *Atlas des décolonisations*, 18.
92. Peyroulou, "Setif and Guelma."
93. For more on Sétif, see Thomas, "Colonial Minds," 140–75; Clayton, "Sétif Uprising"; Evans, *Algeria*; Jauffret, *La Guerre d'Algérie*; Pervillé, *Pour une histoire*; Planche, *Sétif, 1945*; Rey-Goldzeiguer, *Aux Origines*.
94. Lewin, *Le Retour des prisonniers*, 88–89; Cochet, *Les Exclus*, 36.

CONCLUSION

1. See Lawler, *Soldiers of Misfortune*; Echenberg, *Colonial Conscripts*; Thomas, "Vichy Government"; Mabon, *Prisonniers de guerre "indigènes."*
2. See Jennings, *Vichy in the Tropics*; Ginio, *French Colonialism Unmasked*; Laskier, "Between Vichy Antisemitism"; Jackson, *France*; Marrus and Paxton., *Vichy France and the Jews*; Zuccotti, *Holocaust, the French*; Josephs, *Swastika over Paris*; Adler, *Jews of Paris*.
3. Jackson, *France*; Durand, *La Captivité*; Moore and Fedororwich, *Prisoners of War*.
4. Ginio, *French Colonialism Unmasked*.
5. Scheck, *French Colonial Soldiers*, 430.
6. Ginio, *French Army*.
7. Lonsdale and Low, "Introduction."
8. Digo for the absent governor general to ministre des colonies, 22 December 1944, SHD, 5H16.
9. Ginette Eboué, captivity report, 11–13.
10. Ginette Eboué, captivity report, 13–14.
11. Buffon, "Félix Éboué," 142; Fontaine-Eboué, "Unesco Aid."

BIBLIOGRAPHY

ARCHIVAL SOURCES

Archives Départementales des Ardennes, Charleville-Mézières, France
    W series: Public records dating from July 10, 1940
Archives Départementales de la Charente, Angoulême, France
    W series: Public records dating from July 10, 1940
Archives Départementales de l'Eure et Loir, Chartres, France
    J series: Private archives
    W series: Public records dating from July 10, 1940
Archives Départementales de Gironde, Bordeaux, France
    W series: Public records dating from July 10, 1940
Archives Départementales de Haute Saône, Vesoul, France
    13 Av: Oral history series
    J series: Private archives
    1 PJ series: Local press
    W series: Public records dating from July 10, 1940
Archives Départementales des Landes, Mont-de-Marsen, France
    RS Series: Prefectoral correspondence
Archives Départementales de Loire-Atlantique, Nantes, France
    J series: Private archives
    W series: Public records dating from July 10, 1940
Archives Départementales de Loiret, Orléans, Franc
    R series: Military organizations, wartime
    W series: Public records dating from July 10, 1940
Archives Départementales de la Marne, Châlons-en-Champagne, and Reims
    W series: Public records dating from July 10, 1940
    Z series: General administration, subprefectures

Archives Départementales de la Mayenne, Laval, France
    W series: Public records dating from July 10, 1940
Archives Départementales de la Meurthe-et-Moselle, Nancy, France
    W series: Public records dating from July 10, 1940
Archives Départementales de la Nièvre, Nevers, France
    W series: Public records dating from July 10, 1940
Archives Départementales des Pyrénées-Atlantiques, Bayonne and Pau, France
    W series: Public records dating from July 10, 1940
    H Series: Hospital records
Archives Départementales de la Seine, Paris, France
    Z series: General administration, subprefectures
    Fi series: Documents, maps,
Archives Départementales de la Somme, Amiens, France
    W series: Public records dating from July 10, 1940
Archives Départementales de la Vienne, Poitiers, France
    J series: Private archives
    W series: Public records dating from July 10, 1940
Archives Départementales des Vosges, Epinal, France
    W series: Public records dating from July 10, 1940
Archives Départementales de l'Yonne, Auxerre, France
    W series: Public records dating from July 10, 1940
Archives Nationales de France, Pierrefitte-sur-seine, France
    AJ series: Miscellaneous funds, laws and decrees
    F1a series: Ministerial archives, Ministre de l'Intérieur
    F7 series: Ministerial archives, Ministre de l'Intérieur, Police
    F9 series: Military affairs
    F41 series: information
    72AJ series: Comité d'histoire de la deuxième guerre mondiale
Archives Nationales d'Outre-Mer (ANOM), Aix-en-Provence, France
    FM/1affpol series: Political affairs
    Alg/gga series: Government General of Algeria, Vichy. 1940/1943
    Slotfom series: Ministère des colonies, direction des Affaires politiques, service de
        liaison avec les originaires des territoires français d'outre-mer
    Bib series: Publications from the colonies
Archives Nationales du Sénégal (ANS), Dakar, Senegal
    D series: French West Africa, military affairs
    G series: French West Africa, political affairs

Archives de l'Ordre de la Libération (AOL), Paris, France
  Dossier "Félix Eboué"
Bibliothèque de Documentation et Information Contemporaine (BDIC), Nanterre, France
  Fonds Vichy disques
  O 14168: Report Comité d'Aide et d'Assistance Coloniale, 1914–15
  Q 16314: Colonial exhibition, 1931
  S Pièce 8551: Training manuals
  S Pièce 11562: Training manuals
Bundesarchiv-Militärachiv, Freiburg, Germany
  RW series: Defense and armaments, Second World War
National Archives, Kew, United Kingdom
  FO series: Foreign Office
Service Historique de la Défense (SHD), Bureau des archives des victimes des conflits
  contemporains (BAVCC), Caen, France
  P series: Second World War, Vichy, free French, provisional government
  40R series: Individual capture cards for colonial prisoners of war by colony
Service Historique de la Défense (SHD), Vincennes, France
  H series: Second World War in the Empire
  K series: Private archives
  N series: Second World War, 1939–June 22, 1940
  NN series: Third Republic, supplementary archives
  P series: Second World War, Vichy, free French, provisional government
  R series: Naval Archives, Second World War
  T series: Records of the general staff, French Army

Published Works

Abbal, Odon. *Soldats oubliés: Les prisonniers de guerre français*. Bez-et-Esparon: E&C
  Editions, 2001.
Ade, J. F., and Michael Crowder. "The 1939–1945 War and West Africa." In *History of
  West Africa*, vol. 2, edited by J. F. Ade and Michael Crowder, 596–621. London:
  Longman, 1974.
Adler, Jacques. *The Jews of Paris and the Final Solution: Communal Response and Internal
  Conflicts, 1940–1944*. New York: Oxford University Press. 1987.
Ageron, Charles-Robert. "L'Exposition coloniale de 1931: Mythe républicain ou mythe
  impériale?" In *Les Lieux de memoire*, edited by Pierre Nora, 493–515. Paris: Gal-
  limard, 1997.
———. "Vichy, les Français et l'empire." In *Le Régime de Vichy et les Français*, edited by
  Jean-Pierre Azéma and François Bédarida, 122–34. Paris: Fayard, 1992.

Aissaoui, Rabah. "Exile and the Politics of Return and Liberation: Algerian Colonial Workers and Anti-colonialism in France during the Interwar Period." *French History* 25, no. 2 (2011): 214–31.

Aldcroft, Derek. *From Versailles to Wall Street, 1919–1929*. London: Allen Lane, 1977.

Aldrich, Robert. *Greater France: A History of French Overseas Expansion*. Basingstoke: Macmillan, 1996.

Aron, Robert. *Histoire de Vichy, 1940–1944*. Paris: Arthème Fayard, 1954.

Auvray, Lucien. *Du Désastre à la victoire: Souvenirs de guerre 1939–1945*. Paris: Pensée Universelle, 1980.

Azéma, Jean-Pierre, and François Bédarida, eds. *Le Régime de Vichy et les Français*. Paris: Fayard, 1992. Azéma, Jean-Pierre. *From Munich to the Liberation 1938–1944*. Paris: Éditions du Seuil, 1979, translated by Janet Lloyd. Cambridge: Cambridge University Press, 1984.

———. "Vichy et la mémoire savante: 45 ans d'historiographie." In *Le Régime de Vichy et les Français*, edited by Jean-Pierre Azéma and François Bédarida, 23–44. Paris: Fayard, 1992.

Barasz, Johanna. "Un vichyste en Résistance, le général de La Laurencie." *Vingtième Siècle. Revue d'histoire* 94, no. 2 (2007): 167–81.

Barker, A. J. *Behind Barbed Wire*. London: B. T. Batsford, 1974.

Barnett, Michael. *Empire of Humanity: A History of Humanitarianism*. Ithaca NY: Cornell University Press, 2011.

Beaudza, Louis. *La Formation de l'armée coloniale*. Paris: L. Fournier, 1939.

Beaumont, Joan, Lachlan Grant, and Aaron Pegram, eds. *Beyond Surrender: Australian Prisoners of War in the Twentieth Century*. Carlton, Australia: Melbourne University Press, 2015.

Berlan, Hélène, and Etienne Thévenin. *Médecins et société en France: Du XVIe siècle à nos jours*. Toulouse: Editions Privat, 2005.

Bernhard, Patrick. "Borrowing from Mussolini: Nazi Germany's Colonial Aspirations in the Shadow of Italian Expansionism." *Journal of Imperial and Commonwealth History* 41, no. 4 (2013): 617–43.

Betts, Raymond F. *France and Decolonialism, 1900–1960*. London: Macmillan, 1991.

Bilé, Serge. *Noirs dans les camps Nazis*. Monaco: Le Serpent à plumes, 2005.

Billig, J. "Le Rôle des prisonniers de guerre dans l'économie du Reich." *Revue d'Histoire de la Deuxième Guerre Mondiale* 37 (January 1960): 53–76.

Blanc, Brigitte, Henry Rousso, and Chantal de Tourtier-Bonazzi, eds. *La Seconde guerre mondiale guide des sources conservées en France 1939–1945*. Paris: Archives Nationales, 1994.

Bloch, Marc. *L'Etrange défaite: Témoignage écrit en 1940*. Paris: Société des Éditions Franc-Tireur, 1946. https://www.ebooksgratuit.com.

Boittin, Jennifer Anne. *Colonial Metropolis: The Urban Grounds of Anti-imperialism and Feminism in Interwar Paris*. Lincoln: University of Nebraska Press, 2010.

Bories-Sawala, Helga. "Les Prisonniers français dans l'industrie de guerre allemande." In *La Captivité des prisonniers de guerre: Histoire, art et mémoire 1939–1945*, edited by Jean-Claude Catherine, 95–104. Rennes: Presses universitaires de Rennes, 2008.

Buffon, Lucette. Félix Éboué: Le franc-maçon. Témoignage. *Bulletin de la Société d'Histoire de la Guadeloupe* 143–44 (2006): 141–44.

Carlier, Claude, and Guy Pedroncini, eds. *Les Troupes coloniales dans la Grande Guerre*. Paris: Editions Economica, 1997.

Chafer, Tony. *End of Empire in French West Africa: France's Successful Decolonisation?* Oxford: Berg, 2002.

Charbonneau, Jean. *Les Contingents coloniaux: Du soleil au gloire*. Paris: Imprimerie Nationale, 1931.

Clayton, Anthony. *France, Soldiers and Africa*. London: Brassy's, 1988.

———. "The Sétif Uprising of May 1945." *Small Wars and Insurgencies* 3, no. 1. (1992): 1–21.

Cochet, François. *Les Exclus de la victoire, histoire des prisonniers de guerre, déportés, et STO 1945–85*. Paris: SPM, 1992.

———. *Soldat sans armes, la captivé de guerre: Une approche culturelle*. Paris: CNRS éditions, 1998.

Cochrane, A. L. "Tuberculosis among Prisoners of War in Germany." *British Medical Journal* 2, no. 4427 (November 1945): 656–58.

Cohen, William B. "Malaria and French Imperialism." *Journal of African History* 24, no. 1 (1983): 23–36.

Convention (IV) respecting the Laws and Customs of War on Land and Its Annex: Regulations concerning the Laws and Customs of War on Land. The Hague, October 18, 1907. https://ihl-databases.icrc.org/ihl/intro/195.

Convention Relative to the Treatment of Prisoners of War. Geneva, July 27, 1929. https://ihl-databases.icrc.org/applic/ihl/ihl.nsf/intro/305.

Cooper, Frederick. *Citizenship between Empire and Nation: Remaking France and French Africa, 1945–1960*. Princeton NJ: Princeton University Press, 2014.

———. *Decolonization and African Society: The Labor Question in French and British Africa*. Cambridge: Cambridge University Press, 1996.

Cooper, Frederick, and Ann Laura Stoler, eds. *Tensions of Empire: Colonial Cultures in a Bourgeois World*. Berkeley, California: University of California Press, 1997.

Correa, Sílvio Marcus de Souza. "O 'combate' às doenças tropicais na imprensa colonial alemã." Translated by Derrick Guy Phillips. *Historia ciencias saude-Manguinhos* xx, no. 1 (March 2013): 69–91.

Coutau-Bégarie, Hervé, and Claude Huan. *Lettres et notes de l'Amiral Darlan*. Paris: Economica, 1992.

Crowder, Michael, ed. *Colonial West Africa: Collected Essays*. London: Cass, 1978.

Daniels, Marc. "Tuberculosis in Europe during and after the Second World War." *British Medical Journal* 2, no. 4636 (November 1949): 1065–72.

de Boisboissel, Yves. *Sous les couleurs de France et le fanion de Mangin: Peaux noires, coeurs blancs*. Paris: Peyronnet, 1954.

de Gaulle, Charles. Speech on the BBC, June 18, 1940. http://www.charles-de-gaulle.org/pages/l-homme/dossiers-thematiques/1940–1944-la-seconde-guerre-mondiale/l-appel-du-18-juin/documents/l-appel-du-18-juin-1940.php.

Deroo, Eric, and Antoine Champeaux. *La Force noire: Gloire et infortunes d'une légende coloniale*. Paris: Editions Tallandier, 2006.

———. "Panorama des Troupes coloniales française dans les deux guerres mondiales." *Revue Historique des Armées* 271 (2013): 72–88.

Dower, John. *War without Mercy: Race and Power in the Pacific War*. New York: Pantheon Books, 1986.

Doze, Martial. *Le Général Mazillier (1862–1937): Les Troupes coloniales sous la IIIe république (Reconstruction de l'empire. Victoire de 1918)*. Paris: L. Fournier, 1939.

Duboc, Général. *Méharistes coloniaux au Sahara: Valeureuse épopée de nos héros coloniaux*. Paris: Fournier, 1946.

Durand, Yves. *La Captivité: Histoire des prisonniers de guerre français, 1939–1945*. Paris: FNCPG-CATM, 1981.

———. *La Vie quotidienne des prisonniers de guerre dans les Stalags, les Oflags et les Kommandos 1939–1945*. Mesnil-sur-l'Estrée: Hachette, 1987.

Echenberg, Myron J. *Colonial Conscripts: The Tirailleurs sénégalais in French West Africa, 1857–1960*. London: James Currey, 1991.

Evans, Martin. *Algeria: France's Undeclared War*. Oxford: Oxford University Press, 2012.

———. "Culture and Empire, 1830–1962: An Overview." In *Empire and Culture: The French Experience, 1830–1940*, edited by Martin Evans, 1–23. London: Palgrave MacMillan, 2004.

———. *The Memory of Resistance: French Opposition to the Algerian War, 1954–1962*. Oxford: Berg, 1997.

Fall, Babacar. "Le travail forcé en Afrique occidentale française (1900–1946)." *Civilisations* 41 (1993): 329–36. https://doi.org/10.4000/civilisations.1717.

Fargettas, Julian. *Les Tirailleurs sénégalais: Les soldats noirs entre légendes et réalités 1939–1945*. Paris: Tallandier, 2012.

Fauchère, A, and A. Galland. *La France d'outre-mer illustrée*. Paris: Ed. Blondel La Rougery, 1931.

Fell, Alison S., and Nina Wardleworth. "The Colour of War Memory: Cultural Representations of Tirailleurs Sénégalais." *Journal of War & Culture Studies* 9, no. 4 (2016): 319–34.

Ferrières, Gabrielle. *Jean Cavaillès: Philosophe et combattant, 1903–1944*. Paris: Presses Universitaires de France, 1950.

Ferris, Elizabeth G. *The Politics of Protection: The Limits of Humanitarian Action*. Washington DC: Brookings Institution Press, 2011.

Fetter, Bruce. "Changing War Aims: Central Africa's Role, 1940–41, as Seen from Léopoldville." *African Affairs* 87, no. 348 (July 1988): 377–92.

Fishman, Sarah. "Grand Delusions: The Unintended Consequences of Vichy France's Prisoner of War Propaganda." *Journal of Contemporary History* 26, no. 2 (1991): 229–54.

———. *We Will Wait: Wives of French Prisoners of War, 1940–1945*. New Haven CT: Yale University Press, 1991.

Fishman, Sarah, Laura Lee Downs, Ioannis Sinanoglou, Leonard V. Smith, and Robert Zaretsky, eds. *France at War: Vichy and the Historians*. Brussels: Complexe, 2004.

Fogarty, Richard. "Out of North Africa: Contested Visions of French Muslim Soldiers during World War I." In *Empires in World War I: Shifting Frontiers and Imperial Dynamics in a Global Conflict*, edited by Andrew Tait Jarboe and Richard S. Fogarty, 1–20. London: I.B. Tauris, 2014.

———. *Race and War in France: Colonial Subjects in the French Army, 1914–1918*. Baltimore: Johns Hopkins University Press, 2008.

Fogarty, Richard, and Michael A. Osborne. "Constructions and Functions of Race in French Military Medicine, 1830–1920." In *The Color of Liberty: Histories of Race in France*, edited by Sue Peabody and Tyler Stovall, 206–37. Durham NC: Duke University Press. 2003.

Fontaine-Eboué, Ginette. "Unesco Aid for African Liberation Movements." *Courier*, November 1973.

François, Jean-Jacques. *La Guerre de 1939–1940 en Eure-et-Loir: Le courrier des lecteurs*. Luisant: La Parcheminière, 1999.

Frank, Sarah. "'Meet the New Empire, Same as the Old Empire': Visions and Realities of French Imperial Policy in 1944." In *Reading the Postwar Future*, edited by Kirrily Freeman and John Munro, 79–95. London: Bloomsbury, 2019.

Gayme, Evelyne. *Les Prisonniers de guerre français: Enjeux militaire et stratégiques (1914–1918 et 1940–1945)*. Paris: Economica, 2010.

Gervereau, Laurent, and Denis Peschanski, eds. *La Propagande sous Vichy, 1940–1944*. Nanterre: BDIC, 1990.

Geyer, Michael. "Humanitarianism and Human Rights: A Troubled Rapport." In *The Emergence of Humanitarian Intervention: Ideas and Practices from the Nineteenth Century to the Present*, edited by Fabian Klose, 31–55. Cambridge: Cambridge University Press, 2016.

Gildea, Robert. *Marianne in Chains: In Search of the German Occupation of France, 1940–45*. London: Macmillan, 2002.

Ginio, Ruth. *The French Army and Its African Soldiers: The Years of Decolonization.* Lincoln: University of Nebraska Press, 2018.

——. *French Colonialism Unmasked: The Vichy Years in French West Africa*. Lincoln: University of Nebraska Press, 2006.

——. "Marshal Pétain Spoke to School Children: Vichy Propaganda in French West Africa, 1940–1943." *International Journal of African History Studies* 33, no. 2 (2000): 291–312.

Girardet, Raoul. *L'Idée coloniale en France 1871–1962*. Paris: Hachette, 1972.

Goebel, Michael. "Spokesmen, Spies, and Spouses: Anticolonialism, Surveillance, and Intimacy in Interwar France." *Journal of Modern History* 91, no. 2 (2019): 380–414.

Grellet, Isabelle, and Caroline Kruse. *Histoire de la tuberculose: Les fièvres de l'âme 1800–1940*. Paris: Editions Ramsay.

Guillaume, Pierre. *Du Désespoire au salut: Les tuberculeux aux 19e et 20e siècles*. Paris: Aubier, 1986.

Hanotaux, Gabriel, and Alfred Martineau, eds. *Histoire des colonies françaises et de l'expansion de la France dans le monde*. Vols. 2, 3, and 4. Paris: Société de l'histoire nationales, 1929–31.

Harrison, E. D. R. "British Subversion in French East Africa, 1941–42: SOE's Todd Mission." *English Historical Review* 114, no. 456 (April 1999): 339–69.

Hassett, Dónal. *Mobilizing Memory: The Great War and the Language of Politics in Colonial Algeria, 1918–39*. Oxford: Oxford University Press, 2019.

Hazeaux, Roger. "Carnets de guerre et souvenirs de captivité en Allemagne." *Horizons d'Argonne* 87 (2005): 91–124.

Herf, Jeffrey. *Nazi Propaganda for the Arab World*. New Haven CT: Yale University Press, 2009.

Histoire et épopée des Troupes coloniales. Paris: Presses Modernes, 1956.

Hitler, Adolf. *Mein Kampf.* Complete and unabridged. New York: Reynal and Hitchcock, 1941.

Hoffmann, Stefan-Ludwig. "Introduction: Genealogies of Human Rights." In *Human Rights in the Twentieth Century*, edited by Stefan-Ludwig Hoffmann, 1–26. Cambridge: Cambridge University Press, 2011.

Horne, Alistair. *To Lose a Battle: France, 1940*. London: Macmillan, 1969.

Hull, Isabel V. *Absolute Destruction: Military Culture and the Practices of War in Imperial Germany*. Ithaca NY: Cornell University Press, 2005.

Huré, General C. R. *L'Armee d'Afrique 1830–1962*. Paris: Charles-Lavauzelle, 1977.

Jäckel, Eberhard. *Frankreich in Hitlers Europa: Die deutsche Frankreichpolitik im Zweiten Weltkrieg*. Vol. 14. Stuttgart: Deutsche Verlags-Anstalt, 1966.

Jackson, Julian. *France: The Dark Years, 1940–1944*. Oxford: Oxford University Press, 2001.

Jauffret, Jean-Charles. *La Guerre d'Algérie par les documents*. Vincennes: Service historique de l'armée de terre, 1990.

Jeanmot. *Les Prisonniers de guerre dans la deuxieme guerre mondiale: Plan d'études*. Vincennes: Service Historique de la Défense, 1956.

Jennings, Eric T. *Free French Africa in World War II: The African Resistance*. Cambridge: Cambridge University Press, 2015.

———. *Vichy in the Tropics: Petain's National Revolution in Madagascar, Guadeloupe, and Indochina, 1940–44*. Stanford CA: Stanford University Press, 2004.

Jennings, Eric Thomas. "Extraction and Labor in Equatorial Africa and Cameroon under Free French Rule." In *Africa and World War II*, edited by Judith A. Byfield, Carolyn A. Brown, Timothy Parsons, and Ahmad Alawad Sikainga, 200–219. New York: Cambridge University Press, 2015.

———. "Remembering 'Other' Losses: The Temple du Souvenir Indochinois of Nogent-sur-Marne." *History & Memory* 15, no. 1 (Spring–Summer 2003): 5–48.

Jones, Heather. *Violence against Prisoners of War in the First World War: Britain, France, and Germany, 1914–1920*. Cambridge: Cambridge University Press, 2011.

Josephs, Jeremy. *Swastika over Paris*. London: Bloomsbury, 1990.

Kedward, H. R. *La Vie en Bleu: France and the French since 1900*. London: Allen Lane, 2006.

———. *Occupied France: Collaboration and Resistance, 1940–1944*. Oxford: Wiley-Blackwell, 1985.

———. *Resistance in Vichy France: A Study of Ideas and Motivation in the Southern Zone, 1940–1942*. Oxford: Oxford University Press, 1978.

Krooth, Richard. *Arms & Empire: Imperial Patterns before World War II*. Santa Barbara CA: Harvest, 1980.

Laborie, Pierre. *L'Opinion française sous Vichy*. Paris: Editions du Seuil, 2001.

Lacaze, Marcel-Eugène. *La Guerre européenne et le tirailleur Sénégalais*. PhD thesis, Faculté de Médecine de Bordeaux, 1920.

La Gorce, Paul-Marie de. *L'Empire écartelé, 1936–1946*. Paris: Denoël Editions, 1988.

Laskier, Michael. "Between Vichy Antisemitism and German Harassment: The Jews of North Africa during the 1940s." *Modern Judaism* 11, no. 3 (1991): 343–69.

Lasswell, Harold D. *Propaganda Technique in World War I*. 1927. Reprint, Cambridge MA: MIT Press, 1971.

Lawler, Nancy. "The Crossing of the Gyaman to the Cross of Lorraine: Wartime Politics in West Africa, 1941–1942." *African Affairs* 96, no. 382 (January 1997): 53–71.

———. "Reform and Repression under the Free French: Economic and Political Transformation in the Cote d'Ivoire, 1942–45." *Africa* 60, no. 1 (1990): 88–110.

———. *Soldiers of Misfortune: Ivoirien Tirailleurs of World War II*. Athens: Ohio University Press, 1992.

Lawrence, Adria. *Imperial Rule and the Politics of Nationalism: Anti-Colonial Protest in the French Empire*. New York: Cambridge University Press, 2013.

Lebovics, Herman. *True France: The Wars over Cultural Identity, 1900–1945*. Ithaca NY: Cornell University Press, 1992.

Le Naour. *La Honte noire, L'Allemagne et les Troupes coloniales française 1914–1945*. Paris: Hachette Litteratures, 2003.

Le Service des prisonniers de guerre en zone occupée. Paris: Direction du service des prisonniers de guerre, 1942.

Lewin, Christophe. *Le Retour des prisonniers de guerre français: Naissance et développement de la Fnpg, 1944–1952*. Paris: Publications de la Sorbonne, 1986.

Lonsdale, John, and Anthony Low. "Introduction: The Second Colonial Occupation." In *History of East Africa*, vol. 3, edited by D. A. Low and Alison Smith. Oxford: Clarendon Press, 1976.

Luguern, Liêm-Khê. "Ni civil ni militaire: Le travailleur indochinois inconnu de la Seconde Guerre Mondial." *Le Mouvement Social* 2–3, no. 219–20 (2007): 185–99.

Lunn, Joe. "'Les Races Guerrières': Racial Preconceptions in the French Military about West African Solders during the First World War." *Journal of Contemporary History* 34, no. 4 (October 1999): 517–36.

———. *Memoirs of the Maelstrom, A Senegalese Oral History of the First World War*. Oxford: J. Currey, 1999.

Lüsebrink, Hans-Jürgen. "Les Troupes coloniales dans la guerre: Présences, imaginaires et representations." In *Images et colonies: Iconographie de propagande coloniale sur l'Afrique française de 1880 à 1960*, edited by Nicolas Bancel, Pascal Blanchard, and Laurent Gervereau, 74–85. Nanterre: BDIC, 1993.

Mabon, Armelle. "La Singulière captivité des prisonniers de guerre coloniaux durant la Second Guerre mondiale." *French Colonial History* 7, no. 1 (2006): 181–97.

———. *Prisonniers de guerre "indigènes" visages oubliés de la France occupée*. Paris: La Décourverte, 2010.

Mabon, Armelle, and Martine Cuttier. "La Singulière captivité des prisonniers de guerre africains (1939–1945)." In *Les Prisonniers de guerre dans l'histoire: Contacts entre peuples et cultures*, edited by Sylvie Caucanas, Rémy Cazals, and Pascal Payen, 27–45. Carcassonne: Les Audois, 2003.

MacKenzie, S. P. *The Colditz Myth: British and Commonwealth Prisoners of War in Nazi Germany*. Oxford: Oxford University Press, 2004.

———. "The Treatment of Prisoners of War in World War II." *Journal of Modern History* 66, no. 3 (September 1994): 487–520.

Maghraoui, Driss. "The 'Grande Guerre Sainte': Moroccan Colonial Troops and Workers in the First World War." *Journal of North African Studies* 9, no. 1 (2004): 1–21.

Makepeace, Clare. *Captives of War: British Prisoners of War in Europe in the Second World War*. Cambridge: Cambridge University Press, 2017.

———. "Going 'Round the Bend' in Prisoner of War Camps." *Lancet* 390, no. 10101 (September 23, 2017): 1483–84.

Mangin, Charles. *La Force noire*. Paris: Hachette, 1910.

Manifestations et allocutions du maréchal Pétain. Paris: Editions Libraire Joseph Gilbert, 1940.

Mann, Gregory. *Native Sons: West African Veterans and France in the Twentieth Century*. Durham NC: Duke University Press, 2006.

Marrus, Michael, and Robert O. Paxton. *Vichy France and the Jews*. 1990. Reprint, Stanford CA: Stanford University Press, 1995.

McMeekin, Sean. *The Berlin-Baghdad Express: The Ottoman Empire and Germany's Bid for World Power*. Cambridge MA: Harvard University Press, 2010.

Meynier, Gilbert. *L'Algérie révélée: La guerre de 1914–1918 et le premier quart du XXe siècle*. Paris: Librairie Droz, 1981.

Michel, Henri. "La revolution nationale latitude d'action du gouvernement de Vichy." *Revue d'histoire de la Deuxième Guerre mondiale* 21, no. 81 (1971): 3–22.

———. *Vichy: Année 40*. Paris: Robert Laffont, 1966.

Michel, Marc. *Les Africains et la grande guerre: L'appel à l'Afrique, 1914–1918*. Paris: Karthala, 2003.

Michel, Raphaël. "Les Prisonniers de guerre de la Somme de la Seconde Guerre Mondiale." Master's thesis, Université de Picardie Jules Verne, 1999.

Ministre de la guerre. *Manuel élémentaire à l'usage des officiers et sous-officiers appelés à commander des indigènes coloniaux (Indochinois—Sénégalais—Malgaches) dans la métropole*. Paris: Imprimerie Nationale, 1923.

———. *Manuel l'usage des troupes employées outre-mer*. Paris: Imprimerie Nationale, 1923.

Monteath, Peter. "Australian POWs in German Captivity in the Second World War." *Australian Journal of Politics and History* 55, no. 3 (2008): 421–33.

Moore, Bob. "The Treatment of Prisoners of War in the Western European Theatre of War, 1939–1945." In *Prisoners in War*, edited by Sibylle Scheipers, 111–26. Oxford: Oxford University Press, 2010.

Moore, Bob, and Kent Fedororwich, eds. *Prisoners of War and Their Captors in World War II*. Oxford: Oxford University Press, 1996.

Morrow, James D. "The Institutional Features of the Prisoners of War Treaties." *International Organization* 55, no. 4 (Autumn 2001): 971–91.

Motadel, David. *Islam and Nazi Germany's War*. Cambridge MA: Harvard University Press, 2014.

Nelson, Keith L. "The 'Black Horror on the Rhine': Race as a Factor in Post World War I Diplomacy." *Journal of Modern History* 42, no. 4 (December 1970): 606–27.

Ngalamulume, Kalala. "Keeping the City Totally Clean: Yellow Fever and the Politics of Prevention in Colonial Saint-Louis-du-Sénégal." *Journal of African History* 45, no. 2 (2004): 183–202.

Palmieri, Daniel. "How Warfare Has Evolved—A Humanitarian Organization's Perception: The Case of the ICRC, 1863–1960." *International Review of the Red Cross* 97, no. 900 (2015): 985–98.

Paulmann, Johannes. "Humanity—Humanitarian Reason—Imperial Humanitarianism: European Concepts in Practice." In *Humanity: A History of European Concepts in Practices from the Sixteenth Century to the Present*, edited by Fabian Klose and Mirjam Thulin, 287–312. Göttingen: Vandenhoeck and Ruprecht, 2016.

Paxton, Robert O. *Parades and Politics at Vichy: The French Officer Corps under Marshal Pétain*. Princeton NJ: Princeton University Press, 1966.

——. *Vichy France: Old Guard and New Order, 1940–1944*. 1972. Reprint, New York: Columbia University Press, 2001.

Peabody, Sue, and Tyler Stovall, eds. *The Color of Liberty: Histories of Race in France*. Durham NC: Duke University Press. 2003.

Pearson, Chris. "'The Age of Wood': Fuel and Fighting in French Forests, 1940–1944." *Environmental History* 11 (October 2006): 775–803.

Pedroncini, Guy, ed. *Histoire militaire de la France*. Vol 3, *De 1871 à 1940*. Paris: Presses Universitaires de France, 1992.

Pervillé, Guy. *Pour une histoire de la guerre d'Algérie, 1954–1962*. Paris: Picard, 2002.

Peschanski, Denis. *La France des camps: L'internement 1938–1946*. Paris: Gallimard, 2002.

Pétain, Philippe. "Le lancement de la collaboration avec l'Allemagne." Speech October 30, 1940. Fonds Vichy disques de la BDIC, 2018. https://www.ina.fr/audio/phd95079031/.

Peyroulou, Jean-Pierre. *Atlas des décolonisations: Une histoire inachevée*. Paris: Autrement, 2014.

——. "Setif and Guelma (May 1945)." SciencesPo. March 26, 2008. https://www.sciencespo.fr/mass-violence-war-massacre-resistance/en/document/setif-and-guelma-may-1945.

Planche, Jean-Louis. *Sétif, 1945: Histoire d'un massacre announce*. Paris: Pérrin, 2006.

Pollard, Miranda. *Reign of Virtue: Mobilizing Gender in Vichy France*. Chicago: University of Chicago Press, 1998.

Rabinow, Paul. *French Modern: Norms and Forms of the Social Environment*. Chicago: University of Chicago Press, 1989.

Recham, Belkacem. *Les Musulmans algériens dans l'armée française (1919–1945)*. Paris: L'Harmattan, 1996.

Rey-Goldzeiguer, Annie. *Aux Origines de la guerre d'Algérie, 1940–1945: De Mers-el-Kébir aux massacres du nord-Constantinois.* Paris: La Décourverte, 2002.

Rives, Maurice, and Robert Dietrich. *Héros méconnus, 1914–1918, 1939–1945: Memorial des combattants d'Afrique noire.* Paris: Association française Frères d'armes, 1993.

Roos, Julia. "Women's Rights, Nationalist Anxiety, and the 'Moral' Agenda in the Early Weimar Republic: Revisiting the 'Black Horror' Campaign against France's African Occupation Troops." *Central European History* 42 (2009): 473–508.

Rousso, Henry. *The Vichy Syndrome, History and Memory in France since 1944.* Translated by Arthur Goldhammer. 1987. Reprint, Cambridge MA: Harvard University Press, 1991.

Roux, A. Charles. *L'Appel de l'Afrique noire à la France.* Lyons: Éditions France-Colonies-Travail, 1939.

Scapini, Georges. *Mission sans gloire.* Paris: Morgan, 1960.

Scheck, Raffael. *French Colonial Soldiers in German Captivity during the World War II.* Cambridge: Cambridge University Press, 2015.

———. "French Colonial Soldiers in German Prisoner of War Camps, 1940–1945." *French History* 24, no. 3 (2010): 420–46.

———. *Hitler's African Victims: The German Army Massacres of Black French Soldiers in 1940.* Cambridge: Cambridge University Press, 2006.

———. "The Prisoner of War Question and the Beginnings of Collaboration: The Franco-German Agreement of 16 November 1940." *Journal of Contemporary History* 45, no. 2 (2010): 364–88.

Senghor, Lamine. "The Negro's Fight for Freedom." Speech at the League against Imperialism meeting in Brussels, Belgium, 1927. BlackPast. August 11, 2009. https://www.blackpast.org/global-african-history/1927-lamine-senghor-negro-s-fight-freedom/.

Sharp, Lee. *The French Army, 1939–1940.* Vol 1. Milton Keynes: Military Press, 2002.

Siegfried, André. *De la IIIe à la IVe Republique.* Paris: Editions Grasset, 1956.

Stora, Benjamin. *La Gangrène et l'oubli: La mémoire de la guerre d'Algérie.* Paris: La Découverte, 1998.

Streit, Christian. "Prisonniers de guerre allies aux mains des Allemands." In *La Captivité des prisonniers de guerre: Histoire, art et mémoire 1939–1945,* edited by Jean-Claude Catherine, 29–40. Rennes: Presses universitaires de Rennes, 2008.

Sumner, Ian. *The French Army, 1939–1945.* London: Osprey, 1998.

Suret-Canale, Jean. *French Colonialism in Tropical Africa, 1900–1945.* Translated by Till Gottheiner. London: C. Hurst, 1971. Originally published as *Afrique noire occidentale et centrale 2: L'Ere coloniale, 1900–1945* (Paris: Editions Sociales, 1964).

Thobie, Jacques, Gilbert Meynier, Catherine Coquery-Vidrovitch, and Charles-Robert Ageron, eds. *Histoire de la France coloniale 1914–1990.* Vol. 2. Paris: Armand Colin, 1990.

Thomas, Martin. "After Mers-el-Kébir: The Armed Neutrality of the Vichy French Navy, 1940–43." *English Historical Review* 112, no. 447 (June 1997): 643–70.

———. "At the Heart of Things? French Imperial Defense Planning in the Late 1930s." *French Historical Studies* 21, no. 2 (Spring 1998): 325–61.

———. "Colonial Minds and Colonial Violence: The Sétif Uprising and the Savage Economics of Colonialism." In *The French Colonial Mind*. Vol. 2, *Violence, Military Encounters, and Colonialism*, edited by Martin Thomas, 140–75. Lincoln: University of Nebraska Press, 2011.

———. *The French Empire at War, 1940–1945*. Manchester: Manchester University Press, 1998.

———. "Le Gouvernment de Vichy et les prisonniers de guerre coloniaux français (1940–1944)." In *L'Empire colonial sous Vichy*, edited by Jacques Cantier and Eric Jennings, 305–30. Paris: Odile Jacob, 2004.

———. "Les Prisonniers coloniaux." In *La France pendant la seconde guerre mondiale: Atlas historique*, edited by Jean-Luc Leleu, Françoise Passera, and Jean Quellien. Paris: Fayard, 2010.

———. "The Vichy Government and French Colonial POWs, 1940–1944." *French Historical Studies* 25, no. 4 (Fall 2002): 657–92.

Twomey, Christina. *The Battle Within: POWs in Postwar Australia*. Sydney: NewSouth Books, 2018.

Vourkoutiotis, Vasilis. *Prisoners of War and the German High Command: The British and American Experience*. New York: Palgrave Macmillan, 2003.

Wallace, Geoffrey P. R. "Welcome Guests, or Inescapable Victims? The Causes of Prisoner Abuse in War." *Journal of Conflict Resolution* 56, no. 6. (2012): 955–81.

Waltzog, Alphonse. *Les Principaux accords du droite de la guerre sur terre*. Berlin: Librarie Franz Valhan, 1942.

White, Owen. *Children of the French Empire: Miscegenation and Colonial Society in French West Africa, 1895–1960*. Oxford: Oxford University Press, 1999.

Wylie, Neville. *Barbed Wire Diplomacy: Britain, Germany and the Politics of Prisoners of War, 1939–1945*. Oxford: Oxford University Press, 2010.

———. "The 1929 Prisoner of War Convention and the Building of the Inter-war Prisoner of War Regime." In *Prisoners in War*, edited by Sibylle Scheipers, 91–108. Oxford: Oxford University Press, 2010.

Zuccotti, Susan. *The Holocaust, the French, and the Jews*. Lincoln: University of Nebraska Press, 1999.

Zürcher, Erik-Jan, Léon Buskens, and Tilman Lüdke. *Jihad and Islam in World War I: Studies on the Ottoman Jihad on the Centenary of Snouck Hurgronje's "Holy War Made in Germany."* Leiden: Leiden University Press, 2016.

INDEX

Page numbers in italics indicate photos.

ethnic groups, 10; conflict between, 93; of NCOs, 36, 87; suitability of, for service, 26–27; working outside Frontstalags, 100–101

Eure-et-Loir, work in, 100–101

Faidherbe, Louis, 26
family, ideology of, 164–66
Fashoda expedition, 26
Fell, Allison, 273n25
Fillet, Warrant Officer, 126
First Office, 233
First World War: colonial troops in, 27–33, 36, 72, 74, 135–36, 273n25; colonial unity and, 37–38; colonial veterans of, 98, 212, 247, 248; disease and, 135–36; forced labor and, 98–99; French language and, 36; Islam in, 204, 217–18; legacies of, 257; POW treatment in, 17, 31–32, 42, 60, 63; veterans of, in WWII, 67
Fishman, Sarah, 259
Fleury Les Auchais, 134–35
Fogarty, Richard, 273n25
food: and agricultural labor, 100–102; colonial POWs cooking, 86, 103, 116; colonies producing, 29, 38, 86, 164; employers paying for, 113–14; escape and provisions of, 173, 174; French providing, 85–86, 113–15, 149, 164, 179, 218, 242, 261, 263; as gift, 115, 151, 152, 155–56, 164; POWs receiving, from home, 155, 164, 169, 218; lack of, 70–72, 84–86, 96, 123, 148, 199, 244, 246; misappropriation of, 159, 160; morale linked to, 86, 240, 245; as motivating tactic, 75, 114–15, 211; Muslim observance and, 86, 218–19; raiding for, 248; rationing, 160, 192, 193, 244, 248; Red Cross providing, 84–85, 104, 105, 114, 152, 159
forced labor: in colonies, 24, 97–98, 110–11, 264; in forests, 110; under Free French

and Vichy, 98, 110–11; in Germany, 192, 193–94; military service as avoidance of, 25; payment for, 115–16; racist deployment of, 110–11; vs. republican values, 264; resistance to, 111, 223; Scapini on, 99–100

forestry work, 107, 108–11, 112–13; in Africa, 110–11; escape attempts from, 109–10; isolation of, 108; payment for, 117–18
Fort d'Uvegney, 103
"Four Freedoms" speech (Roosevelt), 232
Fourth Office, 233
framework for POWs, 51–78; administrative, 63–70; empire's place in, 52–59; legal, 59–63
France: Africans' place in Empire of, 244; anti-British feeling in, 185; colonial history of, 24, 37–38; colonial POWs politicized by, 22; colonial subjects in, after 1942, 195–96; cost of occupation of, 54, 56, 77, 112–14, 117–18, 121; food provided to POWs by, 85, 86; and German POWs in WWI, 31–32; German suspicion of, increasing, 201; and government-in-exile question, 52–53; "greatness" of, as imperial, 3–4, 7, 33; invasion of unoccupied zone of, 23, 192; liberation of, 243–46; mass graves in, 46; as mother, 166; non-white citizens ignored by, 92; opposition stifled by, 40, 203; pride of, in colonial troops, 25, 49, 222–23; provisional government of, 14–15, 24, 144, 222, 244–45, 246–47, 255, 258; race and belonging in, 5; "racial enlightenment" of, 29; refugees in, 51; size of, in 1931, 38; southern zone of, 145–46, 231; terrorism on behalf of, 253–54; values of, 25, 34–35, 162–63, 204; as "zone of suffering," 163–64; zones of, 1, 51. See also French aid to colonial POWs; Vichy regime; work in occupied France

Franco, Francisco, 56

Franco-German Armistice, 1, 51, 52; colonies in, 185; demarcation line created by, 176–77; French Armistice Delegation and, 64; Geneva Conventions and, 61, 77; legal issues arising from, 77; renegotiating, 56–57, 64, 66–68, 70, 186, 189; signing of, 257; terms of, 54, 77

Franco-Prussian War (1870–71), 25, 26

Free French, 3–4, 263; in Brazzaville, 52, 55–56; British support for, 55; Dakar attack by, 58; forced labor deployment by, 110–11; de Gaulle as leader of, 54–55; veterans, repatriation of, 246

Fréjus, 142–43, 146

French aid to colonial POWs, 151–80; Allies' landing in North Africa and, 179–80; bottom-up, 170–78, 179; difficulties in shipping, 157–58, 179–80; in escaping, 170–78, 179; individual vs. group assistance, 155–56; paternalism of, 151–52, 155, 157, 162–64, 165–70, 179–80; top-down, 152–60, 179–80; Vichy propaganda linked to, 152–53, 154–55, 164, 229. See also food

French Armistice Delegation, 64

French Army: as alternative to forced labor, 25; branches of, 27; dissolution of, 192; ethnic groups deemed suitable for, 26–27

French colonies: British blockade of, 55, 186, 237; colonial troops as propaganda for, 25; continuing the war from, 52–54; First World War and, 37–38; food production by, 29, 38, 86, 164; foreign interest in, 203; French surveillance of, 223; fundraising in, 156–57; gender imbalance in, 39–40; German interest in, 206; German propaganda in, 185, 186–87, 203, 225–26; infantilizing subjects in, 165–66; location and groupings of, 9–10; loss of, 179–80, 184, 191–92, 200–201; metropolitan commitment

to, 169; obedience of, 207; returning to "colonial normalcy," 245, 255, 259; revolts in, during WWI, 29; role of, in collaboration, 184–91; Vichy supported by, 55; Vichy vs. Free French, 4, 51, 53–56, 58, 63, 93, 184, 188, 207–8; and violence of colonization, 248; violent repression in, 253–54; wages in, 200; West African veterans shaping, 274n31. See also forced labor; Free French

French Equatorial Africa, 4, 9; forced forestry labor in, 110–11; de Gaulle supported by, 55, 207; inability to return to, 242–43; wages in, 200

French fleet, sinking of, 4, 58, 185

"French greatness," 3

French language, 35–36

French locals, contact with, 78, 83–84, 255, 262–63; in church, 218; escapes and, 172–73; French reducing, 6, 199–200; and funerals for POWs, 130; humanitarianism arising from, 152; "improvement" through, 165; by literate POWs, 89–90; loyalty maintained by, 8, 20; racism and, 116–17; sexual, 166–67; in war vs. peacetime, 4. See also white women; work in occupied France

French navy, 53, 54; British bombing of, 4, 58, 185; scuttling of, 192

French North Africa, 9, 10, 28; aid parcels to POWs from, 156, 157–58; Allied control of, 243; Allies landing in, 144, 161, 179, 184, 191–92, 231; Armistice supported by, 55; German inspections in, 187; German interest in, 186–88, 203–5, 214–17; German propaganda concerning, 161, 164, 178, 186–87, 190, 203–6, 211–22, 225–28, 262; land gifts in, 241–42; loyalty of POWs from, 161; maritime traffic in, 187–88, 231; moving government to, 54; other European claims to, 161, 203; POWs from, as camp

police, 90–91; tuberculosis among
POWs from, 136; uprisings in, 53
French Red Cross, 22, 85; CCAPG and, 154;
couscous meals provided by, 227; escapes
aided by, 174; food provided by, 84–85,
104, 105, 114, 152, 159; Frontstalag access
of, 61, 88, 154, 158, 184; Henry Eboué
and, 104, 105; politicization of, 153; and
religious observance, 218; shipping aid
parcels, 157–58
French Union, 264
French West Africa, 9, 28, 207; Armistice
supported by, 55; attitudes to war in, 40;
defense of, 187; documentation of POWs
from, 68–69; Islam and, 219–22; joining
Allies, 192; morale of soldiers from, 43;
peacetime code, 33; propaganda in, 262;
propaganda to POWs from, 213; riots
in, 29; trade unions in, 119; troops from,
stationing of, 42; tuberculosis in, 135, 136
Frobenius, Leo, 30
Frontstalag 184A, 109, 112, 213
Frontstalag 194 (Nancy), 127
Frontstalag Onesse-Laharie, 109–10
Frontstalags: administration of, 63–70, 85,
86–87, 125; agricultural labor as relief
from, 101–2; aid parcels shipped to, 157–
58; camp police of, 16; canteens in, 86,
116; civilian visits to, 62; classes at, 165;
discipline in, 88–89, 125–30, 171, 265;
evacuation from, 141–45; food payments
to, 114; Franco-German cooperation in
building, 76–77; French visits to, 61–62,
66, 80, 89, 109, 158, 184; as German
enclaves on French soil, 74; guards'
behavior in, 72, 73–74; ICRC visiting,
61, 80, 109; infrastructure of, 75–76, 78,
81–82; internal hierarchies of, 71, 86–96;
internal police of, 90–91; layout of, 76;
locations of, xii, xiii, 11, 78, 158; medical
personnel at, 132–33; movement to and
from, 13, 79–80; Normandy landings

and, 201; prisoners' positions in, 2, 16,
86–90; propaganda tours of, 213; Red
Cross access to, 61, 88, 154, 158, 184; size
of, 80; spies in, 216; terminology for,
11–12; violence in, 72, 123–30, 148–49,
167, 265; white POWs released from, 21.
See also murders of POWs
Frontstalags, conditions at, 22, 75, 79–96,
258; clothing, 81, 83–84; cold weather,
81, 82–83, 91, 94, 96; after D-Day, 244;
deteriorating, 148; and heating fuel, 83,
108, 109; improving before visits, 80;
nationality correlating to, 83; overcrowding, 83; POWs' ability to affect, 89–90;
sanitary, 82; sleeping arrangements, 83,
87; variations in, 81. See also food
fuel, 83, 108

Gabon, 9
Gassam, Deguety, 134
gender, paternalism and, 165–70, 259
Geneva Conventions, 20–21, 23, 59–61, 62,
106, 111, 183, 263; applicability of, 60–61,
79; Armistice and, 61, 77; dissemination
of, 42; emergency humanitarianism
and, 163; on escapes, 171; financial
responsibilities according to, 77, 112;
on food, 84; on forced labor, 98, 99,
100, 115; German compliance with,
62–63, 73, 114, 149; on humanitarian
intervention, 153, 158; and the "man
of confidence," 87; stipulations of, 61,
77, 81, 124; suspension of, 48; violence
allowed by, 128, 171
German Armistice Commission (Waffenstillstandskommission), 64, 186, 188, 216
German captors. See guards, German
German High Command (OKW), 62,
66, 233; on beard-wearing, 219; peace
settlement resisted by, 186; POWs
classified by, 72–73; and prisoner labor,
99; on prisoner self-improvement, 168

extras, 228; as first permanent African troops, 26; health of, 135–36; hivernage of, 31, 42; indigenous officers of, 36; mandatory service of, 33; morale of, 227; revolt by and massacre of, 249–51, 252; use of, in other colonies, 26

Senghor, Lamine, 30, 275n28

Senghor, Léopold Sédar, 14, 269; on camp food, 86; on escapes, 172; on forestry work, 109; friendship of, with German guard, 15; Ginette Eboué and, 14, 269; on godmothers, 167; and *Négritude*, 93; on Poitiers, 82, 286n21; Red Cross aid and, 159

Service diplomatique des prisonniers de guerre. *See* Scapini Mission

Service du travail obligatoire (compulsory work service), 194

Sétif protest and massacre, 253–54, 267

sex and sexuality, 32, 166–67

shell shock, 134

shoes, 84, 109

Siegfried, André, 274n33

slavery, abolition of, 97. *See also* forced labor

Socialists, 33

Solferino, 81, 89

"solidarity," 3–6, 58–59, 115, 130, 143, 155, 157, 262–63; ebbing of, 121; and escape, 172; French superiority and, 117; limits of, 210–11, 232, 250; loss of, after war, 253, 254–55, 261, 264–65; postcolonial, 264; of suffering, 57, 262

Somme, POW housing in, 75

sources, 11–18, 125–26, 136–37, 139–41, *140*, *178*, 260, 274n27, 274n33

southern zone, 145–46, 231

Soviet Union: colonists opposed to, 225, 226; Geneva Conventions not signed by, 81; POWs from, 21, 49, 61, 73, 81, 120, 123, 147, 192–93

Spahis, 28

Spain, 161, 229

Speer, Albert, 193, 194

Speith, Officer, 125, 129

spying, 89, 104, 223; material benefits of, 224; and spy craft training, 214–17

Stalag III-A, 213, 215, 217

Stalag VII-A, 72, 215

Stalingrad, battle of, 3, 120, 184, 192

Stoler, Ann, 17

strikes, labor, 119

subjects, colonial, 34, 35, 260–61, 266

Sudan (Mali), 9, 206, 208–9, 243; correspondence of soldiers from, 43; homecoming to, 239

Sudau, Corporal, 125

Suret-Canale, Jean, 55

surveillance and discipline, 5, 20, 22, 88, 223, 242, 246, 251, 253, 261

symbolic role of colonial troops, 33, 209–10, 262–63

Syndicat agricole africain, 110

syphilis, diagnosing, 138

Syria, 9, 55, 189

systemic neglect theory, 18

Tall, Seydou Norou, 40, 208, 220–21

Tayeb (murdered prisoner), 127, 129, 167

Tell, Eugénie, 268

theft of aid, 16, 89, 158–60, 221

Thémia, Léopold, 104

Thiaroye barracks revolt and massacre, 249–51, 252–53, 254, 267, 274n27

Third Republic: Colonial Exhibition of, 37–38; colonial troops and, 26–33; "decadence" of, 24, 166, 204, 259; individualism of, 164–65; between the wars, 33–39

Thomas, Martin, 11, 131, 225

"Three Glorious Days," 55–56

Tirailleurs sénégalais. *See* Senegalese infantrymen

tobacco, 86, 152

Todt, Fritz, 99, 193

Todt organization, 99, 193, 194, 199, 245, 265

To order or obtain more information on these or other University
of Nebraska Press titles, visit nebraskapress.unl.edu.

CPSIA information can be obtained
at www.ICGtesting.com
Printed in the USA
LVHW091317150721
692799LV00001B/17